Borowski:
A Canadian Paradox

By
Lianne Laurence

The Interim
Publishing Company

LIFE ETHICS CENTRE

Borowski:
A Canadian Paradox

By Lianne Laurence

Published by:
The Interim Publishing company
104 Bond Street
Toronto, Ontario
Canada
and
Life Ethics Information Centre
104 Bond Street
Toronto, Ontario
Canada

First Edition, April 2004

Printed in Canada

Book Design and Typesetting by David Bolton

Cover Design by Mary Ellen Tardif

National Library of Canada Cataloguing in Publication

Laurence, Lianne, 1959-
        / by Lianne Laurence.

Includes bibliographical references and index.
ISBN 0-9692988-8-9

    1. Borowski, Joseph. 2. Pro-life movement—Canada—Biography. 3. Cabinet min-
isters—Manitoba—Biography. 4. Legislators—Manitoba—Biography.
5. Businessmen—Manitoba—Biography.
I. Title.

FC3378.1.B67L39 2003   971.27'03'092   C2003-906910-9

To Mom and Dad
The joy is in the sharing of the feast.
Alun Lewis

Acknowledgements

Jim Hughes, President of Campaign Life Coalition, was the prime mover behind the Joe Borowski biography; without his inspiration and determination, the writing of this book would not have been contemplated, let alone have come to fruition. Nor would the book have been possible without the cooperation of the Borowski family, and particularly that of Joe's wife, Jean, who provided numerous scrapbooks of clippings, photographs, and patient answers to seemingly endless questions. Thanks also to Joe's daughters, Debbie, Karen and Sandra, for their frankness and unfailing courtesy. My debt to the work of Professor F. L. Morton cannot be overstated; as the footnotes attest, I relied heavily on his 1992 book, *Morgentaler v Borowski: Abortion, the Charter and the Courts*, published by McClelland and Stewart Inc. (Toronto). (Other sources include Catherine Dunphy's 1996 biography, *Morgentaler, A difficult hero*, published by Random House of Canada (Toronto), Anne Collins's 1982 book, *The Big Evasion, Abortion, the issue that won't go away*, published by Lester & Orpen Dennys Limited (Toronto), the 1994 edition of Michael Mandel's *The Charter of Rights and the Legalization of Politics in Canada*, published by Thompson Educational Publishing Inc. (Toronto), and Basilian Fr. Alphonse de Valk's 1974 *Morality and Law in Canadian Politics*, published by Palm Publishers (Montreal).) The Manitoba Legislative Library and the Archives of Manitoba proved invaluable sources of material, as did Fr. de Valk's private archives in Toronto, to which I was granted full access. Father de Valk also gave wise and timely advice and incisive editorial direction, which, along with the thoughtful comments and suggestions of Dr. David Dooley, greatly improved and enriched the manuscript; my sincere thanks to both. I would also like to express my gratitude to the following people, without whose contribution the book would not have been completed, or would have been much the poorer: Richmond Cochrane, C. Edward Collins, Leeda Crawford, Gilles Grondin, Pat Loughran, Marlene MacKalski, Joe Pope, and, of course, all those who freely and generously shared their memories of Joe Borowski and his times. Thanks to the Grey Nuns in Winnipeg for their warm hospitality, and to Councils of the Knights of Columbus, especially Council 3881 of Oakville, Ontario, for their support of this project. Many thanks also to Paul Tuns, for his inspiration in the titling of the book, and for his editorial suggestions while fine-tuning the manuscript, and to the gracious and talented Mary Ellen Tardif for designing the book's cover. The work done by David Bolton, *Interim* Publishing's production manager, went beyond heroic. I don't think it is possible to thank him adequately for his contribution, not only for his fine design, but more to the heart of the matter, for his kindness, his grace-under-pressure, and his impeccable competence in dealing with the varied and oft-changing demands of getting the book to press. Finally, the support and sacrifice of the editor during the writing of this tale is beyond calculating. As well as providing encouragement and clear-eyed insight and direction, Deirdre Collins-Seke accomplished the arduous task of editing, and dealt with antic equipment and vexatious logistics with patience, perseverance, and good humour. Thank you.

L. Laurence

Contents

Contents

Foreword

Joseph Paul Borowski was one of my heroes and a great friend. He was a complex, yet simple man who loved and respected life and family. Joe and I didn't always agree on the tactics or strategies or rhetoric which would be most effective for the Canadian pro-life movement. To a certain extent, he felt that it was necessary to respond immediately to all threats to human life and sometimes this created problems for himself, his family and the rest of the movement.

Borowski was a catalyst, a disturber who caused as much aggravation to his fellow pew-sitters as to those promoting anti-life, anti-family agendas. He believed in comforting the afflicted and afflicting the comfortable. But in the early days, without Joe's leadership, which grassroots Canadians saw as a beacon of hope, the daily press would have all but ignored pro-life activities.

Joe was a prayerful man who practised his Catholic faith on a daily basis in political and private life. He was not part of the often seen phenomenon of avowedly religious people who leave their beliefs at the legislature door. He was "lunchpail" Joe, someone who could especially identify with "blue collar" families.

The night before his funeral, as his body lay in the casket before the altar in his parish church, I took the opportunity to sit alone in a pew, praying for his family and reflecting on the profound impact Joe had on the battle to protect the little guy. Joe Borowski was a simple man who was a giant in the struggle to restore legal protection for the lives of unborn children, and defend the handicapped and elderly at risk.

He is greatly missed.

Jim Hughes

National President
Campaign Life Coalition
Toronto, Ontario

They tried, yet in vain, to tell me
Of joy in words sounding joyful—
Here am I taught, at last,
Here, in this sadness-filled tale.

Friederich Hölderlin

Part 1

The pilgrim from Thompson

Chapter 1

The wandering Joe

I spent my hungry young years running wild,
There was a lot I had to do,
And I spent cities like a handful of change,
But I never stopped looking for you.
Tom Paxton

"...we didn't think we were poor or we didn't think we were rich,
we were just, just there."
Jean Borowski

ON MARCH 31, 1965, JOE BOROWSKI BOARDED A GREYHOUND BUS for the 14-hour ride down from Thompson, Manitoba, to the province's capital of Winnipeg. The good-natured 32-year-old with the booming voice and wide grin was about to begin his public life—a remarkable career that would ultimately pit the plain-spoken, strapping miner against the Dominion of Canada itself.

But on this blustery March day, as Joe Borowski waved to the news photographer and kissed his wife, Jean, goodbye before swinging with easy grace onto the crowded bus, his mission, though clearly focused, was of a smaller scope. The pilgrim from Thompson was on his way south to demand that his town be granted the right of self-government—and he had a petition signed by 1,700 of its residents to back him up.

Joe Borowski had struck out on his own at the age of 14, working in bush camps across Canada but it was only some 12 years later, when he was hired on as a hard-rock miner in the booming frontier town nearly 400 miles north of Winnipeg, that his restless spirit met its match. Scratch the surface in Thompson and you hit permafrost, but plunge a mineshaft 4,000 feet below ground and you will tap into one of the richest bodies of nickel ore in the world.

When Joe arrived in Thompson in 1958, hundreds of men who thronged to the north to make good money lived in tents provided by the International Nickel Company (Inco). Two years earlier this company had signed an agreement with Manitoba's Liberal government to provide the infrastructure for the settlement, which was named after the company's long-serving chairman, John Thompson. According to the terms of the agreement, Thompson would be run by an administrator, not by an elected council.

This may have been a tolerable state of affairs when Thompson was just a tent city, but as the nickel proved prodigious, as miners sent for their families and houses sprang up and roads and sidewalks laid over the boot-sucking, thick, black mud, as church buildings loomed over the landscape and schools were built to take in the burgeoning number of children, then the people who had seen the town grow wanted to have a say in their community.

Six years after landing in Thompson, during which time he bought a house and settled with his wife and three daughters, Joe Borowski, union man and irrepressible entrepreneur, realized that someone had to explain to the Conservative government that the needs of the north were being overlooked. Someone had to tell them just what the people of Thompson were after. Joe would go.

The singular beauty of the Saskatchewan landscape perhaps goes unnoticed by those who live and work there, as it is in human nature to grow accustomed to nature's largesse. The startlingly blue vastness of a cloudless prairie sky, the rippling gold of the whispering, rolling land and the glorious snow that muffles all harshness in its chilly embrace: it was to vistas such as these that Joseph Borowski, senior, and his wife Bernice travelled with their two small sons in 1930.

The Borowskis had met and married in Bialystok, Poland, a town northeast of Warsaw, not far from the border of Belarus. For the first seven years of their married life it was their sorrow to remain childless, but once Isaac and then Frank were born, Joseph and Bernice began to think about opportunities for their children. It seemed to Joseph, the eldest son of a member of Poland's land-ed gentry, that there was little future in his country. Ambition for their children compelled the Borowskis to emigrate to Western Canada. They settled near the village of Wishart, Saskatchewan,[1] about 65 miles northeast of Regina.

Joseph Borowski was not a farmer by training or inclination; in a province renowned for fertile soil, his allotted portion was poor, hilly, bush- and rock-riddled. "He had that kind of luck," his son Joe remarked years later.[2] Still, despite having to pay one-third of his crops to the Canadian Pacific Railroad as rent, the elder Borowski managed to coax enough food from the miserly ground to support his growing crop of children. Bernice gave birth to Walter a year after they arrived in Canada; in 1932 Joe was born, followed in quick succession by Mary, Helen, Lillian, Wallace, Matilda and Irene—five boys and five girls in all.

The Borowski *père* was a strict disciplinarian and a hard work-er. He may have been temperamentally disposed to be the latter no matter what his circumstances, but life on the Saskatchewan prairies in the 1930s reinforced this disposition. The family would not survive unless he, his wife, and all his children laboured 'by singing light'. A winter's day in Saskatchewan left one not only fig-uratively but literally breathless, as the icy air lunged for the warmer recesses of the lungs. Joseph Borowski enterprisingly bat-tled the cold by building a closed-in cutter for eight, complete with a small heater, drawn by two horses. He added another room to the one-room log cabin that he bought for $50 when they first arrived.

He would take time from his labour to tell elaborate stories, holding his children entranced with his vivid descriptions. He told tales of his boyhood, spinning yarns of escapades of his family and friends, who by the 1940's were enduring the Nazi horror. Perhaps it was from his father that Joe inherited his ability to speak elo-

quently and ardently. His younger sister Mary Seidlak maintained
that Joe was like his father in many ways; there were frequent
eruptions between the two. His mother, quiet and gentle, aroused
only admiration in her restless fourth child.[3]

Twenty-six miles north and west over the windswept prairie
from Wishart lay the town of Wynyard. About nine miles south
from there dwelled the Zelinski family. While the Borowski clan
grew in number, and Borowski children scampered through the
straw, burrowed tunnels in the snow, cleared brush, plucked
chickens, drove the cutter to Mass, or trudged over three miles to
school near Wishart, the 13 Zelinski children were in turn doing
much the same things, milking cows every morning and trudging
three miles to their school.

The Zelinskis differed in some respects from their neighbours.
For one thing, Barbara Zelinski was not expected, as many wives
were, to help in the fields along with her husband. Instead, she
presided over the kitchen and the home, a gargantuan task in
itself. The days melded into an endless round of preparing food,
washing dishes and caring for one baby after another. In the meantime, her husband toiled on the land, using horses to furrow the
ground. "He was a hard, hard-working man," his daughter Jean
said. "He was such a worker that we remember a lot of times we'd
call him—supper's ready—to come and eat, and he'd finally come
and he'd be so tired that he literally fell asleep at the table."
Everything they needed they grew themselves, except coffee and
sugar.[4]

Preoccupied with school, chores and family, Jean Zelinski was
only vaguely aware of the world beyond Wynyard. In the horse-
and-buggy days, twenty-six miles might as well have been a thousand. "I didn't know Wishart at all—I heard of it, but who went
there, what for?" It was only after she left her father's farm at age
15, travelled to Toronto to live with her uncle and find work, and
returned two years later for a holiday, that the town of Wishart, or
more accurately, its nearby inhabitants, became significant to her.

Her friend Sandy had a date with Frank Borowski, so Jean and
one of her brothers caught a ride with her into Wynyard. Frank
arrived, but not alone. He had brought along a brother who, too,
was home for the holidays from the bush camps of Ontario.

Jean didn't think much of blond Joe Borowski, who topped her
five feet 10 inches by a mere four inches. "I always liked the dark-

er guys, you know, black hair and brown eyes, and he had green eyes... After I thought he was real handsome, but at the time I thought, 'He reminds me of a spoilt brat'." This fellow also had a curl that hung down on his forehead that he kept brushing away; Jean suspected he was trying to draw attention to his locks. She discovered later that Joe was conscious of that curl and hated it.

Ah well, the path of true love never did run smooth. Her brother, anxious to meet his own date, left Jean with the Borowski boys. "I remember thinking, I don't like this and I don't like that." Despite her discontent, however, Jean made plans to date Joe the next week.

As the days passed, she reconsidered. After all, she was only in Saskatchewan on a holiday. She was a city girl now, having braved the hugeness and bustle of Toronto, and these farm dances, dusty, dirty and sweaty, no longer had the appeal of old. Moreover, she would be going back to Toronto. Why get involved?

Saturday night arrived. Jean instructed her mother to tell the Borowski boys that she and Sandy were not at home. They heard a knock upon the door, and ran upstairs and hid, satisfied they had eluded their erstwhile suitors. Then came her mother's voice: "Gina! Gina!"

"We could have killed her!" remembered Jean. But as Barbara Zelinski told her daughter later, there's a code of conduct to be followed in this world; certain civilities cannot be abandoned at one's whim. If she made a date, she kept it; if she wanted to break it, then she had to do it herself, not leave it to somebody else. Those boys, her mother said, had come a long way to pick them up. "So we learned our lesson."

It proved to be a fortuitous intervention. That night Jean really enjoyed being with Joe and things evolved from there. Even though Joe soon left for work in the bush camps, and Jean travelled to Vancouver with a friend, they corresponded faithfully, and when at home together, they went out.

What Jean didn't know was that Joe was nearly a year younger than she. His air of easy confidence—and the fact that he had his own truck—led her to assume he was at least 24 years old.

He had packed enough experience into his first 18 years of life to warrant such an assumption. From his infancy, according to his sister Mary, Joe had displayed an independent personality, and an unwillingness to follow anyone else's advice. "He had a very strong will of his own." Moreover, he had chafed under the natural order that assumed his brothers, because they were older, knew better. He quit school after Grade 6. "Rather than try and be the fourth kid, little kid...he wanted to go and try his hand at life. So one day he comes to me and he says, 'I'm leaving home' and he got a bag and threw a few things into it and took the horse and drove into Wishart and left the horse at the stable, hopped on the train and took off..."

His father was concerned enough to contact the RCMP, Mary said, but they advised the elder Borowski "to leave him, because if he's not happy at home he's going to run away again so just let him go and [then] when he's ready he'll come. So about a month later I got a letter from him, he was working on a ranch," having assumed, she laughingly recalled, the alias of Jim Rogers.

At age 14, Joe graduated to lumber camps, and worked his way from Ontario to British Columbia. In the rough frontier town of Prince Rupert he was employed on the fishing trawlers, and cooked in a restaurant. He was a good cook, too. From camp to camp, town to town, the 'handsome rover' grew to manhood, acquiring a reputation for toughness among a crowd not known for its shrinking violets.

Joe also had a reputation for frugality. He may have been temperamentally disposed to good husbandry, but early in his life Joe also received advice from an older Polish labourer: "It's not what you earn, it's what you save, that counts," and the younger man took this admonition to heart. Thus he had enough cash to buy a real diamond engagement ring for Jean Zelinski when she agreed to marry him.

Jean did not aspire to either marriage or diamond rings—oh, no.

"That's the last thing I really wanted. You know, a lot of girls in school would say, 'Oh, I'm just going to go and marry so-and-so,' and I used to think, why would you want to do that for, why would you want to get married and start a family? ...It's better being single; you do what you want.... And my girlfriend would say the same thing about marriage—what for?"

Two years after they first met, Joe and Jean attended a friend's wedding. The fragrance of romance was in the air, love lingered on the breeze, the newly married couple danced so well and everyone looked happy and festive. That night Joe asked Jean to marry him.

"And I said yes," Jean remembered, wonderingly, "And I could-n't believe I said that."

The next order of business was the ring, and on a trip to Regina before Joe left for work, he insisted they get one. "I says, 'I'm not looking for any ring, if you want a ring you go and get it,' so he left me in the car and he comes out with this ring and I looked at it—Gee, it's probably not even a real one." Jean scratched the gemstone on the window of Joe's truck while he was checking under the hood. As everyone knows, a real diamond will cut glass. It made a mark! "So I thought, oooohhh."

A real diamond wasn't the biggest surprise in store for Jean Zelinski. She found out how old Joe really was. It disturbed her enough that she thought of backing out, but her father said, "A good man is hard to find. It's like finding a diamond in the sand."

"I said, '*What?*'

"'He's going to be a good man,' he says, 'looks like a good man.'

"I said 'Man?! He's a kid!'"

Her parents took to Joe right from the start, but they didn't push their seventh child to wed. After all, marriage is a lifetime commitment. "They said, 'It's up to you, if you have any doubts, you can walk out, even out of the church, but once you say yes, if you're going to do it in front of the priest, that's it for life and don't you forget it.'

"And that's what's scary, really, because you thought, well, what if it doesn't go? What if I have to leave and go some place strange and I don't like it? Because I was very attached to the family."

Nevertheless, on August 20, 1952, Jean Zelinski married Joe Borowski.

She wore a wedding dress she bought in Wynyard, the only one of the three available dresses to fit her generous frame. The groom was attired in a sober suit. The Catholic wedding Mass took place in the morning, and the wedding celebration on the Zelinski farm in the afternoon. In the house, a band played for the older folks, and out near the granary, on a platform erected by Jean's dad, another musical group churned out tunes more to the tastes of the young. Home-brew flowed like water and food abounded. Relatives from Ontario, their long journey endured, settled down with a sigh into the lavish welcome like ships anchored in a safe harbour.

The next day, according to custom, the bride and groom served breakfast to the family and friends who had served them the day before. Then it was the Borowski family's turn to host yet another dance for the newlyweds; more food, more homemade whiskey, more dancing and merriment as the hot August sun sank slowly into the deepening red of the west, and the first, fixed stars took their appointed places in the mysterious darkness of 'this inverted bowl we call the sky'.

Thus fortified, Joe and Jean Borowski, aged 19 and 20 years respectively, hopped in their truck and drove west to begin their married life.

It was going to be quite a ride.

By the time Jean and Joe arrived in the port city of Vancouver in their pickup, they had $20 between them. Calling home for help was unthinkable; instead, they booked into an inexpensive hotel and began to look for work. It wasn't long before they were both employed, Joe as a cook and Jean as a waitress in a drive-in.

One day, Joe met a man looking for a vacuum cleaner salesman. Although Joe had sold nothing in his life, he was game to give it a try. The man had confidence in the friendly Polish-Canadian, and sent him across to Vancouver Island. Jean stayed behind, content with the drive-in job that netted her a couple square meals a day and a few tips. She was startled to see Joe walk in the door merely a week later. "C'mon, we're leaving," he said. "But I'm not finished," she retorted.

"You don't need this job," Joe said, and fished in his pocket and pulled out a wad of cash—$400 in commission sales. "Good-bye girls, I'm gone!" Jean waved as they swept triumphantly out the door and down to the head office, where the boss buoyantly assured them that Joe was such a natural salesman, "he could sell deep freezers to the Eskimos."

In the next year and a bit, they lived all over Vancouver Island: Port Alberni, Oyster Bay, Nanaimo. Joe kept selling vacuum cleaners, while Jean, although she detested selling, tried her hand at peddling Avon. She preferred the Island to Vancouver, where the rain drove her batty and the fog was sometimes so thick that Joe would walk in front of the car to see where to go, with Jean driving closely behind.

As Joe's sales tapered off, Jean heard of a new restaurant opening in Whitehorse. She left to check it out, while Joe got a job
cooking at an army base. Recognizing his culinary skill, the army
asked him to cook for the soldiers then at work upgrading the
Alaska Highway. Of course, he would need an assistant. And so the
Borowskis moved up to Mile 1083 of the famous road to feed the
36-man crew.

It was an idyllic life. The men appreciated Joe's largesse in the
kitchen, his amply stocked larder, vats of chocolate milk and freshly baked donuts, and they appreciated Jean's offers to mend torn
shirts or replace errant buttons. It was a land of plenty, where
moose and bear meat often supplemented the menu. Rambling
over the hills 'where sang the larks', Jean gathered mushrooms as
big as fists, pails full, and kept a wary eye out for roaming black
bears that were wont to paw through the garbage. A visiting cadre
of army officers came to dine; they complimented the chef on the
bear roast, but the mushrooms they politely declined. Unabashed,
the Borowskis and the crew dug in with relish.

Once they encountered a grizzly bear, a huge fellow who tow-
ered over the cab of the pickup; they just kept driving, Jean
remembered. As the season drew to a close, the boys kept a watchful eye on Jean, helped her with the clothes basket and in the
evenings they played cards and some of the men brought out their
guitars and sang. The summer waned, the sun flickered slowly
out, and as the nights grew longer, Jean grew heavier, and her
body thickened in a particular way and she realized that she was
pregnant. And so they returned to Wynyard, having saved up
enough money to build a little home. Joe started a cattle business
and when Debbie was born in December of 1953 they decided to
open a restaurant in Wynyard.

More cooking and cleaning, only now with an infant daughter
and without the majestic surroundings of the wilderness and clear
mountain air. It was relentlessly hard work, opening at 8:00 in the
morning and closing at midnight. Various siblings pitched in to
help at the popular "Hawaiian Retreat,"—which had a reputation
for its Hawaiian punch, a codeword for home brew—but after a
year the Borowskis had had enough. They were on the road again,
this time moving to Regina, where they stayed with Joe's sister
Mary and her husband, Ted, before moving into a trailer. Joe went

off to work in the potash mines in Esterhazy but was hired for mines that were situated closer to Saskatoon, so the Borowskis moved their trailer to that city.

Work in the potash mines was fitful, so Joe applied for a job as a mechanic in a soon-to-be-opened mine near Sault Ste. Marie, and was hired. But when the opening of those mines was delayed, he applied in Thompson, Manitoba and was taken on by Patrick (Paddy) Harrison, a Quebec contractor doing the initial drilling for Inco.[5] Joe Borowski took the train to Thompson in 1958 and found a situation very much to his liking, a place where a man could work hard and earn good money.

He "worked like a damned fool," Joe told reporter Ted Allen years later. With the Harrison company implementing a bonus system and an incentive, he could pull in $1,500 a month working seven days a week, 12 hours a day. "It's a shallow, cool mine and I got a job underground as a stope leader," Joe said. "I can honestly say it was the job I was most content with. It was certainly the best mine I ever worked. It was the hardest physical work I ever did, but I ate well, slept well and was paid well."[6]

The rolling stone had finally rolled home.

Notes
Chapter 1
The wandering Joe

[1] Interview with Mary Seidlak, February 2002.
[2] "Meet Joe Borowski," Ted Allen, *Winnipeg Tribune*, December 6, 1969.
[3] Interview with Mary Seidlak, February 2002.
[4] Interview with Jean Borowski, February 2002.
[5] Op. Cit. "Meet Joe Borowski," Ted Allen, *Winnipeg Tribune*, December 6, 1969.
[6] Ibid.

Chapter 2

This modern fret for liberty

Alone stood brave Horatius
But constant still in mind
Thrice thirty thousand foes before,
And the broad flood behind.
"Down with him!" cried false Sextus
With a smile on his pale face;
"Now yield thee," cried Lars Porsena
"Now yield thee to our grace!"

Thomas Babington Macaulay
Horatius at the Bridge

"We are not Moses and his followers and we will not wait forty years for the promised land of free government."

Joe Borowski

THE EARTH PARTS RELUCTANTLY WITH HER RICHES. IT TAKES THE BRAWN of men and the leverage of machines and blasting powder to plunder her treasures. The Inco mines in Thompson throbbed with activity 24 hours a day, seven days a week, while the train regularly disgorged men eager for work. For some it was their final journey. The earth fights back, and some men pay for her precious metals with their own life's blood.

Despite the danger, the men kept coming. There was work to

be had: not only did the Thompson site have a surface and pit mine, but a smelter as well.[1] The early years of living in tents, where the meagre warmth of a heater in the middle of this makeshift domicile evaporated quickly in the deep winter nights, and the bedding froze to the canvas walls, soon gave way to a more settled existence. Bunkhouses provided the quasi-comforts of home, but were not enough. The workers wanted a life in Thompson; they wanted their families with them. The occasional weekend together in the neighbouring town, The Pas (about 100 miles southwest), did not bode well for domestic stability.

In June of 1961 Jean Borowski, who had been living in a trailer in Saskatoon while her man Joe plied shovel and pit-drill deep in the stopes of the Inco mines, stepped onto the railway platform in Thompson. She cradled 14-month-old Sandy in her arms, while six-year-old Debbie and Karen, four, stood beside her regarding their new home with curiosity. Jean had packed what she could and sold the trailer and car—what was the point of having wheels in a town where there were next to no roads?

The blackflies swarmed, and the mud, black as a bat's eyes and so thick it seemed alive, clung to her boots and clogged the stroller's wheels—but far worse than all this was the fact that the Borowskis were homeless. Thompson was growing so fast by then that the contractors just couldn't keep up, and the house she had expected to move into had not yet been built. Jean and Joe were forced to share a tiny two-bedroom apartment, offered by a friendly miner, with not only him, but another family waiting for a house. It was Jean's first, undeniably dramatic, experience of typical frontier hospitality: everyone looked out for one another, and what scarce accommodations were to be had in those chaotic years were offered as refuge for the shelterless. In the case of the Borowskis, the landlord, who worked the midnight shift, took the couch, they occupied one bedroom, and the second couple, with their two tots, holed up in the other.

It took three weeks and Joe's persistent calls before the builders called to say the house was ready. Jean took Debbie by the hand and trudged through the mud to find the foreman. "I said who I was and I said, 'I'm looking for which house is mine,' and he said, 'I'm not sure, it's one of those three, and then he looked at the invoices, and said, 'The middle one is yours.'" The next day, between the neighbours and all the people who kept coming to ask, "Do you need anything, do you need anything?" they managed to get their furniture—ordered from Sears and delivered by train and stored until this fateful day—moved through the hurly burly of construction and the never-ending mud, into their new home. "We set up the beds and we hooked up the stove and when Joe came home from work, we ate in that house that same day...it was so exciting," Jean recalled.

It was all "young, young couples with little kids, on both sides, and as they moved in there'd be more young couples with little kids." One of the women would watch the littlest ones while the others would head down to the Hudson's Bay store with their strollers for provisions. More often than not, milk, bread, eggs, and flour would be sold out until the next shipment. "I'm telling you...you really had to think and plan and then you'd come to the conclusion you better start baking your own bread."

Winter came, with more snow than Jean had ever seen before and temperatures of 40 to 50 below zero for days on end. It, too, took getting used to and planning, because she had to walk every-where and be ready to make her move when the weather broke.

What the Thompson wives didn't plan for was the whistle—the signal that there had been an accident at the mine. "We were always scared. Whenever you heard a whistle blow, you were scared because something was happening...you couldn't wait for your men to come home. When they're gone there, you're always worried."

Once Joe was hit by falling rock; it tore a hole in his helmet and grazed his head. He was off work for about a week, his wife recalled. Often he'd come home with a blue tinge to his face, the result of inhaling noxious gas. It seemed natural that his concern about safety would draw him into the politics of mining.

What first sparked Joe's ire were the events of May 1960, when Inco assumed full control of the mining operations, taking over from contractors such as Paddy Harrison. Not only did the new company cut wages from $2.00 to $1.83, and abolish the bonus system—reducing the maximum monthly salary to $600 from a possible $1500—but it displayed, as far as Joe was concerned, a disregard for the men's safety and a callous attitude towards its employees.[2] Other miners felt the same way; labour unrest became endemic. Joe himself told a writer years later, "[T]he joke in Thompson was that there were three shifts, one coming to

Thompson, one working, and one leaving Thompson. The turnover was incredible." [3]

Because of their difficult and dangerous work, miners look after each other. The natural union that bound them together underground began to take political form above ground. At the Borowski house, the worried men argued and debated about what to do in the face of a seemingly impervious, imperious corporation.

Added to their burden was a long-simmering union dispute between the International Union of Mine, Mill and Smelter Workers (Mine-Mill)—which had negotiated the contract that Joe, and many of his brothers, found so odious—and the United Steelworkers of America, which was pushing to take over in Thompson.

According to Leon Lavasseur, who was the parish priest in Thompson from 1960 to 1969, the struggle between the two unions could be traced back to Sudbury in the 1950s. While Mine-Mill "was not as powerful a union" as the Steelworkers, there was "a deep policy decision by Inco to keep the Steelworkers of America out of the labour scene in Thompson." Lavasseur recalled that when the Steelworkers contrived to buy a house, it had to arrange the purchase through a third party—such was the determination of the company, which controlled the administration of the town, to frustrate the union's organization at every turn.

Lavasseur remembered Joe Borowski as "a deep thinker, focused on the essentials of life as opposed to the peripheral" and a man who "attached a lot of importance to honesty." Because of his seriousness, "he was like a leader who hasn't got too many followers because he's too far to the left or to the right."

Inco "tried to be fair," but the core issue was self-determination, observed the former parish priest. Joe's deepest grievance was that he and his fellow citizens were not permitted to govern their affairs, as was their right in a free and democratic society. Former Filipino dictator Ferdinand Marcos apparently remarked that his people would "rather live in a hell run by 1,000 Filipinos than a heaven run by one American," laughed Lavasseur, adding: "There was a bit of this in Joe."

When the long-running feud between Mine-Mill and the Steelworkers erupted into out-and-out warfare in Thompson, the organic solidarity between miners was rent apart. Joe Borowski was not a man to back down from a fight. He chose his side. He "was not a front man for the Steelworkers by any means," Lavasseur recalled, "but he saw that they had more power and more strength to [stand] up to the big man, the big boss." Moreover, Joe was disgusted with what appeared to be collusion by Mine-Mill with Inco, to lock Steelworkers out of the Inco camp in 1958 and 1959. "This made me wonder what kind of a union Mine-Mill really was," he wrote in an undated pamphlet. From the covertly acquired bungalow dubbed "The Steel House", the Steelworkers began in October 1961 to organize in earnest, attempting to gain what is the life's blood of any union: enough members to certify.

"It was dirty work, I mean they fought tooth and nail," Jean Borowski remembered. Threats and intimidation were not unheard of, and the turnover in Thompson was so high it was a war of attrition as well as a war of words and on occasion, fists. Finally, in April 1962, the men voted nearly six to one to accept the Steelworkers. And so Local 6166 was born.

The warm August sun smiled down on Thompson, but the light of summer days did little to dispel the tension felt by the town's nearly 1,900 disgruntled mine and surface workers. For the Steelworkers, 1964 was the summer of discontent—the culmination of months of frustrating negotiations. It was the first time the union tested its mettle in the complex and bitter labour smelter that was Inco's Thompson operation. Joe Borowski was part of a union team that had been negotiating with Inco since January of that year, but when the existing contract expired at the beginning of March, no agreement had been reached. The men were as unhappy as the day was long, and the days grew longer and longer.

On July 19, the workers rejected a proposal authored by a provincially appointed conciliation board[4] and about two weeks later they voted to strike, at which point a final negotiating team was dispatched to Winnipeg in a last desperate effort to reach an agreement. A wildcat strike on August 10 added to the Steelworkers' difficulties. Speculations circulated that it was due to the machinations of Mine-Mill, insinuating itself in to the present labour crisis like the proverbial dirty shirt. But Steelworkers held the day, as the men refrained from further such actions. On August 12, they gathered at the airport and union headquarters to meet their team.

The efforts had failed. Even though Inco had capitulated on some demands, agreeing to an 11.5 per cent wage increase over the next three years, it wasn't enough. That night, in a secret ballot, the Steelworkers Union voted to strike.

The mine in Thompson fell silent.

Thompson itself became a ghost town, as men thronged to the train station or the airport; there was no road out of the town, the nearest began 60 miles away. Faced with an uncertain future, nearly 1,500 workers took whatever way they could out of the beleagured community. "All of a sudden people started leaving and they'd beg you, just take over my mortgage, you can have my house, just take over my mortgage," Jean Borowski remembered. "If...you'd spent too much and you had all these bills, the strike pay wasn't enough, and they couldn't keep up."

For the Borowskis, leaving was unthinkable. Joe was vice-president of the union; he had commitments and obligations. And he had a business to attend to, although one wonders if he rang up many sales in his souvenir and import store while the strike was on. Perhaps the men fleeing Thompson spent their last bit of cash on a nickel souvenir, a reminder of where they had been and perhaps would never be again.

For Joe, the fight with Inco was deeply personal. He had to settle his own score with the company for the difficulty he had renting space for his fledgling enterprise—a difficulty he attributed directly to Inco's influence. The company ran the town, he figured, and it was Joe's strong suspicion that it wouldn't have minded running him right out of it.

In this battle, Joe developed a *modus operandi* to which he remained true throughout his erratic and turbulent public life: he brought everything out in the open. Not for him the furtive backroom politics, the behind-the-scenes deal, the hushed negotiations and nuanced compromise. Perhaps it is true that the better part of valour is discretion, but for Joe, revelation trumped all. That which was hidden was laid bare, and he shouted his grievance from the rooftops.

At least the people could see for themselves what was going on, and make up their own minds.

On April 25, 1963, Joe purchased advertising space in The *Thompson Citizen* and under a heading, "Citizens of Thompson, For your Information," he printed his letter to Sterling Lyon, Manitoba's attorney-general, in which he detailed his difficulty setting up his souvenir store. He was told space could not be rented to him, as he would be in direct competition with another business. The manager of the prestigious Thompson Plaza prohibited another tenant from sub-letting to him.

A week after Joe mailed his letter to Lyon, he was barred from the Inco camp by the Inco Security Police—even though he had been peddling his wares there for nearly seven months. This, too, he reported to the citizens of Thompson. In a letter to the editor dated May 23, 1963, Joe described what happened when he tried to talk to the security chief about the situation. "In a venomous seizure, Mr. Munn had me thrown out of his office, with this promise, 'If I have any more trouble from you, you shall never enter this camp again.'"

Why, asked Joe, did Inco have difficulty in keeping men when there were 500,000 unemployed in the province? "The answer," he wrote, "is quite obvious to anyone who has lived at the Inco camp: 1) the prison type police restriction governing movement to and in camp; 2) un-justifiable restraint of liberties and rights of the individual; and 3) substantial grease-soaked food." Warned Joe: "As long as our democratic rights are denied and tramped on by petty bureaucrats we shall never have labour peace in Thompson."

Come the summer of 1964, Joe's prediction seemed justified, with the workers' strike the jewel in the crown of civic frustration. This was distinguished by being "probably the most orderly major strike in the history of Canadian mining" and could be likened to a "cold war."[5]

Even a cold war has its casualties, and as the strike entered its second, third and finally fourth week the men grew restive. With the bitter tang of fall in the air, the prospect of a prolonged stand-off struck chill in the hearts of many. On September 8, the workers who remained in Thompson voted by an 80 per cent majority to accept the company's offer, and a disastrous winter siege was averted.[6] The Inco employees had 21 days to return. Trains and planes heading north to Thompson were packed: an exodus in reverse.

Joe Borowski, too, went back underground. But he was, according to his wife, considered a troublemaker, a vocal protester whose prominence in the union and vehemence regarding safety in the mines, not to mention his fulminations over his souvenir business, marked him as a man with whom to be reckoned. Reflecting on these days later, Joe described himself as "a poor man's Ralph Nader."[7] Not only that, but the hard-nosed bargaining skills of his union team had netted a generous settlement for the workers, while Joe himself discovered later that Inco had neglected to include holiday pay on bonuses, thus owing the workers a total of $875,000 when the computations were complete.[8]

In January 1965, a miner, and a friend of Joe's, was killed by falling rock. Joe believed the accident could have been averted, and subsequently stated publicly that he himself had reported the area was unsafe the previous day.[9] Summoned to an inquest into the man's death, he accused Inco of negligence.

A month later, he was fired for insubordination. One account of the incident relates that Joe was ordered to work in an area he thought was unsafe. "Like hell," was his response.[10] Bill Smith, who mined alongside Joe down on level six, recalled at least one occasion when Joe, a stope leader, prevented his men from working when he judged the conditions to be hazardous.[11] Joe launched a grievance through the union.

In the meantime, Joe worked part-time for the Steelworkers at their Sudbury office and concentrated on his import and souvenir business. His location problem had been solved when the owner of the bowling alley, Mr. Morgan, offered him a small space upstairs. The store, recalled Jean, was a "beautiful" idea. They sold jewelry, watches, and lighters with Inco insignia. The most popular items by far were the souvenirs Joe crafted himself, including various mineral samples embedded in lucite, a clear plastic. The fact that Joe had access, through sympathetic engineers, to supposedly top-secret core samples, and that he sold these as souvenirs, drove ever deeper the wedge of mistrust between him and the company.[12]

"He'd just make all these things." Jean said, "He'd come up with ideas, you know, what do you think of this one, then he cut out wood and he'd shellac it and he'd mount a buffalo on it with the Inco thing. And the Mounties got hold of that and they said, what a good idea for a going away present for their staff and they'd order these things and we'd put their pips on it, the Mountie symbol."

In April 1965 Joe designed a nickel medal with the help of his oldest daughter. On one side, the face of a miner, sketched by Debbie from a photograph of Joe himself, and on the other, the visage of Sir John A. MacDonald, Canada's first Prime Minister and one whom, according to Joe, all Canadians should admire.

Miners especially should appreciate Sir John A. It was during the construction of the trans-continental railroad that "a dynamite blast accidentally exposed a vein of copper-nickel ore," Joe noted in a flier promoting his medal. This discovery "led to the establishment of the largest nickel complex in the world, at Sudbury, Ontario," with Thompson the second largest.

The nickel medal was a bestseller, especially among the miners who dropped by the store to find gifts for their families. Karen, the Borowskis' middle child, who at five years old could scarcely reach the cash register, proved to be her father's daughter in her salesmanship, telling the customers, "Oh, I think your mother would like this," and the men, lonesome for their kin and outnumbering the women in Thompson 20 to one, listened, believed, and bought.

While Joe worked into the night polishing and gluing souvenirs for his store, he was also polishing and piecing together a political philosophy. The emergence of Joe Borowski, businessman, did nothing to diminish the vitality of Joe Borowski, workingman, or as he phrased it, "the guy who carries the lunch pail."[13] The battle between the Steelworkers and Mine-Mill, the running encounters with Inco, the strike, the fatal accidents in the mines, and finally, his sacking, had sharpened to a dangerously razor-thin edge the already acute sense of justice that was his birthright.

In 1965 in Manitoba, it appeared to Joe that the regular guy, the working stiff, had only one place to go politically. The Liberals had signed away his local civil rights when it entered into the infamous agreement with Inco in 1956. And despite his admiration for the Conservative Prime Minister of his youth, John Diefenbaker, Joe Borowski was fed up with the indifference to northern travails so often exhibited by Duff Roblin's Tories.

In fact, years later he described his affiliation with the

Conservatives in terms of disillusionment. In that party he was "just a robot. When they snapped their fingers I got up and when they snapped them again, I sat down. The big boys ran the show; we were the workhorses. We went around and put up the posters and hauled the people to the polls and they'd pat us on the back, give us a bottle of whiskey and that was the end of it for four years."[14]

When he got involved with the Steelworkers, Joe read the Labour Act passed by the Cooperative Commonwealth Federation (CCF) when that party was in power in Saskatchewan. (The CCF later reinvented itself as the New Democratic Party or NDP.) The radical bill appealed to him, and he realized that the Tories would never support such legislation.[15]

The only place that Joe Borowski could be was in the New Democratic Party.

In the spring of 1965 a mimeographed six-page booklet appeared in limited circulation in Thompson. Staff apologized for the misspellings and badly worded phrases in this "hastily written first edition" of *The Democrat*, but added, "you must remember that we have been subjected to much abuse ourselves in the past few weeks and we make no apology for our efforts to combat and destroy its source. May God bless our little but defiant paper."

That little but defiant paper turned out to be the official voice of the Thompson New Democratic Party, itself defiant and little, but growing rapidly.[16] By the time *The Democrat* hit the streets, the NDP claimed it was well on the way to having 300 members. The party could trace its inception to meetings in Joe Borowski's living room, where frustration finally crystallized into action. "Let's not just talk, let's do something," was her husband's oft-repeated exhortation, remembered Jean Borowski.

The neophyte association had pledged "to combat and destroy" what they saw as the intransigence of Inco and the Manitoba government in not acceding to the demands of Thompson residents for self-government. "For half a decade, this new city has lived under the iron grip of an isolationist minded company, jealous of anything which might dilute its control," wrote executive member John Taylor.

The original 1956 agreement that Inco signed with the Liberal government headed by Premier Doug Campbell stated that the "townsite will not be incorporated as a municipal district, city, town or village unit, until in the opinion of the province and the mining company the time will have arrived when such action should be taken."[17]

But as Inco pointed out, as well as sinking mine shafts, it sank nearly $8.5 million dollars into providing infrastructure for Thompson, including the building of "roads and sidewalks, sewers, drainage system, water treatment plant, schools, and a civic administration building that houses the jail and fire hall."[18] It did not think, insofar as corporations are capable of thought, that Thompson was a company town. Certainly, if it was, it was a very ungrateful one.

Not everyone agreed with Joe's vision for Thompson, nor did everyone view the formation of the NDP as a breakthrough for democracy. The wives of party members held a perogy sale in the plaza to raise funds and were harassed by a "well-known Conservative," Jean related. He was "just wild," and yelled at prospective customers: "Don't buy from them, don't buy from them, they're Communist!" Her friend was truly alarmed, but Jean laughed. "I says, 'Never mind, just ignore it—consider where it's coming from.'"

In March 1965, Municipal Affairs Minister Robert Smellie and Inco agreed to form a five-member advisory council for Thompson. The members would be chosen from a slate of 17 nominees, who would be recommended by the union, the Chamber of Commerce and Inco. The advisory council would live up to its name, in that the members would have no power, but work with and advise the town administrator, Carl Nesbitt, who was regarded as able and competent. After two years, the situation would be reviewed.

Joe excoriated this proposal, inasmuch as a proposal can be excoriated. In a letter to the *Thompson Citizen*, he called the agreement "unfair" and "a violation of our cherished Bill of Rights."[19] "We can do one of two things," he wrote, "allow the present system to continue, which incidentally is very efficient, or we can insist on an elected council. What this simply boils down to is efficiency versus the right to democracy."

Opposition was not confined to the members of the NDP. "Everybody kept saying," recalled Jean Borowski, "we have to do something, we have to do something, so what can we do?" Joe initiated a petition calling for self-government for Thompson within the year, with an elected council of six people. By the end of March, 1,700 people had signed.

The advisory council was to be appointed on April 2. On the last day of March, Joe packed his suitcase, took the petition and an eiderdown sleeping bag, and hopped the bus south to Winnipeg.

Notes
Chapter 2
This modern fret for liberty

[1] According to miner Bill Smith, Inco's Thompson operation was the first mine to run both a pit and surface mine at the same time. (Interview with Bill Smith February, 2002.)

[2] Op. Cit., "Meet Joe Borowski," Ted Allen.

[3] Anne Collins, *The Big Evasion: Abortion, the Issue that Won't Go Away* (Toronto: Lester and Orpen Dennys Limited, 1985), p. 6.

[4] *Thompson Citizen*, August 2, 1964

[5] *Thompson Citizen*, September 10, 1964.

[6] The union itself later admitted that the strike was "more of a protest action against the excessive cost of living …than a disapproval of the contract arrived at by the negotiators. ("Thompson strike over, work starts Wednesday," *Winnipeg Tribune*, September 8, 1964.)

[7] Op. Cit., Anne Collins, p. 7.

[8] "The outsider moves in," Pat Annesley, *Maclean's*, December, 1970, p. 42.

[9] Op. Cit., Anne Collins, p 7.

[10] Ibid. "The outsider moves in," Annesley.

[11] Inteview with Bill Smith, February, 2002. Smith contended that Joe may well have been motivated more by political considerations than concern for worker safety.

[12] Interview with Bob Mayer, February, 2002.

[13] "Meet Joe Borowski," Ted Allen

[14] "Anti-abortion stand restated," *Winnipeg Free Press*, September 10, 1971.

[15] "Nothing fazes the honerabul Joe Borowski," Douglas Sagi, *The Canadian Magazine, Winnipeg Tribune*, June 12, 1971, p 27.

[16] The party's original executive was Joe Borowski as president, Fred Allen as secretary, Lloyd Hamilton as treasurer and John Taylor, organizing chairman. ("Thompson NDP's form executive committee," *Thompson Citizen*, March 2, 1965.)

[17] "An elected council for town of Thompson," Val Werier, *Tribune*, April 7, 1965.

[18] *The Northern Miner*, as quoted on Inco's website.

[19] "NDP opposes advisory plan," *Thompson Citizen*, March 11, 1965.

Chapter 3

The freelance wave-maker[1]

> But hark! The cry is Astur:
> And lo! The ranks divide;
> And the great lord of Luna
> Comes with his stately stride....
> He smiled on those bold Romans,
> A smile serene and high;
> He eyed the flinching Tuscans,
> And scorn was in his eye.
>
> Thomas Babington Macaulay
> *Horatius at the Bridge*

> "Well, they laughed at him—who are you? So Joe says,
> 'Fine, until there're changes
> I'm going to stay right here on the steps.'"
>
> Jean Borowski

DUFFERIN "DUFF" ROBLIN, CONSERVATIVE PREMIER OF MANITOBA IN 1965, was a polished and seasoned politician, known for the forcefulness and eloquence of his oratory, but lacking that elusive quality referred to as charisma—a self-described "bit of a dry stick."[2] Ironically, the man whom Joe Borowski regarded as hopelessly charmed by big business and arrogantly out of tune with the difficulties of the blue collar life was himself considered by the Tory old-guard as a "left-wing radical." Roblin was elected, on his 37th birthday, as leader of the provincial Conservatives after a bitter leadership battle in June of 1954. His first speech in the 1955 assembly was described in the *Free Press* as "a swerve to the Left."[3]

Roblin supported assistance to old-age pensioners and penal reform, policies that were also advocated by the CCF. He was elected as premier in 1958 with a minority government; among the opposition was the 22-year-old Edward Schreyer, who, as the CCF member for Brokenhead, was the youngest person ever to be elected to the Manitoba legislature.

For the better part of a year, the CCF found itself in the awkward position of voting with the Tories on several motions, until at last the government fell in the late spring of 1959. However, it returned again with a secure majority in the May election. Lloyd Stinson, a CCF member who lost his seat, recalled some years later a headline following the Conservative victory: "No sales tax is Tory pledge."[4] As such pledges are wont to do, this one came back to haunt the Conservative premier in the person of Joe Borowski.

That was later: while Joe Borowski was moiling and toiling in the Thompson mine and becoming embroiled in labour disputes, Duff Roblin was enjoying his most popular and productive years as premier. His government built schools, highways, parks, developed northern hydro and embarked on the construction of a monstrously large floodway to contain the annual overflowing of the Red River, which meets the Assiniboine River in the heart of Winnipeg. This last project, known formally as the Red River Floodway, is today referred to by most Manitobans as Duff's Ditch, and is arguably the former premier's most significant legacy.

But come the spring of 1965, Roblin had a lot on his mind. His government's popularity was waning, mainly because of its taxation policies and its reluctance to increase minimum wage, defend the rights of tenants, or tackle medicare. The incorporation of the controversial Metro government of Greater Winnipeg also generated hostility from the populace. Moreover, the premier himself was, or so it was speculated, thinking of running for the leadership of the federal Conservatives.[5]

Thus when Joe Borowski came down from Thompson, like a prophet of old, insisting on self-government for his town, Roblin suavely fobbed him off. He met with Joe to receive the petition, but was not disposed to put any effort into the matter. "Mr. Roblin told me he'd like nothing better than to see free elections in Thompson, but he was bound by a contract of the former Liberal government with Inco," Joe told the curious members of the press.[6]

That wasn't enough for Joe Borowski, who spread his sleeping bag on the steps of the Manitoba Legislature to begin his solitary vigil.

Joe had scarcely begun to brave the icy April chill when sympathetic Winnipeggers, including many university students, ever sensitive to protest and injustice, rallied round, bringing coffee and sandwiches to nourish his body, and whiskey to bolster his spirits.[7] While Joe discussed the issues with visitors to the legislature, the media debated and speculated on the legitimacy of his cause. *Winnipeg Free Press* labour reporter Dudley Magnus cautiously opined that a "status quo" group in Thompson was really at the heart of the present impasse. It was a labour issue, he wrote, because Joe had the unofficial backing of the United Steelworkers of America—even though Joe was at pains to point out his protest was his own initiative.

Winnipeg Tribune writer Val Werier pointed out the oddity that Thompson would have an elected school board in the fall of 1965. "Here is an anomaly. If the town is ready for representative government in school management, why not in municipal affairs?" he questioned. Moreover, many of the 8,500 Thompson residents were ratepayers: 1,200 owned homes. "In this day and age, it is incongruous to have taxation without representation."[8]

Public interest was high, and the media monitored Joe's activities with zeal. When he left his post to attend Mass at St. Mary's Cathedral, the press snapped a picture of his sign: "Gone to Church."[9] When his 11-year-old daughter Debbie made the 14-hour train ride down from Thompson to join him, reporters were there.

When Joe decided to call his hero, Martin Luther King, then engaged in civil rights protests in Baltimore, Maryland, the incident appeared in the paper. Joe, who placed a long distance call to the Lord Baltimore Hotel, just missed the famous minister. Unperturbed, he later abandoned the idea, "as I didn't want to raise the racial element when it isn't a racial issue."[10]

He was also noticed by a number of legislators, including Ed Schreyer, who spoke up in the House on Joe's behalf, and Liberal leader Gildas Moldat, who questioned what was to become of Thompson's desire for self-government.

Joe vowed to stay "until I achieve my objective or until I'm dragged by the heels and thrown into jail," as he told Frank Sullivan, of the *Winnipeg Tribune*, early in his protest.

But while the spirit is willing, the flesh, exposed to the chill of a Manitoba spring, is weak. It was, as someone pointed out to him, the worst time of year to picket out of doors. "Unfortunately, democracy knows no seasons," Joe replied.[11] But he came down with the flu and packed up his sleeping bag on April 8 after huddling inside it for 12 hours trying to shake the bug. Declared Joe, "I am sure that my cause would not be aided if I were to invite martyrdom by remaining outside while suffering from a cold and flu."[12] He had spent six nights sleeping in the windy vestibule and seven days pacing back and forth on stone-grey steps.

That same day Robert Smellie announced the appointment of the five-member advisory council in Thompson, while NDP leader Russ Paulley informed the House of Joe's decision to go home, adding that "it was only at the urging of myself and my group that he agreed to end his vigil…."[13]

Apparently, the wily Duff Roblin also had something to do with Joe's quitting his legislative protest, or so he claimed. Some 30 years later, Roblin reminisced in his memoirs that he sent George Johnson, then Minister of Health and a medical doctor, to pay a visit to Joe. Johnson convinced the feverish protester that he was suffering from pneumonia, and he further persuaded Joe to check himself into the hospital. Joe did not return to the legislature.[14]

Joe himself, in retrospect, wondered if the effort had been worth it. He viewed his protest as ineffective, as he told *Free Press* reporter Dudley Magnus.[15] Moreover, he was subjected to further petty persecutions upon his return, including difficulty obtaining a permit to put up a billboard advertising his business. The first commercial highway sign to adorn the roadside adjacent to Thompson, it was destroyed by vandals soon after it was constructed.[16] Joe offered a reward for information leading to the apprehension of the culprits. Meanwhile, he was still unable to lease space in the Thompson Plaza.

However, Len Steven, United Steelworkers of America prairie region supervisor, lauded Joe's efforts, publicly stating that his picketing "drew nation-wide attention to the fact that a private company can come into Manitoba and not only run the town, but run the people."

A tangible result of Joe's highly visible campaign was that

Thompson's civic election came sooner than expected. This historic event took place in the fall of 1966. Excitement was in the air as Thompson's citizens felt the exhilarating pinch and pull of the democracy for which they had so long sought and fought. It was to be expected that Joe Borowski would be there, plunged in the thick of the politicking, perhaps running for office, as the town prepared to elect its first mayor and six councilors. But where was he?

Joe had tasted the beguiling fruit of protest and had returned for more. When elections came to Thompson in 1966, he was camped 600 kilometres to the south, on the steps of the Manitoba legislature, complete with signs and his trusty sleeping bag. This time, it was a little more personal. "Our premier is greedy and money hungry," read one of Joe's placards.

What precipitated the latest siege was the Roblin government's announcement that the cabinet would have a pay increase as of September 1, 1966. For the premier, it was a raise from $14,500 to $18,000. For cabinet members, the annual $12,500 climbed to $15,000.[17] In the meantime, the efforts by NDP members to increase the province's minimum wage from 92 cents to $1.50 had been stonewalled by the Conservatives. (The Liberals too had pushed for a minimum wage increase, but had suggested that $1.25 per hour was more feasible.) To Joe, the cabinet pay raise was unconscionable.

This time, he was a seasoned picketer, ready for the long haul, telling a *Free Press* reporter when he began his protest on September 20, 1965, that he was going to stay until Roblin and the cabinet rescinded their 25 per cent pay raise, or increased the minimum wage. Joe had given the premier fair warning, calling Roblin a day before he arrived on the legislature steps to give him a last chance to redress the situation. Evidently, Duff turned down the opportunity.[18]

None too happy with Joe's reappearance, Roblin had a relatively cordial exchange with the protester on the steps of the legislature. He didn't mind the picket but he didn't want the mess—Joe was to put his bag away when he wasn't using it.[19] After this, by all accounts, Duff ignored the northern menace. Thus began a provocative standoff.

Many Winnipeggers seemed glad to have Joe back, and gave him tangible support; a group of high school students and others joined him to sleep overnight that Saturday, only to be awakened at 7:30 a.m. by the police, who had been called in by the legislature commissionaires. Not only did Winnipeg city police officers arrive, but members of the RCMP also showed up. Joe was appalled by what he saw as harassment instigated by Roblin himself. "If he doesn't like us here, he knows what he can do. This isn't Moscow or Alabama," he said, and added, "The mere presence of police at any picket line is intimidation."[20]

Joe's next move left government a little nonplussed; on October 2, with the help of students, he moved a trailer onto the steps of the legislature, eliciting a few comments, including a "very interesting" from a cigar-chomping Sterling Lyon.[21] Duff had admitted his right to be here, Joe reasoned, "and surely he would not want me to sleep on the hard concrete and get pneumonia when it gets to 20 below."[22]

Pneumonia or not, Public Works Minister Stewart McLean was miffed. Cabinet, he stated ominously, would be discussing the matter, but the public relations surrounding Joe and his trailer had become undoubtedly touchy, complicated and delicate. Before the aghast gaze of the Tories, Joe Borowski was evolving into a hero of the people, achieving greater status by the day. He may have gone too far, but the government didn't want to make a martyr of him.[23] The affair of the trailer began to take on a hue of buffoonery which was enjoyed by press and Winnipeggers alike, the former writing stories with headlines such as "Trailer for sale or rent?" Joe was told to remove it, a directive with which he did not comply, and in the wee hours of October 5, his mobile home was borne away—with Joe inside it.

"I was still in bed in my pajamas. I didn't even get a chance to brush my teeth. It was a rough ride down the steps..." Joe later charged. The order to remove the trailer came from the provincial cabinet, said sources close to the government. "I think it was most uncharitable of Mr. Roblin and his regime to kidnap me so unceremoniously."[24]

Joe was undeterred, or rather, his supporters were. The trailer was hauled by his fans from the nearby parking lot back to the steps of the legislature. Joe did not stop them. It was taken away again on October 17, and at that point, Joe went to the RCMP with the idea of prosecuting the government for illegally moving his property.[25] He vowed to resist—by force, if necessary—any further attempt to deprive him of his digs.

On October 19, under the watchful eye of the RCMP plain-clothes officers, public work officials attempted to tow the trailer with a government car. Joe, barefoot, leaned against the car, shivering in the early morning chill, clad only in pajama top and trousers. When Stewart McLean arrived on the scene and confronted him, Joe told the Public Works Minister to "go to hell."[26]

As the cars of the early morning government commuters backed up behind the obstruction, and the sound of horns honking rose thin and imperious in clear frosty air, Joe Borowski fought the law. The government car was unhitched, Joe sat on the cross bar of the trailer, and finally ten public work officials lifted the trailer, and Joe along with it, and carried it away. Now shod and wearing a jacket retrieved from the trailer by a supporter, he "disappeared down the road, arms akimbo", but vowed, "I'll be back, you goon."[27] Two days later he returned, reverting to his sleeping bag.[28] In the rough-housing over his mobile abode, a petition of about 10,000 names against the cabinet salary increase had disappeared, and the television set had been broken, claimed Joe.[29]

His vigil continued peacefully for about three weeks, until one night he returned from dinner with a friend only to find that his mattresses, sleeping bag, suitcases and picket signs had disappeared. It turned out they had been locked up in the provincial garage; Joe had been given a warning a fortnight previously to leave the steps.[30]

What next? He tried to lay charges with the RCMP to retrieve his goods but these attempts failed. The next time Joe appeared on the steps, his wife Jean was by his side. Bereft of equipment to shield them from the bitter Winnipeg winds, the couple sought refuge in the lobby. At midnight all unauthorized persons were required to leave the building. Joe and Jean Borowski did not move.

It was show time. The RCMP arrived, and after two hours of wrangling and negotiations, Joe was arrested. He did not struggle, but neither did he cooperate, and it took two burly officers to drag the hefty protester from the vestibule into a waiting patrol car.[31]

Meanwhile, Jean observed the fracas, calmly smoking a cigarette on the lobby bench. "They told us to leave…and I said, 'No,' I said, 'I'm a taxpaxer, I can be here, this building's as much mine as yours'—where it came from, I don't know." She did not plan to get arrested—few people do—but once Joe disappeared, the RCMP "got a lady officer and she says, 'Well, your husband is in jail and he's going to stay there and now it's up to you, do you want to come peacefully or do we have to take you by force?' I said, 'Oh, if he's in jail, I guess I'll go too.'"

Joe settled down in his cell and was soon sleeping the sleep of the just. But Jean, confined in the women's wing, was shaking like "jelly." When that steel door slammed behind her, "I thought I'd just died." The compassionate matron kept Jean with her all night, rather than sending her to a cell. They played cards and Jean smoked to calm her nerves. (She and the matron corresponded for years afterward.) In the morning, Joe's wife had to breakfast with the inmates. "These women, they looked so hard, and you had big slices of toast and mugs of coffee and one says, 'Are you going to eat that toast?' I said, 'No.'—'Oh, you're too good for us?' You know, my heart was pounding like you wouldn't believe."

The Borowskis were brought before a magistrate November 15, charged with obstructing an RCMP officer in his duty, and released. Joe, when he heard of Jean's fright, said only, "Well, what are you scared of?"

Jean flew home and Joe soldiered on alone. Deprived of his belongings, he picketed all day and slept elsewhere at night. As he tramped back and forth on the legislature steps, his thoughts dogged him. What difference was his protest making? He had received an enormous amount of publicity. And there had been noises from the Tories that the minimum wage would probably be increased.

Joe had said from the outset that he would end his protest if the minimum wage were increased, if the cabinet repudiated their salary increase, or December 20, whichever came first. But once again, the willing spirit bowed to the tyranny of the flesh; this time, Jean succumbed. Having been left to look after the store since September 20, and following two trips down to Winnipeg, one of which ended in the trauma of arrest, she developed pleurisy and took to her bed, closing up the souvenir shop.

On November 25 Joe flew back to Thompson.

What had he accomplished? *Maclean's* magazine chose him as one of the "outstanding Canadians of 1966" and "the year's most obviously disgusted taxpayer." The government's throne speech in December 1966 included a promise to raise the minimum wage to $1.00 an hour. Moreover, some thought that Joe's stand was instrumental in the government preparing a bill to establish the office of a provincial ombudsman.[32]

Less rewarding results were special regulations passed by the

Conservatives in March of 1967, which pundits attributed to government nervousness generated by the Borowski pickets. The rules prohibited any "sign or notice" being erected on or in government grounds that was not issued from the government itself, and banned parking and loitering on government lots and properties from midnight to 7 a.m.[33]

This is what Joe Borowski had wrought. Not bad for a self-described "freelance wave-maker." But the '60's, that decade of protest, were not over yet.

Despite the campaign promise during the 1959 election that there would be no sales tax, no such promise was made in the 1966 campaign, and the Tory government, which still held a working majority following the election on June 24 of that year, finally bit the bullet. A sales tax of 5 per cent became effective June 1, 1967.

Joe Borowski regarded the tax as illegal because the people didn't vote for it, nor were they given a chance to do so.[34] His method of protest was, as usual, direct and to the point. He refused to collect the reviled tax from his customers—instead, he paid it out of his own pocket, remitting more than $20,000 over the years.[35]

One freezing winter afternoon, a well-wrapped customer climbed the stairs to Joe's cosy souvenir shop above the bowling alley. After pulling off his gloves, stamping the snow from his boots and brushing off his greatcoat, the man deliberated over several items before finally purchasing a $3 medallion. Unbeknownst to Joe, the man was a tax department undercover agent. Joe was summoned before Judge N. G. MacPhee in a Thompson court on January 19, 1968, where James Constable testified that when he bought the medallion, Mr. Borowski had not charged him sales tax. Joe pleaded not guilty, but was convicted. He was fined $25 or seven days in jail.

He chose jail and served his time at The Pas. As one editor observed: "What did amuse us was the mild revenge he took against the Establishment in forcing them to fly him to jail in The Pas for only seven days. The cost of police escorts, plane fares, meals and ground transport to the Government of Manitoba probably proved a sweetener in his bitter cup."[36] In February, Joe was back in court on a second charge of not collecting the sales tax. He provided his own defense and pleaded not guilty. Again, he was convicted. The sentence, however, was more severe: $50 or 21 days in jail.[37]

Back in The Pas for a longer stay, Joe sent a letter to Manitoba Attorney-General Sterling Lyon, condemning the jail as a "filthy Conservative fire-trap" and "unsanitary rat hole."[38] He did not expect special treatment, nor was Joe Borowski the kind of man whose heart would bleed for the penalized. As he noted later, "When I see the five million people living in misery and poverty, in shacks, honest people, trying to meet their family responsibilities with dignity, when I see them treated the way they are by the various levels of government, I can't begin to sympathize with the people in prison."[39]

But the conditions at The Pas provincial jail—where the maximum stay was three months—were in violation of basic human rights, he charged. Less than a year later, Joe would describe to his intrigued colleagues in the Manitoba legislature his jailhouse experiences. The prisoners themselves had rated The Pas as one of the worst in Canada. The 1917 building was poorly ventilated, and 50 to 70 men were crammed into a space of 30 by 35 feet, with only two toilets. The inmate was given one dirty blanket when he arrived and that was his only bedding. Joe wasn't even given a pair of shorts. "You were given a pair of pants and a shirt and you wore this thing until you left."[40] If a fire broke out, the men would surely perish, as "the fire escape door is always blocked by beds because there's so many prisoners in there… there's just enough space for you to walk in sideways and get on your bed."

More frightful yet than The Pas was the local Thompson jail. "In a mining town you have to appreciate there's a lot of drinking and fighting, so Friday night and Saturday night the business is very good and there could be 15 or 20 people put into this place," Joe explained. "There's no mattresses in there so the boys spend the night standing up, and the worst part of it is they make the prisoners take their shoes off, so you're standing on cold concrete all night…I know what it's like because I've spent one night in there, standing in your bare feet on concrete and guys throwing up all over the place. They throw up on you and the place stinks."[41]

Yet the punishment meted out by the crown neither deterred nor rehabilitated him. The recidivist Joe was charged yet a third time in the summer of 1968. He was found guilty, and this time slapped with a stiff fine of $200, which he again refused to pay. Jean found an envelope slipped under the door of the souvenir shop, with $200 in bills stuffed inside. Scrawled on the outside was the message, "from the boys."

Joe was then serving a month's sentence, but not at The Pas. Because he wanted to work, he was sent to the provincial institution at Dauphin. "It's only 75 cents a day," he shrugged. "Nobody does this for the money. They just want to get out and do some work." At the Pas, "you get up in the morning at 6:30 or 6:15; you eat breakfast, you lay around; you eat lunch, you lay around; you eat supper and you lay around. It drives you up the wall."[42]

At the Dauphin jail, which prisoners rated as one of the best in Canada, conditions were much improved. "And I think the reason for it, first of all, is that you can get a second helping of food at Dauphin...the second thing is you can get out and work. I spent a month there and in that month we dug 700 bags of potatoes, 300 bags of onions and all kinds of other things that we did, you know, cutting the lawn and raking. And when the month was gone I lost weight, I had a nice tan and I felt good. No kidding. When I got out of there I had no grudge, you know, I didn't go out hating the government or hating the police or hating anybody. I spent a month in and to me it just seemed to fly."

At Dauphin, Joe enthused, "facilities there are excellent. The place, I think, is twice the size of The Pas jail, for example, but there's only 28 prisoners. You have your own cell, two men to a cell; you have your own toilet and sink in each cell, you have a television and radio—this is a luxury I agree—but nevertheless, it's there."[43]

When Joe got out of jail, the sales tax was still there. It seemed inconceivable that his actions would have any influence on the matter. What did he gain, except a certain working knowledge of the best and the worst jails in Manitoba, and an added burnish to his reputation as a man of conviction? He didn't seek notoriety by his actions, but that was one thing, if nothing else, that he achieved in his latest struggle with the state.

A little notoriety goes a long way, and as Joe spent 1968 in and out of jail, the political pendulum in Thompson swung further and further to the left, as dissatisfaction with the Conservatives deepened. Finally, in early 1969, Gordon Beard, the Conservative MLA for the riding of Churchill (which at that time included Thompson) resigned in protest over the government's lack of action in the north. A by-election was set for February 20, 1969.

Who best to run for the NDP but the well-known champion of the working class, Joe Borowski?

But "he said, no way, no," Jean Borowski remembered. "He just felt that he wasn't qualified and he was involved in the union and we had a business—we had a good thing going." Moreover, she recalled, the United Church minister in Thompson was also involved in the NDP and the Borowskis thought he would be the best man to run.

The minister, however, had a caveat: he needed the permission of his congregation in order to stand for election. Moreover, he was convinced that Joe was the better choice. Finally, Joe proposed that if the preacher could not obtain permission, then he, Joe, would run as the NDP candidate.

He was "so confident" that the minister would get permission that he began to think up slogans for the other man's campaign, Jean said. When the cleric walked into their home a few days later and without further ado said, "Joe, you're in," her husband was dumbfounded. "I can't believe, I just can't believe it," he said. "Oh my God, what am I going to do?"

Joe seemed to be the only one among his colleagues and friends with any apprehension about his nomination. Jean, for her part, "couldn't think one way or the other. I had no idea what we were getting involved in, really. We weren't political people—the union's one thing, but politics—what? You voted for whatever your parents voted, or you got to know the man, you voted for him, but that's about it." Nevertheless, everyone who heard the news was excitedly optimistic. "Oh sure, Joe, he can do it, he can do it."

Sid Green, then NDP MLA for Inkster and lawyer for the United Steelworkers, and Russ Paulley, NDP leader and MLA for Radisson, both thought they had a winner in Joe, Jean recalled. Joe knew the miners, he was a Steelworker, he was a businessman, and his stints at the legislature, and most particularly, his landing in jail for not collecting the sales tax had burned his image into the mind of the public.

For good or ill, Joe accepted the challenge. He plunged into that fast-moving, turbulent river that was political life in Manitoba in 1969 and started swimming for his life.

Notes
Chapter 3
The freelance wave-maker

[1] Op. Cit. "Meet Joe Borowski," Ted Allen.

[2] "The Roblin Decade," Lloyd Stinson, *Winnipeg Free Press*, February 27, 1971

[3] Ibid.

[4] Ibid.

[5] Ibid.

[6] "Legislature camper gets long lease from Smellie," *Tribune*, April 2, 1965.

[7] "Camper at legislature has not so quiet night," *Tribune*, April 4, 1965.

[8] "An elected council for town of Thompson," Val Werier, *Tribune*, April 7, 1965.

[9] *Tribune*, April 5, 1965.

[10] "Picket walks and walks, tries to phone Martin Luther King" Don Newman, *Winnipeg Free Press*, c. April 6, 1965.

[11] "Flu hits picketer Borowski," *Free Press*, c. April 7, 1965.

[12] "Borowski quits with a cold," *Tribune*, April 9, 1965.

[13] Ibid

[14] Duff Roblin *Speaking For Myself, Politics and Other Pursuits*, (Winnipeg: Great Plains Publications, 1999), p. 216.

[15] "Says legislature camping didn't pay," *Free Press*, c. April, 1965.

[16] *Nickel Belt News*, September 14, 1964.

[17] "Premier and cabinet boost own salaries," *Free Press*, c. September 12, 1966.

[18] "Camper to stage protest," *Free Press*, September 20, 1966.

[19] "Make your bed Duff instructs messy camper," *Tribune*, c. September 21, 1966

[20] "Pay critic hurls charges at police," *Free Press*, c. September 26, 1966.

[21] "Picketer warm, snug in camper," *Tribune*, October 3, 1966.

[22] "Borowski gets roof," *Free Press*, October 3, 1966; "Picketer warm, snug in camper," *Tribune* October 3, 1966.

[23] Ibid.

[24] "I was kidnapped, says Joe Borowski," Sheldon Bowles, *Free Press*, October 5, 1966.

[25] "Trailer for sale or rent?" *Tribune*, October 17, 1966.

[26] Ibid.

[27] Ibid.

[28] He returned the ill-used trailer to the owner, garage mechanic Les Hansell.

[29] "Trailer for sale or rent?" *Tribune*, October 17, 1966.

[30] "While Joe is out, his tent is folded, " *Free Press*, November 9, 1966.

[31] "Borowski, wife held after 'sleep-in' bid," Michael Kostelnuk, *Free Press*, November 15, 1966.

[32] "Citizens, take heart. People can fight back," *Maclean's Report*, February 1967.

[33] "No watching the sunrise in the part," Val Werier, *Tribune*, March 17, 1967; "Could 'unfriendly' gov't hit pickets" Dudley Magnus, *Free Press*, March 18, 1967.

[34] "The outsider moves in," Pat Annesley, *Maclean's*, December 7, 1967 p. 42.

[35] Ibid.

[36] "Cale's comments: A matter of principle," *Coin, Stamp and Antique News*, March 9, 1968.

[37] *Nickel Belt News*, February 14, 1968.

[38] "Borowski raps 'filthy' conditions at The Pas jail," *Tribune*, March 5, 1968.

[39] *Hansard*, May 5, 1969, p. 1918.[40] Ibid.

[40] Ibid.

[41] Ibid. p. 1919.

[42] Ibid.

[43] *Hansard*, May 5, 1968, p. 1920.

Chapter 4

Deep down you're NDP too

But fiercely ran the current,
Swollen high by months of rain,
And fast his blood was flowing;
And he was sore in pain,
And heavy with his armour,
And spent with changing blows;
And oft they thought him sinking,
But still again he rose.

Thomas Babington Macauley
Horatius at the Bridge

"But let's put this thing in perspective.
There are almost four billion people in this world who've
never even heard of Joe Borowski, let alone Walter Weir."
John Robertson[1]

ONCE RESOLVED TO THE COURSE, JOE SET ABOUT CAMPAIGNING VIG-orously in the vast Churchill riding, which covered nearly all of northern Manitoba. He expected little trouble from the Liberal opponent Gary Walsh, and from the Conservative candidate Mike Klewchuk.

It seemed to Jean that his green and black signs were everywhere. Joe canvassed three-quarters of the voters in Thompson, all the voters in Lynn Lake and Churchill and over half the voters in Gillam and Snow Lake.[2] Sid Green, well-known in Thompson, knocked on doors on Joe's behalf, and his campaign was managed by neighbour and former NDP candidate Wilf Hudson.

Thompson parish priest Leon Lavasseur presided over the town hall meeting at which all candidates gave their views. There were at least 400 people packing the high school gymnasium that night, he recalled. Joe, for his part, had to answer questions about his opposition to the sales tax. He and the government had "reached a compromise" in November, was all he would reveal.[3]

Joe was door-knocking in Churchill when he called home and received the news he'd half expected but still dreaded: Dr. Blaine Johnston had entered the race as an independent candidate. He was a formidable opponent, a doctor who had been in Thompson since 1957, and was chief-of-staff at the Thompson General Hospital. He had been elected to town council in the first municipal elections in October 1966.[4] Moreover, Joe suspected Inco and its supporters were quietly backing Johnston.

"When I told Joe, he said, 'Well, that's it…I haven't got a hope in hell'—that's exactly what he said," related Jean. So sure was Joe that he abandoned his plans to campaign on the far-flung reserves, and returned to Thompson. "He went to see Blaine and they shook hands because we knew him, he was our doctor…Joe said, 'Good luck, and may the best one win.'"

Joe did not publicly admit his trepidation but he believed a doctor would easily defeat an ex-miner in a town like Thompson. "So election night, we couldn't believe the results as they were coming," Jean said. At 10 o'clock, Johnston arrived at the NDP headquarters, as his own headquarters were deserted. "You know, Joe'd be ahead and he'd be ahead, just going back and forth, back and forth." At that point in the evening, Joe was leading by 21 votes and he wanted to leave, but Johnston said, "I'm staying 'til the end—I have to know who's going to win."

The tired Borowskis went home, and Johnston came and sat with them. "Our phone was ringing off the hook." Ed Schreyer, by then an MP in Ottawa, was one of the callers. "He says, 'Joe, when you're leading by 21 votes, you're not going to lose 21 votes—I'm telling you right now, you're in.' Of course the Conservatives were going crazy. They wanted a recount and a recount and a recount and…Joe'd go ahead, they'd recount, Joe would lose, and Ed was the only one who kept saying, 'Joe, believe it.'"

The following day, the press reported Joe's slim 23-vote win, and the plans for a recount the next week. Voter turnout had been 66 per cent, the highest ever for the riding of Churchill. When ballot boxes arrived from Pukatawagan and Laurie River, and the results tabulated, Joe's lead dropped precariously to only 14 votes.[5] An official recount was scheduled for March 13, and in the meantime, Dauphin Judge Lorn Ferg ruled that Joe could not take his seat in the assembly.[6]

Joe called Sid Green to represent him at the recount, and, over 30 years later, the former NDP Minister remembered that day. At one point, there was a ballot that was clearly marked for Joe, but which also bore "a little, a little mark." It had been rejected. Green questioned why, and accepted without comment the argument that the small mark disqualified it. "But Joe, you know, there could be problems in his mind." When they broke for lunch, Joe reproved him: "You didn't put up much of a fight."

"He was wondering whether he'd got a good enough lawyer, and I said, 'Joe, the status quo is we win...if we change the status quo, I don't know what happens...' And his face lit up... And sure enough, in the afternoon a ballot came up for Johnston with an x *and* a little mark, and they threw it out—and Joe winked at me."

In the end, Joe emerged the winner, by 21 votes. He himself credited his win to an inspired remark he made at a public meeting: if Dr. Johnston won the election and took off to Winnipeg, who then would be the doctor in Thompson? It was this astute observation, Joe believed, that sank deep into the consciousness of the townspeople and dictated the results.[7]

Whether this was the case or not, Joe Borowski took his seat in the Legislature as Member for the Churchill riding in 1969 on March 19—the day reserved in the Catholic Church for the feast of his patron, St. Joseph.

The press had already pegged Joe Borowski as a colourful personality, and now it kept close tabs on his performance in the House. Joe, from day one, did not disappoint.

He was himself, however, disappointed—as he declared in his maiden speech—that his "old friend and tormentor, Mr. Duff

Roblin" was not there. Roblin had left the Manitoba legislature to run for the leadership of the federal Conservative party in 1967, only to lose to Robert Stanfield. He then ran as the Conservative candidate for Winnipeg South Centre in 1968 and was decisively defeated. Roblin himself looking back on his political life, was philosophical about his defeat; things just didn't work out.[8]

A more partisan view was that "when marking their ballots on June 25, 1968, the good people of Winnipeg South Centre may have had visions of Joe Borowski on the Legislative Building steps protesting the sales tax and Cabinet Ministers' salaries. Perhaps Joe defeated Duff."[9] Be that as it may, Roblin subsequently accepted the presidency of Canadian Pacific Investments in Montreal and was appointed to the Senate in March 1978.

Thus when Joe arrived triumphant, Manitoba's premier was Walter Weir, a former undertaker from Mindosa, who had been in power since November 25, 1967. Despite Duff's absence, Joe quickly found his footing as a member of the opposition. He had a natural oratorical gift, a shrewd business sense, a commitment to the "guy who carries a lunch pail to work" and, what his colleague Sid Green described as "street smarts."[10]

He was upbraided, shortly upon his arrival, by Conservative Thelma Forbes, for using "unparliamentary language." Joe said "damn" not once, but twice, in a speech expressing his disgust for doctors who chose to opt out of the provincial medicare plan. "When I was elected to this House I did not realize that I would have to go to finishing school to be able to speak here," Joe shot back. "I'm a working man and I have been all my life, and you'll forgive me if I can't use the flowery, the meaningless euphemisms that we have heard from across the House."[11]

The bill being debated was an amendment to the 1967 Medicare Act, which would make premiums mandatory for all Manitoba residents—yet doctors could opt out and charge an extra 15 per cent. Ironically, all the doctors in Thompson, including Blaine Johnston, announced their intention of following the latter course.

Joe followed Sidney Green's lead in suggesting that if the doctors "really want to practise medicine under their beloved free enterprise system," they could build their own hospitals, or be charged a fee for using existing hospitals. "You can't have it both ways; either you are for free enterprise or you are for socialism, but the way it is being practised in this country up until now, it's rugged free enterprise for us little guys and creamy socialism for the rich," he charged. "We're one of the richest nations in the world and yet we are the recipient of second-class, dollar-oriented medical care."

When Liberal member Laurent (Larry) Desjardins pressed Joe on whether or not he thought that doctors "be forced to belong to the plan", Joe retorted, "...if we are compelled by law, by this very legislature, to pay premiums, I see nothing wrong—these aren't God's chosen people, the doctors—if we are compelled by law to pay premiums, I see nothing wrong with compulsion for the rich."[12] It was not the last time Joe would tangle with Larry Desjardins in the House.

Another thorn in his side was Sterling Lyon. Joe got a taste of the attorney-general's caustic style when he questioned what seemed to be a paltry amount of money relegated to the branch of northern affairs. Lyon rose to his feet to "tell my honourable friend what he should know as the member for Churchill, and I hope that his education will be improved by the time I sit down."

Lyon then proceeded to explain that the branch under discussion was established well before Joe Borowski "had anything concrete, ill or otherwise, to do with the north, in order to bring, primarily, municipal services to many of the remote areas." The north received its due share of dollars in the budgets of individual departments, Lyon said, describing these minutely before concluding, "fairly elementary—I would say kindergartenish—for anyone who wants to take an interest in it, but for the honourable member to stand up tonight and say that this is a shocking vote for Northern Affairs because of the small amount, it means that the honourable member does not know, does not comprehend what this branch is supposed to be doing."

Joe was flushed with anger when he rose to his feet. "Let me first of all thank our clever wise guy there for venting his spleen on me. I'm a new member here and I know you are right; I don't know, that's the reason I stand up to ask him these questions. He doesn't have to get smart about it and start treating me like a juvenile."

"That's what you are," retorted Lyon.

When Joe snapped back that the best person to "refute that garbage that you're telling us" would be former Tory MLA Gordon

Beard, who "quit because he couldn't stomach the crap that you give us," Lyon complained to the chairman that this had now become "a question of civility in the House."

This prompted Saul Cherniak, NDP member for St. John's, to intervene on his colleague's behalf. "It would be helpful if all members of this House listen carefully to what the attorney-general said, including himself. He provoked exactly what he got, and if that's the way he wants to conduct himself, he'll get those answers, I'm sure."

"If I get them, Mr. Speaker, and if this House has to be subjected to the kind of incivility of language made by the honourable member, he won't be here," said Lyon.

"Mr. Chairman, it sounded almost like a challenge," replied Joe, "and if this was five years ago I'd invite him to throw me out. I could handle two smart alecks like that."[13]

Thus did Joe painfully gain experience of the roughhouse ways of the Manitoba Legislature. He also suffered disillusionment. "I used to think all these men who sat in the House were God-like creatures, orators. And I get into the Legislature and find jackasses and drunks. Falling asleep in the House, going through their bills, making paper darts."[14]

Yet Joe seldom seemed fazed by the antics, political or otherwise. He did not cease to ask questions on issues significant to his constituents. Among these happened to be one of the more controversial Conservative proposals: an extensive plan to flood Southern Indian Lake as part of a hydro scheme. The high-level diversion would create a man-made lake of nearly 1,800 square miles, and displace two communities of about 600 self-sufficient aboriginal people.

There was a certain amount of public unease about the plan; opposition members charged that they were given little information, and that alternatives to the flooding had not been thoroughly investigated. Joe, forced to confine his remarks to tourism in his first speech in the House, facetiously suggested that the government change the name of Southern Indian Lake to "Lake Auschwitz" since its plan, if adopted, would wipe out two communities with the stroke of a pen. "And who knows, we may even get tourists from Europe coming down here to see our own home-made Auschwitz."[15]

But he was to offer far more substantive criticism of the hydro scheme in the coming days, albeit expressing frustration that the government was not more forthcoming with facts regarding the consequences of the flooding. The primary consideration, he noted, was the welfare of the natives living there who would be forced to relocate. "...The Indians have stated time and again...that they will not move. And if they're not going to move—it's easy enough to say, well, we'll force them out, we'll use brute force like people do in some countries. But it's a serious problem and it's something that you're going to be faced with."

Other considerations were the water supply to the town of Churchill, which would be greatly decreased, and the diversion of water to the Burntwood River, which flows near Thompson. And there was speculation that Sherrit Gordon, a mining company, had discovered an ore body in the area that would, if the proposal became a reality, be under water. That could leave the government vulnerable to compensation claims by the company, and if the former passed that on to Manitoba Hydro, well, Joe said, "Who's Manitoba Hydro? It's our money."[16]

He spoke often and always to the point. He spoke most frequently for his people in the north. Following the death of a miner as the result of a blasting accident in the Inco mine, he asked for a permanent mining inspector in Thompson.[17] He had campaigned on this very issue, and had mentioned it earlier in the House, only to have Mines Minister Harry Enns discount it because of the possibility of coercion, an idea Joe scornfully dismissed: "We've called Inco a lot of names but you in effect are saying that this company is so rotten that by putting an inspector in there these guys are going to coerce them." Surely the inspectors have "enough backbone" to investigate a mining accident fairly, and if not, "fire them and put somebody in there you could trust," Joe advised. "Maybe you'd consider taking somebody out of this House and making them an inspector, one of your backbenchers perhaps."[18]

He denounced the disgraceful conditions of northern roads, and blasted the Conservative government for squandering the province's resources by cutting the mineral tax in half—this done in 1966 by Sterling Lyon, then Minister of Mines and Resources. Mining companies, Joe maintained, don't need an incentive: tax them, especially his alma mater, Inco. "Nobody leaves a gold mine, and in the case of nickel, it is a gold mine."[19]

Joe also drew attention to the dearth of doctors in the north, and the unique difficulties northerners faced regarding medical care. Here he ran into heated debate with Larry Desjardins, the Liberal from St. Boniface who would figure prominently in the political fortunes of the NDP in the years ahead. When Joe suggested that, since northern Manitobans must pay a medicare premium, the government must then guarantee them transportation to get to a doctor, Desjardins erupted.

"What you're asking for is impossible. It's impossible…They have a special fund for emergency—and they've flown Eskimos up here to different hospitals—they're going to do that, but if we're going to state this principle that we have to deliver everybody to a doctor, where are you going to stop?"[20]

Joe then spoke about the problems facing the town of Churchill, "one of the oldest, dirtiest slums in Manitoba" and charged that the government wasn't doing enough.

"Why don't you pay your taxes?" snapped Desjardins. "Maybe we'll do more, for God's sake."[21]

Joe also put forward a resolution to have the minimum wage increased from $1.25 to $1.50, and used the opportunity to reveal, for those unaware of the fact, that the chairman of the minimum wage board was also the president of the Manitoba Progressive Conservative Party, G. Campbell MacLean, and therefore a "party stooge."

"No, no. It can't be the same MacLean!" other members cried.[22]

In his denunciation of the government on that particular occasion, Joe gave full vent to his own political philosophy: "We heard the Minister of Transportation talk about serfs away back in England several hundred years ago, and he tried to point out to this House that every time we bring any social measures, that you're really somehow infringing on the rights of a person and that you're not doing them any favours. The Minister implied that this thing was as a result of some socialistic measures, but the fact is when these serfs existed and lived in England it was a free, rugged, wheeling-dealing free enterprise system, just as we had…

"It wasn't a socialist system that enslaved them. It was a free enterprise system and today in Manitoba, and as a matter of fact across Canada, we see it. It's not called that any more, they've got a different name for it, but the end result and effect on these people…is the same, because when you're living in a shack, a filthy shack; and you get a pay cheque of $50 a week and you pay all the deductions...what have you got left?

"And really, what good is that right to vote, this political freedom, when you get that kind of pay cheque? This is economic slavery and I think, if I was faced with the prospect of choosing political freedom or economic freedom, I think I would choose economic freedom. What good is a vote when your family is starving?"[23]

Joe's speech was curtailed when Sterling Lyon jeered, "You Marxists haven't had a new idea for 200 years." Flustered, Joe admitted he had a few other things to say but he'd forgotten them, "thanks to the red herring over there" and almost sat down without putting forward his resolution, remembering his stated purpose just in time. His pithy remarks, however, were recorded in the press.

As Joe and other NDP colleagues such as Sid Green (Inkster), Sam Uskiw (Brokenhead), Saul Cherniak (St. John's), Ben Hanuschak (Burrows) laboured in the House as members of the Honorable Opposition, the party braced itself for a leadership race. Former leader A.R. "Russ" Paulley had narrowly defeated Sid Green in a leadership battle a year earlier, and, according to one commentator, may not have won except for the "unique campaign promise" that he would resign within a year in order that Ed Schreyer, who at that time was an NDP MP for the federal riding of Selkirk, Manitoba, would be able to stand as a candidate.[24]

The leadership convention was to be held June 28, 1969 but was moved abruptly ahead three weeks when Premier Walter Weir called a snap election for June 25. Sidney Green and Ed Schreyer were the two rivals for the leadership, but strangely enough, they travelled together to keep expenses down. It was during the trip from Thompson to The Pas that Schreyer got to know Joe, who drove them those 100 or so miles over a rough northern road.[25]

Ed Schreyer's political views fell more into Joe's pattern of thinking than did Sid Green's, especially on the issue of public funding for parochial schools, which both Borowski and Schreyer supported, but Green adamantly opposed. "Schreyer fully expected that Joe would support him," Green related, "and when Joe nominated me, he was astonished."[26]

Joe described Green as "the most dynamic [MLA] in the legislature...Sid is the kind of person who can go out and knock hell out of the Tories."[27] Moreover, Joe knew Sid far better than he knew Ed Schreyer; he had been a colleague of Sid's in the legislature, and Green had campaigned for him in Thompson.[28] Green considered himself and Joe to be "very close" friends.

But when Joe stood up at the June 7 NDP convention to nominate his friend for leader of the party, his words caused only consternation among Sid Green's supporters.

"Joe said—and he pointed at Schreyer right on the stage—Joe said, 'If the *Winnipeg Free Press* is in favour of that man, you had better be suspicious of him,' and people started to boo. And you know, the whole audience was at least two-thirds Schreyer and that was, they considered, a low blow," said Green, adding, "It really wasn't lower than the blows that were being leveled the other way."

Joe's caution was that the party not let the media unduly influence the election: Schreyer had been championed as the front-runner. But his remarks backfired, or were misconstrued, a problem that would plague him for most of his life. The CBC panelists covering the convention variously described his speech as "a classic *faux pas*" and a "major political blunder"; one commentator confessed to being "incredibly shocked at such a nominating speech."[29]

Green himself was unperturbed. "A lot of people blamed my defeat on Joe," he said matter-of-factly. "Now, that's not true. He didn't cost me those votes because those people who were annoyed with that remark were Schreyer's supporters."[30]

With or without Joe's support, by the end of the convention, Ed Schreyer was the undisputed leader of the Manitoba NDP, with 506 votes to Green's 177. But there was no time to savour the victory; Schreyer, Green and Borowski, among others, were off and running in the campaign for the provincial elections, a scant three weeks away.

Notes
Chapter 4
Deep down you're NDP too

[1] "Another view, John Robertson" *Winnipeg Tribune*, February 22, 1969.

[2] "Borowski says he is confident of win" *Thompson Citizen*, February 19, 1969.

[3] "Four candidates meet in debate Sunday at high school," *Thompson Citizen*, February 18, 1969.

[4] "Dr. B. Johnston a surprise candidate," *Thompson Citizen*, February 5, 1969.

[5] "Borowski's lead cut to 4 votes," *Free Press*, February 26, 1969.

[6] *Winnipeg Tribune*, March 8, 1969.

[7] Interview with Jim Hughes.

[8] Op. Cit., Duff Roblin, *Speaking for Myself*, p. 174.

[9] "The Roblin decade," Lloyd Stinson, *Free Press*, February 27, 1971.

[10] Interview with Sidney Green, March 2002

[11] *Hansard*, March 26, 1969, p. 750.

[12] Ibid. p. 752.

[13] *Hansard*, April 24, 1969, pp. 1607, 1608.

[14] Op. Cit., "The outsider moves in," Pat Annesley, p. 42.

[15] *Hansard*, March 19, 1969.

[16] *Hansard*, April 24, 1969, p. 1576.

[17] *Hansard*, April 29, 1969, p. 1712.

[18] *Hansard*, March 24, 1969, p. 678.

[19] Ibid.

[20] *Hansard*, May 8, 1969, p. 2022.

[21] Ibid. p. 2027.

[22] *Hansard*, April 22, 1969, p. 1517.

[23] *Hansard*, April 22, 1969, p. 1519.

[24] James A. McAllister, *The Government of Edward Schreyer, Democratic Socialism in Manitoba*, (McGill-Queen's University Press, 1984), p. 19.

[25] Interview with Edward Schreyer, March 2002.

[26] Interview with Sidney Green, March 2002.

[27] *Winnipeg Free Press*, June 9, 1969.

[28] Interview with Ed Schreyer.

[29] *Thompson Citizen*, [undated; c. June 9, 1969.]

[30] Interview with Sidney Green.

Chapter 5

The legend

And now he feels the bottom;—
Now on dry earth he stands;
Now round him throng the Fathers
To press his gory hands.
And now, with shouts and clapping,
And noise of weeping loud,
He enters through the River Gate
Borne by the joyous crowd.
Thomas Babington Macauley
Horatius at the Bridge

"Borowski was absolutely more popular
than Schreyer or myself—not as a leader but as an MLA.
He was probably the most popular of all of us."
Sid Green

ON JUNE 25, 1969—FIFTY YEARS TO THE DAY THAT THE WINNIPEG General Strike came to an end—the NDP swept into power in Manitoba for the first time. City editor of the *Winnipeg Tribune* at the time, Peter Warren remembered the party's victory as a complete shock: "Schreyer got elected and all hell broke loose. The *New York Times* sent a reporter—my God, the socialists have made their benchmark in North America."[1]

It was a precarious benchmark. Ed Schreyer's party had captured 28 seats of a 57-member House. The Conservatives held 22, the Liberals 5. There was a lone Social Credit member and Gordon Beard, the former Tory whose resignation led to Joe Borowski's election in February 1969, reappeared in the Legislature, this time as an Independent candidate for the riding of Churchill.[2] Joe, who ran in the new riding of Thompson, had won handily.

Schreyer himself was taken aback. He thought the NDP would form the official opposition—that, too, would have been a first. To actually form the government was "unexpected—I could sense that we would do well, but not that well."[3]

There was a brief period of uncertainty immediately after the election, as former Conservative premier Walter Weir attempted to form a coalition government with the Liberals. That plan was nixed when Larry Desjardins, calling himself a Liberal-Democrat, joined the Schreyer caucus. As one commentator noted, "His move gave Schreyer control of the Legislature. But, as later events were to prove, it also gave Desjardins control of the NDP."[4]

As the neophyte premier selected his cabinet and began the first of what would ultimately be eight years as Manitoba's leader, Canadian society was itself undergoing a radical social transformation engineered in main part by Liberal Prime Minister Pierre Trudeau.

And the change wrought by the Liberals could accurately be termed a "revolution" according to historian Fr. Alphonse de Valk, "in view of the age-old traditions which have been attacked and overthrown in such a short period of time."[5] On May 14, 1969, the federal government passed the Omnibus Bill, which, among other things, amended the Criminal Code to permit abortion under certain conditions, namely, if a committee of physicians deemed such an action necessary to preserve the "life and health" of the mother.[6]

The legalization of abortion was "one of the rare examples of a legal reform which stirs up more controversy after the law has been amended than before," wrote Fr. de Valk.[7] But that controversy, which would one day rise up as 'a tide in the affairs of men' with such force and ferocity as to wholly engulf Joe Borowski and his family, was for him now only the distant murmur of an uneasy sea.

Manitoba had scarcely recovered from the shock of an NDP government when Schreyer named his Ministers. "Because it was a rag-tag bunch of people who were elected, the big thing was, well...what's going to be his cabinet?" Peter Warren recalled. When Joe Borowski was named Minister of Transportation "everybody was surprised," Warren said. "They were absolutely shocked. How do you take a miner...and make him Cabinet Minister?"

Ed Schreyer's executive council was noteworthy for a number of other reasons. The 13-member cabinet was the youngest in Manitoba's history, with an average age of 43.[8] Schreyer was 33 years old, Joe was 37, Sid Green, initially Minister of Health and then Minister of Mines, was 39, Howard Pawley, Minister of Municipal Affairs, was 34.[9]

The cabinet was also remarkable for the variety of ethnic groups represented, but, indeed, some analysts viewed the triumph of the NDP itself as a marked demographic swing that the cabinet merely, albeit faithfully, reflected. "It was a victory of the poorer parts of the province—the marginal farming areas and the working class areas of Winnipeg—over the well-to-do farming areas of the southwest and the wealthier suburban areas of Winnipeg. It was also a victory produced by a successful voting coalition of ethnic minorities, the traditional outsiders in Manitoba society and politics....It was a victory too, for the party supported by organized labour over the parties supported by the business community."[10]

Thus, it was not surprising that the cabinet roll call "read like a battle hymn of the unwashed—four Anglo-Saxons, three Jews, two Ukrainians, one French Canadian, one Pole, one Icelander and one Austrian German (Schreyer)."[11]

The premier maintained that he always had it in the back of his mind to appoint Joe to the cabinet if and when the NDP formed the government. Joe was from the north, and Schreyer was determined to have representation for that region at the cabinet level. Sid Green, however, recalled that his boss had some doubts about Joe, mainly connected to the infamous nomination speech. "Schreyer thought that Joe displayed an error in judgment and asked me whether he should be in the cabinet. And I said that, certainly, Joe would be a good Cabinet Minister." Green also was of the opinion, and there seems considerable evidence to support it, that Joe was the most popular MLA in the NDP government—a popularity he already enjoyed in June of 1969 when the government came to power, and which grew in the next two years.

Joe was, Green said, a "champion of the underdog", a populist, renowned for the great lengths to which he would go to fight for the little guy.[12] He had a reputation for unassailable integrity, and for a forthrightness that often bordered on tactlessness—an attribute which at this point in his career drew more admiration than ire from the general populace, and which was happily exploited by the media.

Or was it? Therein lies subject for debate. The press had a complex relationship with Joe, as complex as the man himself. "He did have a knack for getting media attention, and that's more than half the battle, up to a point," Ed Schreyer noted. But whether Joe manipulated the media, or ever intended to, he would not grant: "They needed each other." The growing phenomenon of "hotline shows" was a medium tailor-made for the personable, off-the-cuff, blunt and opinionated Joe Borowski. "He loved the hotline shows," Schreyer said, "He developed quite a following."

Peter Warren, who did openline radio for nearly 35 years, concurred. He first noticed Joe during the latter's camp-out in 1965, and by now considered Joe his friend. "I'm a journalist, and I've done the scumbags of the earth and I've done the captains and the kings, and somewhere in between you find a genuine human being, and Joe was it."

Joe was successful on openline radio "because he was Joe Six Pack," Warren surmised. "I mean, you don't take a, to use the vernacular, a Polack miner from Thompson and suddenly he's meeting the Queen, and so every Joe Six Pack, Joe Borowski with an ethnic name like that, a miner, a Polack, a guy who was still rough around the edges for awhile, epitomized for a whole generation of guys out there, down the mine or on the farm fields or whatever, what could be accomplished by running for public office. Joe ran, nobody gave him a chance in hell, the world flipped when...Schreyer named him to cabinet and he turns out to be a bloody good Cabinet Minister. And there's a lesson in there somewhere."[13]

The Winnipeg press corps, observed one commentator, was "pro-Joe almost to a man."[14] Yet, it is arguable that he was treated with a *soupçon* of disdain. And the newsmen were sometimes left to wonder: Was Joe really only what he appeared to be, a regular guy who spoke for the legions of other regular guys—or was he an extraordinarily shrewd politician, and they dupes in his hands?

"I don't think that Joe thought about what he was doing and how it would be effective. I think that what he did was totally natural, that there was no amount of manoeuvring or trying," observed Sidney Green. "He did what he did, he flew off from the seat of his pants and because of what he was, and what he felt, he made the news. He would not try to manipulate a reporter. He would just do what he wanted to do, and because of what he did, he got the press."[15]

Pundits of the day weren't so sure. When Joe advised NDP delegates to ignore the press during his ill-fated convention speech, he did so "knowing full well" that such a statement would guarantee him full coverage, wrote John Robertson. "He knows that he is bigger than the press, with the people who count...his people...the ones who clap him on the back and shout 'Atta boy Joe'....

"I kid you not when I say that there is no limit to the political heights Joe Borowski is capable of attaining. He has none of the deficiencies that 'do in' other politicians...deficiencies such as higher education, polished wit, a firm grasp of the intricacies of parliamentary procedure, or a measure of sophistication that would set him apart from the people who vote for him.

"Joe personifies the little guy who has been getting a lot of lousy breaks from life and has decided to take things into his own hands."[16]

At his physical prime and riding the crest of his wave of popularity, Joe Borowski did, indeed, take many things into his own hands.

Steven Ashton was 11 years old when his family moved to Thompson, but decades later he could still remember the drive. When his mother turned their '64 Buick Le Sabre onto Highway 391, she thought there was something wrong; this rutted, dirt road could not possibly be the highway. But it was, and the Ashtons got stuck twice on their maiden voyage to Thompson.

Some three years later, Steve Ashton watched with awe as Highway 391 was paved, and Highway 6, which runs through the interlake and is a direct link between Thompson and Winnipeg, was constructed in less than two years. Moreover, the single-lane World War II bridge over the Burntwood River was replaced by a double-lane bridge.

The politically precocious teenager knew who was responsible for these developments: Thompson MLA and Minister of Highways, Joe Borowski, and his premier, Ed Schreyer. Steve Ashton lost no time in joining the NDP—Joe's party. He had seen with his own eyes the "people of that day who took the North's frustration and did an amazing number of things in a very short period of time."[17]

Described by an NDP party insider as the "consummate politician," Ashton had, by 2002, been in public life for over 20 years, having been elected as MLA for Thompson six times. He was also Minister of Highways at that time, occupying the same office that his political mentor, Joe Borowski, worked in some 30 years earlier. He did not mind invoking the name of Borowski, in fact, was glad to do so—despite the events of late 1971 and beyond.

"The easiest thing for me to do would be to say, 'Oh well, Ed Schreyer—' and leave Joe Borowski out, because you know Schreyer was the premier and we don't want to get into….the polarizing impact. I never shy away from it; I sometime surprise people when I say, 'Yeah, Joe Borowski's one of the reasons I joined the NDP.'

"And they don't get the point…because whatever Joe did afterwards, never took away from that for me or a lot of people in Thompson who, whether they agreed with Joe or not, would still say, he was a damn good MLA—excuse the language, but ….that's kind of the language Joe would have used."[18]

"We have always alleged that, with the exception of the present Highways Minister [Steve Ashton], Joe was the best Highways Minister the province has ever seen," recalled Bob Mayer, a lawyer, NDP member and long-term Thompson resident. "He actually drove the roads. He made his deputy take the phone out of the deputy's car and put it in his car, and he drove the roads. And he stopped at every camp that road contractors were running, just to see what was going on.

"In Thompson, he'd call me up and he'd say, 'Bob, we're going on a little bit of a tour…and you're driving.' I said, 'Okay'—some God-awful time…like 8 o'clock Saturday morning. We'd drive out to a construction camp, Joe would walk in—he wanted to be there around breakfast time—sit down, talk to the guys. [He] didn't go see a foreman or anything, just walked into the camp…and says, 'How are you guys eating?' 'Very well, Mr. Borowski, we're eating very well, we're getting steaks.' 'Good, cause,' he says, 'that's what I'm paying for.'"

A memory that lingered in Mayer's mind was the time he and Joe drove to Soab Lake, about 60 kilometres south of Thompson. They "picked up the highways engineer, visited the camp, asked the guys the questions about what they were eating, and now we're going fishing, so okay. Pulls over and looks at the access to Soab Creek and Joe gets out of the car; we've got a brand new highway—just been poured. He kicks a piece out of it, and this is asphalt, so he calls the engineer over and says, 'How long does it take for this stuff to dry?' 'Oh,' he says, I think it was 'ten days.' 'Why are we letting people drive on it?' 'Oh, no, it's set in two days, no problem.' He says, 'Then why have I just been able to kick a big piece out of this road?' And so he kept doing it, and he kicked his way just about [across] the road, he was just butting this asphalt out with his boots. The engineer did NOT have an answer for that."

It turned out that the oil they bought in Saskatchewan did not meet the specifications required, and did not bind with the soil of northern Manitoba. When Joe told the company bosses that he wouldn't be paying for the oil, they threatened to sue; whereupon, Mayer maintained, Joe turned around and said he would sue them for forty miles of road that wasn't worth a dime. The company capitulated.

Borowski also turned his scrutiny on his own department, Ashton recalled. "We were not exactly Nova Scotia, where the highways crews changed every election, depending on who was elected, but I know a lot of people who said that it was not until Joe Borowski came along that the highways department really started moving into the modern era."[19]

He was praised as "one of the more effective Ministers in the Schreyer government. He is a good administrator and organizer and gets things done," noted a *Tribune* editorial. "He has saved the province $1 million by introducing a new tendering system on highways construction. His toughness with the Traffic Act enforcement has cut accident fatalities by 26 per cent."[20] It was on Joe's watch that laws were passed requiring motorists to reduce speed approaching a stop sign, and dotted lines painted on the highways.

But then there were always those *other* incidents that, not unlike a sudden summer twister created by a drop in barometric pressure, blew up in furious gusts from Joe's uniquely calibrated personality. And like a summer twister, they raised considerable dust, debris and noise, and were just as suddenly gone, leaving one to wonder what had happened. There were enough of them to prompt one newspaper to dub Joe Borowski "the Minister of Highways and Uproar."[21]

One such incident was the lost key. Joe discovered in late January 1971, that the master key for the legislative buildings had been missing since the middle of the month. He had received the public works portfolio in November of 1970, in addition to highways, and was in that capacity responsible for security and maintenance of all government buildings. He promptly suspended the chief security guard for five days, and issued a public appeal that the key be returned.

By the time the key was recovered on February 16, (sent back anonymously) Joe had suspended another security officer and received 30 keys in the mail from, as he described it, "Liberals, Conservatives and other kooks."[22] He also ordered a full-scale investigation when a "professional lock pick" was found in the cafeteria of the Highways Services Building.[23] Joe hinted darkly at political espionage, and by the time the key had been recovered, he alleged that some documents—"so important there will be repercussions in the House"—had been tampered with.[24]

The episode highlighted the differences between the Highways Minister and his more low-key boss, Ed Schreyer, who, according to one reporter, viewed Joe's exertions with "bemused detachment."[25] Some people, the premier commented, "have the urge to play James Bond" but he practised open government. "To my mind there is not any clear and present danger of important secrets of state being discovered."

Scarcely had the hubbub over the missing key died down than Joe became embroiled in a public relations tempest.

"Joe flew by the seat of his pants, and sometimes that type of flight was right and sometimes it was demonstrably wrong," remembered Sid Green. "He made a statement once reflecting on drunken Indians and it was a statement which was totally unacceptable, and he wouldn't take it back. And finally I drafted a statement for him. I was the only one who could put into words something that he could accept as not being a back-down... He finally made the statement and an apology, without using the word apology, which I don't think he would have used."[26]

This particular trouble began when the *Winnipeg Free Press* published remarks Joe made at a NDP meeting. He spoke about the brush-clearing contracts the NDP had negotiated with the native people in his constituency—a pilot project he had initiated, and of which he was especially proud, as it provided an opportunity for self-sufficiency to the people living on northern reserves.[27]

In speaking about the progress of the clearing, Joe said that the Indians weren't bound by the clock, but worked long days when necessary, then took one week a month off to visit their families, buy groceries, and get drunk. They were, he said, hard to get up in the morning.

Joe mentioned in passing that the security guard who had been suspended for five days during the missing key fiasco was a disabled war veteran. He had received a complaint that a guard who had been "crippled" in the war could hardly be expected to provide satisfactory security.[28]

The *Free Press* article attributed those words to Joe, and this, coupled with the comments about natives, prompted cries of protest from all quarters—including from veterans' associations, and from members of the NDP caucus, particularly Labour Minister Russ Paulley and Rupertsland MLA Jean Allard. The howls of protest reached such a pitch that Joe offered to resign. However, three NDP aldermen and one MLA present at the fateful meeting issued their version of events, and after Joe himself read a statement clarifying what he said, the caucus was mollified and convinced that the popular Minister had been misquoted.[29]

An angry Joe accused the *Free Press* of attempting "the most beautiful political assassination by a politically racist" newspaper. The less dramatic Schreyer exonerated the paper of any deliberate attempt to mislead. However, "it's no secret some of their stories are calculated to provide great difficulty for the government and compound misunderstandings." *Free Press* publisher Richard

Malone shrugged off the accusation of bias: "Any politician who puts his foot in his mouth claims afterwards that he was misquoted."[30]

Once more, the press corp marveled, Joe Borowski had nimbly negotiated a particularly perilous turn on the road of public opinion. It was not as if people hadn't heard Joe's opinions before and been left to ponder, abhor or applaud his views—which were sometimes, in fact, contradictory. In the opinion of Sid Green, Joe "didn't have any coherent political philosophy."

He decided issues on a case-by-case basis. He fully supported Trudeau's handling of the FLQ crisis in the fall of 1970, when the Prime Minister responded to the kidnapping of Quebec Minister Pierre Laporte and British diplomat James Cross by invoking the War Measures Act on October 16. Joe Borowski wired his approval and thanks, and offered Trudeau some advice: "When you catch the abductors, execute the bastards." The telegraph office wouldn't accept that last word, and substituted "butchers."[31]

Joe was also a monarchist, and displayed in his office the white hardhats that had adorned the royal heads when the Queen and her family toured the Thompson mines as part of the Manitoba centennial royal tour in July of 1970.[32] A press photo during that visit caught a mesmerized Joe gazing raptly at Her Majesty, with an undeniable look of admiration.

One telling incident signaled the direction in which his life was about to move, and was often later referred to by the press for that precise reason. One Saturday morning in May of 1971, about 60 members of a "women's liberation" group converged on the legislature grounds, bearing coffins and intending to meet with René Toupin, Minister of Health. But the building was locked—on the order of Public Works Minister, Joe Borowski. He had not intended to lock out the group, Joe later explained, but gave orders to bar the demonstrators, who were agitating for abortion on demand, because he did not want the legislature "desecrated by having buckets of blood and coffins" brought in. When he realized the women were to meet with a department of health representative, Joe countermanded his edict, but "the second order never reached the proper party."[33]

Irene Boxer, the protesters' spokeswoman, complained to Joe about the lockout and his subsequent remarks on the radio. Joe apologized for the mistake, in a letter. Then he clearly stated his convictions. The women claimed he had insulted them during the course of his radio remarks: "My answer is that it's impossible to insult any abortion group." Moreover, "I have heard of the perverted rationale and psychology used to justify abortion for convenience sake. The sinister minority of which you are a part is made up of the same ultra-liberals who say everything is relative and permissiveness is the new religion." Moral degeneracy, wrote Joe, "makes you a slave, not free."

"So lady, when you speak of me or the Church forcing our moral standards on you, remember we have a greater responsibility than you. I was elected by the people in a free and democratic election and therefore have earned the right to try and set moral standards, and so has the Church, which speaks for even more people than any elected government in the world."[34]

This latter statement drove the press wild. "Joe Borowski claims right to set moral standards," trumpeted the *Free Press* headline, and printed the entire text of his remarks. "Joe sees 'moral toboggan slide,'" was the heading for the article in the *Tribune*, which printed most of the letter as well. Moral outrage at his views pervaded both accounts.

"Has there ever been anybody in politics, anywhere in the world, remotely like Joe Borowski?" questioned political columnist Charles Lynch, and answered his own question: "No. No way."[35] Lynch catalogued a series of "Borowskisms" which included Joe's condemnation of the movie *Joe* as a smorgasbord of pornography—the Swedes then objected to his use of the word "smorgasbord."

"Having insulted everybody, he shouldn't have a friend left," Lynch wrote. "But how come so many Manitobans call him 'good old Joe'?"

Joe would have had his own answer to that, but he was not overly preoccupied with his public image. He was too busy cleaning up the departments of public works and highways, and routinely, putting in 12 to 18 hour days.

He was fully aware of the department's power to corrupt. "I've had a whole bunch of propositions from people who offer me a piece of the action for giving them advance information on where highway construction is going to take place. There's a lot of money been made in this province that way," he confessed to *Maclean's* reporter Pat Annesley, "...It makes you think sometimes. I guess that's why the premier appointed me to highways. Because he figured I was incorruptible."[36]

Schreyer remembered that about Joe. "He liked to always say that later, that I used to describe him as 'incorruptible.' Certainly that adjective fits. Of course, that I could say about all my colleagues, but certainly in his case it was sort of obvious... And making him Minister of Highways was just the nice icing on the cake, because there had been long-standing rumours and suspicions—only a few of which were well-founded, only a few—that there was a certain amount of hanky-panky going on in road construction. So I knew if there was, he'd get to the bottom of it."[37]

Notes
Chapter 5
The legend

[1] Interview with Peter Warren, February 2003.

[2] "How Manitoba turned 100 by standing on its head," Douglas Marshall, *Maclean's*, December 1970.

[3] Interview with Ed Schreyer.

[4] Op. Cit., "How Manitoba turned 100…," Marshall.

[5] Alphonse de Valk, *Morality and Law in Canadian Politics: The Abortion Controversy* (Montreal: Palm Publishers, 1974), introduction.

[6] The bill also permitted homosexual acts in private between persons 18 years and older.

[7] Ibid.

[8] "NDP cabinet is youngest for Manitoba," Chuck Thompson, *Tribune*, July 10, 1969.

[9] The rest of the cabinet, for the remaining term of 1969 was as follows: Saul Cherniak, 52, Minister of Finance; Russ Paulley, 59, Minister of Labour; Al Mackling, 41, Attorney-General; Sam Uskiw, 35, Minister of Education; Rene Toupin, 35, Minister of Consumer and Corporate Affairs; Fr. Phill Petursson, 66, Minister without portfolio; Len Evans, 39, Minister of Mines and Northern Development; Peter Burtniak, 43, Minister of Tourism; Saul Miller, 52, Minister of Education.

[10] Nelson Wiseman, "Social democracy in Manitoba," as quoted in Ken Coats and Fred McGuinness, *Manitoba, the province and its people* (Hurtig Press, 1987), p. 125.

[11] Op. Cit., "How Manitoba turned 100," Douglas Marshall.

[12] Interview with Sidney Green, March 2002.

[13] Interview with Peter Warren, February 2003.

[14] Op. Cit., "The outsider moves in," Annesley

[15] Interview with Sid Green, March 2002.

[16] "Another view," John Robertson, *Winnipeg Tribune*, June 10, 1969.

[17] *Hansard*, November 7, 1996, p. 4854.

[18] Interview with Steve Ashton, March 2002.

[19] *Hansard*, November 7, 1996, p. 4854.

[20] "The Borowski affair," *Tribune*. May 14, 1971.

[21] "The world of Joe," *Tribune*, September 10, 1971.

[22] "Borowski says key back but documents disturbed," *Tribune*, February 16, 1971.

[23] "Borowski fears security breach," *Tribune*, February 3, 1971.

[24] Ibid.

[25] "Schreyer not a James Bond," *Free Press*, February 6, 1978.

[26] Interview with Sid Green, March 2002.

[27] "Indians sign highway pacts worth $51,000," *Free Press*, September 15, 1969.

[28] "Borowski flaps at all and sundry," *Free Press*, February 18, 1971.

[29] "Borowski to remain in cabinet," *Free Press*, February 25, 1971.

[30] Ibid.

[31] "Execute abductors, Borowski tells PM," *Tribune*, October 17, 1970.

[32] Op. Cit., "The outsider moves in," Annesley

[33] "Lib lockout just a mistake?" *Tribune*, c. May 14, 1971.

[34] *Free Press*, May 14, 1971.

[35] "There's never been anyone quite like Joe," *Free Press*, February 20, 1971.

[36] Op. Cit., "The outsider moves in," Annesley.

[37] Interview with Edward Schreyer, March 2002.

Chapter 6

The road to Dauphin

"If the Opposition doesn't like it, they can go to hell."
Joe Borowski

"If he really thought he was right, there was no
way you could get him to apologize.
There's no way. He wouldn't apologize
in order to ease a situation."
Ed Schreyer

"He was certainly a person whom I would
want on my side if I were in a fight.
There is nobody I would want more to be on my side…"
Sid Green

THE SLEEPY CITY OF DAUPHIN NESTLES ON THE MANITOBA PRAIRIE JUST a hundred miles east of the Saskatchewan border. It is as likely, or unlikely, a place as any for corruption to spin an ugly web in which to ensare the hearts of men: "irregularities" had long been suspected in the Dauphin district highways department.

The Tories, under Walter Weir, had pursued their own inquiries into alleged skullduggery, but whatever insights they gleaned as a result of their efforts were never made public.[1]

Then along came Joe. He had received complaints about Dauphin's highways department soon after he came to office. An RCMP investigation was launched, and in February the district engineer, Ray Daniels, was suspended, only to resign two days later.[2] Charges of breech of trust and theft were subsequently laid against him. Dauphin highways department foreman, Ronald Aube, also faced a breech of trust charge, and by mid-August, a further six department employees had been suspended, demoted or dismissed for a variety of offenses—including allegedly doing work at Daniels' ranch on government time.[3]

Fair enough. But one hot August afternoon, opposition members questioned Joe about the Dauphin investigation. He happily responded with a brief summary of an RCMP report, and noted that, as well as charges already laid, fraud charges could well be expected. He then freely speculated on the roles of Walter Weir, Harry Enns and Stewart McLean, all of whom served as Highways Ministers during the years under investigation, 1962 to 1968. "I don't know to what extent they were involved; they were Ministers and it seems to me that they knew or should have known what was going on. My only suggestion would be that perhaps the present Leader of the Opposition [Weir] and the Member for Lakeside [Enns] should be suspended from the Legislature pending an investigation." (McLean, who was the Public Works Minister responsible for turfing Joe and his trailer off the legislature ground in 1966, was not reelected in June of 1969 and was at this time a circuit magistrate in Saskatchewan.)

Weir was immediately on his feet, demanding a retraction: unless the Minister had charges to lay, the idea of a suspension from the House was "completely out of order."[4] At that, Joe upped the ante. The RCMP report, he retorted, contained "charges made publicly....of kickback, kickback to the Conservative government."

Premier Schreyer hastily intervened, pointing out that the matter was before the courts, and "we should take great care to observe the well-known practise....that matters that are *sub judice*...not be a subject of further comment in this Assembly."[5]

Too late. The House erupted. Speaker Ben Hanuschak pressed Joe for a retraction. "When the court finds the Leader of the Opposition innocent, I'll be very happy to apologize and withdraw," said Joe. When pressed further, he replied, "Mr. Speaker, I answered the question that was asked of me, a question I promised to answer for several months now and if the Opposition doesn't like it, they can go to hell."[6]

Amid the rising voices and tempers, Weir threw a rulebook into the middle of the chamber, and shouted at the speaker, "You have an obligation without delay or further pussyfooting around to 'name' the Minister" (a procedure that results in the offending member being temporarily suspended from the House). For his part, Hanuschak beseeched Joe repeatedly to comply with the request made of him. Joe sat mute and intractable. Finally, it fell to House Leader, Sid Green, to enforce the rules and move that the honourable member be suspended for the remainder of the sitting.[7]

Outside the Legislature, an angry Joe spoke to eagerly gathered newsmen. "If the House won't permit me to speak the truth, then I don't want to sit in the G–d—ed House." He vowed he would not return until the session was prorogued or dissolved. But then came Finance Minister Saul Cherniak and other Cabinet Ministers, and they spirited Joe into his office and locked the door.[8]

Perhaps Walter Weir would not have pressed the moment to its crisis had the NDP government itself not been in the throes of a crisis of its own—over Bill 56, the measure to provide public automobile insurance. The bill had been vociferously and noisily protested by the province's insurance agents—including the entire village of Wawanesa, headquarters of the Wawanesa Mutual Insurance Company—who were aided by the *Free Press*, which dubbed the government "Red Ed and his Raiders." Schreyer, acutely conscious of his razor-thin majority, had been wooing both Independent Gordon Beard and Liberal Democrat Larry Desjardins, whose votes he needed to pass the bill.[9]

It was rumoured that some NDP caucus members wanted to force a non-confidence vote on Bill 56, convinced they would return after an election with a majority government. Joe, recalled Schreyer, held to this opinion, but the premier was absolutely opposed to the idea. "I didn't want to play dice like that," he said, "I wanted to avoid the stigma of instability before causing it if I could help it, so I tried desperately to put the measure through."[10]

Thus it was that Joe, following that locked-door meeting, returned to the House that same afternoon, despite his intention to boycott. And he voted, along with Desjardins and Beard, on August 13 for Bill 56, which passed 29-27.[11] Autopac, as the public car insurance is referred to, is still in force.

It is reported that at the end of that stormy day, an unknown citizen wrote a message with magenta lipstick on the rear window of a government car: "Good work, Joe."[12]

Back in Dauphin, the wheels of justice were rolling, rolling, rolling. Ray Daniels was ultimately convicted of one count of breech of trust (for instructing an auto shop employee to change an invoice to cover up damage to a government vehicle) and fined $250.[13] Ron Aube was acquitted and reinstated.[14]

Meanwhile, a civil service commission dealt with the six Dauphin employees whom Joe had variously dismissed, suspended or demoted. All were reinstated in October 1970, at full pay. Three of the men were disciplined but assessed greatly reduced penalties from those originally ordered by the Highways Minister.[15] The commission's rationale for this was reported to be that the men were acting under orders from superiors Daniels and Aube.[16]

The civil service commission was also critical of the internal workings of the highways department, citing examples of senior officials approving payroll even though they had no way of verifying the amount of hours worked[17] and a lack of supervision generally.[18] Joe admitted that his department was prone to "sloppy" operations but that he was trying to change that.[19]

Joe had agreed to abide by the commission's findings, but he was far from happy with the results. The Dauphin "scandal" was proving frustrating. That whisper of rumoured wrongdoing had not yet found full voice; the dark hints of a deeper malfeasance still remained, in large part, only suspicions—hard evidence was maddeningly elusive.

A few days after the ruling, Joe ordered a number of men from Dauphin to be transferred north. Productivity in the district was down as a result of the investigation and the factions among the crew. Borowski was now accused of penalizing the men for refusing to testify against Daniels and Aube.[20]

The Dauphin investigation took on a bizarre and unpredictable turn when one of the dismissed employees, Norm Anger, himself took Borowski to court.[21] On October 9, he swore out a charge against Joe Borowski under the Vacations with Pay Act, claiming that the Minister failed to pay him the four per cent of his salary between April 1 and August 10, 1970.[22] Reinstated in mid-October by the commission, Anger was one of the men under orders to transfer north.

It was obvious that Anger's case was "malicious in nature," represented a personal vendetta against the Highways Minister, and should be dismissed, argued Joe's lawyer, Mel Myers.[23] However, Magistrate F. M. Manwaring concluded that, since it was not shown that revenge was a motivation, the case could be heard.[24]

Now Joe was angry, and didn't mind who knew it. "If that bastard hears the case, I'll have him defrocked and debarred," he declared in an interview with two reporters. As far as Joe was concerned, Manwaring's decision was "judiciously improper" and based "on political considerations." Expanding on this theme in a radio broadcast, Joe opined: "Well, one can read many motives into it. The fact that [Manwaring] is a loyal Conservative and had been appointed by a Conservative administration can't be overlooked."[25]

Moreover, Joe said, if the allegations regarding vacation pay were true, the government should be charged, not him personally. "What do I have to do with pay?"[26]

Such audacity provoked near apoplexy in some quarters, but Joe was unperturbed. "It's funny, every time I make a statement, there's always some donkey around asking for an apology," he said in a news conference March 17. It seemed simple to Joe: there were "too many people in high places" who believed that judges should have "some type of papal immunity...even judges can make mistakes."[27] The trouble was that Joe, as a Cabinet Minister, technically did have the power to do exactly what he had threatened to do—remove Manwaring from the bench.

The next day an application was filed in the Court of Queen's Bench on behalf of Norm Anger, claiming Joe Borowski was in contempt of court. He was to appear on March 31 to answer the civil charge.

Meanwhile, Attorney-General Al Mackling was under pressure to do something about his flamboyant colleague. The Law Society of Manitoba urged him to "take appropriate action" at this "dangerous and reprehensible....undermining of the independence of the judiciary." Mackling was also given advice by one who had formerly occupied the same office—Sterling Lyon. Joe's "threat", sputtered Lyon, was "a throwback to the most barbaric and autocratic societies of the dim past....it is intolerable in a free society. I, for one, cannot stand idly by and witness the degradation of our judicial system."[28]

Joe was conscious of the irony of his position, as he noted in a public statement: "I, who have often been called the Spiro Agnew of Manitoba because of my complete and almost blind support of the police and the courts, now stand accused of being contemptible of that very institution." Cooler heads recognized the same: Joe Borowski, Minister of the Crown, had an unassailable faith in the system. His was not the nature of an anarchist. An editorial in the *Winnipeg Tribune* dismissed the more vehement reactions to Joe's statements, such as the call for his resignation by then Liberal leader Israel Asper, (later president of CanWest Global and owner of the *National Post* newspaper), as mere politicking. "Whatever else Joe Borowski may be—hot-tempered, stubborn, even rude by establishment standards—he stands firmly for law and order. To suggest his outburst was solely a challenge to the majesty of the law ignores the whole context of which the outburst was an integral part."[29]

The fair-minded Mackling commented to the press that he had "sympathy" for Borowski over these "most unusual and interesting" proceedings emanating from the Dauphin case. It was unusual, Mackling said, "for a Minister of the Crown to be sued personally for something for which the government is responsible."[30] Speaking in the House, and under immunity, the attorney-general was less circumspect. While not wishing to "cast reflection on the discretion of the magistrate", the whole court proceedings which allowed Anger's civil suit were "asinine."[31]

And as Joe and Jean Borowski headed to Queen's Bench for the contempt hearing, Mackling walked beside them. When his decision was handed down April 28, 1971, Justice Israel Nitikman found Joe Borowski guilty of contempt. He gave Joe a suspended sentence of one year, and ordered him to give an "unreserved" apology to Magistrate Manwaring within 60 days. Failure to do so would be a violation of the terms of the suspended sentence and Borowski could be brought back to court for further penalty.[32]

Justice Nitikman's 33-page judgment was severe: the threat to have the magistrate defrocked and debarred was "unbelievably outrageous." Joe Borowski "made a malicious and shocking charge. It would be inexcusable even as infantile rudeness. The statement was not only intemperate and insulting, it denigrated the reputation of integrity and probity the courts of this province have always justly enjoyed and taken pride in."

The justice did note that Joe was "genuinely convinced the proceedings against him by Mr. Anger were motivated solely by the latter's desire to harass and embarrass him." But this was no justification for a contempt of court "so disputably self-evident I would have hoped that at the commencement of the hearing Mr. Borowski would promptly have admitted and tendered a genuine and unreserved apology."[33]

Joe's conviction of contempt did not prevent him from sitting in the legislature. Premier Schreyer did not comment beyond saying, "I don't think his position in the Cabinet is materially affected."

Nevertheless, a deadline loomed: an apology from the quick-tempered Borowski to Judge Manwaring within 60 days. It was a situation to be delightfully savoured by both the press and public. The suspense built, the days passed, the mercurial Minister remained morosely mute, and the question on many people's minds was: What would he do? Would he apologize, or wouldn't he?

Those who knew Joe, if only by reputation, knew that he meant what he said, and stood by it come what may. He was, Ed Schreyer said, "probably the most stubborn person I ever met in my life." Moreover, "if he really thought he was right, there was no way you could get him to apologize. There's no way. He wouldn't apologize in order to ease a situation—he would only apologize if you could demonstrably prove that he was wrong in what he said." Had Schreyer ever had an opportunity to present Joe with such a proof? "No. It's not that easy."[34]

Those who knew Joe personally knew what mettle he had. "No matter what particular thing Joe believed in at the time, he'd go to the wall for it," recalled Thompson lawyer Bob Mayer. And Mayer knew too, what a lot of people at that time had gleaned: "Joe didn't pay fines." Period. He would go to jail, as he did with the sales tax, rather than pay a fine.[35]

And when it came to the Anger debacle, Joe held true to form. He would not apologize.

He was, however, vindicated. On June 2, 1971, Joe was acquitted of the charge of withholding vacation pay from Norm Anger. Ruling on the case was Chief Magistrate Harold Gyles, who termed the affair "regrettable." Joe personally could not be considered the employer in terms of administration of vacation pay, and there was no evidence that he had "deliberately intervened" to withhold the vacation pay.[36]

Once acquitted, Joe lost little time in dealing with the thorny issue of the required apology to Magistrate Manwaring. On June 5, he released a 6-page letter to Justice Nitikman stating that he would not comply, and, furthermore, "the real culprit" in this affair was Manwaring himself.

Joe fully expected to go to jail as a consequence of his refusal to comply. He did not, contrary to how it might appear at first, make the decision lightly. Later that day, in an impromptu news conference at a labour convention, he nearly broke down, and had to pause three times to regain his composure. The tears came when he was asked about his family; they were "glad it was over" but had suffered months of anguish over the affair. It was to prevent them further grief that he chose not to appeal the contempt of court ruling. Finally overcome, Joe had to stop talking to the reporters, whom, one scribe noted, "he blames for a lot of his trouble."[37]

Joe also told the newsmen that he fully expected to resign from cabinet if sent to jail. His boss declined to comment: Schreyer noted only that the original Anger case was "clearly a frivolous and vexatious matter."[38]

In his letter to Justice Nitikman, Joe wrote that he had been accused, in that the charge of withholding vacation pay, of "the ultimate crime in the labour movement (beating a working man out of his just wages)." Not only had he been "compared to Hitler, Stalin and other assorted degenerates" but his family had gone through "living hell for nine months" for which state of affairs, Joe, concluded Manwaring should apologize.[39] The "only way the damage can be repaired is by the voluntary departure of the magistrate—so that he can never again disgrace the courts which I have the highest respect for, even though they are politically appointed and occasionally are guilty of outrageous conduct."

Such was the record of events when Joe Borowski appeared before Justice Israel Nitikman on June 30, having refused to comply with the order to apologize to Magistrate Manwaring. Justice Nitikman then drew his own line in the sand: he refused to send Joe to jail. "Imprisonment for you obviously would not be a deterrent—it would delight you."

Instead, the judge fined Joe $1,000. If he refused to pay it, the Court was instructed to appoint a receiver of his assets and thereby wring the money from him. In this way, Justice Nitikman said, he circumvented Joe's obvious desire to be a "hero-martyr" and deprived him of an opportunity to continue "grandstanding tactics" from a penal institution funded by Manitoba taxpayers. Joe, in an outburst, told the judge not to impute motives, but was warned to keep quiet.[40]

Schreyer stood by his embattled colleague, saying that Joe's position in cabinet was not in jeopardy as the Highways Minister had not been sent to jail. This drew sharp criticism from the Toronto *Globe and Mail*, which viewed Joe's "snarling fight with the courts" as "deplorable" and Schreyer's decision to support him as politically motivated.[41]

Despite the *Globe and Mail*'s deploring, Joe had support from more people than just his premier. No sooner had the sentence been made public than calls and money poured in, along with a bouquet of pink peonies from the Benedictine Sisters.[42]

Joe cheekily designed an orange-and-black button, which declared "I gave"—anyone who made a donation to the cause could sport this memento. Ontario labour leaders started a "Borowski Bucks" campaign, which drew about $200.[43] Even his political foes came to Joe's aid. Tory backbencher Art Moug quipped that Joe, as the "best showman" the government had, should be supported, and sent $10 across the floor. Joe sent back $9 in change and one of the buttons, which Moug pinned to his lapel.[44]

It was not long before Joe had received enough money to pay the fine, and more besides.

Despite the *Globe and Mail*'s tut-tutting, and the severity of Justice Nitikman's reproof, Joe was more popular than ever: Manitoba's Golden Boy, he was seemingly politically indestructible.

Notes
Chapter 6
The road to Dauphin

[1] "The Dauphin highway workers, a tangle that goes back a long way," *Tribune*, October 24, 1970

[2] "Road official at Dauphin suspended," *Free Press*, February 11, 1970.

[3] Ibid.

[4] *Hansard*, August 5, 1970, p. 4192.

[5] Ibid. p. 4193.

[6] Ibid. p. 4195.

[7] "Naming of Borowski puts House in uproar," Eugene Weiss, *Tribune*, August 5, 1970.

[8] Ibid.

[9] "How Manitoba turned 100 by standing on its head," Douglas Marshall *MacLeans*, December 1970 p. 36.

[10] Interview with Ed Schryer.

[11] Ibid, p. 37.

[12] Op. Cit., "The outsider moves in," Annesley, p. 42.

[13] "Dauphin road man fine $250.00 for breach of trust," *Tribune*, January 18, 1971.

[14] Op. Cit., "The Dauphin highway workers, a tangle."

[15] "Borowski action reversed: six employees reinstated," *Free Press*, October 15, 1970.

[16] Op. Cit., "The Dauphin highway workers, a tangle."

[17] "Borowski action reversed: six employees reinstated," *Free Press*, October 15, 1970.

[18] Op. Cit., "The Dauphin highway workers, a tangle."

[19] Ibid.

[20] Ibid.

[21] Anger was initially dismissed for "allegedly leasing equipment to the highways department, and receiving payment for the leasing of a back-hoe and its operation. ("Decision on Dauphin firings soon," *Tribune*, October 12, 1970.)

[22] "Borowski charge," Egon Frech, *Free Press*, October 10, 1979.

[23] "Borowski case delayed," *Free Press*, November 3, 1970.

[24] "The Borowski affair," *Tribune*, editorial, May 14, 1971.

[25] "Contempt decision deferred," *Free Press*, April 1, 1971.

[26] "Magistrate shouldn't hear case," *Tribune*, March 17, 1971.

[27] "Minister repeats objections," *Free Press*, March 18, 1971.

[28] "Lyon's letter requests action," *Tribune*, March 18, 1971.

[29] "The Borowski affair," *Tribune,* editorial, May 14, 1971.

[30] "Contempt action sought," *Free Press*, March 19, 1971.

[31] "Court action flayed," *Free Press*, May 7, 1971.

[32] "Conviction of Borowski won't affect MLA status," *Tribune*, April 29, 1971.

[33] Ibid.

[34] Interview with Ed Schreyer, March 2002.

[35] Interview with Bob Mayer, March 2002.

[36] "Borowski acquitted in 'regrettable' case," *Tribune*, June 2, 1971.

[37] "To quit if goes to jail," Charles Thompson, *Tribune*, June 5, 1971.

[38] "Improper for cabinet to take sides: Schreyer," Ron Campbell, *Free Press*, c. June, 1971

[39] "Complete text of Borowski letter," *Tribune*, June 7, 1971.

[40] "Borowski fined $1,000," Egon Frech, *Free Press*, June 30, 1971.

[41] Editorial, *Globe and Mail*, July 2, 1971.

[42] "Borowski won't appeal sentence," Tribune, July 2, 1971.

[43] "Borowski gets $200," *Free Press*, July 9, 1971.

[44] "Second Tory offers aid to Borowski," *Tribune*, July 8, 1971

Chapter 7

The Fall

It seems so far away,
and everything seemed
so far behind—
Now I can see clearly.
And I forgot to pray for everything
that's tearing in my mind—
Things I once held dearly....
M. J. Laurence
Hearts are breaking

"The only real enemies he had were in
the pro-choice movement. They hated him."
Sid Green

ON MAY 17, 1971, THE *WINNIPEG FREE PRESS* PUBLISHED AN INTER-view with Anne Ross, the executive director of Mount Carmel Clinic, a medical center in Winnipeg's impover-ished north end. While the clinic provided legitimate health care services to the poor and disadvantaged, it also offered contracep-tives and abortion referral services.

Ross divulged during the interview that Mount Carmel Clinic had been sending pregnant women to an abortion provider in the United States. At this time, the law said abortion was permitted in

Canada only if a committee of three doctors agreed that the continuation of the pregnancy would endanger the expectant mother's life or health. According to Ross, the amount of time the committee took to process these applications was unbearable for some women, hence, the clinic sent them to New York (which had a year earlier passed the most liberal abortion law in the United States) for a total cost of $450 to $500 U.S. per person.[1]

That May, Joe Borowski received a telephone call from a doctor—who remained anonymous—who accused him and the NDP government of hypocrisy because it paid a portion of the fee for these abortions; that is, the $63.75 which medicare at that time alloted for "therapeutic" abortions. Joe, incensed both at the charge of hypocrisy, and at the possibility that the government was indeed doing that of which the doctor accused it, resolved to investigate the claim.[2] The result was that on August 13, Joe sent a letter to the United Way director E. F. Paterson, asking that the charity stop all funds to Mount Carmel Clinic, which, he wrote, was involved in "illegal pimping for abortionists."[3]

"I am sure the United Way fund was never intended to: a) become involved in abortion; b) be party to an illegal act," penned Joe, and added, "Regardless of what one thinks of abortion (which I personally consider a savage, inhuman butchery), the fact is that it is illegal in Canada." Joe sent copies of his letter to Health Minister René Toupin and Winnipeg mayor Steve Juba, as the clinic received municipal funds as well.[4] He also sent a copy to Attorney-General Al Mackling to determine the legality of the actions of the Mount Carmel Clinic.[5]

As events gathered momentum, the press kept close watch—perhaps the newshounds had picked up the intoxicating scent of a potentially huge controversy, one that would see political bloodletting before its resolution.

On August 17, the *Free Press* carried a story relating Joe's remarks on a radio call-in show, in which he again denounced Ross's actions, which, he said, could prove to be in violation of the Criminal Code. He opposed public funding of the clinic, or of any abortion-providing institution. "Abortion is murder...I don't care how you slice it...Murder in a back alley and murder in a hospital bed is still murder." The mail he had received at his office was about nine to one in favour of his position.[6] He had also expressed his confidence that the directors of the United Way, whom he described as "pillars of the community" would make a decision to cut funding to the Mount Carmel Clinic "within the next few days."[7]

Alas, that confidence proved to be misplaced. On August 21, the president of the United Way of Greater Winnipeg was quoted in the press as seeing no reason why Mount Carmel should be cut off from financial aid. "The only question we have to concern ourselves with here is whether the clinic is breaking the law, and obviously it isn't, because therapeutic abortions are perfectly legal," was the response of Art Coulter, who, incidentally, was also executive secretary of the Manitoba Federation of Labour and a Winnipeg metro councillor.[8]

On August 25, the *Tribune* reported that Joe Borowski had declined an invitation to be the keynote speaker for the United Way kick-off campaign, explaining in a letter to campaign organizer William Brown that he had been "unofficially" told that the Mount Carmel Clinic would continue to receive funds from the charity. "That being the case, I must regretfully inform you that I will not be making any contribution to the United Way, and will urge my friends and supporters to do likewise."[9]

Opposition to Joe mounted: a *Free Press* editorial reprimanded Joe for his stand,[10] and a September 3 demonstration of women on the steps of the legislature, brought a petition of 1,000 signatures demanding that Joe resign and apologize to Anne Ross. The delegation missed the premier, but delivered its petition, along with a letter that excoriated Joe's comments as "malicious and slanderous attack" on both Mount Carmel and its director. The group vowed to "pursue this matter relentlessly until Mrs. Ross receives either a written retraction or an apology from the government of Manitoba."[11]

Joe declared that he would not accede to these demands, even if it meant resigning, and that he was going to release a statement the next day "which is going to be a hell of a long way from an apology." He admitted, however, that he had been severely censured in cabinet over earlier remarks about Mount Carmel. What particularly angered his colleagues, apparently, was that he had referred to Anne Ross as the wife of a Communist. (Her husband, Bill Ross, was president of the Manitoba Communist Party.) "Over that, they were incensed, and I can't really blame them," he said.[12]

Joe was true to his word. He sent a memo to the 2,500 employees of the Highways and Public Works Department asking them to voluntarily stop contributing to the Winnipeg United Way campaign.

Mount Carmel Clinic received $50,000 from United Way, as well as $45,000 from the government, wrote Joe. "The Winnipeg United Way has never told its volunteer canvassers, or the contributing public that part of their funds would go towards the running of a disgusting abortion referral business." He described abortion in graphic terms, and wrote that the practise of infanticide in ancient Greece "would bring cries of horror in this day and age but it seems that many people have no such scruples in destroying the fetus at a slightly earlier stage of development." The "screaming minority of abortion on demand" would doubtless approve of the Eskimos' technique of leaving "grandma or grandpa" to freeze to death: "Their rationale was basically the same as the abortionists are using, being old and useless and a burden to us—life is so much more pleasant without them.

"Finally, we are being asked to be accomplices in this medieval act of barbarism by not only forcing our doctors and nurses to commit murder—through abortion, so a handful of cheap, third-rate immoral tramps (also some good women) can escape the consequences of their actions, and to add insult to injury, they are asking that it be included in medicare."

The memo, Joe concluded, "is not a department order or directive—merely an appeal to withhold funds from those involved in or supporting child-destroying barbarism."[13]

On September 3, the government announced a change in policy. Out-of-province abortions would receive funding from medicare only if the criteria required under the Criminal Code were fulfilled: the signature of three doctors that the abortion was necessary because of a threat to the mother's life or health—although, according to Health Minister René Toupin, these need not be signatures of Manitoba doctors. Toupin also announced that Grace and Victoria Hospitals in Winnipeg would start performing abortions, in addition to the Winnipeg General Hospital.[14]

This announcement precipitated vociferous public disagreement between Joe Borowski and René Toupin. Joe maintained that cabinet had agreed to no funding for out-of-province abortions. To pay even a portion of the cost for such abortions was "so repugnant and disgusting and bloody awful that my limited vocabulary fails me to express it," he told the press. "When these immoral, secondary tramps get pregnant and go to New York for an abortion of convenience, it's bloody awful." Ed Schreyer himself had been "dumbfounded" to learn that provincial government cheques were sent to New York abortionists, said Joe.[15]

The next day, the full text of Joe's department memo—that statement "a hell of a long way from an apology"—hit the press. The air was thick with calls for Joe Borowski's head on a platter—or failing that, his resignation.

Conservative leader Sidney Spivak's cries were joined with the multitude. He criticized Joe's memo as "preposterous" and "just an absolute abuse of his rights as a Minister." It was time, opined Spivak, for Schreyer to cease to be "the jellyfish he has been in the past." The premier should either support Joe Borowski in his anti-abortion campaign, or fire him.[16] Whether or not Schreyer read Spivak's comments, the premier publicly rebuked Joe at a meeting with a delegation from the Mount Carmel Clinic on September 7. Although Schreyer did not mention Joe by name, the press inferred that the "tongue-lashing was meant for the Highways Minister and his outbursts would have to stop."[17]

"I am prepared," the premier told the 30 or so members of the delegation, "to witness an unusual degree of dissent, but not in a way that is intolerant of a differing view or in a way that makes it difficult for government policy to be understood…it is not tenable to have two or more different Ministers issuing directives which are contradictory on a single issue."

He had released a warning that day to his Cabinet Ministers that he would not brook any statements contrary to government policy; those who could not comply would be expected to resign. "Intolerance," intoned Schreyer, "particularly on moral issues where there is a wide range of opinion, or degrading or demeaning comments, will not be accepted."[18] He personally did not favour abortion on demand, nor did he believe that "there is sufficient acceptance for more liberal or more progressive abortion laws and that is the policy of this government, bearing in mind it is a federal matter." He was also "at a loss to understand in what way Mount Carmel Clinic is to be regarded as unfit for continued public support." Schreyer declared as void Joe Borowski's inter-departmental memo requesting that his employees not support the United Way campaign.

Joe himself was not present at the meeting. "Why should I go in there and be insulted?" was his comment. When the press played him a tape recording of the premier's words, he was "taken aback", allegedly laughed nervously, but retracted nothing.[19] His now notorious memo retained its validity, he believed, at least until Attorney-General Al Mackling ruled on the legality of Mount Carmel's abortion referral practises. "In the final analysis, it is the employees who will make their decision—my personal request stands." Ultimately, the cabinet would decide if he were fit to remain in office, and it was to meet the next day. "If the premier thinks I am doing something wrong, they can fire me tomorrow— I am wrong occasionally."

On September 8, the cabinet assembled for what proved to be an arduous and lengthy session, over six hours in duration. At 12:45 Joe Borowski left alone, and disappeared into his office. At about three o'clock, he released a statement to the many reporters crowded near his office, but not before his secretary had borne a sealed envelope to the cabinet room. It was official: Joe Borowski had resigned.[20]

He could not accept the cabinet's stand toward "dirty and degrading pornography...Nor can I in good conscience remain in cabinet knowing the permissive attitude of cabinet in regards to inhuman—barbarous destruction of human life through abortion," Joe wrote in his resignation letter. "While I appreciate the wide latitude and tolerance of my colleagues to allow me to speak on most moral issues, often contrary to the majority view, I just cannot bury or abort my principle on this paramount and very basic issue."

While he realized abortion was permitted in Canada through federal law, the province should refuse to pay for "sexual irresponsibility" and, as a "working man's party," the NDP should be more concerned with supplying free prescription drugs to the aged or free dental care to the poor. Moreover, the government should tell Ottawa to build its own abortion-providing hospitals. "I find it abhorrent that their law should force our doctors and nurses to become hired killers in order to fulfill Ottawa's election promise... In conclusion, my dear colleagues, I want to thank you for the many good 'people's' legislation you have passed since July 14, 1969 and for the opportunity of allowing me to bring to fruition some of my own life-long dreams—such as sane and life-saving highway laws and meaningful involvement of Indian and

Metis people in the building of our great North... But I cannot be party to or accept child-destroying legislation in which we are involved."[21]

It was speculated that had Ed Schreyer not accepted Joe's resignation, he would have had a mutiny on his hands, with the revolt coming from both cabinet and caucus. "Too many people have been stepped on," a source was quoted. Speculation included the possibility that if Joe didn't go, Health Minister René Toupin would.[22]

Toupin, himself a Catholic, stated repeatedly that the NDP government would not oppose the federal abortion bill of 1969. He held adamantly to government policy, and was circumspect about his personal views on the matter. Only a little over two months later did Toupin divulge his thoughts about the controversy, when he surprised delegates at an NDP convention by publicly opposing further liberalization of abortion. Then, speaking as the MLA for Springfield, Toupin said he believed a pregnant woman "does not have the right to do away with a life." He also spoke out against euthanasia: "There is also life in the Brandon Mental Institute, and in the Selkirk Mental Hospital. Even for those who beg us to take their lives—in mercy killings—there is life."[23] The beliefs held by Toupin, however, demonstrably did not affect his decisions as a Minister of the Crown. He remained in cabinet.

Joe Borowski did not.

Despite the indisputable signs of the impending and unbreechable rift, many people couldn't believe Joe—not Joe, the beloved working-class hero—would really be out. But he himself had no doubts about his future. "I don't think 10,000 letters on the premier's desk tomorrow morning would make any difference... it has reached the point where I can't reconcile this very basic disagreement."[24]

It was only after Ed Schreyer appeared that afternoon and confirmed that he had accepted Joe Borowski's resignation that people were convinced.[25] The consensus of the cabinet, said the premier, was that the Minister's views were "very intolerant and disrespectful" of those who did not agree with him, and could not be condoned. He had been at times embarrassed by Joe's blunt statements, Schreyer said, "but I want to make it plain that I was a lot less embarrassed than some people seem to think." In fact, until the "irreconcilable difference" on abortion arose, the good Joe had done outweighed any harm.[26]

Colleague Sid Green was not surprised, nor does he remember even trying to persuade Joe to stay, although others recall a delegation going to Joe's home during the crisis to talk to him. "It would not even be a consideration in my mind...if I knew that this was the way he felt, there was no, no persuasion that was going to change him."

"When you ask did I foresee it," Green recalled, "I told people that if they think Joe was a left-wing radical, they were very badly mistaken and that they had something to learn."[27]

Joe's Thompson constituents were unhappy. "People are angry at Joe now, even some of those who are openly known as Liberal and Conservatives but used to come out in support of Joe," said Brian Koshul, editor of the *Thompson Citizen*, and a friend of Joe's, in response to media inquiries. "They feel he betrayed us here...we no longer have a direct pipeline into the cabinet."

But what really perplexed people, in Koshul's view, was the reason Joe left. They would have understood more readily if he had resigned "over a road to Churchill. This abortion thing nobody understands here and people feel Joe was sent into the Legislature to fight for our northern interests there, not for his pet projects."[28]

Wilf Hudson, representative of the United Steelworkers and former NDP candidate, another blunt-spoken northerner, was disappointed that Thompson had lost a Cabinet Minister. "But having talked with Joe this evening, I know that this is a gut feeling with him. I suppose it was also a pretty gutsy thing to resign." All in all, Hudson mused, "Joe will continue to have the support of the people of Thompson. On the matter of roads, and in the cabinet in general, I think he has done a damned good job."[29]

The press gently reminded the public of Joe's zeal regarding road safety. His stringent regulations regarding snowmobiles and cars, his expanded high school driver training programs, all contributed to the province having one of the best records for reducing motor vehicle accidents in North America.[30] Fittingly, Joe's last press release as Highways Minister was a warning about a hazardous facemask for motorcycle helmets. His parting injunction to reporters: "I hope you guys will give good play to that...it could save a life."[31] He hadn't been so conscious of avoiding hazards when it came to his political career. Perhaps it was because he had veered so close to the precipice so many times before, sometimes even clipping the guardrail, always pulling back just in the nick of time, that it took people a little time to realize that Joe was gone. He had finally plunged over the edge. Whether his political life would survive the crash, remained to be seen.

There were those who had noticed a change in him earlier in the year, or so it seemed to them in retrospect. The story goes that Joe Borowski, being somewhat of a wine connoisseur, went to Spain on a buying trip for the liquor commission and came back a changed man—a deeply religious man.[32]

This doesn't exactly fit the recollections of Jean Borowski, who said that her husband had always been a devout Catholic, a man who frequently attended Mass during the week. But she did concede that he had at times been at odds with the Church. "He was strong, and then he was sort of wishy-washy and then, because of the kids, we started going back."

Joe's own account was that he left the Church at age 23, attending Mass only occasionally with his family.[33] As he told writer Anne Collins, it was because he disagreed with the Church's teaching on contraception. "I got married when I was nineteen. And you know, your fertile years—the wife was nineteen—and you've got a lot of fertile years. And I just couldn't see myself having all the children."[34]

In this regard, Joe was a child of his age. The Second Vatican Ecumenical Council was opened in 1962 by Pope John XXIII and closed under Pope Paul VI, in 1965. During the turbulent years following Vatican Council II, speculation was rife that the Church would alter her traditional teaching on contraception.

Jean recalled a confrontation with a bishop who, while teaching a marriage course, had explained the Church's teaching somewhat clumsily, or, one might argue, in a way Joe himself would have explained it. The bishop asserted that if a couple used contraception, the wife could be likened to a prostitute. Joe erupted in fury, and he and Jean left the hall. He accosted the prelate afterwards.

"'How dare you?' he says, 'We're married and she's expecting and you're calling her a prostitute?'" Jean related. "The bishop replied, 'Well, you don't take it in full context of the words, but it's the same principle,' and he says, 'No, it's not, and how the hell would you know anything about it?' and we walked away. That bothered him a long time. He'd go and then he wouldn't go and he was really fighting with himself."[35]

In July 1968, Pope Paul VI issued the encyclical *Humanae vitae*, which affirmed the Church's teaching that contraception is intrinsically wrong and cannot be justified under any circumstances: the use of contraception separates the unitive and procreative aspects of the conjugal act, thus irreparably violating its essential integrity. Prophetically, the pope warned that if contraception were condoned, the sex impulse, released from the moorings of a chaste and exclusive love within marriage, would leave devastation in its wake. Women would be objectified and suffer a degradation hitherto unimagined, marriages would falter and break, the consequences of sexual misconduct would blight the young lives of countless men and women, and out-of-wedlock pregnancies would increase. Moreover, a mentality that accepted contraception, Paul VI wrote, would ultimately condone abortion.

When *Humanae vitae* appeared, "Well, I figured that's it, I have no choice," Joe admitted. "It's very clear that the Church will not change for me. And I have to accept the Church on its terms or stay out. And I thought about it and thought that my soul was more important than some hang-up and inconvenience."[36] He began attending Mass regularly, but still deeply troubled over the issue, did not receive Communion.[37]

Finally, Joe made a trip to Fatima in early 1971—possibly as a side-trip on a government sponsored liquor-buying excursion. On February 13, he met a Franciscan priest to whom he confided his uncertainties, and received the sacrament of Confession. Unburdened at last, Joe came back to his Catholic faith with fervour. Since that day, he attended Mass and said fifteen decades of the rosary daily. As he recounted to writer Grace Petrasek years later, at age 39, he felt at peace for the first time in years.[38]

His daughters noticed a difference because when their father came home after this particular trip, instead of the usual curios and mementos he typically brought as gifts, he gave them rosaries.[39] Bob Mayer claimed that he saw a change in his buddy's demeanour. Other NDP cronies noticed too. Joe was attending daily Mass. Gradually oaths and profanities disappeared from his infamous "swears like a stevedore" vocabulary. Mayer was intrigued, and perhaps alarmed, enough to ask Joe's middle daughter, "Karen, what happened?" When she replied that "Dad went on a liquor buying trip to Spain," Mayer laughed, "My first question was, 'What was in the wine?'"

Who knows what moves the hearts of men? And who can presume to chart the mysterious penetration of nature by grace? The facts are these: Joe Borowski returned fully to his Catholic faith at Fatima, the site where the Blessed Mother appeared in 1917 to three children, and through them, exhorted the faithful to do penance and recite the rosary—practices to which Joe Borowski, after his pilgrimage, applied himself with open-hearted ardour. In 1971, Joe's intense opposition to abortion culminated in his resignation from cabinet on September 8, the date on which Catholics celebrate Mary's birthday. It can also be noted that Joe's birthday, December 12, is the feast of Our Lady of Guadalupe, the Patroness of the Unborn. These facts cannot prove the maternal intercession of the Virgin Mary in the life of Joe Borowski, but neither can they be brushed aside, as it is not unreasonable to suppose that their significance was noted by Joe himself, permeated as he was in the Catholic sensibility of the world as sacramental, and of time itself bearing the imprint of divinity.

Joe had resigned from cabinet, but he was still an MLA in good standing, and still a member of the NDP caucus. His faith, expressed particularly in his devotion to the Virgin Mary, arguably both compelled him forward and sustained him along the way, in the battle for justice in which he was now irrevocably engaged.

Notes
Chapter 7
The fall

[1] "Would blacklist clinic," Egon Frech, *Winnipeg Free Press*, August 14, 1971.

[2] Grace Petrasek, *Silhouettes Against the Snow* (Toronto: Interim Publishing Company, 1991), p. 187.

[3] Op. Cit., "Would blacklist clinic," Egon Frech.

[4] Ibid

[5] "Clinic's director replies to letter from Borowski," *Tribune*, August 16, 1971.

[6] "Clinic violating law, charges Joe," *Free Press*, c. August 16, 1971.

[7] "Clinic's director replies to letter from Borowski," *Tribune*, August 16, 1971.

[8] "Way president stands behind Mount Carmel," *Tribune*, August 21, 1971.

[9] "Borowski won't contribute to the United Way," *Tribune*, August 25, 1971.

[10] "A great disservice," *Free Press*, August 25, 1971.

[11] "Protesters miss premier but petition is delivered," *Tribune*, September 3, 1971.

[12] Ibid.

[13] Text of Borowski's memo, *Tribune*, September 4, 1971.

[14] "Abortion coverage now is limited," Katie FitzRandolph, *Free Press*, September 3, 1971.

[15] "Toupin alters billing rules," *Tribune*, September 3, 1971.

[16] "Premier told to support or fire Joe," *Tribune*, September 7, 1971.

[17] "Schreyer tells Borowski to fall in line," Alice Krueger, *Tribune*, September 8, 1971.

[18] "Premier raps Borowski," Katie FitzRandolph, *Free Press*, September 8, 1971.

[19] "Joe taken aback but won't retract," *Free Press*, September 8, 1971.

[20] "Joe made decision on moral issues," Katie FitzRandolph, *Free Press*, September 9, 1971.

[21] "Borowski text," *Free Press*, September 9, 1971.

[22] "Cabinet revolt staved off," Egon Frech, *Free Press*, September 9, 1971.

[23] "Borowski loses first battle," Mike Flynn, *Tribune*, November 26, 1971.

[24] Op. Cit., "Joe made decision," Katie FitzRandolph.

[25] Ibid.

[26] Op. Cit., "Cabinet revolt staved off," Egon Frech.

[27] Interview with Sid Green, March 2002.

[28] "Schreyer to blame, Tory leader claims," *Tribune*, September 9, 1971.

[29] "Thompson people shocked by news," *Free Press*, September 9, 1971.

[30] "Turtle sign came down first," *Tribune*, September 9, 1971.

[31] Ibid.

[32] Interview with Bob Mayer c. March 2002

[33] Op. Cit., Grace Petrasek, p. 189.

[34] Op. Cit., Anne Collins, p. 39.

[35] Interview with Jean Borowski, March 2002.

[36] Op. Cit., Anne Collins, p. 40.

[37] Op. Cit., Grace Petrasek, p. 189.

[38] Ibid.

[39] Interview with Karen Borowski.

Chapter 8

I'm for Joe

Your justice I have proclaimed
in the great assembly,
My lips I have not sealed;
You know it, O Lord.
Psalm 40:9

"But he would have gone far? I doubt that…
I don't believe that Joe would have gone further
than he did. He became a Minister of the Crown—
which is pretty far, by the way."
Sid Green

JOE, THE ULTIMATELY UNCATEGORIZABLE POLITICIAN, HAD REACHED, IN A manner of speaking, a crossroads. Having been ousted from cabinet on a matter of fundamental principle, the most immediate consequence he suffered was material deprivation: his salary dropped from a Minister's annual $24,000 to the lowly $6,900 received by an MLA.[1] His demotion to backbencher would naturally be expected to curtail his political influence. Yet this reality was not immediately apparent, obscured as it was by his immense popularity, his headline-making ways, and his reputation as a politician who "was not for sale."[2]

His political future remained an open question; Joe himself contributed to the public speculation, candidly discussing alternative offers. The first was the request to form a Christian Democratic party in Manitoba, which he considered, but rejected—at least until the NDP policy meeting scheduled for November 1971. Then, he hoped, the Schreyer government would "mend its ways." He was supported in this hope by "a tremendous number of letters from party members and citizens."[3]

When the 500 or so delegates assembled in Brandon for the policy convention that year, they encountered "the awesomely dominant presence of Joe Borowski."[4] He had set up his own "information room", from whence he discussed and lobbied participants on five key issues. As well as advocating a stronger stand against abortion, pornography and welfare abuse, Joe opposed the legalization of marijuana, and supported public aid to private schools—a divisive issue for the NDP caucus.

Joe hinted he would leave the party if it adopted a resolution supporting abortion on demand. He was at the convention to plead that the NDP get "back on the right track. If I fail, then I'll be faced with making the most difficult decision of my life. Leaving the party is almost like leaving your wife."[5]

The lengthy debate over the abortion-on-demand resolution was highly charged. In the end, it was defeated, by 155 to 117—an unexpected result, as nearly 230 of the delegates had earlier signed a petition in support of removing abortion from the Criminal Code. What turned the tide were the remarks of Ed Schreyer in the closing moments of the debate.[6]

In doing so, Schreyer broke his personal silence on abortion. He cautioned delegates not to treat the issue casually or to think they had the solution to a question on which "even the experts are painfully split." While he pointed out that "we're not talking about cutting off a wart...these are human lives we're dealing with," Schreyer opted for maintaining the status quo. "Why can't we live" with current Criminal Code provisions that require a panel of doctors to be consulted, he questioned: it was the "height of egoism" to assume one doctor or individual could decide the matter. Some people "will be impressed that I am looking at the problem of society through the lenses of Roman Catholicism binoculars. But anyone who knows me at all would know better than that."[7]

Whatever the binoculars he had trained on society's problems,

Schreyer's remarks were gratefully acknowledged by Joe Borowski. Rumours ran rife about his possible defection from caucus, but Joe was satisfied enough with the policies of the convention[8] to remain a card-carrying member of the New Democratic Party and MLA for Thompson.

It was not long before the irrepressible northerner was in the headlines again.

On March 27, 1972, Joe Borowski was hanged in effigy on the legislature grounds by an angry group of about 300 protesters. When he attempted to speak to the crowd, amid jeers and boos, demonstration organizers turned off the loudspeaker system.

The people with such hostility to Joe Borowski and who had come to demand—what else—his expulsion from the caucus and an apology, were representatives of the 35,000 native people who were rallying in defence of Dave Courchene, the president of the Manitoba Indian Brotherhood, about whom Joe was, apparently, spreading "malicious lies."[9] Chief Gordon Lathlin said that Joe would no longer be welcome on any of Manitoba's 54 reserves, and accused Premier Ed Schreyer of standing by in "silent agreement".[10]

What had brought events to this sad pass? It began when Manitoba Liberal leader, Israel "Izzy" Asper, toured, along with five Winnipeg newsmen,[11] a northern bush camp for Indians contracted to clear brush for Manitoba Hydro. Asper was shocked at the conditions, which he described as worse than a prisoner of war camp—men living in tents with only space-heaters for warmth and sleeping on spruce boughs.[12]

Joe, who as Minister had initiated the practise of government contracting bush clearing directly to the Indians, scoffed at Asper's concerns, saying that the Indians themselves chose the accommodation. Dave Courchene then jumped in, calling Joe's statement "a damned lie."[13] And the war of words was on.

Joe expanded on his opinion, speculating that Courchene, like Asper, was making political hay of the situation. But far more disturbingly, Joe alleged that the MIB president was exploiting his position and misusing the Brotherhood funds—including grants received from the government—by drawing a fat salary and living the life of Riley. Moreover, Courchene favoured friends and rela-tions on reserves in the south and ignored the north and the majority on the reserves who lived in poverty, charged Joe.[14]

And so the angry delegation converged on the Legislature grounds to defend Courchene. Schreyer defused the situation but made no promise to muzzle Joe Borowski, which, the premier said, would amount to "thought control."[15]

Courchene then accused Joe of McCarthyism for his unsub-stantiated allegations, while Joe challenged the MIB president to open the books of the Brotherhood, as he had promised to do.[16] If the allegations proved untrue, Joe said, he would resign. If irreg-ularities were revealed, Courchene would have to resign.[17]

It was reported that Borowski had sent a letter to federal Indian Affairs Minister Jean Chrétien to demand a public inquiry into the expenditure of tax monies granted to the MIB. The regional direc-tor of Indian Affairs was interviewed and reported that funds were accounted for.[18]

Opinion ran slightly against Joe: his colleague and Minister without portfolio Ron McBryde distanced himself from the Thompson MLA's "intemperate remarks", Conservative leader Sidney Spivak called for his expulsion from the NDP caucus, sec-onded by Liberal leader Israel Asper. A *Free Press* editorial chided Joe for his "shotgun allegations" and his desire that Courchene prove his innocence—"a practise quite contrary to established jus-tice," but concluded that opening the MIB books was now the only way to resolve the matter.[19]

Tribune columnist Frances Russell derided Joe's efforts as "how not to go about investigating organizations." Russell contended that a number of people shared Joe's concerns about the MIB. Some accused the former Highways Minister of being a racist—an unfair charge—but he admittedly had little use for organizations of "professional Indians" like the MIB, which he thought "serve to underline the differences between Indians and whites and thus to throw up obstacles to Indian progress." But, Russell continued, Joe had turned the entire affair into a witchhunt. And "when a witchhunt has racial overtones, there are no responsible partici-pants whatever."[20]

Perhaps opinion would have continued against Joe Borowski—but for the reported death threats. The first disclosure came from Chief George Guimond of the Fort Alexander Reserve, about 70 miles northeast of Winnipeg and the home of Dave Courchene. In a letter to his band councillors Chief Guimond said he received two telephone calls, in which he was told his "head would be blown off" if he spoke out publicly about the Borowski-Courchene dispute.[21] Brian Koshul, managing editor of two Thompson newspapers, also reported receiving death threats at home, just after the edition of the *Nickel Belt News*, which published parts of the 1971-1972 annual report of the MIB, was on the streets. More accurately, his wife Sharon was told by an anonymous caller one evening that her husband would "not be home tonight. We're going to blow his head off." The caller said that Koshul was "a G–d—ed liar and we know how to handle G–d––ed liars and Indian-haters."[22] Koshul said he saw no facts indicating the MIB was corrupt. What he published, however, did indicate an ineffective use of government funds.[23]

Jean Borowski remembered the night when a car pulled up outside the Borowskis' home in La Salle, a town just south of Winnipeg. "I went to the door and there were five big Indians—men. I said, 'This is it, this is the end.'" The men said they wanted to see Joe.

"I just said, 'Joe, there's somebody here to see you,' so Joe comes, looks out and says, 'C'mon in.'" Jean thought only, "Oh my God, my kids are in bed," but the men walked in and shook Joe's hand. They had come to see her husband—"everybody knew where Joe lived"—to tell him that "it's about time that somebody spoke up and somebody listened—this is happening all the time."[24]

With reports of death threats, public opinion veered towards Joe, who, despite the fact that he had been declared *persona non grata*, slipped up to the Fort Alexander Reserve to talk to Chief Guimond, a move that further incensed the Brotherhood. The Chief himself said Borowski's accusations were not true, but "there's no way that I will stop anybody who wants to criticize or say what he wants to say over the issue. If the taxpayer wants to know how this money (MIB funds) is spent, he has a right to see."[25]

The immediate resolution was that the MIB board of directors—not Chief Dave Courchene—requested an independent audit by Ottawa of provincial and federal funds, after which, it would decide what financial statements to release.[26]

Schreyer thought this entirely suitable, although whether the matter would then be settled, he could not predict. "I have no way of knowing. I suppose that some of the questions would never be answered in any case."[27]

In the meantime, the gulf between Joe and Ed Schreyer's NDP government remained bridged by only the frailest of ties. In January 1972, Joe again announced that he had received offers from all major parties—presumably, this included federal NDP— to run in the federal election. He had refrained from making a commitment until the issue over provincial funding for private schools had been settled. "After that battle has been fought, then I'll know where I stand."[28]

That fragile bridge connecting Joe to the NDP caucus finally came crashing down with the government introduction of a bill which would replace Manitoba's film censorship board with a film classification system. The censorship board itself had not always operated as stringently as Joe would have liked. He had been outraged when the movie *Joe* passed through the board—enduring the genial scoffing of his supposedly more enlightened colleagues. But to disband the censorship board was, in his view, a grave mistake, and would lead to moral ruination.

When the bill passed, Joe quit the caucus. "This government," he asserted, "is going to turn our theaters into smut hostels and transform Manitoba into a cultural desert—a socialist Death Valley where decency and respect will die of moral scurvy, where human dignity will perish."[29]

While now outside caucus, Joe still did not feel it necessary to relinquish his NDP party membership; he therefore carried the strange appellation Independent-New Democrat.

His departure from the caucus left the House with government and opposition tied at 28 seats each, with only the vote of the speaker separating the former from defeat.[30] While Schreyer deftly navigated through these treacherous political waters, he had to keep a wary eye out for the torpedoes fired by the one-time stalwart defender of his government. For Joe, freed from the shackles of any loyalty or bond to the provincial NDP caucus, was at liberty to hammer the government at every turn. And he proceeded to do so, prompting the speculation that his real genius lay in opposition.

Moreover, he attempted any possible means to get abortion de-insured under the provincial medicare scheme. He tried first to take the government to court, but following legal advice that this was impossible, he announced in early February 1973, that he was going to stop paying medicare premiums. He hoped that, in so doing, the government would take *him* to court.

He was prepared to take the fight all the way to the Supreme Court, and had recently formed a group—Alliance Against Abortion—to provide funding for the campaign.[31] Joe also introduced a private member's bill that would mandate the removal of abortion from the medical procedures insured under medicare.

Meanwhile, the time of reckoning between Joe and the NDP party was approaching. The first move went to Joe, when he endorsed Trudeau's Liberal party for the federal election in the fall of 1972. He himself would not be running, but would campaign on behalf of the Liberals, although only as the lesser of two evils, Joe announced. He could not countenance the policies of NDP leader David Lewis, especially regarding abortion and marijuana. While he did not agree with Trudeau on a number of things, Joe said that the Prime Minister had stated he would not liberalize the abortion law and he was opposed to the legalization of marijuana. "I'd sooner," said Joe, "have the government give the money to the corporate bums than to the abortionists and drug addicts."[32]

This ended the somewhat unbelievable rumour that Borowski was being considered for another cabinet post. Schreyer had not commented on the rumour, except to say he was waiting for Joe's announcement regarding his intentions in the forthcoming federal election.[33] Now, it was clearly impossible for Borowski to return to cabinet. "No one can be in the cabinet who is supporting another party," Schreyer retorted to reporters' questions. Would Joe be returning to caucus, he was then asked. Sounding a tad exasperated, the premier replied: "No one of my other colleagues, in cabinet or in caucus, are supporting another party; I don't see how I can make an exception."[34]

Not long afterwards, the NDP executive in Thompson saw fit to tighten the screws. While expressing regret that such an action was necessary, the executive passed as resolution that the provincial party executive not renew Joe's NDP membership—unless he signed a statement declaring his support for the party. Nowhere was it stated why this had to be done, and the party executive was at pains to point out it was not because of Joe's views on abortion or pornography, as his "position on these matters was accepted as a legitimate right of any party to express his view."[35]

The ultimatum didn't bother Joe: it "may not come to that." He was willing to sign but his assent was contingent on events at the upcoming party convention. He was keeping a close eye on the next NDP convention and if the resolutions supporting abortion and the legalization of marijuana were passed, he would leave. But he did consider it "a lack of courtesy" on the part of the executive not to tell him directly of its decision, but to leave him to hear of it through the media.[36]

In Thompson, there was a certain coolness towards the unpredictable MLA. Despite Borowski's qualified support of the party, Wilf Hudson was "a little disturbed by Joe's fickleness" pointing out that it was the Trudeau government that legalized abortion.[37]

The editor of the *Thompson Citizen*, Brian Koshul, attempted to identify Joe's true political philosophy. Tracing his evolution from a Diefenbaker federal Conservative, a Ross Thatcher provincial Liberal and NDP hero, Koshul wrote that Joe's political life had taken "more turns than a wine steward's corkscrew. Today this so-called radical is regarded by many in this province as a reactionary, the Ernest Manning of Manitoba...a bible-thumping, hippy-hating, enemy of pot-smoking, pro-abortion women's libbers and their natural allies, the university professors." While Joe had "settled down considerably from his younger hell-raising days," Koshul contended that "basically, his political philosophy hasn't changed that much from his Saskatchewan Thatcher Liberal days."[38]

But, warned the editor, it behooved the NDP to remember that Joe Borowski was the reason they held Thompson, and that "without him as a candidate, they have absolutely no chance of retaining the seat in the next election."

Nevertheless, they had to try, for Joe Borowski decided early in 1973 to pack it in and leave the NDP completely. When he announced his intention to stop paying medicare premiums, Joe also announced that he would not rejoin the party, for the simple reason that "I don't think they'll want me."[39] Moreover, his disgust with his former colleagues increased daily. In April, he publicly blasted Health Minister René Toupin, declaring that the

Springfield MLA was a "two-faced double crosser," who had incensed not only Joe himself but "many good French Catholics" of his constituency.[40] Toupin had promised to support the Borowski private bill to de-insure abortion, Joe alleged, but instead the Health Minister voted for a six-month's delay of the bill.

Despite this legislative defeat, Joe was ready for battle in the upcoming June provincial election—"I will do everything and anything I can to get rid" of the NDP, he vowed. "They have got to be defeated or we will be left with nothing in this province but prostitutes, perverts and homos."[41]

Yet, a month later, Joe revealed himself to be capable of self-doubt and even discouragement. What precipitated this momentary and public hesitation was a meat boycott instigated by a radio hot-line host. Within two weeks, the station apparently received 30,000 letters about the boycott, which prompted Joe to wonder.[42] "I never got that much response in two years" of opposition to abortion and pornography, he pointed out. "I really have reservations whether I'm serving the public or stating my own views....I don't feel I have the right or responsibility to go on tilting at personal windmills."[43]

Joe would run if he received a response from the public indicating they were behind him, he said, adding somewhat bitterly, "It seems that human life is of less concern than the price of meat."[44]

One can only conclude that there was an upswing in verbal support, because when the provincial election was held June 28, 1973, Joe was indeed listed as an Independent candidate. He brought the battle to the streets of Point Douglas, and his opponent was incumbent NDP member, Fr. Don Malinowski, a priest of the Polish National Church, who was married and the father of two children.

Why did Joe choose to run in Point Douglas? He wanted to run primarily on the issues of abortion and pornography, he wanted to run against the NDP, and he chose to do it the hard way—this, according to his family. And as Bob MacKalski, one of the founding members of Alliance Against Abortion, recalled, the group thought that Point Douglas was an area where Joe would have a lot of support. The constituency, in Winnipeg's north end, was poverty-stricken, and encompassed neighbourhoods consisting mainly of Polish and Ukrainian Canadians, as well as areas with a high population of native people and Metis. It also contained within its boundaries the infamous Mount Carmel Clinic.

Joe's daughters, enlisted to help with door knocking, remembered vividly the rough and tough campaign. Their dad had his headquarters on Selkirk Avenue from whence they went forth with a campaign worker. "I remember him saying, 'Okay, we'll go in there and drop off the pamphlets, but if there's a problem, here's the key, to run back to the car and honk the horn and stay in the car,' and I'm thinking, 'What?'" Sandy recalled. "And it was hot and it was really smelly and I didn't know what we were doing there."[45]

Bob MacKalski, too, remembered walking the streets, knocking on doors with Joe. "We sure worked hard at that." But the hours and days of tramping through the bleak and sometime squalid streets of Point Douglas did not pay off. Joe lost by a two-to-one margin. It was a "sad commentary" on a community "more interested in filling its stomach and getting something for nothing than in the evils and immorality in our society," he said.[46]

He also had harsh words about the newly elected MLA: "He has preached against pornography and abortion every Sunday in his parish and then he says the opposite in the Legislature. He'll have to answer for that some day." In Joe's opinion, it was the popularity of Ed Schreyer and the NDP that led to Fr. Malinowski's victory and his own defeat.[47]

Schreyer, who was reelected with a majority of five seats, was himself taken aback by Joe's trashing at the polls. "I knew he had a very substantial following, so all the more reason why I was quite surprised with the actual results of the '73 election," the former premier said. "The hot-line following didn't translate into votes." For Sid Green, the reason for this was simple. "He got beat by Don Malinowski, who was a nobody. I mean, compared to Joe, Don Malinowski was a nobody." But Don Malinowski was the candidate for the NDP, and that's why he won. Green shrugged: the same thing happened to him, when he ran as a candidate for the Manitoba Progressive Party, which he was instrumental in founding. "I was winning every election—in one year I got the biggest majority of anybody—but when I left the NDP, I got beat," Green recalled. He paused, and added, "Joe did better than I did, by the way. Joe did reasonably well."[48]

In Green's view, Joe had gone as far in politics as he could go.

"He was too unpredictable and people would be concerned that they wouldn't know what was going to happen if he went any further. And in order to go further, there has to be a certain feeling of security with the people around you."[49]

Joe Borowski was out of the Legislature. And out of a job. He was 40 years old.

Notes
Chapter 8
I'm for Joe

[1] "Borowski to keep seat as MLA for Thompson," Alice Kreuger, *Winnipeg Tribune*, September 9, 1971.

[2] Interview with Fr. Morand, February 2002.

[3] "Borowski may form Christian Democrats?" *Tribune*, September 29, 1971.

[4] "Two forces meet at Brandon," Frances Russell, *Tribune*, November 20, 1971.

[5] "Joe hints he'll quit as NDP meets," *Tribune*, November 19, 1971.

[6] "Borowski says 'thanks boss,'" *Tribune*, November 22. 1971.

[7] Ibid.

[8] Marijuana and pornography were not discussed; public aid to parochial schools, according to press reports, was referred to the Legislature on a non-partisan basis. ("Abortion, schools dominate issues," *Free Press*, November 22, 1971.)

[9] "Chiefs tell Borowski he's no longer welcome," Wally Dennison, *Free Press*, March 28, 1972.

[10] Ibid.

[11] "Milk frozen, bedrolls wet," *Free Press*, March 13, 1972.

[12] "Courchene 'playing politics': Borowski," *Free Press*, March 18, 1972.

[13] Ibid.

[14] Op. Cit., "Chiefs tell Borowski," Wally Dennison; "Indian chiefs to demand that NDP oust Borowski," *Tribune*, March 27, 1972.; "Borowski sticks to his accusations," *Free Press*, March 27, 1972.

[15] "Chiefs tell Borowski he's no longer welcome," Wally Dennison, *Tribune*, March 28, 1972.

[16] "Charges not backed by proof: Courchene," *Tribune*, March 28, 1972.

[17] "Editor claims life threatened," *Free Press*, April 14, 1972.

[18] "Funds spent properly, department says," *Free Press*, March 28, 1972.

[19] "A solution," *Free Press*, March 30, 1972.

[20] "Borowski and the Brotherhood," *Tribune*, April 4, 1972.

[21] "Chief alleges threats," *Free Press*, April 11, 1972.

[22] "Editor says story led to death threat," *Tribune*, April 14, 1972.

[23] "Editor claims life threatened," *Free Press*, April 14, 1972.

[24] Interview with Jean Borowski, March 2002.

[25] "Borowski visit upsets Indians," Nick Van Rijn, *Tribune*, April 29, 2002.

[26] "MIB asks government audit," *Tribune*, April 14, 1972.

[27] "Ottawa to audit books: Schreyer," *Tribune*, April 15, 1972.

[28] "Borowski confirms federal seat offers," *Tribune*, January 28, 1972.

[29] "Exit Joe," *Time Canada*, editorial, July 10, 1972.

[30] Ibid.

[31] The founding members of the Alliance were listed as: Ken Dedrick, Moose Jaw, Saskatchewan; Bob MacKalski, Winnipeg; Fern Marion, Winnipeg; René Andre, Winnipeg; and Brian Borowski (no relation) ("Borowski to with hold medicare premiums to fight abortion," Alice Kreuger, *Free Press*, February 10, 1972).

[32] "Borowski backing Liberals," *Free Press*, September 11, 1972.

[33] Ibid.

[34] "No cabinet role for Borowski seen after his Liberal move," *Free Press*, September 12, 1972.

[35] "Sign or, Borowski told," *Free Press*, November 21, 1972.

[36] "Must take NDP pledge or else," *Free Press*, December 12, 1972.

[37] "Discussion on Borowski status mounts," *Free Press*, December 22, 1972.

[38] Editorial, *Thompson Citizen*, c. December 1972

[39] "Abortion law test possible," *Tribune*, February 10, 1973.

[40] "Seeks defeat of government," *Free Press*, April 10, 1973.

[41] Ibid.

[42] "Borowski undecided on seeking re-election," *Free Press*, May 29, 1973.

[43] "Borowski may not run," *Tribune*, May 29, 1973.

[44] Op. Cit., "Borowski undecided."

[45] Interview with Sandy and Debbie Borowksi, February 2002.

[46] "Ex-cabinet Minister hunts job," *Free Press*, June 30, 1973.

[47] "Joe's defeat marks end of era," *Tribune*, June 29, 1973.

[48] Interview with Sid Green, March 2002.

[49] Ibid.

My hand made all these things
When all of them came to be, says the Lord
This is the one whom I approve
The lowly and afflicted man
who trembles at my word.
Isaiah 66:2

Part II

The pilgrim for life

Chapter 9

The real Joe

"There is only one adventurer in the world, as can be seen very clearly in the modern world—the father of a family....Everything is against him.... Men, events, the events of society, the automatic play of economic laws. And, in short, everything else. ...He alone is literally 'engaged' in the world, in the age. He alone is an adventurer."

Charles Péguy, Clio 1[1]

WHEN JOE WAS APPOINTED HIGHWAYS MINISTER IN THE SUMMER OF 1969, the Borowski family accepted the inevitable: they packed up and left Thompson, but not without a wistful backward glance. They had been there 11 years; Karen and Debbie were in high school, Jean was involved in the parish, bowling, bingo and any number of other activities.

They were known there, and Joe, the prophet in his home country, was just Joe. While the girls might get teased at school the odd time when their dad was protesting or locked up in jail, they had that implacable right of birth conferred without question on the veteran settlers of a frontier town. They belonged because they had been there as long or longer than anyone else, and there was very little Joe could do that would shake the solidity of that civic foundation.

It was different in the south. Because Joe and Jean did not want to live in the city, they finally settled in La Salle, a French community about 15 miles southwest of Winnipeg. They purchased ten acres on the banks of the La Salle River, not realizing at the time the area had been nicknamed "Snob Hill" by the kids at the local school, as the residents consisted mainly of airline pilots and politicians.

No matter; the property pleased them greatly, and Joe, with the help of his daughter Karen, set about constructing a sauna down by the riverside, and later, when he discovered golf, a three-hole golf course. When the Borowskis moved down the road some years later, Joe repeated the procedure: installing a sauna in the basement of his new home, and laying down a nine-hole course on the grounds.

The Borowski *filles* had a difficult time adjusting to life in La Salle. They were not French, they hailed from Snob Hill, and their father was constantly in the news. "You'd go to bed with the national or the local and you'd hear Dad," said Sandy, "and wake up with the CJOB action line with Dad on—it just seemed that way." This was daunting enough when Joe garnered headlines for his statements as Highways Minister, but when the controversy turned to abortion, his daughters were called upon to argue the case with people who didn't want to confront Joe himself.

"If you want to be a renegade and be out there and outspoken," asserted Sandy, "you're much better off to be a single person than to have a family, absolutely, because they're the ones—people will not have the nerve to say it to you, but they will say it to your kids." But, as all Joe's daughters pointed out, they believed that abortion is wrong because it is wrong, not because that was what their father believed.[2]

They also dealt with people's perceptions of their father. "They wanted a traditional Archie Bunker," mused Sandy. She recalled that after her father's death, a woman commented that Joe sounded "almost scary...judgmental" on the radio. "I says, really, when you think of it, you're being as judgmental as what you were thinking he was... And I said to Debbie, what do you have to prove to these people—yes, I'm a normal person, and my dad was normal? It's almost like the whole defence thing comes back up."

But people thought as they would, and naturally wondered, when they heard his bluster, what it would be like to live with Joe Borowski. What was he really like?

He was all that he was in public: strong-willed, opinionated, honest, scrupulously honest. But he was also fundamentally good-natured and not given to hysterics, in fact, was "calm as a cucumber," said Jean.

She herself noted the difference when Joe was in the public eye. "The focus was there...Actually, he was gentle, but when you heard him speaking, you'd think there was a different person there. I'd think, 'what are you doing?'" In person, Joe was "very generous and attentive" and soft-hearted: "I mean, he'd cry at a movie. Before I'd even think of tears coming, he'd be gone already." He was sensitive and sentimental, the social director of the family, the one who organized family celebrations, and as Sandy pointed out, "the total opposite of a bigot."[3]

He would go out of his way to help people, said his daughter Debbie. She remembered the time her dad saw a man in shoes so worn he had stuffed them with newspaper to keep out the mud and grime. Joe "ran into Woolworths on Portage Avenue and bought the guy some rubber boots." After Joe died, Sandy added, people would tell them all the things he had done for them. While he was a Cabinet Minister, word got out to "go to Joe." He would do what he could. "He was known for that, whatever it was, it could be totally unrelated, they would write to him—they had trouble with their landlord, they had trouble with their lawyer, they had trouble with immigration."

He was never one to hold a grudge, nor to bar from his friend-ship those whose views differed from his. "I didn't see Joe very much after he left the New Democratic Party but we were never, ever on anything but friendly terms," recalled Sid Green, "There was never anything but good relations between myself and Joe, even on those questions over which he left the party."[4]

Bob Mayer, who had introduced himself to the young Borowski when the latter was camping on the steps of the Manitoba legislature, described Joe as "friendly, friendly as hell." Mayer, who remained with the NDP and in Thompson, continued to count Joe among his boon companions. Ed Schreyer, too, remained close to Joe throughout his life, emerging at various points from relative obscurity to make significant contributions to the Borowski saga.

But while there was no definite estrangement from his union and NDP friends, Joe's life had taken a definite turn. In the organic development of his new vocation, old affections gradually weakened, past ardours cooled, and the pull of former desires and associations imperceptibly eased.

What a lot of people didn't understand or sympathize with was the reason why he left the cabinet. "When he quit over the abortion issue, people figured, what a stupid man, to give up a job like that, that they'd give their eye teeth for—over a stupid abortion issue? What's the matter with him?" Jean Borowski elaborated. "The families have said it, the friends have said it and the neighbours have said it: 'What's wrong with you? …Why would you give up a job like that? It's once in a lifetime.'"

She knew that Joe had to do what he thought was right. But it was unnerving to watch his political career accelerate on its downward trajectory. "Here we were, out in the middle of nowhere, and, what are you going to do, what do you do? We were talking one night, went for a walk…I says, 'What are we going to do?' and he says… 'What kind of a job would you do after being a Highways Minister? What would you apply for? The Pope?'"

Joe considered opening a spa in La Salle. He had a long-standing interest in health foods and nutrition, principally because he had suffered from colitis since his mining days in Thompson. He had even contrived to grow his own vegetables in the thin layer of soil available above the permafrost; tilling sucker fish into the ground as a fertilizer. "He was the only guy who had a garden you could actually eat food from, up north," Debbie laughed, though the smell of his innovative fertilizer did not endear him to his neighbours.

Jean, too, pondered their circumstances. "I kept thinking, what else can we go to? We've been in the restaurant [business], and we've been in the government and we've been in the mines, we've been in a cattle business, what, what else? … So he thought, well, we'll just wait and see, we're going to do a novena and see what happens."

Despite the insecurity, it was a blessed relief for Jean to be free of the constraints and responsibilities of political life, and the attendant social obligations, which had caused no little tension in the Borowski home. "Oh sure, we'd have clashes, especially during the government, all these different social events—I hated it with a passion, I really did, because it was so meaningless, these cocktail parties…for what? I would rather go on out there and golf or play ball in the evening. And there was another Minister's wife, she was the same: 'What are we doing this for, they want the man, they just want to see what we're doing. Phony, isn't it…'"

Joe had a signal, a tug on his ear, which he would use if he were being bothered by someone in a conversation, and as Jean recalled, he frequently had recourse to it during government parties. "He'd just go like this—and I'd manage in time to approach and say, 'Hey, we gotta go, look at the time.' I could spot him across the room."

When Joe was Cabinet Minister, they dined out at a particular restaurant where the waiters came running, the maitre d' hovered, and the meal was offered on the house. "And Joe said, 'Hey, I'll tell you what I'd rather do, there's a family over there, give them the meal'—'Oh, no, no, Mr. Borowski, this is for you.' Right after he quit the government, Joe says, 'Let's go back to that same restaurant,' and it was as though they didn't know us. And we found this out very quickly—once he was a Minister, we had cousins, we had people say, 'Oh, I know Joe, I know his son'—we'd hear this on the bus, we'd hear this just in casual conversation… Everybody wanted to be there, but after…it's just as though you don't exist anymore.

"You're gone. There's somebody else that's the Minister now."

The insincerity of it all bothered her husband. "He said, 'Why can't people just be honest about it?' He hated liars, he hated liars with passion, even with the kids: 'Don't lie to me…don't cover it up, be straightforward.'"

So there he was, 'without maps or supplies, a hundred miles from any decent town… attempting the impossible.' But unlike the average man, Joe Borowski did not turn and run. He thought and prayed.

It seemed as though the answer came when Jean's brother-in-law called up with an invitation to become a salesman with a new insurance company, Pioneer Life. Joe took the job.

He was selling and selling well and the money was good, recalled Jean, but "it wasn't long before he thought, hey, there's something not quite right, kosher, about all this. He had this feeling and he had this feeling and again, he said, … 'The top guys prance around like they know it all and you don't quite know it, and they don't give you a straight answer.'" It appeared to Joe that the company was presenting false information, over-projecting possible returns for investments.[5] "He tried to pin them down," said his wife, "and…he wouldn't give up: how about this and how about that, and he kept asking and asking and finally he said, 'I'm not getting the answers, I'm quitting, this is it,' and he did, he quit.

"And it wasn't long before the company went under."

His daughters remember this episode as well. The idea that people had invested their hard-earned money in an insecure company on his recommendation and for his livelihood galled their father. "It was Joe, honest Joe," said Debbie, "He could've had a million jobs because of his reputation—what a spokesman. He could've sold tires, he could have sold ice cream cones."

After Joe quit and before Pioneer Life folded, he tried to make amends by going back to everyone he dealt with to urge them to back out of their investments. "Because who do you sell first to?" said Jean, "Family, friends. And he started telling them, 'You've got to sell, what I'm telling you is good, because I think…things are happening.' And the ones that didn't—lost."

Joe lost, too. Once again, after two years selling for Pioneer Life, he faced the question of how he was going to earn a living. "He really believed in a man providing for his family and he would do any kind of a job," said Debbie, who was in her early 20's at the time and had moved into Winnipeg.

The idea returned to capitalize on the years of research and experience Joe had accumulated in his search for respite from his ailments. He was well versed in the science of nutrition and had developed a number of theories on diet. He had read and studied extensively about vitamins, and extolled their efficacy, as well as promoting the virtues of organically grown products.

Thus it was that, with their options dwindling, Joe and Jean decided to open a health food store. With typical zeal Joe augmented his already formidable knowledge by obtaining his master's degree in herbology through correspondence. He was required to manufacture salves, ointments and medicines. "I remember coming home on weekends, Mom's perogies and stuff, and there's Dad boiling some strange herbs because he had to make stuff…you'd go, 'Oh no'…in a few minutes, 'Put this on your skin or taste this,' some kind of brittle bark, yewww," Debbie recalled.

On May 2, 1977, preparations were completed and the

Borowski Health Food Store officially opened, with Ed Schreyer there to cut a ribbon to which Jean had stapled perogies (which, contrary to what some might believe, are indeed a health food— when made with whole-wheat flour).

The first tiny store on St. Anne's Road was supplied with Joe's own manufactured Golden Boy vitamins. Sourdough bread, yoghurt chips, soy coffee, cabbage rolls made from brown rice, fertilized eggs rounded off an inventory of more traditional health food fare.

On sale, too, was *The Borowski Cookbook*, a compilation of ethnic recipes with healthy and natural ingredients substituted for other, allegedly toxic substances. As well as recipes, the cookbook featured commentary by Joe on health food and politics, and the politics of health food. It was frustration and anger with the latter and "a lot of prodding from family and friends" Joe wrote, that caused him to undertake the "heavy task of writing a genuine, natural food, ethnic, health cookbook, which completely expels from all recipes, the odious Big Three: white flour, white sugar and brown chocolate."

This publishing phenomenon sold out within 90 days of hitting the stands in May 1977, necessitating a second press run of another 5,000 copies of the slim, spiral-bound volume.

Thus it was that Joe Borowski embarked on an entrepreneurial path to which he remained faithful for the rest of his days. His evolution as proprietor of a health food store, as master herbologist, and later, as iridologist (a science that diagnoses health problems by looking at the eye), appeared to be divinely inspired.

There were a number of benefits. Joe enjoyed the work; he could render assistance to people suffering from numerous ailments; and the store provided a stable income while at the same time left him free to pursue his pro-life initiatives. "I'm financially independent, and I have no employee or labour problems."[6]

Unfortunately, he was still expected to pay taxes. This, then, was the next battle Joe Borowski chose to wage against the culture of death. Once engaged, the formidable apparatus of the state creaked and clanged into motion, and once in motion, bore down on Joe Borowski with unstoppable and relentless intent.

Notes
Chapter 9
The real Joe

[1] As quoted in "The secret path: a Catholic response to the New Age," Stratford Caldecott, *The Chesterton Review*, November 2001, p. 489.

[2] Interview with Sandy and Debbie Borowski, February 2002

[3] Interview with Jean Borowski, February 2002

[4] Interview with Sid Green, March 2002

[5] Interview with Sandy and Debbie Borowski, February 2002.

[6] Op. Cit., Grace Petrasek, page 188.

Chapter 10

Joe and the tax collectors

"I'm expecting anything…they seem to have more
power than the RCMP or the government, so I'm
expecting any kind of dirty tricks."
Joe Borowski[1]

"We want to know what you have, Mr. Borowski."
Mr. Craig Henderson, Esq.,
Judgment Creditor,
Government of Canada

WHEN JOE BOROWSKI DECLARED IN THE LEGISLATIVE ASSEMBLY OF Manitoba on May 4, 1973, that he was not going to pay income tax, his credentials as a practitioner of non-violent civil disobedience were already firmly established.

As early as 1965, he had taken as his mentor Martin Luther King, Jr., the black civil rights leader who declared: "I will not and cannot obey an evil law, therefore civil disobedience is the only alternative left to me." King was assassinated in Memphis on April 4, 1968, at the age of 39; when Joe heard the news, he broke down and sobbed uncontrollably.[2]

Joe's first attempt to apply the principles of civil disobedience in his battle against legalized abortion was to refuse to pay medicare premiums. His next step was even more drastic.

"I'm serving notice on this spiritually dead and cowardly government that so long as one cent and one dollar of this money is used to pay, subsidize, finance child murder, legalized child murder, without due process of law, no matter what the price or the consequences, I will refuse to pay one penny of income tax or any other tax, even if it means going to jail."[3]

Thus did Joe inform his colleagues in the Manitoba legislature of his intentions. His late afternoon announcement had been preceded by an uproar in the House which began when Joe introduced the subject during the discussion on the health department's budget estimates. "I want to talk about ruthless and politically sanctioned child murder that is enthusiastically and financially supported by the NDP government..." At that, the chairman demanded a retraction: "The honourable member accused members of that side of the House of being child murderers."[4] "Murderer" was a word explicitly proscribed in Beauchesne's Rules of Order, along with other "abusive and insulting" language.

"He's not accusing an individual of being a child murderer," spoke up the member for the Winnipeg constituency of Riel, Donald Craik, "He's saying that government policy endorsed by the present government is condoning child murder. And if he wishes to say that, I don't see that you can accuse him of calling an individual a murderer."

Joe complied: "I withdraw the remark and suggest that this government through the medicare premiums and through other taxation is paying for child murder and that is a fact."[5]

Needless to say, his statement renewed the furor. Attorney-General Al Mackling leapt up. "His rephrasing is no better than his first expression, and it is an offence to the rules. He's accusing this government of breaking the law, and that is absolutely unparliamentary."[6]

When order was restored, Joe pointed out that the recent Supreme Court decision in the United States, the *Roe v. Wade* decision of January 22, 1973, which struck down any state law restricting abortion as unconstitutional—"is a storm warning to Canada...It won't be long before the bootleg barnyard swirl of that decision washes over the border..."[7]

Abortion was just the beginning and anyone who can't see that was "just plain crazy," Joe contended. Legislation advocating euthanasia had been introduced in Florida, and he documented a case where a handicapped infant had been left to starve to death in an American hospital. "It is because of this toboggan slide towards the Hitler-type of treatment and a solution towards the unwanted and unloved and the old and the weak, that I raise my voice in protest here today."[8]

With this declaration, Joe ceased to file his income tax returns—a more serious offence than filing a return while refusing to pay the outstanding tax. His last return filed was for 1971.[9]

The challenge was out, the gauntlet flung down.

The tax department lost little time responding. Despite the fact that he had paid income tax while on payroll as an MLA, Revenue Canada issued a claim against him for $20,000[10]—a "deliberately inflated" amount, as Joe pointed out in a later court appearance.[11]

Tax officials also managed to obtain an order to garnishee 50 per cent of his income. While he remained a salesman for Pioneer Life, the tax department managed to extract $16,000 from his commission.

On May 12, 1975, Joe was convicted on two counts of failure to file a 1973 income tax return, and ordered to pay $25 or spend five days in jail on each count.[12] Joe chose jail. He also pointed out to Judge Mitchell that the government had chosen to ignore violations by abortionists of Section 251 of the Criminal Code, while expending an inordinate amount of time and energy pursuing him. "If the government is not disposed to see to it that its laws are respected, how can it expect a mere citizen to obey these laws...I must protest against the destruction of thousands of lives. One day we shall have to render an account of our acts; at that moment, I want to be able to say, Lord I have sought to observe your commandments."[13]

Joe served his time in jail, reportedly only two days[14] and on October 21, 1975, he was convicted of failure to file a 1974 income tax return, and fined $200 or 20 days in jail.[15] Again, Joe chose jail.

A period of relative calm followed; in a subsequent court appearance, Joe speculated that Revenue Canada "received a great deal of flak and anger from the public" because of this heavy-handedness, and that officials had lain low, and considered other tactics.[16]

Be that as it may, in 1978 things began to heat up. Revenue Canada put a lien on the Borowski property in La Salle early that year, even though the property belonged not to Joe but to his wife and daughters.[17] In July, Joe was informed by letter that unless he filed his tax returns, he could be prosecuted without notice, and if convicted, face a sentence of a fine of up to $10,000 and a maximum jail sentence of six months.

In August, in an attempt to collect an alleged $9,200 in back taxes for 1975 and 1976, of which Joe hadn't even heard at this point, the tax collectors registered a claim on his house. Joe was adamant about his non-co-operation. "I have refused to file any forms since 1973. As long as they use tax money to subsidize child murder, I'll not file any forms."[18]

It wasn't until the early winter that Joe heard anything more.

Then the tax department moved in.

In the early hours of November 16, 1978, tax collector Douglas Shackell, accompanied by sheriff's officer Walter Budge, came looking for Joe's assets. Shackell was armed with writs of seizure from the Manitoba Court of Queen's Bench and the Federal Court in the amount of $32,440.52.[19] The two men seized Joe's new car from the auto shop where it was being serviced. It was a four-door 1978 Volare—the first car he had ever owned that had air conditioning. "The rats could have taken my old car but they waited until we got a new one," Joe lamented, and observed that there was little he could do: "These thugs have got the law on their side."[20]

The taxmen then headed to Joe's health food store, where they presented him with a departmental requirement for information. Joe refused the request to disclose his assets. Twice, he asked the men to leave and when they did not, he finally—as he himself testified later—took Shackell "by the arms and propelled him toward the door and pushed him out the door." Shackell laid a charge of common assault against Joe the next day, and went to see a doctor, who later testified that the taxman had a bruise, 2.5 by 3 inches, on the back of his left triceps muscle.[21]

When Joe was hauled into court on the assault charge some five months later, he pleaded not guilty. He told Judge Ian Dubienski that he had not fought a man since his days as a nickel miner in Thompson: "If I assaulted that clown, I can assure you he would be on crutches and wearing home-made teeth."[22]

Moreover, he disputed the testimony of Budge and Shackell concerning his utterances on the fateful day. The two alleged that Joe had said "tell Trudeau to lick my –––" and used the words "G–d–––." "To use God's name in vain is a mortal sin," said Borowski; he hadn't done so, he told the Court, for many years. He might have said "damn" but not anything more. He recalled saying "I don't want Trudeau's boot-lickers in my place"—the other statement was "outrageous. I resent such words being attributed to me."[23]

Despite the genuine meekness Joe displayed when confronted by Revenue Canada's representatives, he was found guilty of assault and sentenced by Judge Dubienski to 50 hours of community service to be completed over a period of three months, and a year's probation. While Joe expressed resolve that he would not comply if the agency was pro-abortion or involved in "unethical" practises, ultimately he served his time at the Holy Family Nursing home.[24] He was also enjoined not to talk to the media, but returned to court to argue that he was thus hampered in his role as president of Alliance Against Abortion, especially in view of the upcoming federal elections. Judge Dubienski agreed and amended the order; Joe was to keep silent about his community service work while performing it.

Was there a hidden, more sinister motivation behind the renewed zeal of the tax department? Joe was convinced of it, and his claim is plausible.

On September 5, 1978, Joe had filed a statement of claim in a Regina courthouse, seeking to have therapeutic abortion committees declared illegal. He was represented in his action by Regina constitutional lawyer Morris Shumiatcher, and backed financially by Alliance Against Abortion. Joe expected the court case would cost about $50,000 and would be heard in the summer of 1979. In Joe's view, the seizure of his car was unquestionably related to the lawsuit. The tax department "haven't bothered me for the last three years. But now that we've raised money for our lawsuit, they're coming around again."[25]

Such words seemed prophetic. On November 27, 1978, Joe was

summoned to the Federal Court for an examination of discovery in front of Commissioner Allan Rouse.

The grilling by tax lawyer Craig Henderson involved questions of such specificity, including queries about 22-carat gold coins and their whereabouts, that Joe was convinced that somewhere along the line, the federal agents had tapped his phone.[26] He bore up admirably under Henderson's badgering. How much did he sell his home for when he sold it to his wife? Joe did not recall. Would he go home and search his records? No. "I can get an order of this court if I wish, compelling you to answer that question."

"What is the point of it? The house does not belong to me. You have no right to it."

And on it went. Where did Joe get the money to buy his car (which by that time had been seized by the government).

"I'm 44 years old." Joe exclaimed, showing some impatience, "I have worked all my life. I have saved money throughout the years, unlike some people, and I had savings, have had savings and have savings."

Despite Henderson's persistence, Joe was tight-lipped about his assets. "I am not," he told the government representative, "going to make your job easier to hang me." But he was candid about the activities of Alliance Against Abortion, and the impending court challenge. He revealed that the group had about $45,000 in its account at Holy Spirit Credit Union. Henderson followed up with alacrity. Was Alliance Against Abortion a registered charity? No. "So the funds that are solicited are held in your name, is that correct?"

"No, they are held in the name of The Alliance Against Abortion."

"But you are The Alliance Against Abortion?"

"Well, I am the president. We have a group of people that created the organization in '73. They elected me as president."

When Henderson's questioning could unearth no further information, the proceedings were adjourned, with Henderson vowing to obtain an order compelling Joe to cooperate. Later that same day, the federal tax department seized $32,000 from the Alliance Against Abortion. It was a declaration of war.

Joe hired lawyer Murdoch MacKay to act on his behalf, and within 10 days the money was returned. According to MacKay, the tax officials "looked at the situation, used common sense and came to the conclusion that the monies were trust monies collected for a specific purpose and not funds belonging to Mr. Borowski personally."[27]

That left the original combatants back circling each other on the dusty field. True to his word, Henderson sought to obtain an order from Justice C. Rhodes Smith compelling Joe to provide information on his assets. Joe objected that such a tactic was "a circumvention of normal judicial process."

In the end, despite the judge's misgivings, Henderson emerged with an order compelling Joe to respond to those questions pertaining to his assets that he had hitherto refused to answer. April 3 found the two men again in front of Commissioner Allan Rouse, and Joe made quick work of the day's proceedings.

The seizure of his car "was probably the only legal thing that they have done in this entire episode," Joe admitted. But the tax department sold it for $4,400 at a public auction, and only gave him credit for $3,200—which meant $1,200 had somewhere disappeared. "This is an example of the way the tax department deals with the public. I'm not prepared to cooperate with them in any way, shape or form. I am not going to give them money so they can kill more babies."

The commissioner had barely time to warn Joe that refusal to comply with the order was contempt of court, before Joe was on his feet and out the door. "That's all I have to say to this federal kangaroo court hearing. Good day, gentlemen."

On June 14, 1979, Joe appeared before Justice G. A. Addy, where he was obliged to "show cause" why he should not be held in contempt. He came prepared. He had hoped to have Fr. Patrick Morand, whom he had befriended some years previously, make a presentation as "friend of the court." The judge disallowed that request, on the grounds that Fr. Morand was not a member of the bar, although the priest could give character evidence or general evidence for Joe. This refusal seemed to nonplus Joe, who stated he had checked with Morris Shumiatcher and thought he was entitled to have one person assist him in making a submission. The Church's position on abortion, which was what Fr. Morand would address, was part of his defense.[28]

"Well I can tell you right now that I know the Church's position on abortion, because I am a Roman Catholic myself, and I am not unsympathetic at all with the Church's stand on abortion," responded Judge Addy. But that stand "has nothing to do with the question as to whether or not you have properly or improperly refused to answer questions put to you in an action as a judgment debtor. That is a completely different matter."[29]

In front of a courtroom packed with his supporters, some of whom had come from Regina, Joe proceeded to make his case. He first read into the record a speech he had made on March 20, 1973, in the Manitoba Legislature, when he introduced his private member's bill to delete abortion from medicare. The bill, Joe noted, was defeated by only one vote.[30]

But Justice Addy interrupted Joe's oration after some forty minutes, overcome with exasperation. "I fully appreciate your stand regarding abortion," he commented testily, "It is a crime against humanity, it is immoral, shocking and it is scandalizing, and it's murder, and everything else, but I cannot for the life of me see what connection that has with the contempt of court offence with which you are charged."[31]

Implicit in Joe's response was a plea for patience on the part of the judge; explicit was his promise that upon the completion of his presentation, which he expected to take an hour, his motivation for his extraordinary conduct would be clear. "You are going to be sending me in all probability to jail, and I think that you are entitled to know why I choose this course of action. And I think the public is entitled to know why I choose to deliberately disobey a law, which you have indicated, and counsel has indicated, is very serious, more serious because I happen to have been in politics. And you know the worst criminal in this country has his day in court."[32]

Thus appeased, Judge Addy subsided for the moment, and Joe again took up his speech. But it wasn't long before the querulous judge interrupted once more, "I cannot for the life of me see what connection it has, except that you have just stated that you are deliberately disobeying this particular Order of the Court, because you do not agree with the federal laws on abortion… haven't you got anything else to say except that abortion is a bad thing, it is a horrible thing, it is murder… I am convinced that you are convinced… now what else do you have to say?" Furthermore, Justice

Addy said, the courts are not constructed to provide a political platform, "and you are reading a political speech."[33]

Joe, nevertheless, persevered, and read his remarks in full. Justice Addy remained unimpressed, stating that it was only because Joe Borowski had no legal counsel that he had allowed such leeway.[34] But when Joe proposed to read excerpts from the Nuremberg trials, another outburst ensued from the judge, "We are not going to go into the Nuremberg trials, that lasted for two years or four years, I don't want to listen to that."[35]

Joe then attempted to read excerpts from the *Handbook on Abortion* by John Willke. The judge ruled it irrelevant. Next, Joe tried to read into the record some remarks by physicians in Washington, and the judge had had enough. "I am not interested, look it, I am not interested in providing you with a forum to put certain things on record... I am interested only in how much punishment you should get for having disobeyed a specific order to answer a specific question put to you. Nothing else but that."[36]

When Joe outlined his grievances against the tax department, the judge dismissed them, saying Joe had had full right of appeal and did not avail himself of it. As far as Justice Addy was concerned, those matters had been decided, and he did not wish to go into the merits of those proceedings. Moreover, Joe could have sued the tax officials if he thought any seizures were illegal.

"Sue them?" asked an incredulous Joe, "They have got millions of dollars to fight me, they could break me and put me in the poorhouse in a year's time if I had turned around and took them to court for every illegal act."[37]

Finally Joe wanted to read the transcript of the examination that transpired between Henderson and himself, but Justice Addy again objected, "I am not interested in reports from court proceedings, you tell me what you have to say."[38]

Joe retorted that he had intended to bring in cases of civil disobedience, but that Justice Addy wasn't interested. That's right, the judge concurred, he wasn't interested "unless it has some bearing on the reason why you disobeyed this order."

"Disobedience has bearing I suggest, and if you don't want to hear it, then I have nothing else to say."[39] When the judge pressed him as to whether he intended to continue his disobedience, Joe pointed out that he had made his position "half clear" and not been given an opportunity to close, "I have nothing further to say."[40]

Judge Addy found Joe guilty of contempt of court, and adjourned the proceedings until June 22 for sentencing.

On that day, Joe confined his remarks to a brief statement of intent. He was using "a civilized and accepted method for protesting a law which I consider, and most Canadians consider, evil and destructive of human life." He realized that disobeying a court order was a serious matter, but "if people in Germany had disobeyed the law, we might not have had the gas chambers."[41]

Now it was the judge's turn, and although he was convinced of Joe's sincerity, it was in his mind "nothing short of absurd" to withhold income tax because of an objection to the abortion law. If allowed, such a state of affairs would lead to "complete anarchy... You are not being ordered to obey a law against which you object," Judge Addy ruled. "The Income Tax law has absolutely nothing to do with the law on abortion."[42]

Joe seemed to be "deliberately attempting to create a public furor by openly defying and challenging a court order... You haven't indicated the slightest repentance, the slightest intention of complying with the order."[43] If he was determined "to make a martyr" of himself then so be it; "you will of course have to suffer the consequences," which could, the judge warned, be ongoing. A further order could be applied for, and "if you again refuse, you can go again to jail."[44]

"I will refuse," said the unyielding Joe.[45]

Judge Addy sentenced Joe with a fine of $800 and 14 days in jail, plus another 90 days in jail to be served consecutively with the 14 if the fine remained unpaid. Among the 45 supporters gathered in the courtroom were two priests, Fr. Pat Morand and Fr. George Svoboda, and a number of nursing women, some of whom, newspaper reports tell, wept openly when the sentence was passed.[46]

Joe was taken away in handcuffs to serve out his time in Headingly Correctional Institute, a provincial jail about three miles west of Winnipeg and, for those with a good arm, a long stone's throw from the trans-Canada highway.

Whether or not Joe Borowski would have been jailed indefinitely is a subject that must be left, in the words of the poet, in the realm of 'infinite conjecture.' In the realm of concrete, historical facts, it happened that a group, calling itself "Friends of Joe" sprang into existence that July, formed with the express purpose of raising money to pay Joe's back taxes.

According to the group's spokesman, Winnipeg lawyer Ernie Wehrle, "Friends of Joe" was of the mind that the former Highways Minister would be much more effective out speaking to the public than rotting in jail. Pro-lifers across the country would turn up in droves to hear Joe speak. And Joe himself had promised that he would accept liberty if a settlement were worked out with the federal agencies.

Not that Joe was rotting in jail. He was doing a fair bit of mission work among his fellow prisoners. "Just this past Sunday I managed to get six inmates to attend Mass in our kitchen area—(a first for Headingly)," Joe wrote in a personal letter. "One even asked to go to confession."[47]

Joe himself received Holy Communion daily from either Fr. Morand or Fr. Svoboda; the former also took it upon himself to smuggle in health food—considered contraband—to the inmate with the finicky stomach. The prison diet, high in starch, potatoes and glutenous white bread, exacerbated Joe's colitis, resulting in a certain level of discomfort. Fr. Morand, being a priest, was not frisked and had freedom of access, and he was more than willing to engage in such mildly subversive activities on Joe's behalf, secreting in his communion kit bananas, sunflower seeds and other delicacies provided by Jean.[48]

The good priest also prevailed upon the Cardinal of Winnipeg, Archbishop George Flahiff, to visit the famous prisoner. Surprisingly, the Cardinal, a reserved man who seemed more at home among his scholarly tomes than among putative criminals, agreed. Cardinal Flahiff, remembered Fr. Morand, "had never been in a jail, had never even seen a jail" and he reacted strongly. When they approached the prison, "I let the Cardinal go ahead of me and then the door shut behind me." The prelate gave a start: "He says, 'Don't slam the door like that.' I says, 'I didn't slam it, that's automatic.'

"It really hit the Cardinal that these men were in cages, really, and he said to me—that was typical of the Cardinal—he said, 'Why do they paint everything in the same dull grey colour?' So you know, his heart really went out, and then he was really impressed with Joe, behind bars because of his convictions."

In the meantime, "Friends of Joe" was diligently raising money and negotiating with Revenue Canada and finally reached a settlement on Joe's behalf. Joe contemplated his forthcoming court challenge: it could be a long, drawn-out affair and Joe vowed that he would pay his income tax with interest when his case on behalf of unborn children was decided at the Supreme Court.

He stayed in jail most of that summer. It was, as Joe noted, "a little hard on the family—but they understand and 'offer it up.' We all know God is not deaf or blind. He has good reason to send us these little crosses."[49]

Notes
Chapter 10
Joe and the tax collectors

[1] "Alliance group regains account," *Tribune*, December 6, 1978.

[2] Interview with Sandy and Debbie Borowski, February 2002.

[3] *Hansard*, May 4, 1973, p. 2427.

[4] Ibid. May 4, 1973, p. 2421.

[5] Ibid. p. 2422.

[6] Ibid. p. 2422.

[7] Ibid. p. 2425.

[8] Ibid. p. 2426.

[9] "Borowski firm on tax," *Winnipeg Tribune*, May 12, 1973.

[10] Alphonse de Valk, *Joseph Borowski and the Trial of the Century* (Edmonton: Life Ethics Centre, 1983), p. 9

[11] Trial transcript, Federal Court application for *ex parte* order, Judge C.R. Smith, February 22 1979, p. 22.

[12] Trial transcript, Federal Court, June 14, 1979.

[13] Op. Cit. Alphonse de Valk.

[14] Ibid.

[15] Ibid. Trial transcript, June 14, 1979.

[16] Trial transcript, Federal court application for *ex parte,* order, Judge C.R. Smith, February 22 1979, p. 20.

[17] Op. Cit. Alphonse de Valk.

[18] "Taxmen eye Borowski's home," *Tribune*, August15, 1978.

[19] "Borowski convicted of assault," *Free Press*, April 19, 1979.

[20] "Borowski loses round with taxman," *Free Press*, November 17, 1978.

[21] Op. cit. "Borowski convicted of assault."

[22] "Borowski will obey order if it's ethical," Ron Campbell, *Free Press*, April 21, 1979.

[23] Ibid.

[24] "Borowski's media gag is loosened," *Tribune*, May 4, 1979.

[25] "Borowski launches anti-abortion battle," *Free Press*, Sept 6; "Borowski loses round with taxman," *Free Press*, November 17, 1978.

[26] Ibid

[27] "Alliance group regains account," *Tribune*, December 6, 1978.

[28] Trial transcript, Federal Court of Canada, Trial division, between *Her Majesty the Queen*, and *Joseph Paul Borowski*, before Justice G. A. Addy, June 14, 1979, pp. 19 and 20.

[29] Ibid. p. 20.

[30] Ibid. p. 22.

[31] Ibid. p. 36.

[32] Ibid. p. 37.

[33] Ibid. pp. 43-44.

[34] Ibid. p. 45.

[35] Ibid. p. 57.

138

[36] Ibid. p. 58-59.

[37] Ibid. p. 65.

[38] Ibid. p. 68.

[39] Ibid. p. 68.

[40] Ibid. p. 69.

[41] Transcript of judgment of trial, Federal Court of Canada, Trial Division, between *Her Majesty the Queen* and *Joseph Paul Borowski*, before Justice G. A. Addy, June 22, 1979, p. 3.

[42] Ibid. pp. 3-4.

[43] Ibid. p. 5.

[44] Ibid. pp. 5-6.

[45] Ibid. p. 6.

[46] "Borowski jailed for contempt," Steve Pona, *Free Press*, June 23, 1979.

[47] Letter dated July 31, 1979 to Basilian Father Leonard Kennedy.

[48] Interview with Fr. Morand, February 2002.

[49] Letter dated July 31, 1979 to Basilian Father Leonard Kennedy.

Chapter 11

The end of the beginning

"The purpose of the case is simply
to convince the court that the unborn child
is an individual and that he has a right to life."
Morris Shumiatcher

"I sat there for as long as I could take it.
I've never seen that kind of attitude in a court before."
Joe Borowski

"Oh, he wanted money. He wanted money."
Fern Marion

WHILE JOE ENDURED THE ATTENTIONS OF THE INDEFATIGABLE agents of Revenue Canada, he also pursued his dream of reversing the legalization of abortion.

Supported morally and financially by his friends in Alliance Against Abortion, Joe tried everything he could think of to stem and turn the legal and social tide that had swept away the traditional protection for the child in the womb. But, in his own words, "after years of agitating, advocating, writing and arm-twisting, there wasn't even a hint of any possibility of any changes either provincially or federally... There was obviously not going to be any resolution through the political process."[1]

As this became increasingly clear, Joe turned again to the courts. When he formed the Alliance Against Abortion in 1973, his initial action was to refuse to pay medicare premiums. But his hope that the NDP government would prosecute him and therefore, the matter would end up in the courts, remained unfulfilled.

Joe's quest to challenge the law itself led him to Morris Shumiatcher, a renowned constitutional lawyer who practised in neighbouring Saskatchewan. In retrospect, it seemed inevitable. The diminutive Shumiatcher possessed a formidable intellect, and was, by the time Joe sought him out, a "living legend of the Canadian bar," having argued his first case before the Supreme Court at age 25. From a Jewish family in Calgary, Shumiatcher became, at age 29, the youngest lawyer ever in the Commonwealth to be appointed King's Counsel.[2]

He embraced left-wing politics in his youth, and for five years was executive assistant to CCF premier Tommy Douglas, in which position he drafted the Saskatchewan Bill of Rights—the first such bill introduced in the country. Shumiatcher later became disaffected with the CCF-NDP and publicly critical of the welfare state. He gently chided Douglas for suffering from "political nymphomania—he just couldn't say no to his people."[3]

Most important of all for Joe Borowski's purposes, Morris Shumiatcher was personally opposed to abortion. He spoke out against the Canadian Bar Association's push for a more liberal abortion law in the 1960s, and when Joe met him, was a member of the national Coalition for Life.[4] He was not cowed by controversy; quite the opposite. Shumiatcher confessed in an interview that, "I find that more often than not the popular view is not the proper or honest view. ...I like to think of myself as a sort of gadfly on the flank of the nation."[5] Shumiatcher, himself, had pondered, independently of Joe Borowski, the possibility of a legal challenge to the 1969 abortion law using the Canadian Bill of Rights. But he had gone no further than contemplating a possible legal strategy when he received a call from the former Highways Minister of Manitoba.[6] He invited Joe to Regina to talk further.

The meeting, which occurred most likely in late 1977, proved to be fortuitous. Joe was impatient and completely resolved to the course. He was ready to bankroll a court challenge to the abortion law, however long and costly such an enterprise would be.

"Joe Borowski told me, passionately, that he wanted me to stop the slaughter immediately," Shumiatcher related years later.[7] "And, if abortions could not be stopped, he at least wanted me to end the spending of public money to pay to kill babies. This was strong stuff—and the demands that Borowski was making were challenging. There would be many obstacles to overcome if one were to achieve Joe's heart's desire."

Shumiatcher saw opportunity along with the obstacles. Here was a case, he later declared, that could prove as significant to Canadian jurisprudence as *Dred Scott* was to American legal history—a strange and strangely prophetic comparison. The Supreme Court of the United States had declared, in *Dred Scott*, that African Americans were not full members of the human race, and therefore could be held as chattels.[8] Joe's invitation was nothing less than an attempt to change the course of history. Shumiatcher did not turn it down.

Fern Marion, a courtly French Canadian with an infectious laugh and an appreciation for a good story, could not recall exactly when he and his wife, Jeanne, first ran across Joe Borowski. But the association went back many years. Jeanne's sister had met Joe in the mid-fifties, in the Sutherland Trailer Court of Saskatoon, where Joe ran a little convenience store. She and her husband had struck up a friendship with the Borowskis, and had kept in touch with them ever since. The Marions had followed Joe's public protests and subsequent political career with an interest spiced with this personal connection. They admired what he said and his forthright style, even though they had reservations about the NDP. But the couple, devout Catholics and parents of six children, really sat up and took notice when Joe resigned from cabinet over abortion. Fern Marion was one of the original members of the Alliance Against Abortion.

The Marions also only vaguely recalled the date of a certain meeting to which they were summoned; it was sometime in the mid-to-late-seventies. They didn't realize when they accepted the invitation that they were only two of about 15 or so people handpicked by Joe Borowski to help him with his court case. But they remembered clearly why Joe asked them to his home at La Salle.

"Oh, he wanted money," laughed Fern Marion. "He wanted money."[9]

The couple was mystified as to why Joe had included them in his plea. Fern worked as an administrator for the City of St. Boniface. It seemed as though the others present that evening were professionals—lawyers, doctors. "How come we were invited with all those other bigwigs?" Jeanne thought at the time. "We don't fit in here."

Then Joe came out, Fern recalled, and "he said he was expecting a thousand dollars from everyone. I looked at her…"

"We were poor," interjected Jeanne.

"And I said, 'Where …where are we going to get a thousand dollars to give to that?' Then we came home and we said, you know–"

"We borrowed it, or we had enough in our…" said Jeanne.

"Might have had enough," interrupted Fern, "It was almost to the point where we would have had to borrow it. We didn't have money in the bank—we were just struggling."

The Marions, however, believed so strongly in Joe's efforts to defend unborn children that they were determined to come up with a thousand dollars. It was a contribution, in their minds, worth every penny and infinitely more. Although admittedly "poor as church mice," they were the first to donate the requested amount.

That night, also sitting quietly among the bigwigs, was a diminutive nun with bright, intense brown eyes and a sweet smile. Sister Rose Bouchard did not know Joe Borowski personally, although she had met the family occasionally. She had heard him on the radio and wondered, "Who *is* that guy?" But he asked her to come to the meeting: why, she could not say. "You know how it is, they kind of pick you off," she laughed.

She also could not recall exactly when the meeting was held, but thought it was the late seventies. Joe also announced at that time that he was not going to file his income tax returns, and that he fully expected to end up in jail as a consequence. He asked those present to be his financial support.

As a member of a religious congregation, Sister Rose had taken a vow of poverty—as Joe well knew—and was in no position to donate a thousand dollars. "And he turned to me and said that instead, he would appreciate me saying a thousand rosaries." She agreed. Over the course of the next year, Sister Rose said three rosaries a day for the intentions of the pro-life efforts in which Alliance Against Abortion was engaged. From time to time, Joe would ask her if she was keeping to it. She also agreed, as a sideline to her work as a speech therapist at St. Amant Centre in Winnipeg, to keep track of the donations for Alliance Against Abortion.

The active solicitation of funds had gone on for nearly a year before Morris Shumiatcher filed the first motion on behalf of Joe Borowski in the fall of 1978. By then, Alliance Against Abortion had amassed close to $40,000, largely due to Joe's indefatigable efforts, including speaking engagements, newsletters and advertisements. It seemed a sufficient amount—but unknown to those who were moved to contribute so generously, the battle had just begun, and the rapacity of the litigation courts had not yet been revealed.

On September 5, 1978, Morris Shumiatcher filed a Statement of Claim at the Court of Queen's Bench in Regina, Saskatchewan. (It had been decided in the interests of economy, to pursue the lawsuit in Regina. It was much less expensive for Joe to travel the 320 miles from his home to Saskatchewan's capital than for Shumiatcher and his associates to sojourn in Winnipeg.) The Borowski case was simple: the plaintiffs sought a declaration that the 1969 amendments to the Criminal Code which permitted abortion under certain conditions, were in violation of the Canadian Bill of Rights—which guarantees the right to life of every individual. Shumiatcher planned to use expert testimony to the advances in medical knowledge, specifically in the areas of fetology, genetics and ultrasound, to prove irrefutably that the child in the womb is an individual and therefore has the right to life.

Joe also sought a permanent injunction to prevent the Finance Minister of Canada from providing public money for abortions.

At that time, abortion was an indictable offence under Section 251 of the Criminal Code. However, the 1969 amendments (subsections 4, 5, and 6) permitted abortion if done by a doctor in an accredited hospital, and if a "therapeutic abortion committee", consisting of three medical doctors, issued a certificate asserting that the continuation of the pregnancy would endanger, or would likely endanger, the life or health of the mother.

For Joe's case to succeed, Shumiatcher had to prove not only that the child in the womb was a unique individual, but also that the Canadian Bill of Rights took precedence over the Criminal Code and "the right to life prevails over the right to kill by abortion."

The Crown's response to the Statement of Claim was somewhat obstructionist. Crown lawyers argued that the lawsuit should be heard not in the provincial high court, but in the Federal Court. This, according to F. L. Morton, in his 1992 study of abortion law and the Charter, was "clearly a delaying tactic."[10] Determining what disputes fell under the jurisdiction of the Federal Court and which should more properly be heard in the provincial superior courts had become, by 1978, "one of the murkiest issues in Canadian law," Morton wrote. The statute "was unclear and there was a welter of conflicting precedents."[11]

The delaying tactic proved to be successful, as the issue of jurisdiction occupied the attention of both the Saskatchewan high court (Court of Queen's Bench) and the Saskatchewan Appeal Court for the better part of two years. Both these courts ruled against the Crown. On April 1, 1980, Justice J. Hughes found that the Saskatchewan Court of Queen's Bench indeed had jurisdiction to hear Borowski's case. The Crown appealed, and in November 1980, the Saskatchewan Appeals Court, too, ruled 2-1, in Joe's favour.

Although it was batting 0 for 2, the Crown appealed to the Supreme Court. But now, realizing that the jurisdictional question was proving a flimsy basket for all its disputational eggs, it also argued that Joe Borowski had no standing to challenge the abortion law. The issue of standing, as Morton explained, is akin to jurisdiction—a "threshold" issue, "a legal question that a judge must answer first… before considering the substantive issues raised by the case."[12] It took a further six months for these questions to wind their way to the Supreme Court. On May 27, 1981 Joe Borowski and Morris Shumiatcher appeared, for the first time but not the last, before the highest court in Canada.

In the meantime, Joe had been fighting the battle on other

fronts. Having been faced with the renewed enthusiasm of Revenue Canada, he had spent the summer of 1979 in jail for refusing to provide information on his financial assets. When a repetition of this grim scenario was precluded by the formation of the "Friends of Joe", who settled the dispute directly with Revenue Canada, he was left free to concentrate his efforts on the health food store and the adjoining pro-life store, which he had acquired for the administration of Alliance Against Abortion. Joe became the unofficial spokesman for the pro-life movement in general in Manitoba—a fact that sometimes caused quiet consternation among his more tactful colleagues.

Nevertheless, despite differences, either of style or tactics, the pro-life groups in Manitoba—including Joe Borowski and the Alliance Against Abortion—united in early 1979 in opposition to a free-standing clinic in the city's downtown.

Anna Desilets, who at the time was president of the Manitoba League for Life, found out from an anonymous source that an abortionist, Dr. Richard Boroditsky, along with Dr. John Tyson, head of Obstetrics and Gynecology at the Health Sciences Centre, had proposed to set up an abortion and birth control clinic. Anna, a mother of six children and former teacher, had had little to do with Joe Borowski personally, and had not met him until the late '70. "My main knowledge of him was from the media, and Joe was nothing if not forthright and spoke from the hip," she laughed, "and so the picture you got from the media was of a very brash, loud, harsh person, those are the adjectives I think that first come to mind. And when I met him personally, I was astonished, because he was not that kind of person at all. I found him soft-spoken, very, very devout and I liked him."[13]

Now Joe and the League joined forces, along with Physicians for Life, Coalition Against Abortion, and Pregnancy Distress Centre, to battle this newest anti-life threat. Forming the Ad Hoc Committee Against Abortion Clinics, they called a press conference to denounce the proposal and to warn that an abortion clinic in Winnipeg would mark Manitoba as the "abortion centre of Canada."[14] Ultimately, Conservative Health Minister "Bud" Sherman nixed the proposal, stating he, and most of his colleagues in Premier Sterling Lyon's government, were opposed to "abortion on demand."[15]

Aside from emergency rallying points such as this, Joe Borowski and Alliance Against Abortion maintained a certain autonomy, as did other local pro-life groups, most of which came into being in the mid-seventies. Unlike other groups, however, it seems that the Alliance Against Abortion was an informal creation, more of a permanent ad hoc committee to provide support for Joe than anything else. He was the front man, the visible presence, the one who took the risks and the initiatives. Sometimes the initiatives were pure Borowski and not the Alliance Against Abortion. Such, it seems, was the case when, in early May of 1981, Joe embarked on a 90-day fast to protest the lack of protection for the unborn child in the proposed Charter of Rights.

This was the Charter that, in the fall of 1980, Prime Minister Pierre Trudeau had threatened to impose unilaterally, despite strong provincial opposition. (Whether the Liberal government had the legal and conventional right to do so had just been argued in April 1981 before the Supreme Court of Canada.) Thus it happened that when Joe Borowski's number was drawn, and the Supreme Court prepared to hear Morris Shumiatcher's arguments as to why his client should be permitted to challenge the abortion law, Joe had already been without food for four weeks.

Despite his weakened state, Joe travelled to Ottawa for the May 27 hearing. Once seated in that hallowed room, he watched as Morris Shumiatcher was subjected to intense questioning, especially from Chief Justice Bora Laskin.

Shumiatcher remembered the day well. "Borowski sensed the tenor of the Chief Justice's sharp questions. He must have felt he might lose the day. Out of the corner of an eye, I noticed him approaching me. I thought he had some words of instruction for me. I turned to him, but he ignored me, and from the aisle under the nose of seven justices, he began to address the Chief Justice.

"'Do you realize,' he said in a firm, assertive voice, 'that every day 150 unborn children are being killed? This case is urgent...'

"Taken aback by this sudden explosion, the Chief Justice told my client to please sit down."[15] Joe desisted for a moment, but felt compelled a second time to interrupt, and at this point, Laskin ordered his personal doorkeeper to escort Joe outside.[17]

Thus, Joe Borowski became the first, and to this day, the only person ever ejected from the Supreme Court of Canada.

"It was humbling," Shumiatcher admitted. "But it did afford me the opportunity, in apologizing to the Court, to tell the judges that

Joe was in the 28th day of his hunger strike…and he was really not himself. The Chief Justice graciously said he understood."[18]

With anger providing a rush of adrenaline that temporarily staved off the effects of his fast, Joe returned to Winnipeg, where he told reporters that the "constant interruptions and interjections by Judge Laskin" persuaded him that his case was not receiving a fair hearing. "It is obvious to me that this court has no interest in my rights as a citizen or in the rights of the 1,500 souls who are aborted every year."[19]

"I sat there for as long as I could take it. I've never seen that kind of attitude in a court before." So frustrated was he that Joe confessed publicly he was considering abandoning the courts altogether to "seek justice by other means." Shumiatcher, bereft of his choleric client's presence, continued, presenting "with much trepidation" his arguments why Joe Borowski, citizen, should be permitted to challenge the abortion provisions to the Criminal Code. Then he packed his bags and returned to Regina to await the Court's decision.

Seven months later the Supreme Court handed down its ruling. On December 1, 1981, the Court decided, 7-2, in favour of Joe Borowski: he could proceed with his legal challenge to the abortion provisions in the Criminal Code. The question of jurisdiction, the judges ruled, was in the Borowski case no different from two cases argued immediately prior to it, and whatever was decided in those cases would apply to Borowski as well. In this it was ruled ultimately that jurisdiction properly belonged to the provincial superior court.

According to F. L. Morton, the decision on standing in the Borowski case was noteworthy for a couple of reasons. One was that the Chief Justice Bora Laskin, hitherto known for being an "activist" judge and one whose decisions clearly favoured an expanded role for the judiciary, wrote the dissenting judgment (with which Justice Antonio Lamer concurred). It was expected that Laskin would side with a broad interpretation of the rules of standing.

Even more unexpected, the justice who penned the majority ruling, Roland Martland, was reputed to be a staunch defender of judicial restraint. Yet Martland, with his decision, expanded the right to standing beyond what had been formerly allowed.[20] In order to establish standing, proof of a legal dispute must be provided, and the aspiring litigant must also show that he is party to that dispute. In Borowski, the problem was demonstrating how Joe Borowski was personally affected by the subsections of the Criminal Code that provided grounds for legal abortion.[21]

Adding piquancy to the phenomenon of the surprising and opposing decisions of Martland and Laskin was the fact that the former had been passed over by Prime Minister Trudeau in 1974 in favour of the latter for the position of chief justice. In appointing Laskin, who at that point had been on the Supreme Court a mere four years, Trudeau violated the unwritten convention governing the appointment. It ought to have been Martland—an Anglophone judge who had the most seniority.[22] It was clear, wrote Morton, that the Prime Minister favoured Laskin because the justice held views that in many ways so neatly corresponded with his own. Trudeau advocated a strong central government and championed civil liberties; Laskin's judgments tended to support these positions.[23]

Roland Martland, in expressing the majority decision[24] noted that the legislation being challenged—the 1969 amendments to Section 251—was "exculpatory in nature" and "provides that in certain specified circumstances conduct which otherwise would be criminal is permissible." Therefore, Martland observed, "it is difficult to find any class of person directly affected or exceptionally prejudiced by it who would have cause to attack the legislation."[25]

But most importantly, the legislation "to be attacked," wrote Martland, "has a direct impact on the unborn human fetuses whose existence may be terminated by legalized abortions. They obviously cannot be parties to proceedings in court and yet the issue as to the scope of the Canadian Bill of Rights in the protection of the human right to life is a matter of considerable importance. There is no reasonable way in which that issue can be brought into Court unless proceedings are launched by some interested citizen."[26]

It was therefore his opinion, and an opinion with which six of his colleagues on the Supreme Court concurred, that the court open its doors to Joe Borowski.[27]

Joe Borowski, naturally, was pleased to win his day in court, even though, as he expressed to writer Anne Collins years later, it had taken over three years "and cost $100,000." Such a situation was, in his view, "outrageous. You can talk about democracy, you can talk about judicial process and freedom, but what freedom is it if... in order to exercise it you have to have $100,000?"[28]

Meanwhile, the course of history continued. Events that would not only prove to have radical significance for Borowski's court action, but would also ultimately reconfigure the Canadian political and judicial landscape almost beyond recognition were already in full play: the federal government was fully engaged in machinations to patriate the Canadian Constitution, a Constitution that would include an entrenched Charter of Rights and Freedoms.

Notes
Chapter 11
The end of the beginning

1 Op. Cit., T*rial for Life*, Vol. 1, [Trial transcripts] (Winnipeg: Alliance Against Abortion, 1984), p. 272.

2 F.L. Morton, *Morgentaler v. Borowski: Abortion, the Charter and the Courts* (Toronto: McClelland and Stewart Inc., 1992), p. 89.

3 Morris Shumiatcher, *Welfare: The Hidden Backlash* (Toronto: McClelland and Stewart, 1971), p. 10.

4 Op. Cit., Morton pp. 90-92

5 Op. Cit., Morton, p. 90.

6 Op. Cit. Morton, p. 92.

7 "I set before you life and death: Abortion—Borowski and the Constitution," Morris Shumiatcher, *University of Western Ontario Law Review*, 24 (1987) p. 1.

8 Toronto Right to Life Association newsletter, c. 1979.

9 Interview with Fern and Jeanne Marion, March 2002

10 Op. Cit. Morton, p. 93.

11 Ibid.

12 Ibid. p. 96.

13 Interview with Anna Desilets, February 2002.

14 "Pro-life Leagues foresee Manitoba being centre for abortions in Canada," *Free Press*, March 16, 1979.

15 "Sherman provides powerful support for pro-life groups," *Tribune*, August 17, 1979.

16 Op.Cit., Shumiatcher, p. 3.

17 "Angry Joe Borowski back in city to 'seek justice by other means,'" John Sullivan, *Free Press*, May 29, 1981.

18 Op. Cit., Shumiatcher, p. 3.

19 Op. Cit., Sullivan. "Angry Joe Borowski back in city."

20 Op. Cit., Morton, pp. 100-103.

21 Op. Cit., Morton, pp. 95-96.

22 Ibid. p. 72.

23 Ibid. p. 73.

24 The Supreme Court at the time consisted of Bora Laskin, Willard (Bud) Estey, William R. McIntyre, R.G. Brian Dickson, Jean Beetz, Antonio Lamer, Julien Chouinard, Ronald Martland and Roland A. Ritchie.

25 Transcript of Judgment, *Minister of Justice of Canada and Minister of Finance of Canada v. Borowski et al.* (1982) *Western Weekly Reports*, p. 115.

26 Ibid. p. 116.

27 The Borowski decision, Morton commented, paved the way for greater "judicial policy-making" than ever before, because it created a "broad right for citizens to go to court and demand that the judges force the government to 'behave constitutionally.'" (Morton, p. 103.)

28 Op. Cit., Collins, *The Big Evasion: Abortion, the Issue that Won't Go Away* p. 49.

Chapter 12

The Charter and the fast

...who have watched his mold of man, big-boned
and hardy handsome, pining, pining...
Gerard Manley Hopkins
Felix Randal

"He just looked at me, and smiled
a tired, hungry little smile."
Paul Sullivan[1]

"I don't give a damn about my life...
500,000 dead through abortions in
Canada to one life as a sacrifice is a bargain."
Joe Borowski [2]

WHEN JOE BOROWSKI LANDED IN JAIL IN 1978, HE USED THE OCCA-sion to read the life of Mahatma Gandhi, the founder of civil disobedience in the modern era, who became, along with Martin Luther King Jr., a model. Joe was impressed with Gandhi's use of hunger strikes, or more accurately, fasts, as a means of both self-purification and advancement of the cause of India's independence.

The idea of a protest fast lay tucked away in his mind until the dispute arose over the issue of protection for the unborn child in the proposed Charter of Rights and Freedoms. Then, incensed by what he perceived as the intransigence of the federal Liberals, and particularly Prime Minister Trudeau, in their insistence that the Charter was neutral on abortion, Joe decided to put this hitherto unused weapon in the arsenal of the conscientious objector to use.[3]

"If Trudeau gets away with changing the Charter of Rights, there will be unrestricted abortion," Joe predicted to the press, when embarking on his fast May 1, 1981. "The Charter will be a death sentence for hundreds of thousands of unborn children."[4]

Joe took up his fast four days before IRA member Bobby Sands died, at age 27, in Long Kesh prison in Northern Ireland after a hunger strike of over two months, having rejected pleas from many, including the Vatican, to end his action. Did the press envision a similar fate for Joe Borowski? And did the use of a fast by a man imprisoned for alleged terrorist acts (Sands had, at the time of his death, served five of a 14 year prison sentence for possessing a gun) in some way tarnish Joe's efforts?

Because of the media's lame attempt to connect him with the IRA, the timing of his protest was not fortuitous, conceded Joe. "The IRA revolts me. Certainly, Sands' fast is hurting me, but at least it shows people that there are some causes worth dying for," he commented. Bobby Sands had lasted 66 days, "and he was drinking water and salt, the worst thing he could have been taking."[5]

Joe himself subsisted only and entirely on six or seven glasses a day of a "vile concoction"[6] of lemon juice, distilled water, herbs and cayenne pepper.[7] As the days passed and Joe grimly and faithfully kept fasting, the possibility of his demise increased. "I know I could lapse into a coma and die in my sleep," Joe confessed to a reporter on the 12th day of his fast. "But people get killed in a war, and this is a war. Trudeau declared it, and I'm simply responding."

Joe's action, he had to admit, was itself limited by the natural moral law that he was compelled to obey. "If I had my way, I'd hang on until Trudeau changes his mind or I die, but I'm a practising, loyal Catholic. Suicide is against my religion. I'm not prepared to give up my eternal soul for this issue. There's a risk, but the risk is not as great as mountain climbing."[8] Nevertheless, if he did inadvertently succumb, so be it: "If my death will stop the destruction of the unborn, it will be a bargain," he said.[9]

Joe entered the Charter waters late in the fray. Trudeau had begun to lay the groundwork for an entrenched Charter of Rights as early as 1967,[10] but the political genesis of the battle over the amendment of the Canadian constitution was the 1976 election of René Levesque and the separatist Parti Québécois.[11]

The resulting anxiety over national unity provided the impetus for Trudeau's Liberals to bring the constitutional question to the forefront. A federal Task Force on National Unity was created and became a receptacle for any number of proposed constitutional reforms. Meanwhile, a slow economy, wild inflation, and labour unrest wrought havoc. The chickens came home to roost in the spring of 1979, when Trudeau *et al*. were ejected from power to make way for Joe Clark and the Conservatives.

Nine months later, Clark himself and his minority government were summarily dismissed by a non-confidence vote. Trudeau was back in power just in time to campaign in Quebec's sovereignty referendum in May of 1980, and promised a "renewed federalism" if Quebeckers repudiated Levesque's proposal of "sovereignty association." When the voters of Quebec did exactly that, though by a slim margin, the Liberals lost no time in launching an initiative for constitutional reform in answer to, in the words of Prime Minister Trudeau, Quebecers' "massive support for change within the federal framework."[12]

Trudeau was convinced that cross-Canada bilingualism was the surest way to confound and combat Quebec nationalism. When it came to framing a new constitution, he was willing to negotiate anything, he announced in the House of Commons, except a strong federal government and entrenched language rights in the Charter.[13] He saw that his plans would come to naught if the federal Liberals considered themselves bound by the unwritten convention that any constitutional amendments required the unanimous consent of the provinces.[14]

The Prime Minister thus intimated that, if the provinces proved recalcitrant, his government would proceed unilaterally. After a September 1980 first Ministers' conference broke down with no agreement—and during which the hostility between Trudeau and

Levesque was so palpable that Roy Romanow described them as "two scorpions in a bottle"[15]—the Prime Minister announced that his government was going to press on without provincial support.

Trudeau introduced draft legislation for constitutional reform—legislation that had as its cornerstone an entrenched Charter of Rights and Freedoms—on October 6, 1981. However, he had only the support of the federal NDP and two provinces: Ontario and New Brunswick. All other provinces, and the federal Conservatives, were opposed to the plan. The bill was referred to a special Joint House of Commons and Senate Committee after three weeks of intense and frequently acrimonious debate. Trudeau wanted the Committee to produce its report by December. But in this he was thwarted by the opposition, which, abetted by the media, forced the government to open the debate on the proposed constitutional amendment and the Charter, to public, televised hearings.[16]

The hearings began November 6, 1980, and lasted until February 13, 1981, during which time the Committee received over 1000 written briefs and heard over 100 oral presentations.[17]

A majority of the submissions came from an "impromptu coalition of human rights, feminist and native groups" whose "common denominator… was their lack of interest in the amending formula and provincial rights but commitment to a strong Charter."[18]

Not all those who appeared before the Joint Committee came to praise the proposed Charter of Rights and Freedoms. One group, in particular, came to bury it, or hoped to do so. Campaign Life was one of the few of either groups or individuals who opposed the Charter.[19]

In 1981 Gwen Landolt was the mother of four young children, a lawyer and veteran pro-life activist. She had been involved in political action on behalf of the unborn child ever since 1973, when she returned from the States, where her husband had been pursuing post-graduate studies, to discover to her horror that Canada had legalized abortion.

Landolt, a precocious overachiever who entered law school at age 19 and was one of four women among 110 men in her graduating class at the University of British Columbia's law school, recalled the halcyon days of the late 1970s and early 1980s, when the pro-life movement gained strength, savvy and political clout. This momentum culminated in the fervent, ferocious and exhausting lobbying efforts against the Charter.

Tall and articulate, Landolt's poise and self-possession concealed a rapier-sharp wit and a shrewd political sense. She foresaw the damage that would be done if the Charter of Rights and Freedoms were entrenched. It was she, along with Paul Formby, national coordinator of Campaign Life of Canada, who spearheaded the campaign to de-rail, if at all possible, the Liberals' plan. On January 8, 1981, Landolt headed the delegation that presented Campaign Life's brief to the Joint Committee of the House of Commons and Senate. She was accompanied by Campaign Life national president, Kathleen Toth of Edmonton Alberta and Ontario psychiatrists, Dr. Edward Rzadki and Dr. Michael Barry.

The pro-life group objected ardently to an entrenched Charter, Landolt told the Committee, because "it would give rise to a shift in power from Parliament, which is subject to public opinion, to the Supreme Court of Canada, which is not. This shift in power would then open the door to a wide list of areas in which, for the first time, the judiciary, rather than the legislature, would have the final say."[20]

Unlike the American system, where the President's nomination of a Supreme Court justice is subject to Senate approval, the Canadian system lends itself to great abuse of power, Landolt warned. Judges are appointed to the Supreme Court of Canada by the Prime Minister and his Cabinet, and the appointment "is absolute and is not subject to confirmation or rejection from any authority, such as Parliament." An entrenched Charter could only be altered by constitutional amendment, and that would be a long, arduous and drawn-out process.

If, however, Parliament did decide to entrench the Charter, "then it is absolutely necessary to the pro-life people of Canada that the present proposed Charter of Rights must be amended for us to provide protection for the unborn child."[21] The sections to be amended were 1 and 7, Landolt outlined. Section 1, if not amended, would give the Supreme Court "unprecedented wide and sweeping powers to make political decisions. The court need only to decide what, in its opinion, was generally accepted in a free and democratic society and that would be that." (Section 1 read: "The Canadian Charter of Rights and Freedoms guarantees the rights and freedoms set out subject only to such reasonable limits as are generally accepted in a free and democratic society with a parliamentary system of government.")

Turning to Section 7, Landolt acknowledged that the government had as yet resisted the ongoing lobbying efforts regarding the wording of this clause, which read: "Everyone has the right to life, liberty and security of person and the right not to be deprived thereof except in accordance to with the principles of fundamental justice." The Advisory Council on the Status of Women (ACSW) had been pressuring the Liberals to change "everyone" to "every person."

Before dealing with the substance of this argument, Landolt sought to forestall any assumption by the Committee that the views of ACSW—whose members were government appointees— represented those of Canada's female citizens, an assumption that would be "insulting." Women, observed the canny lawyer, "are as diverse as men and vote and think, as do men, according to their own social and economic backgrounds and not according to their sex." On the abortion issue especially, "the majority of women are deeply and irrevocably opposed to the extremist feminist view as espoused by the Advisory Council, that the unborn child should be denied all civil rights, should be denigrated and abandoned on the alleged grounds that it is a so-called woman's right."

Landolt then argued that even though Section 7 referred to "everyone" rather than "every person" that wording alone "in no way assures the right to life of the unborn child will be protected." It was essential that Section 7 "spell out, in exact language, that the 'right to life' shall include the right to life of the unborn child, conceived but not yet born."[22][23]

What was behind this lobbying over a single word in the Charter?

Not only had ACSW requested the change in the wording of Section 7, from "everyone" to "every person," but so had the National Action Committee (NAC), and the National Association of Women and the Law (NAWL). As author F. L. Morton pointed out, none of these groups mentioned, in their formal presentations, that preserving access to abortion was the underlying motivation for this request. But abortion advocate Doris Anderson, then president of ACSW, did admit to the press that her group was lobbying for the words "every person" in order to "exclude the possibility that the courts may uphold the rights of fetuses."[24]

The dispute over wording was significant, explained historian and Basilian priest Alphonse de Valk, who, at the time of the Charter battle, was principal of St. Joseph's College at the University of Alberta. The confidence of feminist groups that the word "person" would be interpreted to exclude the unborn child followed from the 1973 *Roe v. Wade* decision of the U.S. Supreme Court, he wrote. That decision ruled that "the unborn are not 'persons' and as only persons qualify for protection under American law, the unborn may be killed with impunity." It might be argued that Canada had its own rules, but "once the Canadian Supreme Court comes to be the all powerful instrument for the interpretation of the Charter, as it is bound to become if the Charter is approved, the U.S. legal precedent is likely to be of immense influence."[25]

The Canadian Abortion Rights Action League (CARAL) made the point to the Joint Committee. Author Morton contended that the CARAL delegation had the forthcoming Borowski legal challenge in mind when it asserted that the word "everyone" in Section 7 "is completely open to litigation and to the argument that somehow Parliament intended to create rights in the fetus or embryo, and if Parliament does not intend that then we suggest they must include a section which explicitly states that."[26] CARAL wanted to see a new section stating that "nothing in this Charter is intended to extend rights to the embryo or fetus nor to restrict in any manner the right of women to a medically safe abortion" as an ironclad guarantee that Section 7 "cannot be misinterpreted."[27]

The government itself was wary that an American influence of a slightly different sort might come to bear. This became clear in another skirmish over the wording of the Charter, concerning the phrase "principles of fundamental justice" in Section 7. NDP MP Svend Robinson, in his January 27 submission to the Joint Committee, argued for the addition of the words "including the principles of due process of law" to Section 7. This would, declared the pro-abortion MP for Burnaby, "permit some expansion by the courts if necessary of the concept [with respect to] the questions of life, liberty and security of person."[28]

This, too, seemed a somewhat obscure point for the uninitiated, but as Morton explained, the reasoning behind Robinson's request had to do with the distinction between "procedural due process" and "substantive due process"—a distinction the government itself had considered. Barry Strayer, Jean Chrétien's Assistant Deputy Minister in charge of public law, insisted that the words "fundamental justice" would "cover the same thing as what is called procedural due process, that is the meaning of due process in relation to requiring fair procedure." What the government intended by avoiding the phrase "due process of law" was the possibility of an American interpretation of that phrase, or, as Strayer put it, "the concept of what is called substantive due process, which would impose substantive requirements as to the policy of the law in question."[29] (In other words, the judges could rule on the substance of the law.)

The fierce debate on the issue of protection of the unborn child did not obscure the general impression received by the government (although how much this was orchestrated by the media has not yet been fully investigated) that the idea of an entrenched Charter of Rights and Freedoms was gaining popularity among the people. Thus reassured, the Liberals re-jigged their original version and in February of 1981 introduced a Charter that, according to Morton, met the approval of special interest groups: civil libertarians, natives, and feminist groups.[30]

As for abortion, the government claimed the Charter was neutral on the issue. This claim was denounced by pro-life commentators, who foresaw that the Charter could easily end up "a dangerous anti-life document" in the words of Fr. de Valk. He excoriated the Liberal government for its exclusion of the unborn child from protection under the law. Its determination to entrench this exclusion in the Charter of Rights "in full knowledge of its abominable consequences" could only be seen as "a provocation."

When the Liberals liberalized the abortion law in 1969, it could be argued that MPs were confused about the medical and legal issues surrounding abortion, the pro-life forces were "weak and inarticulate," and the "official voice of the Catholic Church …was practically inaudible." Therefore, it was not impossible to excuse that debacle "on account of confusion and ignorance." But 12 years later, it was clear that the 1969 amendment was a failure, wrote the priest. "Health" had come to encompass social and economic circumstances; the "idea of careful counseling has proven illusory;" and "therapeutic" abortion committees "rubber stamp everything before them." In the previous year, the number of recorded abortions was 65,000. And altogether, a modest estimate of the number of lives snuffed out by abortion since 1969 was 500,000. Yet, Fr. de Valk charged, the Liberal government "not only intends to carry on as usual but now proceeds to ensure that the process, for all practical purposes, will be irreversible."[31]

Garnet Bloomfield was, in 1981, a 50-year-old Baptist and a Liberal backbencher for the riding of London-Middlesex. It was his first foray into federal politics, and the term he spent in the House of Commons, while the Charter fight roiled around him, was to be his last. He had been drafted into federal politics by none other than Senator Keith Davey, who had convinced the popular county reeve to run for the Liberals. But Bloomfield warned them beforehand what could happen. "You see, there was always the unwritten rule that if you behaved yourself and didn't cause any problems you'd get the promotions, and if you caused problems, you wouldn't. But I didn't really live by that rule. I lived by the rule, I served God first and the party came second—so if they liked it, okay, and if they didn't like it, it was still all right with me."[32]

Bloomfield remembered Gwen Landolt and fellow lawyer John Stephens speaking to the interparty pro-life caucus about the perils of the proposed Charter. It was in the spring of 1981, "and I wrestled with that…for several weeks. And finally I was sitting in Sunday school class one day, and, I think it's Proverbs 24—the 10th, 11th and 12th verses—it talks about those that are in danger of death, and if you don't do something about it, you'll be held accountable to God, and so my wrestling was over. I said, 'I know what I've got to do now.'"

Bloomfield did not go public with his opposition to the Charter at that time, as he perceived if he did so, "I'd lose all my rapport with the caucus. So I was desperately trying to do something in the caucus right to the last."

About 40 Liberal MPs, many of whom were Catholic, opposed

the Charter out of pro-life convictions, Bloomfield recalled. Then came the chilly spring day when Catholic MP Ursula Appolloni (York South-Weston, Ontario) came running into the caucus meeting, pulling imaginary manacles off her wrists and proclaiming exultantly, "We're free! We're free!"

Ms. Appolloni's elation was the result of a call she had received from the Archdiocese of Toronto. Cardinal Carter "has issued a statement to the *Catholic Register* to the effect that he is convinced that the Charter is neutral on abortion," she related to her colleagues in an excited memo dated March 31, 1981. "He further adds that it is wrong for people to accuse those who support the Charter of immorality, inasmuch as the Charter itself entrenches many moral rights."[33]

The news broke on April 3, 1981: Cardinal Carter announced that he did not oppose the Charter, having been convinced, after a private meeting with Trudeau, that it would not open the door to abortion on demand.[34] "While I am not satisfied with the protection accorded the unborn," he stated, "I do not consider the proposed Charter as worsening the position [on abortion] and, because of its many positive values, I do not oppose its passage on moral and religious grounds." Going even further, the prelate prohibited the handing out of Campaign Life literature at any of the parishes in his Toronto archdiocese.[35]

Gwen Landolt was incredulous. "[I]n 10 years of fighting abortion, it never entered my mind a Catholic cardinal could take the stand Carter has taken. We believed we were making the only possible moral response when all of a sudden we find the huge cannons of the Catholic Church blazing at us—no warning, no dialogue, nothing. We're dumbfounded."[36]

Campaign Life coordinator Paul Formby (who was, at the time, a Basilian seminarian—a fact he prudently concealed from the media, but which he could not conceal from the Cardinal) was also flummoxed. "We think it comes down to the fact that our lawyers say the Charter is not neutral on abortion, that it will pave the way for the Supreme Court (of Canada) to strike down abortion laws and to provide, in essence, abortion on demand—and the Cardinal has said the opposite."[37]

Fr. Alphonse de Valk publicly questioned the Cardinal's actions. "The attack upon Campaign Life by means of ecclesiastical prohibition which accompanies this opinion seems to indicate that the Cardinal would like his archdiocese to believe that his opinion on the Charter is the only legitimate one," the priest wrote in a letter published in the April 25 *Globe and Mail*. One could further infer that the Cardinal thought that members of the Liberal Party should not be held accountable for the Charter as it now stood.

Speculation was rife that the Cardinal had issued the ban on Campaign Life literature because the political lobbying group had recently targeted the pro-Charter premier of Ontario, Conservative Bill Davis. The Cardinal, it was suggested, was sensitive to the political repercussions of such actions at a time when the archdiocese was doing its own quiet lobbying for the full public funding of Catholic schools. The rumour was categorically denied by a "source close to the Cardinal."[38]

Whatever his motivation, Cardinal Carter's action wrought anger, dismay and bitterness among pro-life advocates—particularly with the 10,000 supporters of Campaign Life. Moreover, it left many of his priests in confusion, as pointed out by Jim Hughes, Toronto chairman of Campaign Life. "I personally have received calls from at least two dozen priests who are very confused and very upset. On Friday it was just manic …they say, 'Cardinal Carter is our boss but we support you—don't give up, redouble your efforts'," Hughes told the press.[39]

Meanwhile, the Canadian Conference of Catholic Bishops (CCCB) also consulted its own lawyers. A legal opinion prepared for the CCCB by Joseph Magnet in March 1981 disputed the claims of Landolt and her colleague John Stephens, but as the latter noted in rebuttal, Magnet at one point referred to "the mother's right to a therapeutic abortion." As Stephens added wryly: "So there it is."[40] Campaign Life's lawyers were left to wonder why the Canadian bishops felt compelled to seek an opinion other than their own. They were further left to wonder why the bishops did not seek this alternative opinion from a lawyer who was unambiguously pro-life.

Shortly after Cardinal Carter's bombshell in April, the House of Commons and the Senate approved the amended Charter.

Later in the 'cruelest month,' the action shifted to the Supreme Court. Manitoba, Newfoundland and Quebec had all contested the legality of Trudeau's plan to change the constitution unilaterally. They also requested a ruling as to whether by so doing, the federal government would violate the unwritten convention that required the consent of all the provinces for any constitutional amendments.[41]

The Supreme Court heard five days of arguments, then deliberated on the question for nearly six months. Meanwhile, Joe Borowski was getting restive. He had not been permitted to address the Joint Committee, and had been forced to watch, from the sideline, the heroic attempts of pro-life lobbyists. He finally had had enough, and following the developments of April, began his fast for life.

The fast "was the bleakest period of our lives," remembered Sandra Borowski.

Her older sister Karen was even more emphatic. "I remember being angry at him... he was trying to send a message and make a stand but all that he was doing was hurting himself. Other people weren't affected the way we were; we had to watch him suffer, we had to watch him get sick. "He almost died... He didn't need to go that far."

As the days passed Joe became weaker and weaker. The cold forced him to wear gloves even as spring was deepening into summer, and the lassitude brought on by hunger compelled him to take to his bed.

Jean Borowski had every confidence in her husband's ability to monitor his health. Joe had "thought of everything and anything that would push it to a head" and the fast, she recalled, was a last ditch attempt to bring attention to the issue of abortion.

But "the girls were getting scared." As the 80th day of his fast approached, Joe had lost nearly 50 pounds. When Dr. Colin Merry, a haematologist from the Health Science Centre drove out to La Salle, bringing with him a colleague who specialized in the effects of malnutrition, the physicians were shocked. Joe's blood pressure was incredibly low and he was losing skeletal and heart muscle mass. Joe could suffer congestive heart failure, Dr. Merry told the grimly determined pro-lifer. He then pulled Jean Borowski aside with fierce insistence: "Do something. He's going to die."

Joe waved these objections aside with his usual sang-froid, but by now, even Jean was alarmed. "I said, 'Joe, you realize how serious it is?' And he says, 'Don't worry about it, don't worry about it.'" By evening, her emaciated husband resembled a corpse; his heartbeat so faint and erratic that Jean failed to detect it: "I couldn't get a pulse." In a state of panic, she called Fr. Morand who came to administer last rites.

Meanwhile, intervention was brewing from another source. A former NDP colleague of Joe's, Harry Shafransky, had called Ed Schreyer, then Governor-General of Canada. Harry explained that Joe had "pushed his fasting to the point of physical damage," Schreyer remembered. He admitted that his first reaction was: "Well, what in the world can I possibly do that would be useful? Then I got the bright idea—because I knew Joe—I got the bright idea to phone the papal nuncio." Soon, the Queen's representative was telling the Vatican diplomat about a particularly devoted son of the Church, a man of "a stubbornness that went beyond description" and his resolve to fast for his unborn brothers and sisters.[42]

"I said, 'We have to do something because his wife is concerned, and she's not one that easily gets concerned, so he's probably pushed it to the extreme where he's on death's bed... I don't know that, but I suspect it.' [H]e was quick-thinking, the papal nuncio. He said, 'Some intervention from the Vatican?'

"I said, 'Precisely.'"

Within eight hours the papal nuncio called Schreyer back with the news that a telegram was coming from Rome, a telegram stating that under no circumstances does the Catholic Church condone or sanction suicide. He called Jean Borowski with the news. But Joe had already called an end to his protest.

He had been persuaded by a Sunday morning conversation with Morris Shumiatcher, who pointed out to his client that if he died, the court case that they had piloted through three years of arduous wrangling in the lower and appellate courts, and which now only awaited the ruling of the Supreme Court in order to be heard, would be extinguished as irrevocably as his life.[43]

The case was in Borowski's name, and no Joe, no go, Shumiatcher pointed out. "I told him that thousands of his supporters whose donations were financing the case would lose the money they had given him to fight their cause. 'Besides', I said, 'I, myself, am not a little piqued that you should have so little faith in your counsel that you feel you can win your case only by starving yourself to death!' That did it. He left his bed and, with his wife, went to church."[44]

"The choice was pretty clear." Joe ruefully admitted. "He asked me if I cared for the publicity I get from fasting or if I cared about the unborn." On July 19, 1981, exactly 80 days since he last ate solid food, Joe took a bite of "the tastiest orange I've ever had in my life."[45]

Joe made it to Mass nearly every day of the fast, even though toward the end, he had to walk with a cane. When he brought his ordeal to a close, Jean took him to see his mother, who was 82 years old and understandably concerned about her son.[46]

It took the 48-year-old Joe several weeks to return to a regular diet, but he never regained the robust physique of his prime, and remained for the rest of his earthly days a markedly slighter man. His family believed that the fast took years off his life. While he was slowly regaining his strength by following a "carefully graduated eating plan,"[47] the Supreme Court justices were mulling over the constitution at the request of the federal government. It was not until September 28, 1981 that their decision was released.

It was held to be the most momentous decision that the Supreme Court had yet made—and with the media attention focused on the court as never before, Chief Justice Bora Laskin permitted television cameras to record the proceedings. However a judge tripped on a sound cable, and cut the audio broadcast.[48]

The Supreme Court ruled 7-2 that a unilateral constitutional amendment by the federal government would violate the unwritten convention that required substantial agreement of the provinces. However, because a convention is not, by nature, enforceable, the Liberals' contemplated course of action was not illegal. As Morton described it, "Ottawa's unilateralism was legal but wrong."[49]

The Court's guarded go-ahead to the federal government paved the way for the historic November 1981 accord, forged during the week of intense politicking and negotiating that was the meeting of provincial and federal First Ministers. The deal-making culminated in a series of informal meetings and communications through the night of November 4 and into the early morning of November 5, from which, tellingly, Rene Levesque was excluded. The Quebec premier, to his stunned consternation, received the news of the agreement that would form the basis of Canada's new constitution along with his morning coffee.[50]

The accord included an amending formula more to the liking of the premiers than had previously been the case, and the addition of the "notwithstanding clause"—now Section 33. This clause ensured that both provincial and federal governments could, by declaring that a statute would operate "notwithstanding" the Charter, protect legislation from being struck down by the courts as unconstitutional. These the premiers lobbied for and received while Trudeau, for his part, insisted that "language rights, minority education and mobility rights" be exempted from Section 33, as well as "those sections pertaining directly to democratic rights" (Sections 3-5).[51]

The Supreme Court was lauded in many quarters for having made the ruling that broke the constitutional logjam and led to the November accord. "Overlooked," observed Charter analyst Morton, "in what the Court did for constitutional reform was what the Court did for itself. It became the first court of any English common-law jurisdiction (and presumably the world) to rule on the existence of an unwritten political convention. Despite the fact that there was no precedent of any court ever doing so, the Supreme Court did so unanimously."[52][53]

The fear that the Charter would lead to "rule by judges" was not confined to the political right, nor to those attempting to protect the child in the womb. Left-wing Osgoode Hall law professor and political commentator Michael Mandel, a proponent of the "right to chose," published a trenchant and stinging critique of the Charter, in which he dated the beginning of the "legalization of politics" from the point at which the Supreme Court consented to address on the question of constitutional convention. It was common knowledge that Ottawa would violate convention by unilaterally amending the constitution, argued Mandel; to ask the court to rule on the matter—more properly the concern of politics, not law—was "extraordinary."[54]

Yet, the justices agreed as one to rule on the question. Mandel contended that they did so because the Liberals "expected" it of them. Motivating the federal response to the Court's decision was the fact that the effectiveness of the soon-to-be-entrenched Charter was contingent on esteem and respect for the judiciary. Trudeau, asserted Mandel, had every intention of using the Court, when the need arose, to overrule legislation—particularly in the area of minority language rights.[55] By ruling on the constitutional convention question, the Court itself departed radically from tradition, but, after the patriation of the new constitution, it could claim the Charter as its authority to nullify offensive statutes.[56]

It was the eleventh hour, and the pro-lifers who had toiled in the heat of the sun were getting desperate in their battle against the Charter. Yet unexpected, but gratefully received, reinforcements arrived.

In Toronto, the editor of the *Catholic Register*, Larry Henderson, who had previously been supportive of the Charter, changed his tune and came out strongly against the legislation in the summer of 1981. He permitted Campaign Life to continue its advertising in the Toronto archdiocesan newspaper, and he exercised his formidable pen on behalf of the pro-life lobby.

Meanwhile, some Canadian bishops still doubted the Liberals. An exchange of correspondence between Archbishop Joseph MacNeil of Edmonton, Alberta, then president of the CCCB, and the Prime Minister was made public in early June. It revealed that the prelate had written Trudeau back in March, asking him to publicly assure Canadians that the Charter "is intended to enhance respect for life from its very beginnings. It would be deplorable if your Charter of Rights could either now or in the future be interpreted in such a way as to broaden the impact and effect of the present abortion legislation which is already, in some of its prescriptions, unacceptable to us."[57]

Archbishop MacNeil was not satisfied when Trudeau fobbed him off by saying the government preferred to leave abortion out of the Charter, the public being evenly divided on the issue. He persevered with a second letter. "There has been mounting evidence supporting the legal opinion that, despite the goodwill and assurances of the government, further interpretation of the Charter could well remove all protection to the right to life of unborn children."[58] Because he had asked Trudeau for a public statement, he was free to release the correspondence to the press, the archbishop wrote.

Campaign Life was gratified by these efforts, in which the president of the CCCB was supported by Cardinal Carter, then in St. Michael's Hospital recovering from a stroke. The Cardinal had had second thoughts about Trudeau's declaration that the Charter was neutral on abortion. The Catholic Church and the grass-roots political lobby group now presented a united front.

However, time was running out. Following the Supreme Court ruling, and the accord of November, the government would brook few negotiations. The last debate on the constitutional package took place at the end of November, and pro-life activists were at their wit's end, trying to exert whatever leverage they could.

Paul Formby, the main lobbyist for Campaign Life Canada and, at the age of 36, a veteran of the Charter battle, arrived in Ottawa one freezing November day with a mandate to lobby the Conservatives. He was to meet Gwen Landolt in the office of Tory MP Doug Roche. When he arrived, a deal had already been struck.

"Gwen was desperate. She knew that this Charter was going to lead to abortion on demand and she had lobbied, on her own, without Kathy Toth or Hughes or me or anybody knowing, doing what she could with Doug Roche," he recalled. The two had agreed that the Conservatives would ask for a clause to the Charter that explicitly stated the Charter would not impair Parliament's ability to legislate on abortion.

Formby figured his people would want more. "We didn't come all the way to Ottawa just for this, we want them to stick their neck out on protection of the unborn." Roche, however, was adamant that the Conservatives would go no further.

"And I started to say, 'But what about Kathy Toth and these people, I'm here representing them, they want you guys to do something more,' and then he started raising his voice, and I said, 'Wait a minute,' and so he and I started arguing really loud and he chucked me out. He said, 'You get out of my office right now.' I wasn't threatening him or anything, I was just saying, we want something and Gwen's sitting there, 'Paul, there's nothing I can do, it's the way it is,' and this guy kicks me out of his office." Formby walked out "into the daylight" and looked back at Parliament.

"I can remember very vividly the feeling I had, that everything in this building is so convoluted, this is our House of Commons ... and there's nothing that is true; they say the exact opposite of what they want, they're using political games."[59] He suspected that the Conservatives were not acting in good faith, but were motivated by a desire to politically embarrass the Liberals. Landolt was not so sure; she knew there were several staunch pro-life politicians in the Conservative caucus and she was willing to give them the benefit of the doubt.

The Roche strategy was bitterly contested within the Tory caucus itself. It was finally agreed that the proposed amendment would be put forward, but if defeated, the Conservatives would vote en masse in favour of the Charter, of which leader Joe Clark was greatly in favour.

Landolt thought the vote would take place on a Tuesday, giving the pro-life groups the weekend to lobby their MPs, but she received a call from a distraught pro-life MP who told her Trudeau had called a vote on the resolution that Thursday.[60]

Conservative MP David Crombie had been elected to put forward the amendment. The member for Toronto-Rosedale had, Landolt observed, an "aura of neutrality" but he was not pro-life. (In his tenure as mayor of Toronto, Crombie was a member of the Amnesty for Dr. Morgentaler group in 1975.)[61]

Crombie had already pointed out to the Joint Committee in January that he wanted to be sure that Parliament, not the courts, would deal with abortion. He was told then by Bob Kaplan, federal solicitor-general, that abortion "is a matter which, in our view, the Charter does not touch and, therefore, does not put it within the competence of a court to determine whether an abortion or a non-abortion law is valid."[62]

On November 27, 1981, Crombie rose in the House to propose the addition of the following clause to the Charter: "Nothing in this Charter affects the authority of Parliament to legislate in respect of abortion." Added Crombie: "It took 350 years to establish the parliamentary system where legislation governing our actions with respect to life and death would be determined not by those appointed by the state but, rather, by those elected by the people themselves."[63]

He also referred to "conflicting legal difficulties" surrounding abortion. The reality of these legal difficulties threw into "doubt" the authority of Parliament in the matter of abortion, Crombie stated: "We want to make it clear that Parliament's freedom to legislate on this matter is unimpaired."

Prime Minister Trudeau himself responded to the resolution. The Charter was, he insisted, "absolutely neutral" with respect to abortion. "In other words, the Charter does not say whether abortions will be easier or more difficult to practise in the future...under the constitution, the House retains the right to amend the Criminal Code, which is the statute affecting the issue of abortion." If it did happen that a judge should conclude that the Charter does "affect certain provisions of the Criminal Code, under the override clause we reserve the right to say: Notwithstanding this decision, notwithstanding the Charter of Rights as interpreted by this judge, the House legislates in such and such a manner on the abortion issue."[64] [65]

The Prime Minister also objected to the amendment on the grounds that if passed, it would give the impression by implication that Parliament's ability to legislate in other areas regarding human life, such as capital punishment and euthanasia, was somehow in question.[66] Moreover, he did not wish to jeopardize the accord reached the weekend of November 4 and 5. While two amendments, "one concerning women and equality between the sexes and the other concerning aboriginal rights and the entrenchment thereof in the Constitution" had been approved after receiving the consent of the nine signatories to the accord, that was quite enough. "Any amendment now which is brought before the House and which does not have the support of the nine premiers, we will vote against," promised Trudeau.[67]

The Crombie clause fell.

Who was left to stand up in the winds that blew then?

Garnet Bloomfield.

The valiant and intrepid backbencher from London county (who, although Baptist, had himself called up Archbishop MacNeil to encourage him in his efforts) finally went public. On November 20, 1981, he announced at a press conference that he would be unable to support the Liberal constitutional bill. He could not support a Charter of Rights that failed to protect the right to life of the unborn. A number of his colleagues had warned him, "Bloomfield, you vote against that main bill and you might as well go home. And I said, 'Well, I'll climb back in my tractor with a clean conscience anyway.'"

Two things happened. One was that "my office went wild"— pro-life people from across the country called or telegrammed their support: "They didn't think there was anybody there."

The other event was that Garnet Bloomfield, in his determination to get an answer from his party, met with Trudeau. Having been rebuffed by Justice Minister Jean Chrétien in his attempt to discuss the matter, Bloomfield went to Senator Keith Davey, who in turn referred him to Trudeau operative Jim Coutts. Bloomfield remembered Coutts telling him, "Garnet, I'm gonna shock you, but a lot of my ancestors were Methodist preachers," before adding, "Would you mind talking to the Prime Minister?"[68]

When the time came, Bloomfield was ushered into an imposing office, and Trudeau came out from behind the massive Sir John A. MacDonald desk and sat down two chairs, and began to talk to Garnet "just like an older brother ... I just looked back and I couldn't measure the time, I was just intent on what he was saying, and he must have talked to me for at least 20 to 30 minutes, reasoning with me why the government was proceeding the way they were."

The passage of more than twenty years since that encounter had not impaired Bloomfield's ability to recall the exchange that then took place between the two men. Bloomfield told the Prime Minister, "We are all known for who we are and what we are and what we stand for and we can destroy that, that ability with our people if we don't vote in support of what they know us for. And he said, 'I know what you're talking about Garnet, I've destroyed at least a third of my credibility in the province of Quebec because I'm a federalist.'"

Garnet replied: "Well, Mr. Prime Minister, I know you did what you believe is right. I guess I'm just asking for the same privilege.'

"And he sat there, and the silence was long and excruciating.

"I wondered what he was going to say finally—because there was no way out of that—and finally he said, 'Well, Garnet, I know you've got deep religious beliefs and you know I'd like you to support the Charter, but I'll understand it if you don't,' and we shook hands."

When Bloomfield returned to his constitutency after the Charter vote, he encountered admiration more than anything else. "Bloomfield, you have set a new standard," he was told, "We can't believe you voted against a major bill of the government."

Twice after that, Trudeau appointed him parliamentary secretary.[69]

Shortly after Bloomfield's press conference, Cardinal Carter, still somewhat debilitated by his stroke, sent a telegram to Trudeau, supporting Archbishop MacNeil, and suggesting an amendment "that nothing in the Charter may be interpreted as infringing on these rights, or at the very least a statement that notwithstanding any provision in the Charter, Parliament shall not be precluded from legislating the rights of unborn children."

It was too late. The finagling, inveigling, politicking and manoeuvring were done. On December 2, 1981, MPs who opposed the Charter had recourse to the only weapon they had left: their vote. When the tally was in, 264 MP had voted in favour of the package, one had abstained, and 24 voted against.

The only two Liberals who voted against the constitution for pro-life reasons were Garnet Bloomfield (London-Middlesex) and Stan Hudecki (Hamilton West). Tory opponents included Len Gustafson (PC, Assiniboia, Saskatchewan) and Douglas Roche (PC Edmonton South). Abstaining from the vote was NDP member for Saskatoon East, Fr. Bob Ogle, who styled his action a "silent protest" against the Charter's lack of protection for the child in the womb.

Gwen Landolt, who had the highest regard for Doug Roche, was mystified when she called him the night before the vote that he was as distraught as he was. "I don't know what to do," she recalled him saying. She was unaware of the pact to which the Tories had agreed: they were obliged to vote for the Charter once their resolution failed. "I said, 'Well, Doug, why are you upset? Of course you have to vote for pro-life, you'd have to vote against the Charter, you know what it's going to do to the unborn.'"[70]

When the roll was called on that fateful day, Roche looked sick. But he voted against the Charter, and, according to Landolt, that ended his political career. He chose solidarity with unborn children over his pledge to party solidarity.

Roche, who formerly had edited the Edmonton archdiocese's weekly newspaper, *The Western Catholic Reporter*, released a statement shortly after the vote. "I maintain that the exclusion of the unborn from a Charter of Rights—written in the year 1981 with all the medical knowledge of the human features of the unborn child—can scarcely be called neutrality. The government turned down every effort to introduce even a reference to the unborn child in the charter, insisting the issue be handled through the Criminal Code."[71]

At this point, any opposition was merely symbolic. The rest, as they say, is history. The British Parliament and the House of Lords subsequently approved and passed *The Canada Act* 1982 on March 29, 1982. Under the terms of this legislation, *The Constitution Act*, 1982, which includes the Canadian Charter of Rights and Freedoms, was proclaimed by Queen Elizabeth II in Ottawa, on April 17, 1982.

Was this a new springtime for the country, or was April again the cruelest month? For good or ill, the federal structure of the dominion had been altered radically. It was, in Landolt's view, "a bloodless revolution...Rarely has a developed nation's constitution been so speedily drafted and implemented."[72]

A whole new Canada had begun, but whether the unborn child would find a welcome there remained to be seen.

Notes
Chapter 12
The Charter and the fast

[1] "Borowski's final protest," *Winnipeg Free Press*, May 12, 1981.

[2] "Borowski on hunger strike," *Free Press,* May 4, 1981.

[3] "Borowski's final protest," Paul Sullivan, *Free Press*, May 12, 19981.

[4] "Joe protesting charter of rights," Ric Littlemore, *Winnipeg Sun*, May 4, 1981.

[5] Op. Cit., Sullivan.

[6] Op. Cit., Littlemore.

[7] Op. Cit., Sullivan.

[8] Ibid.

[9] Op. Cit., Littlemore.

[10] Michael Mandel, *The Charter of Rights and the Legalization of Politics in Canada* (Toronto: Thompson Educational Publishing Inc., revised, updated and expanded edition, 1994), p. 20.

[11] Op. Cit., Morton, p. 104.

[12] Op. Cit., Morton, p. 105.

[13] Op. Cit., Mandel, p. 25.

[14] At this point, any constitutional amendments were also required, under the BNA of 1867, to be passed by the British Parliament before coming into effect. This would come to an end if Trudeau's promise to patriate the Constitution were successful. (Morton, p. 205 and 130).

[15] Op., Cit., Morton, p. 106.

[16] Op. Cit., Morton, pp.108-109.

[17] Op. Cit., Mandel, p. 26.

[18] Op. Cit., Morton, p. 109.

[19] Among others were Alan Blakeney, NDP premier of Saskatchewan, and Edward MacLean, premier of PEI.

[20] Minutes and Proceedings of the Joint Committee of the Senate and the House of Commons on the Constitution of Canada, 34:117.

[21] Ibid., 34:122.

[22] Ibid., 34:123.

[23] Other pro-life groups that appeared before the Joint Committee included Alliance for Life, which requested on December 16 that Section 7 be amended to read, "Everyone from conception to natural death has the right to life." On January 7, the Ontario Conference of Catholic Bishops made the same request. The Coalition for the Protection of Human Life recommended that Section 15, the equality section, be amended to explicitly prohibit discrimination against the child in the womb. (Morton, p. 113.)

[24] "Charter clearly denies rights to unborn," Alphonse de Valk, *Western Catholic Reporter*, January 26, 1981, p. 12.

[25] Ibid.

[26] Op. Cit., Morton, p. 112.

[27] Ibid., p. 113.

[28] (Op. Cit., Morton, p. 114.) Supreme Court Justice McIntyre was to refer to this

very point in his dissenting judgment in the 1988 *Morgentaler* decision. (See Chapter 22, note 39)

[29] Minutes and proceedings and Evidence of the Special Joint Committee, 46:32, as quoted in Morton, p 115.

[30] Op. Cit., Morton, p. 116.

[31] Op. Cit, de Valk, "Charter clearly denies rights to unborn."

[32] Interview with Garnet Bloomfield, September 2002.

[33] It was shortly after this, in April 1981, that the interparty pro-life caucus dissolved.

[34] "Cut ties to anti-abortion group, Carter tells priests," Nora McCabe, *Globe and Mail*, April 3, 1981.

[35] Ibid.

[36] "Cardinal called 'dishonest' by pro-lifer," Tom Harpur, *Toronto Star*, April 11, 1981.

[37] "Cut ties to anti-abortion group, Carter tells priests," Nora McCabe, *Globe and Mail*, April 3, 1981.

[38] Op. Cit., Tom Harpur.

[39] "Carter's flock bickering," Jan Lounder, *Toronto Sun*, April 6, 1981.

[40] Letter from Stephens to Msgr. Dennis Murphy, CCCB general secretary, April 10, 1981.

[41] Op. Cit., Mandel, p.27.

[42] Interview with Edward Schreyer, March 2002

[43] "Borowski calls end to food fast," Ric Littlemore, *Winnipeg Sun*, July 20, 1981.

[44] "I set before you life and death: Abortion—Borowski and the Constitution," Morris Shumiatcher, *University of Western Ontario Law Review*, 24 (1987) p. 3.

[45] Ibid. Littlemore.

[46] "Borowski ends fast after 80 days on doctors' advice," *Winnipeg Free Press*, July 20, 1981.

[47] Ibid.

[48] Op. Cit., Morton, p. 119.

[49] Ibid.

[50] Op. Cit., Mandel, p. 35.

[51] Op. Cit., Morton, p. 119.

[52] Op. Cit., Morton, p. 119.

[53] Michael Mandel's view was that the Supreme Court decision enabled Trudeau to shut-out Quebec, the sole province locked in fundamental conflict with the federal government. Once the Supreme Court sanctioned Ottawa's unilaterlism, Quebec's fate was a fait accompli. (Op. Cit., Mandel, pp. 34-35.)

[54] Op. Cit., Mandel, p. 28.

[55] Ibid. p. 33.

[56] Ibid. p. 35.

[57] "Archbishop asks PM to protect unborn" Tom Harpur, *Toronto Star*, June 5, 1981.

[58] Ibid.

[59] Interview with Paul Formby, September 2002.

[60] Intevew with Gwen Landolt, September 2002.

[61] Catherine Dunphy, *Morgentaler, a difficult hero*, (Toronto: Random House of Canada, 1996), p.140.

[62] Minutes of proceedings and evidence of the Special Joint Committee, 43:46, as quoted in Morton, p. 113.

[63] House of Commons Debates, November 27, 1981, p 13436.

[64] Commons debates, p. 13438.

[65] Justice Minister, Jean Chrétien, had also verbally assured Crombie, in an exchange during the Joint Committee hearings, that the Charter was neutral on abortion. (See Chapter 27, note 34.)

[66] Ibid. The Prime Minister also repeated these points to Cardinal Carter, in a letter received by the latter on December 21, 1981, in which Trudeau was at pains to reassure the Cardinal by pointing out the existence of Section 33.

[67] Pro-life and Christian groups had also been lobbying for an explicit reference, in the Charter's preamble, to the supremacy of God. The Liberals allowed this, in what some commentators saw as merely a tactic to appease the Charter's opponents.

[68] Interview with Garnet Bloomfield, September 2002.

[69] Bloomfield lost in the next election when the Tory Mulroney sweep occurred. From interview with Garnet Bloomfield, September 2002.

[70] "Some dissenting votes over pro-life issue, Stan Koma", *Catholic Register*, December 19-26, p.3.

[71] "The immorality of the Law," presented at Alliance for Life Ontario Provincial Conference, November. 3, 2001, p. 3.; August 1995 brief on the Charter, p. 5.

Chapter 13

The pending assault

Genuine love rises above creatures and soars up to God.
In Him, by Him and through Him it loves all men, both good and
wicked, friends and enemies…. It prays for all, suffers for all…
desires happiness for all, because that is what God wants.
St. Maximilian Kolbe

"I believe he will be converted before he hangs up his spurs. Prayer
will convert Henry Morgentaler. I don't know how it will happen—
God works in mysterious ways."
Joe Borowski

TWO WEEKS AFTER THE PROCLAMATION OF THE CHARTER, HENRY Morgentaler announced that he would open abortion clinics in Toronto and Winnipeg.[1]

Few Canadians during those years would not recognize the name of Henry Morgentaler. The Jewish general practitioner had achieved notoriety for repeatedly and brazenly breaking the law by performing abortions in his Montreal clinic, yet had managed for the most part to evade the grasp of the authorities, with whom, by 1981, he had a long and convoluted relationship. He had also acquired the stature of media spokesperson and principal agitator for the abortion-on-demand lobby. In a 1967 brief, which he presented on behalf of the Humanist Fellowship of Montreal to the Commons Standing Committee on Health and Welfare, then reviewing the abortion law, he proposed abortion-on-demand during the first three months of pregnancy. There, Joseph O'Keefe, Newfoundland Liberal MP (St. John's East) asked the 44-year-old if he would have any qualms about "aborting a baby born of a syphilitic father and a tubercular mother? I am very confident that the majority of doctors who did not have a Catholic conscience would abort the fetus. Would you agree?"

"I would agree definitely," Morgentaler responded.

"Then we would have lost Beethoven..."

"This argument is completely nullified by the fact that if you had had legal abortions you perhaps would not have also had Hitler, or Mussolini, or Stalin, or many other..." Morgentaler countered.

"I think," rejoined O'Keefe, "they have the right to life."

"Therefore it evens itself out."[2]

Agitation for a permissive abortion law in Canada had begun as early as 1959, when *Chatelaine* magazine made the case for legalizing abortions, using arguments and phrases that would become stock propaganda in the abortion advocates' campaign. Canada's law was "the world's harshest" wrote the author of an article in August of that year, and it compelled "desperate women to seek help from a vicious back-room racket that often deals in death."[3]

The following year the United Church jumped on the bandwagon, using its official paper *The Observer* to broadcast its pro-abortion views. But it was the *Globe and Mail* that, through its relentless editorials and skewed coverage of the issue, proved to be "the most formidable protagonist of the legalization of abortion among the general public," according to historian, Alphonse de Valk.[4] The paper routinely quoted estimates of "back-street abortions" for which no source was given and which stretched credulity to the limit, at one point asserting that there were from "20,000 to 120,000 annually." Other abortion advocates used the same tactic; for example, the National Council of Women in its brief to the Commons Committee, put the number at "30,000 to 300,000."[5][6]

Then the lawyers and doctors came on board. In 1963 the

Canadian Bar Association first floated a resolution to legalize abortion under the Criminal Code, one that included a provision to permit abortion if there was reasonable suspicion that the unborn child was mentally or physically defective (this provision, it was claimed, came about because of the thalidomide tragedy of the early '60s). The resolution provoked such controversy and opposition that it was tabled for further study, much to the scorn of the *Globe and Mail*.

That same year the Canadian Medical Association began to discuss legalizing abortion, and the association struck a committee to produce a study of therapeutic abortion and sterilization. The chairman of the committee was self-confessed Toronto abortionist Dr. Donald Low, who also was a member of the CMA delegation to the 1967 Commons Committee reviewing the abortion law.[7]

By 1966 both organizations had come out in favour of legalizing abortion under some circumstances, although they differed over just how the legislation might be drafted. Meanwhile, other social changes occurred in Canada: contraception was legalized in 1967, and the next year, the grounds for divorce were broadened.

In 1967 Lester Pearson's Liberal government convened a Commons Standing Committee to study abortion law reform. After sitting from early October to mid-December, the Committee produced, on December 19, an unexpected interim report that recommended revising the law.

This provided the opportunity for Pearson's impatient new Justice Minister to introduce an Omnibus Bill on December 21, 1967, a bill that included, among its formidable bulk of 72 pages and 104 clauses, revisions to the Criminal Code permitting abortion in some circumstances (and decriminalizing homosexual acts in private between persons 18 years and older).

That, wrote de Valk, made the media sit up and notice Pierre Elliot Trudeau, who had held the post of Minister of Justice for only eight months and who, in referring to his bill's decriminalization of homosexuality, spoke the words that burned themselves into the media's (and presumably, the country's) psyche: "The state has no business in the bedrooms of the nation." A mere four months later, Trudeau became the leader of the Liberal Party and Prime Minister-in-waiting.[8]

From that point the die was cast. The eventual passage of the Omnibus Bill was aided by the stridency of abortion advocates, the confusion and unreadiness of any opposition and the unrelieved propagandizing by the pro-abortion "paper of record", the *Globe and Mail*.

But real responsibility for the passage of the abortion clause on May 14, 1969, fell to the Catholic Prime Minister Pierre Trudeau and his band of Liberals[9]—many of whom, it can be noted with regret, were also Catholic but to whom Trudeau, the putative liberal, denied a free vote. They did not defy their charismatic and autocratic leader.

Henry Morgentaler, meanwhile, had publicly recommended that unborn children 12 weeks old and under be aborted on the demand of the mother. When women began calling him for abortions, Morgentaler refused; he said he did not want to break the law. But, finally he did. On on January 9, 1968, Morgentaler performed an abortion on the 18-year-old daughter of a friend.[10]

By March 1969, Morgentaler specialized exclusively in "family planning," inserting IUDs, performing some vasectomies, but mainly doing abortions, claiming in a 1973 article to have done 5,641 by the vacuum aspirator method, in which he had trained himself, purchasing the equipment from Britain. He had not gone public with his illegal activities, writing anonymously in *The Humanist* in 1970 that "I prefer to live for a cause than be martyred for it."[11]

Despite this preference, Morgentaler's Montreal clinic was raided on June 1, 1970 and he was charged two days later with three counts of criminal abortions. He did not go to trial on these charges until October 18, 1973, both because his lawyer, Claude-Armand Sheppard, counseled delay, and the Quebec government was preoccupied with the FLQ crisis in October 1970. But when his day in court finally arrived, the Crown had added 10 more charges, following an August 15, 1973 raid on the clinic.[12]

Morgentaler had become increasingly vocal and defiant in the months following his first arrest. He was emboldened by *Roe v. Wade*, the American Supreme Court decision that struck down all state prohibitions against abortion, resulting in abortion on demand in that country. He publicly admitted, more than once, that he had done over 5,000 illegal abortions, and more audaciously, the CTV *W-5* program broadcast—on Mother's Day, 1973—a news item that showed him aborting a baby.[13]

The Quebec Crown elected to proceed by "preferred indictments" against the abortionist in the fall of 1973. It was an "extraordinary procedure" used in the October 1970 FLQ crisis, noted author Morton. The Crown thus dispenses with the usual procedure of a preliminary inquiry (the purpose of which is to establish that there is enough evidence to justify a trial) because the delay of such a hearing would "threaten the public good." In the case of Henry Morgentaler, his lawyer's constancy in obstructing the proceedings, and the accused's deliberate and apparently unrepented law-breaking were given as the reasons for the preferred indictments, signed by Quebec's Minister of Justice himself, Jerome Choquette.[14]

On November 13, 1973, the 11-man, one-woman, French-speaking, working-class jury acquitted Henry Morgentaler of breaking the law. His lawyer, Claude-Armand Sheppard, had thought such a verdict entirely possible from the moment presiding Justice James Hugessen permitted a defence based on Section 45 of the Criminal Code, (which allows persons to perform non-consensual surgery in a situation in which another person's life is in jeopardy) and the defence of necessity. The latter defence excuses a criminal act that is done to prevent a greater crime or evil. (A classic illustration of this is someone who trespasses in the course of rescuing another from impending death or harm.) Courtroom analysts criticized the Crown witnesses, one of whom admitted referring women to Morgentaler's clinic, and contended that Crown Prosecutor Louis-Guy Robichaud's personal hostility towards the accused and his lawyer had obscured his good judgement.[15]

Montreal pro-life activist Peter Hopkins, in a detailed report of the Morgentaler trials, pointed out that Sheppard weeded out jury candidates whose opinions on abortion were admittedly "based on religious or moral grounds"; he also rejected all but one of the female candidates. Moreover, Hopkins observed, not only in this trial, but in the two following trials, "the jurors were not sequestered, they went home every evening and returned next morning." Thus, while they waited every morning in the court-house hallway, they could easily mingle with the coterie of feminists and sympathetic media members hovering around

Morgentaler.[16]

However it came about, Henry Morgentaler walked free—that day. Robichaud appealed the verdict, and on April 26, 1974, the Quebec Court of Appeal unanimously ruled that Judge Hugessen had erred in law by allowing the Section 45 defence, and the defence of necessity. Not only that, the Court declared Henry Morgentaler guilty and directed him to return to the trial judge for sentencing.[17] The judgment was controversial; opponents objected that it undermined the jury system. But it was, under Canada's Criminal Code, perfectly legal.[18]

Meanwhile, Morgentaler had been approached by Revenue Canada in February of that year. He owed, according to the tax-man, $355,000 in back taxes, and as a result, his bank account and assets were frozen, his clinic searched and documents seized.[19]

On July 25, 1974, Justice Hugessen sentenced Henry Morgentaler to 18 months in jail, followed by three years' probation. It was a relatively severe sentence, but the judge took note of Morgentaler's "massive and public flouting of the law" which "forced the authorities to prosecute with more vigor and the courts to punish with more severity than would have been the case if he had simply initiated one test case for the pursuit of the ideals which he claims…"[20]

Henry Morgentaler, under sentence, still walked free—pending the decision by the Supreme Court on his appeal. His case was heard by the nine justices of Canada's highest court on October 4, 1974. Courtroom observers thought Morgentaler's lawyer, Sheppard, faltered in this more sterile venue, so at variance with the dramatic scope of the criminal trial. The audacious advocate attempted to "recuse" Justice Louis-Phillippe de Grandpré, that is, have him removed because of bias, (he had spoken publicly against abortion) but his motion was refused. As Morton related, "it was a high-risk tactic, and it seemed to backfire."[21]

The hearing was finished on October 12 but Morgentaler then waited another five months (bail conditions, naturally, prohibited the committing of abortions) until on March 26, 1975, the Supreme Court decision was announced: in a decision six to three, his appeal had been refused.[22] The highest court upheld the

Quebec Appeal Court's ruling that Morgentaler's Section 45 defence, and the defence of necessity, were unacceptable.[23]

Morgentaler, who had fled Montreal for the verdict, returned to that city from Toronto the next day to begin serving his 18-month sentence. After about six weeks in Bordeaux jail, the abortionist was transferred to the minimum-security facility, Waterloo. After about a month at the Waterloo facility, Morgentaler was reportedly manhandled by the guards, thrown into solitary confinement after being forced to disrobe for not obeying a directive, and allegedly suffered a mild heart attack as a consequence. Morgentaler's accounts of the incident differed on occasion, and the authorities at Waterloo denied that he had been mistreated. Whatever really happened, the result was that Morgentaler was taken to hospital, and on doctor's orders, never returned to prison. He spent the remaining seven months of his sentence in a nursing home, from whence he was permitted three times a week to go to the YMCA for rehabilitation sessions. While at the nursing home, he was visited by *Globe and Mail* reporter Richard Cleroux, who described his surroundings as comfortable.[24]

During this time, abortion advocates rallied around his cause. These champions included Laura Sabia, chairwoman of the Ontario Advisory Council on the Status of Women, writers June Callwood and Pierre Berton, Toronto mayor David Crombie, Linda Rapson, a founding member of Doctors for the Repeal of the Abortion Law (DRAL) and wife of Morgentaler's future lawyer, Morris Manning, and Ed Ratcliffe, president of CARAL.[25]

Meanwhile, the Quebec government enforced the law. Morgentaler stood trial for an additional five charges of criminal abortion while still confined. But he was again acquitted on June 9, 1975. This time, the Quebec Court of Appeal upheld the acquittal in a January 20, 1976 decision[26] and the Supreme Court refused to hear the case when requested to do so in February.

Two days after the Quebec Appeal Court ruling in Morgentaler's favour, Ron Basford, the newly appointed federal Minister of Justice, set aside the abortionist's earlier and only conviction by the same court, and ordered a retrial. Four days later, Morgentaler left the Villa Mount Royal nursing home, a free man. His retrial in September 1976 resulted in a third acquittal.

An unusual incident occurred during the course of this trial. An unidentified man at a hotel bar offered a female juror a bribe of

$1,000 to acquit Morgentaler. The agitated juror requested to speak to the judge the next morning and related her experiences to him; she thought perhaps it had been a test of her integrity. Crown Counsel René Domingue, Morgentaler and his lawyer, Sheppard, then met with Judge Ducros in his chambers to hear the story, transcribed by a court reporter. It was decided that the juror be suspended, and that no investigation or announcement of the episode be made until after the trial. No investigation ever occurred.

In another disturbing event, the jurors complained of intimidation, after a young man repeatedly photographed them on their return from their midday meal—this on the second day of deliberations, when the foreman had earlier informed the judge that the 12 were deadlocked. It seemed he was requesting that Judge Ducros declare a "hung jury" but the judge elected instead to send the jurors out to lunch and have them continue their exertions until 4 p.m. If at that point they could not reach unanimity, he would dismiss them as "hung."

Security guards apprehended a man with a camera who claimed to be a Canadian Press photographer; his claim was verified by a woman "who had been seen among Morgentaler's entourage", who was herself, she stated, a CP reporter. The man refused to relinquish the film; the jurors did not want to return to their deliberations unless the film was confiscated; the man asked for, and was provided with, a lawyer; judge, lawyer and alleged photographer conferred; the film was not obtained by the court; the jurors did not want to go back to work; the judge ordered them to do so, and they, at last, reluctantly obeyed.[27] Shortly thereafter, they returned with their verdict of not guilty.

The Bourassa government had begun proceedings on eight other outstanding charges against Morgentaler when, on November 15, 1976, the pro-abortion Parti Québécois came to power. Shortly afterward, PQ Justice Minister, Marc-André Bedard, informed the federal government that Section 251 was not enforceable in his province.[28]

It seemed inevitable that sooner or later, Morgentaler's abortion crusade would bring him to Joe Borowski's backyard. In

1983, Winnipegger Anna Desilets, then executive director for Alliance for Life, was discussing with a friend whether Toronto or Winnipeg would be the next target for a freestanding abortion clinic. She was sure Morgentaler would pick Manitoba because the NDP was in power, and Premier Howard Pawley had appointed pro-abortion Roland Penner, known affectionately as "Red Rolly" as a nod to his days as a Communist in the '60s, as attorney-general. It turned out that Morgentaler intended to set up in both places.

While Penner did not prove as amenable to Morgentaler's crusade as the latter had perhaps anticipated, neither did the pro-life movement—which had burgeoned in the almost 15 years since the legalization of abortion and had achieved cohesion and a certain amount of political clout—intend to let him have his way without a fight.

In Winnipeg, that battle involved Joe Borowski and his Alliance Against Abortion, along with Alliance for Life, Manitoba League for Life, headed by Pat Soenens, and Coalition for Life. But despite their using every available legal avenue to obstruct and delay the clinic opening, on May 5, 1983, Henry Morgentaler opened his abortuary at 883 Corydon Avenue.

Joe Borowski directed picketing and demonstrations from his makeshift headquarters, a mobile home, parked on the lawn of sympathetic neighbours. He had already been warned by city officials to move the mobile home as it violated zoning by-laws, but he wasn't about to give in. He vowed that pickets would be maintained 24 hours a day, but there was no plan to actually block the entrance of the abortuary.

"If anybody is brave enough to go through a picket line to see Dr. Morgentaler, we're certainly not going to stop them. If we can, we will urge them not to go. There is an alternative." There were families willing to help the distressed mothers by taking them in, he added. "And when the child is born, we will take the child off her hands."[29]

Joe had scarcely begun to picket with the other Winnipeg pro-lifers than he was compelled, by happy coincidence, to leave the grim scene for a pro-life venue, and for what could be the most significant two weeks in his life.

His goal of getting the abortion issue into court had finally come to pass. It was his turn now.

Notes
Chapter 13
The pending assault

[1] Op. Cit. Morton, p. 123.

[2] Op. Cit. Catherine Dunphy, *Morgenatler, a difficult hero*, (Toronto: Random House of Canada, 1996), pp. 64-65

[3] Alphonse de Valk, *Morality and Law in Canadian Politics: The Abortion Controversy* (Montreal: Palm Publsihers, 1974), p. 9

[4] Ibid. p. 11

[5] Ibid. p. 23

[6] Ibid. p. 52

[7] Other members of the CMA delegation who admitted to performing illegal abortions were Dr. Douglas Cannell of Toronto, Dr. Aitken, and Dr. Gregg Tompkins of Halifax. The CMA delegation before the Commons Committee, interestingly, did not concur that the legalization of abortion would decrease the number of illegal abortions; Dr. Aitken stated that they had "no way of knowing what effect" the former would have on the latter, and Dr. Tompkins opined that legalization might not change the number of illegal abortions. (Ibid, p. 48.)

[8] Op. Cit., de Valk, p. 57

[9] It was John Turner, also a Catholic, who, as Justice Minister in the Trudeau government, reintroduced the Omnibus Bill in 1969.

[10] Op. Cit., Dunphy, p. 81

[11] Op. Cit., Morton, p. 34

[12] Ibid. pp. 34-35

[13] Ibid. p. 37

[14] Ibid. pp. 46-47

[15] Ibid. p. 49

[16] Peter Hopkins, The Morgentaler Case, (a verbatim report of an eyewitness present at the judicial proceedings in Montreal), (c. 1976, Campaign Life Archives), p. 3

[17] Op. Cit., Morton, p. 59

[18] At that time, an appeal court could "enter a verdict of guilty with respect to the offence of which, in its opinion, the accused should have been found guilty but for the error in law." This section of the Criminal Code (613, 4(b)(i)) was seldom used and its deployment politically risky, as in Morgentaler's case, writes Morton. The outcry that ensued after the Quebec Appeal Court's ruling was upheld by the Supreme Court, eventually resulted in an amendment to the Criminal Code, fittingly dubbed "The Morgentaler Amendment." Introduced by Justice Minister Otto Lang in July 1975, and passed into law some months later, the amendment proscribed the finding of a guilty verdict by an appeals court. If that court found that a jury verdict resulted from an error in law, it could set aside the verdict and order a new trial. (Morton, p. 59 and p. 82)

[19] Ibid. Morton, p. 56

[20] Ibid. p. 62

[21] Ibid. p. 75

[22] The majority included Justices Dickson, Pigeon, Marland, Ritchie, Beetz and de Grandpre. Those dissenting were Justices Laskin, Spence and Judgson.

[23] Ibid. Morton, p. 77

[24] Op. Cit., Dunphy, pp. 141-149

[25] Ibid. pp. 129-30, 138-140

[26] Op. Cit., Morton, p. 84

[27] Op. Cit., Hopkins, The Morgentaler Case

[28] Op. Cit., Morton, p. 86. It should be noted that in January of that year, the Professional Corporation of Physicians of Quebec suspended Morgentaler's license for one year. The corporation's disciplinary committee, after investigating a complaint against the abortionist, deplored "the almost complete lack of a case history as well as the failure to perform the necessary scientific tests…pregnancy test, blood tests" before performing abortions. Morgentaler did not bother to obtain "a pathological examination of the tissues he has removed, nor does he follow up the state of health of his patients after having performed the operation." The committee concluded that Morgentaler had "an attitude which is primarily directed to protecting his fees" – a behaviour that "confers a mercenary character on the doctor/patient relationship." (Judgement, The disciplinary committee of the Professional Corporation of Physicians of Quebec.) Morgentaler's medical practices had received public scrutiny earlier, when the abortionist complained in 1974 to the firm that manufactured the "vacurettes" used in vacuum abortions. He was annoyed that the newest model collapsed under pressure and could not be reused; his allegation upset the company because the disposable, $3.30 vacurettes were not intended to be reused, as doing so could potentially transmit such diseases as viral hepatitis, tetanus, venereal disease and gaseous gangrene. ("Morgentaler re-used instruments despite maker's warning," Tom Pawlick, *Montreal Gazette*, December 24, 1974.) The abortion doctor's fees received attention again during his Ontario trial in 1984, when it was revealed that typically, one abortion was done every 30 minutes, and in some cases, two in a half-hour period, at his Toronto abortuary. Morgentaler was then charging $300.00 for the "procedure." ("$300 abortion every half hour MDs' trial told," Bill Walker, *Toronto Star*, October 24, 1984.)

[29] "Abortion clinic gets permit, but opponents won't give up," *Winnipeg Free Press*, May 6, 1983, p. A8

Chapter 14

The trial begins

"...the multi-faceted elements that go to make up
the drama of this case...
are nothing more than tiny unborn children,
but at the same time
they are nothing less than
our families, our country and our future."
Morris Shumiatcher

NEARLY THIRTY-FIVE YEARS AFTER LEAVING HOME, JOE BOROWSKI returned to his home province. But the man who took his seat in a Regina courthouse on a chilly May day in 1983 was very different from the adventurous boy who shook the Saskatchewan dust from his feet, and whose restless wanderings cut a wide swathe across those vast tracts of land from Ontario to British Columbia. In those days, Joe spoke as readily with his fists as with his tongue.

He was still a fighter, and still driven by an unquenchable thirst for justice that more often than not took notice of the plight of others. But now he was a man refined by fasting, prayer and a deep commitment to the Catholic faith. He was a man who had suffered persecution for his convictions, who had willingly forfeited his career, who had, by default, sacrificed many of the pleasant associations with the comrades of his earlier life, who had endured the derision of the media, and the more subtle persecution by fellow Christians who were not as zealous as he, or who regarded his present quest as just plain wrong-headed.

And he was a man who, it seemed, was willingly joined in the most difficult battle of all: the struggle against himself, against those vices and prejudices and sins that marred God's marvelous creation.

It might have been surprising for those who knew only the public persona of Joe Borowski, but those who knew him better called him a humble man, who readily admitted his faults and who often felt remorse for the rough and ready ways of his tongue and the impatience that sometimes erupted in the face of the provocations and unwelcome constraints of daily life.

When Alliance Against Abortion was formed in 1973, the founding members recognized that the pro-life struggle had an added dimension, recalled Bob MacKalski, a Polish-Canadian like Joe. "[W]e thought that, actually, this was a spiritual warfare," he explained. Therefore, they resolved to try and "have our lives in as good a state spiritually as we could." And with that, "we all improved, I suppose, our lives—not that we had anything to hide."

As was typical, MacKalski recalled, "Joe tended to go an inch or a mile further than any of us. Joe then started to fast entirely all day long Friday…that's each and every Friday. And even if we went out at night, Joe would only break the fast with a glass of water." Joe already attended Mass daily and he began to study the teachings of the Church.

Such was the manner of man who returned to his boyhood province, to where, not but 200 kilometres from the Borowski family farm, the quest into which he had poured his life's energies for the last ten years was to be placed before those who had been selected by the Canadian government to dispassionately administer to her citizens that highly-prized quality of justice.

That the state extend justice to the unborn child was the issue that Joe Borowski, through the dapper and eloquent Morris Shumiatcher, put with urgency before the courts.

About 50 curious spectators and supportive well-wishers crammed into the Court of Queen's Bench courtroom. Outside, picketers from a group styled Citizens for Reproductive Choice sloshed through the wet snow to show their opposition to the proceedings.

Members of the media were also very much in evidence at the trial; among these was renowned Saskatchewan poet and playwright Andras Tahn, who had been dispatched to the Regina courthouse to cover the momentous trial for the Catholic magazine *Our Family*. Tahn penned a vivid description of the major players of these dramatic proceedings.[1] As well as Queen's Counsel Shumiatcher, who, garbed in the black robe of the court and with a generous grey beard, "reminded one of a friendly gnome from a classic fairy tale," the legal team representing Joe Borowski included the 25-year-old Brad Hunter and "the efficient Barbara Henning." Joe himself, "always neatly dressed in a three-piece suit and a tie fastened with a little silver cross, sat behind his legal counsels."

The "Shumiatcher entrance" was generally carried out with such flourish that the spectators gathered "felt sure they were attending a significant event in modern Canadian history." In sharp contrast, "the arrival of Queen's Counsel Edward Sojonky and his young assistant, Mike Kindrachuk from the Department of Justice in Saskatoon, was always subdued."[2] Moreover, the "tall, lean and clean-shaven" Sojonky and his aide seldom looked up during the proceedings to scan either the witness or the judge. "Their taciturn manner became the topic of conversation for the press gallery during a few of the morning coffee breaks as we stood about in the hallways," wrote Tahn.

But during one of these breaks, Edward Sojonky demonstrated that, while he missed few opportunities to batter the Borowski case in the courtroom, he certainly bore no animosity towards the plaintiff, and was capable of breaking out of his serious mien when the occasion required. He and Joe Borowski met, shook hands "and began to chuckle, chatting and exchanging pleasantries," Tahn described, and further speculated: "Their similar backgrounds (they are both originally from southern Saskatchewan) may have contributed to their personal warmth toward each other."[3]

The presiding judge was Justice William Matheson, who had

been appointed a superior court justice only a year earlier. A burly family man in his 40s, father of two children and step-father of two, he was sparing with his comments.

Three groups—Campaign Life Canada, the Canadian Civil Liberties Association and the Canadian Abortion Rights Action League—had in January of that year requested permission to intervene in the trial but had been turned down.[4] Right-to-abort supporters protested their exclusion by parading in front of the courthouse wearing cloth gags over their mouth. Joe Borowski was not impressed, noting to the press that the majority of the protesters were from the United Church of Canada, "which I find shocking. Perhaps they should change their name to the Aborted Church of Canada."[5]

Morris Shumiatcher briefly outlined the history of the lawsuit: Joe Borowski objected to the 1969 amendments to the Criminal Code which allowed for abortion under certain conditions as "repugnant to the right to life conferred upon every individual historically, by section of the Canadian Bill of Rights as it existed when the action was started."[6] He observed that the Minister of Justice "has admitted that more than 1,000 abortions are performed in Canada each week"—a total of nearly 65,000 abortions each year.

Joe was also seeking an order of the court preventing the Minister of Finance from allotting any funds towards provincial health budgets that would pay for abortions.

Because of the unusual delay resulting from the legal questions of jurisdiction and standing, the Charter had come into effect before the case came to trial. The Borowski Statement of Claim was then amended to invoke the Charter. The plaintiff claimed that the therapeutic abortion provisions of Section 251 of the Code "deny the unborn child" Charter rights "in at least four significant areas.

- Children in the womb are denied "the right to life, and the right not to be deprived of life except in accordance with the principles of fundamental justice—Section 7."
- They are also denied "the right not to be subjected to cruel and unusual punishment—Section 12."
- "Denied the unborn children is the right to have someone speak for them before the committee, whose actions almost

invariably result in the issue of a certificate that terminates their life—Section 14."

- And finally, "denied unborn children also is equality before and under the law, and equal protection under the law with out discrimination because of their age—Section 15." (Shumiatcher conceded that this last right would not become enforceable until April 17, 1985.)

Section 251 of the Criminal Code, he said, was silent "concerning the life and health of the unborn child and we contend that if that child is someone, anyone, it is our position that he must also be considered before it is decided to destroy him, or destroy her…These little children are not so small or insignificant we say, that the Canadian Charter of Rights and Freedoms has ignored or forgotten them."[7]

Shumiatcher was "conscious of the very heavy responsibility" he and his associates had in presenting this difficult and important issue to the Court, and they were determined to "fully and fairly present the multi-faceted elements that go to make up the drama of this case. In a sense, those elements are nothing more than tiny unborn children but at the same time they are nothing less than our families, our country and our future."[8]

The evidence of intrauterine life from testimony of various medical experts would assist Justice Matheson in determining whether the unborn child is "anyone" within the meaning of Section 7 of the Charter. "In this case we shall be embarking upon a voyage of discovery…a voyage into the distant stages of our early life," Shumiatcher told the crowded courtroom; a life "that modern science and medicine are now charting with such precision that fancy is being overtaken by fact…. This evidence will be submitted to demonstrate the personality of the unborn child, each unique, and each curiously and wondrously wrought."[9]

Earlier in the proceedings, Crown lawyer Edward Sojonky, who represented the defendants, the attorney-general of Canada and the Minister of Finance of Canada, had objected to Shumiatcher's request to call nine expert witnesses, rather than the maximum of five permitted by Saskatchewan law.

Evidence pertaining to "the meaning of life or perhaps when life begins" was not relevant or admissible, he argued, and therefore no expert witnesses were needed to expound on this point. The question of when life begins was a legal problem: "Whether fetal life or the fetus is a human being, is not a justiciable issue." To listen to evidence regarding intrauterine life would result in "the Court acting as a forum, a commission almost, to ascertain what the law should be"—in effect, a "questioning of Parliament's power."[10]

Sojonky also argued that precedent in Canadian law had determined that the unborn child was not included in the terms such as "person, individual or everyone."[11] Birth is "the line of demarcation at which personhood is realized, at which full and independent legal rights attach."

No court had yet ruled the definition of "everyone" Justice Matheson observed, "in light of the entrenched rights and freedoms guaranteed by the Charter of Rights."[12] The plaintiffs cited the famous "Persons" case—the 1929 Supreme Court decision that women were not "persons" under the law, which was reversed the following year by the Judicial Committee of the Privy Council. "Is that not exactly the same situation we are faced with here?" queried the judge. "Assuming that we are talking about Section 7 of the Charter, are we not faced with the question, does 'everyone' include...unborn children?"[13]

Sojonky contended that the Crown's view was that Parliament "did not wish to have the unborn included in the term 'everyone'" in Section 7.

Shumiatcher argued that with the advent of the Charter, "we are in a different forum." The question before the court was, are the abortion provisions of the Criminal Code in conflict with "the higher law of Canada"—the Charter. "And that is," the lawyer pointed out gravely, "under our constitution, a matter peculiarly and exclusively reserved for this Court."[14]

Sojonky persisted in his objections to the expert witnesses, but Justice Matheson seemed sympathetic to the motion, particularly as the cases the Crown lawyer cited to support his arguments had been decided prior to the Charter. When Sojonky asserted that "we can all anticipate" the medical evidence, the judge replied, "Maybe you can but I don't know how I can without even knowing who these people are."

With that, Sojonky gave up. "I have nothing to add."[15] Shumiatcher was granted permission to call all nine witnesses.

The first witness was Dr. Donald Carnduff, medical director of the second largest hospital in Saskatchewan, the Regina General Hospital. He brought with him minutes of the Therapeutic Abortion Committee (TAC), and a random sampling of cases of applications reviewed by the committee.

Scarcely had Shumiatcher begun questioning the witness as to the workings of the committee at his hospital than Sojonky objected on the grounds that the documents were personal in nature and entering them into the court record was potentially an attack on the privacy of the women involved. This objection was overruled; it was, nevertheless, agreed that any personal medical documents entered into the record would have the name of the patient deleted.

It was Shumiatcher's intention to ascertain just what consideration was given to the applications and what came before the abortion committee.[16] But as it turned out, Carnduff, while he oversaw the committee in his capacity as medical director, was not a member of the committee and often seemed at a loss to answer the lawyer's questions. Nevertheless, as counsel for the plaintiff and the witness methodically examined the documents Carnduff provided, it became apparent that the TAC functioned merely as a rubber-stamp.

In 1982, the committee approved 447 abortions out of a total of 460 applications—95 per cent. The reasons cited were medical, psychiatric, or socio-economic. Dr. Carnduff admitted that the largest percentage of abortions were done for socio-economic reasons, next for psychiatric, and lastly, for medical reasons.[17] He recounted that members of the committee were required only to accept or reject the application, but were not required to indicate the reason why. That was left for the chairman to determine.[18] The committee, testified Dr. Carnduff, generally relied on two or three letters of reference, from the attending physician, and from the doctor who would be performing the abortion, or from a psychiatrist, or both.[19] The certificates were usually signed by Carnduff, even though he was not a member of the committee. The certificate stated that in the opinion of the committee, the continuation of the pregnancy would, or would be likely to, endanger the woman's life or health.[20]

The criteria of medical, psychiatric or socio-economic reasons "are all presumably regarded as part of the concept of the health of the mother," commented Shumiatcher. Had the committee adopted any standard of health?

They had no definition of the word, responded the doctor, nor was one provided in the Criminal Code. The only legal definition available was that of the World Health Organization, which he could not recall precisely, "but it goes something to the effect that health shall be defined as a sense of physical, mental and social well being."[21]

"Do you think any of us in this room would qualify as being healthy on the basis of that definition?"

"No, sir."

Is it possible, Shumiatcher asked, to define health in a meaningful way? "I think that it is possible depending on what you wish to accomplish by a definition," replied the physician. Medical and psychiatric health reasons could be defined fairly well; "I am not too sure about the socio-economic definitions. I am not just too sure where they fit in."

"Would that be within the field of a medical doctor as far as you know?"

"The first two certainly are."

"I am talking about socio-economic particularly," clarified Shumiatcher.

"I think that is probably in the realm of the politicians."

Shumiatcher went through several cases, querying his witness on a number of points, and frequently provoking the ire of Sojonky, who objected that Carnduff was not qualified to answer the questions: "It's not fair, not fair."

"Well, that is what this case is all about, isn't it?" quickly rejoined Shumiatcher, "If you will be fair to the unborn child, I will be fair to the witness."[22]

He stopped at the application of M.B., wherein the doctor wrote that the pregnancy should be "terminated" firstly because "it was a contraceptive failure." Asked Shumiatcher, "Would that have anything to do with the patient's life or health?"

"I don't know. It is one of four items." The other items listed were that the mother had two children already and "couldn't afford a third." Thirdly, she had no man to support her, and fourthly, she was a university student and a new baby "will be in her way to study."[23]

Later, Shumiatcher revisited the contraceptive question when examining in detail the application for a "therapeutic abortion." This form included a question as to whether contraceptive failure had occurred.[24] Why would it make any difference to the life or health of the mother if she became pregnant because of a contraceptive failure, he wondered—could the doctor enlighten the Court about the significance of this? Carnduff could not; he had no further information than that included on the application, other than the general comment that doctors routinely "ask lots of questions."

"Well, do the members of the committee believe that if there were a contraceptive failure a better case would then be made out for an abortion than if there had been no contraceptive use at all?"

"I can't speak for the committee," the witness said.[25]

Was it customary for the Therapeutic Abortion Committee "to see the girl or the woman that is requesting the abortion?"

No, came the answer, but occasionally the committee might request a psychiatric consultation if it "feels that there may be a psychiatric overlay."[26]

Were there any cases where an examination was made "concerning the unborn fetus or child?" asked the lawyer for the plaintiff. No. After the abortion, a pathologist examined the tissue and verified whether or not there were "products of conception" and that in fact, an abortion did take place.[27]

"Would you say then, that under these circumstances, the hospital is more concerned with the dead baby than the live baby?" questioned Shumiatcher.

"There have been a number of leading questions," interjected Sojonky. "Why don't you ask him a non-leading question for a change?"

Justice Matheson concurred. "Well, certainly that last one was leading, Dr. Shumiatcher."

"Yes, I think it was," twinkled the Q.C., "I will withdraw it, My Lord. It was more rhetoric than anything else, I confess."[28]

Shumiatcher questioned Carnduff about the type of abortions done at the hospital. The witness testified that no "therapeutic" abortions were done after the 12th week of pregnancy, and any done after that time were for "a serious threat to the patient's life, rather than to their health," and certainly not for socio-economic reasons.[29] He testified that the abortions were done by the suction curettage method but could not describe it. Abortions by saline solution were proscribed because of the high complication rate.[30] Abortions after 12 weeks were done by injection of various drugs into the uterus; what the drugs were, he did not know.

Crown lawyer Sojonky then briefly cross-examined the witness, who clarified that there was no fee schedule for the abortion as such, but it was included in the hospital budget for outpatient services.

Press reports caught the gist of Carnduff's testimony. *Globe and Mail* reporter Richard Cleroux summarized neatly the proceedings: "By the end of the afternoon, Mr. Borowski's lawyer had established that there is no formal meeting of the Regina General abortion committee; that the authorization forms are signed by Dr. Carnduff and not the members of the committee; that the women involved are never interviewed by the committee; that last year at the hospital there were 477 applications for abortions, of which 460 were granted; that the great majority of these were for socio-economic reasons and not for medical reasons, and that any question of the rights of the fetus was never taken into account by the committee."[31]

The next witness called was Dr. William Liley, a professor in perinatology from Auckland, New Zealand, who had developed the method of prenatal diagnosis known as amniocentesis. Called the Father of Fetology for his contributions to the research and care of the baby in the womb, William Liley was knighted in 1973 and, although not a Catholic, was a member of the Pontifical Academy of Sciences, the oldest and most exclusive science academy in the world.[32]

He was called as an expert witness in the field of perinatal medicine. In response to Shumiatcher's detailed and probing questions, the white-haired New Zealander graciously charted the course of intrauterine (within the womb) life, from the moment of conception, to the journey of the "conceptus" (a small ball of cells resembling a mulberry) in its protective membrane down the mother's Fallopian tube, where it attaches itself into the wall of her uterus, through to its astounding development and growth, until the time arrives when the baby exits the womb—a departure orchestrated by the baby itself, and to whose command the mother's body must comply.[33]

Shumiatcher several times queried if the baby was a separate being from the mother, to which Sir Liley replied in the affirmative. "They are independent individuals but whose tissues are in contact," explained the world-renowned physician.[34] In fact, mother and baby are aware of each other's foreignness and exist in a situation of "armed neutrality" in which the placenta (that is, the protective sac in which the baby lives and which is an organ of the baby) forms a "frontier" of contact between them.[35]

It is the fetus who is in "command" of the pregnancy, who solves his or her "important environmental problems" such as preventing his mother's next menstrual period, Liley told the courtroom. "And this is a remarkable performance when you realize that at this stage the conceptus is little more than the size of a grain of sugar…and yet must influence a mother weighing over a thousand million times more."[36]

In the first weeks of life, the baby's growth is explosive: 90 per cent of the development of the human organism, in a biological sense, occurs during this interlude—what remains will take place outside the womb during infancy, childhood, and adolescence. The fertilized ovum divides into two cells, these into four, the four into eight, and so on, until a total is reached of 30 million million cells, of which the adult human body is comprised. This is accomplished by 45 cell divisions, Dr. Liley explained. Forty-one of these cell divisions are complete by the time we exit the womb.

Dr. Liley, who pioneered remarkable feats done *in utero*, such as blood transfusions for babies affected by Rh factor, explained that by 28 days from conception—at which time the mother might still be unaware she is pregnant—the baby "has a brain, eyes, structures of the inner ear, a liver…kidney rudiments and a heart pumping blood."[37]

But despite the astonishing rate of development in the hours, days and weeks immediately following conception, after that beginning, the life of the unborn child is simply a continuum, he observed. "There is no particularly arbitrary point in it where anything dramatic or different happens. It is just part of an ongoing stream, and although one uses terms like zygote or morula or blastocyst or embryo or fetus, one uses these no more technically or more self-consciously than you would talk about someone being a newborn or an infant or a toddler or an adolescent."[38]

But in much of the evidence, "you were talking about mother and baby," noted Shumiatcher. Why was that? "I have yet to meet any woman, sir, who is expecting anything other than a baby as a result of her pregnancy," was the somewhat dry reply.

Delving further into the area of semantics, Shumiatcher asked what was meant by the phrase "terminating a pregnancy." That is a "careless use of words," responded Liley. Pregnancy does not continue indefinitely, and is "self-terminating." It would be more accurate to refer to "artificial" termination of pregnancy.

Even there, the distinction must be noted between pregnancy, the state, and baby, the entity. In the case of an Rh baby, for instance, a pregnancy might be terminated in a later stage but "we would energetically strive and probably succeed in guaranteeing the survival of the baby." In early pregnancy, however, "this distinction is willfully confused," the doctor testified, and "what one is talking about is strictly not the termination of pregnancy but more particularly the extermination of the baby."[39]

Similarly, the term "therapeutic abortion" refers to a procedure that is not therapeutic for the baby "by any stretch of the imagination" testified the fetologist. It was used, in his view, because it is doctors who carry out abortions.

"And you say it has nothing to do with the baby's therapy?" asked Dr. Shumiatcher.

"Not to my understanding of the word therapy, sir. It has never been a tenet of medical practise that we will kill anything we can't cure."

"And insofar as the mother is concerned, do you say the same thing?"

"Yes, sir." Liley explained that advances in medicine had made it possible to ensure the safety of the mother despite conditions that would formerly have constituted "major hazards to maternal life and health."[40]

In fact, the situation today is "paradoxical" in that "women with the strangest conditions and most serious disorders that you can imaging are having babies—this is the safety of modern obstetrics" while on the other hand, women "with little or nothing wrong with them" are requesting abortion because their child "represents an inconvenience. Naturally," continued the witness, "abortion is safer the healthier the woman you do it in. In other words, the more unnecessary the abortion, the safer it is."[41]

But, he repeated, even if a mother was suffering a serious illness, if she wanted the baby, it was expected that the pregnancy could be successfully managed to ensure her safety, although the outcome for the baby might not be so guaranteed.[42]

It could be observed that continuation of the pregnancy does not represent a threat to the mother—the threat is, rather, "the survival of the child." Thus, Liley objected to the use of the term "therapeutic" in reference to abortion: "one is using the skill and indeed the terminology of medicine to deal with social and economic problems."[43]

Had the doctor ever come across a pregnancy that, if it continued, did in fact "endanger the life or health of the mother and for that reason had to be terminated?" asked Shumiatcher. Not only had he not, Liley responded, but one of his colleagues had deposited 500 New Zealand pounds in the bank, "to be claimed by the first person who could present a pregnancy in which termination was necessary to preserve the life of the mother." The money remained uncollected.[44]

Continuing his discussion of semantics, Shumiatcher remarked that sometimes the unborn child is referred to as a "potential human being." What, he asked the witness, does that phrase mean? "Very little," replied Liley, adding that the phrase is not a biological or medical term, but a metaphysical one. If one wished to philosophize, "which of us would be arrogant enough to say that we have fulfilled all our potential yet?"

But apart from the realm of achievement, "life," patiently explained the doctor, "as we deal with it in biology and medicine...exists only as an attribute of living matter, and in those terms we can define when a human life begins and when it ends, and in between it doesn't develop or grow, it is simply there. What does develop or grow is the physical structure."[45]

What about, persisted counsel for the plaintiff, the phrase "unwanted child." Did the witness have anything to say about that?[46] It would, observed Liley wryly, be more accurate to speak of "unwanting or rejecting parents." Moreover, it seems "quite unfair" that the child is stigmatized because it is unwanted. "After all, we do not blame stolen goods for being stolen." But to use the term "unwanting parents" might "be holding the mirror up perhaps too firmly where it belongs, so it is easier to attach the epithet to the child or baby who is in no position to answer—to attack the fetus."[47]

Lethal for the unborn child, abortion presents hazards for the mother as well, the kindly knight told the Court. "Acute complications" from abortion include but are not limited to "hemorrhage, local tissue damage, uterine perforation and infection or combinations of these." Long-term consequences are infertility, as well as greater susceptibility to miscarriage or premature labour, and "blood group sensitization", the most common being Rh sensitization.

And while he was not the most competent witness in the area, Liley also pointed out that there were "long-term psychiatric *sequelae*" resulting from abortion, women who "are now distraught and have more than sentimental regret of having parted with their baby... The idea that a pregnancy is an event which can, as it were, be expunged from the record—that is not the way nature works," he testified. "As someone remarked...God always forgives, man sometimes and nature never. Unfortunately, it is nature we are dealing with here."[48]

As well as painting a picture of intrauterine life with his elegant descriptions, the fetologist provided a slide presentation for the attentive Court. One gruesome image depicted the severed remains of a 12-week-old aborted baby, a "macabre jig-saw puzzle" in which one could recognize the components of a human fetus, albeit eviscerated and dismantled: limbs, eye, brain, torso, "all have become detached." This slide and others were entered as exhibits; the Court adjourned for the day.

Next morning, Crown lawyer Edward Sojonky swung into action for his cross-examination, having, he said, "a few bones to pick" with the renowned doctor. The lawyer sought a clarification from the physician that the latter believed there were no circumstances in which an abortion would be necessary. Liley countered that such might possibly be necessary in the case of the treatment for pelvic cancer, or in treating an ectopic pregnancy, but in these instances "the unborn happens to get in the way of an act performed for some other...good" and so they would "differ very much from the abortions that people are normally talking about."[49]

Sojonky then took issue with the idea that the unborn child is in command of the pregnancy. What role, then, did the mother play?

"You have just described it, sir, she is the child's mother."[50]

But, persisted Sojonky, "from your evidence, the poor mother is a minority partner." "No, sir. She happens to be a bigger partner. She is no less, or no more and no less a living partner than the other one, party concerned, the unborn child."[51]

A very large bee in the bonnet of the Crown lawyer, and an issue which he circled around and around and returned to again and again with all the persistence of such an insect, was the question: when does the baby in the womb become a "human being"? Even Liley's colleagues could not reach agreement on this point, he suggested to the witness. Some physicians allege they know when life begins, but admit that they cannot determine "when the group of cells becomes a human being."

The witness did not argue the point, but noted that the views in question "alter quite strikingly with circumstance." He elaborated with this story: The teaching films on prenatal life used by his hospital in the '50s and '60s, which came from Europe, the U.K., the U.S.A. and Canada, had as technical advisors the top obstetrical and gynecological specialists in their respective countries.[52] All the films unambiguously and unequivocally taught that a new life begins at the moment of conception, the point at which the ovum is penetrated by the sperm. But that was "before abortion became a social issue," Liley said. Ten or 15 years later, some of these same specialists had abandoned this view, and were "now redefining when life begins." It was his opinion, the witness said, that they had done so in order to justify abortion.

In biological and scientific terms, he asserted, there is no dispute as to when life begins.

"At conception?" asked Sojonky.

"Exactly."

But, the Crown lawyer said, the divergence of opinion is not about when life begins, but when that "group of cells ...becomes a human being."

While Liley conceded that there was an array of views on this question, he spoke clearly of the dangers of this state of affairs. A survey of health professionals in California had elicited a wide range of responses to the question as to when human life begins, he told the Court. Some thought conception, some implantation, others thought live birth, some even thought human life commenced with the ability to communicate by speech.[53]

The concern with such results "isn't just the astonishing arbitrariness of it," Liley emphasized, but "the significance of the disqualification which is to be attached to you if you haven't yet reached the approved age...your life may be arbitrarily forfeit.

Sojonky took another tack. He recalled Liley's description of the conceptus, which begins as one cell. "When does the cell become a baby?" he asked.[54] The common view, responded Liley, was "when one has a recognizable embryo." His view was "based on the fact that once a woman knows she is pregnant, she knows she is expecting a baby and nothing else."

"And when does the cell become a baby, Dr. Liley?" repeated Sojonky.

"It is not a question strictly answerable medically; it is only answerable in human terms."

Then, persisted Sojonky, would it not follow that the question as to when the cell becomes a human being, was also not a medical question?

The cell, rejoined Liley, "is a living human organism."

But "we are really unable to say when the cell becomes a human being, aren't we?" Sojonky queried, "It is a philosophical [and] theological question, isn't it?"[55]

"That applies to humans at any age and in any condition sir," countered the witness. "It is not a problem peculiar to early human life."

"But given what you have said with regard to when the cell does or does not become a baby, you are really unable to assist me and the Court...as to when the cell becomes a human being. It really is the same question, isn't it?" pressed Sojonky.

"No, sir. My point was that it is simply a continuance of existence and development of an individual and as such, it is not possible to put arbitrary divisions on it."

"When does the cell become an individual?"

"At fertilization," Liley patiently responded. At conception, "it is now genetically distinct and a separate individual from its mother."

"I see," the Crown lawyer said, "An individual, but it is not a baby?"

"Not yet, sir, no, nor a teen-ager or anything else."

Sojonky considered: "And we must go further afield, beyond the medical field to determine at what point it is a baby or a human being, don't we?"

"Yes, sir."[56]

Sojonky had other questions for the doctor about his terminology. "Would you agree with me, when you speak of exterminating the baby or killing the baby, those are emotional terms and not medical terms?"[57]

"No, sir, not at all," Liley responded. But apparently, he observed, the "deliberate taking of the life of the baby must not be referred to as an extermination or killing."

Some doctors, pursued Sojonky, "must not consider the termination of pregnancy as being extermination."

They "evade the point rather than deny it," came the rejoinder.

"Are you suggesting that all doctors who perform abortions believe that they are killing babies?" Sojonky enquired.

"They must be conscious of it sir, they prefer not to admit it likely."

When Sojonky pressed him again, Liley was firm: "I cannot imagine that they don't believe it sir, I agree that they don't admit."[58]

At the beginning of his cross-examination, Sojonky was at pains to gain an admission from the witness that his personal belief was that abortion was morally wrong. "Not just simply morally," replied Liley, "but logically wrong also...insofar as professionally, I care for, I look after, I treat babies before birth."[59]

As his grilling drew to a close, Sojonky again returned to the question of morality, reminding the witness of his comment that abortion "was immoral and criminal and arbitrary."

"It would represent a policy which came under those terms if practised in any other age group, sir," retorted Liley.

"And by using the term immoral you concede, Dr. Liley, that a moral issue is involved, is interwoven throughout this, isn't it?"

"It is in all medical care, sir."

With that, Sojonky completed his questioning.

Justice Matheson, who had turned to face the witnesses and had listened attentively to the long and detailed testimony and cross-examination,[60] now had his own questions. Once again, the Father of Fetology was called upon to clarify what conditions "would constitute a threat to the mother's life or health." It seemed to the judge that on his first day of testimony, the doctor was unaware of such conditions, but gave a different response to Edward Sojonky.

Again the knight sought to explain that he was making the distinction between an abortion where the purpose was the termination of a pregnancy, "whether or not one accepts the qualification, extermination of a baby" and other situations such as an ectopic pregnancy or independent treatment of pelvic cancer. "There the purpose of the act is not primarily abortion at all, it happens to technically be one in pursuit of other medical treatment. But where the primary purpose of an abortion is an abortion, I am not aware of any medical field complications that justifies this."[61]

After a few more questions, Sir Liley was dismissed. Without further ado, Shumiatcher called his next witness.

Notes
Chapter 14
The trial begins

[1] Among Tahn's well-known productions was the hit show *Paper Wheat*. His articles on the trial were later published as a booklet, *A Case of Life and Death: the Trial of the Century* (Battleford, Saskatchewan: Oblate Fathers of St. Mary's Province, Marian Press, 1983 and 1984).

[2] Op. Cit., Tahn, p. 12.

[3] Ibid. p. 10.

[4] "Abortion case 'most important' since Riel Trial" *Regina Leader-Post*,
May 6, 1983.

[5] "Pro-choice supporters draw Borowski's wrath," *Saskatoon Star Phoenix*,
May 18, 1983, p. 3.

[6] *Trial for Life*, Vol. 1 and II [Trial transcripts] (Winnipeg: Alliance Against Abortion, 1984), p. 127.

[7] Ibid. p. 128.

[8] Ibid. p. 127.

[9] Ibid. p. 128.

[10] Ibid. pp.106-107.

[11] Ibid. p. 111.

[12] Ibid. p. 112.

[13] Ibid. p. 113.

[14] Ibid. p. 114.

[15] Ibid. p. 124.

[16] Ibid. p. 133.

[17] Ibid. p. 156.

[18] Ibid.

[19] Ibid. p. 139.

[20] Ibid. p. 138.

[21] Ibid. p. 158.

[22] Ibid. p. 143.

[23] Ibid. pp. 147-148.

[24] Ibid. p. 160.

[25] Ibid.

[26] Ibid. p. 149.

[27] Ibid.

[28] Ibid. p.150.

[29] Ibid. p. 162.

[30] Ibid. p. 163.

[31] "Abortion law called rights violation," Richard Cleroux, *Globe and Mail*,
May 10, 1983.

[32] Op. Cit., *Trial for Life*. p. 170.

[33] Ibid. p. 207 and 211.

[34] Ibid. p. 173.

[35] Ibid. pp. 174 and 177.

[36] Ibid. p. 189.
[37] Ibid. p. 190.
[38] Ibid. p. 211.
[39] Ibid. p. 212.
[40] Ibid. p. 188.
[41] Ibid. p. 222.
[42] Ibid. p. 213.
[43] Ibid.
[44] Ibid. p. 214.
[45] Ibid.
[46] Ibid. p. 215.
[47] Ibid.
[48] Ibid. pp. 225 and 226
[49] Ibid. p. 241.
[50] Ibid. p. 243.
[51] Ibid. p. 244.
[52] Ibid. p. 249.
[53] Ibid. p. 247, Nutsan, University of California at Berkeley.
[54] Ibid. p. 248.
[55] Ibid. p. 249.
[56] Ibid.
[57] Ibid. p. 248.
[58] Ibid.
[59] Ibid. p. 239.
[60] Op. Cit., Tahn, p.22
[61] Op. Cit., *Trial for Life*, p. 252.

Chapter 15

The Trial Continues

"After years of agitating, advocating, writing
and arm-twisting, there wasn't even
a hint of any possibility of any change
either provincially or federally and that
is why we are in court today."
Joe Borowksi

THE NEXT WITNESS WAS A YOUNG WOMAN OF 27 YEARS WHO TESTIFIED about her experience when she became pregnant at age 16. The witness, referred to as Mrs. K. to protect her identity, said her mother told her to have an abortion and, in fact, wrote a letter to the family doctor requesting it.

She herself was utterly confused. "…I didn't know what I wanted. I was scared. I really didn't know. You know, I was confused. I was a kid. I didn't know." No one counseled her, she testified, about the possible ill effects of an abortion, either physical or psychological.[1]

She saw a Dr. Sollars within a week. He booked an abortion for the next day, but called that evening to tell her she needed the signatures of two physicians or the abortion would not be done. Her own doctor refused to sign; she obtained a signature from her boyfriend's physician.

On the day she was booked for the abortion, Mrs. K.'s boyfriend dropped her off at the General Hospital at 8:00 in the morning. She was in a room with eight to 10 beds in it. Four other women were there, waiting for abortions. At twenty-minute intervals, one would be wheeled away. When it was her turn, Mrs. K. was given general anesthetic. When she came to, she had cramps and was bleeding. She was discharged by noon, and other than a check-up six weeks later, she never saw Dr. Sollars again, she told the Court.

Six and a half years later, while living common-law with the man she subsequently married, Mrs. K. became pregnant. She carried her baby for about 33 weeks before going into premature labour. She delivered a baby girl, Nicole Lee-Ann, who developed respiratory distress syndrome the next day and died a week later.[2]

Mrs. K. conceived again in 1980, but again went into premature labour, this time when she was five months pregnant. She gave birth to Allen, who weighed a pound and a half and who lived an hour and twenty minutes.

In July of 1981, she was 12 weeks into her third pregnancy since the abortion when she started bleeding. Mrs. K. called her doctor. "I really didn't want to go to the General because it was getting to the point that every time I went in there I never came home with a baby," she testified. She went instead to her doctor's office, where he managed to stop the bleeding and advised her to go home and stay off her feet for a couple of days. But she miscarried two days later.[3]

At this point, she and her husband investigated the possibility of adoption, but because she was able to conceive, the wait was at least five years.

"Do you see any relationship," asked Shumiatcher, "between this sad story of how you had these births, all ending in disaster—did that in your view have anything to do with the abortion you first had when you were sixteen?"

"Yeah, I think it has everything to do with it." Mrs. K. replied, "I think psychologically very much so…when I delivered my first one you know…as soon as I looked at her I wondered what the other one would have been like." In her view, all that happened "is a way of paying me back for what I did to that one."

"What did you do?" Shumiatcher prompted.

"Well, I killed it literally, I took its life." Testifying about her experience, Mrs. K. explained, "maybe it is a way of—you know, like making—not—you will never make up, but, help, you know."

"Is that why you volunteered to come here today?"

"Yes, because I think with any young girl at sixteen, there is nothing more than confusion. You know a lot of these girls don't know and they don't realize what it will do to them later, psychologically especially."[4]

On the "cheerier side," as Shumiatcher noted, what has happened since?

"I'm pregnant again," Mrs. K. said. "I am just starting my fifteenth week. I go by weeks, forty weeks to have a baby and I am only in my fifteenth. I am due the same day my son was born, November 9."

Shumiatcher then turned the witness over to Crown lawyer Sojonky, who made it clear he was not the least bit interested in cross-examining Mrs. K., but did voice his opinion that the testimony was "not at all relevant." Justice Matheson agreed. After mulling over the matter during the mid-day break, the judge wished to clarify matters with counsel for the plaintiff. Was Shumiatcher going to call any further witnesses "of the nature of the last witness?" he asked.

"Oh, yes indeed."

"What relevance is that testimony to the matter—"

"Oh, the last witness?" Shumiatcher sounded surprised. "I'm sorry, you mean Mrs. K.? Oh no, no, that is the only one."

"I am inclined to agree with Mr. Sojonky," said the judge, "in that, the issue that I am required to determine is not in any way influenced by someone's conviction or someone's unfortunate experience one way or the other. That is not the question."

There would be no more witnesses of that type, Shumiatcher assured the judge. However, Mrs. K.'s testimony provided a "sampling of the relationship between that witness and the [Therapeutic Abortion] Committee. I think that is the relevant part."

The next witness was Joe Borowski. The questions established that Joe had not spoken out on the issue of abortion until he became embroiled in the controversy surrounding the Manitoba provincial funding for abortions performed in the States in the spring and summer of 1971, a controversy which culminated in his resignation from the NDP cabinet September 8, 1971.

After that, testified Joe, he spoke out about abortion on a number of "hot lines" and as a banquet speaker, and he also spoke out in the Legislature on the issue, whenever he had an opportunity to do so, which, he admitted was "not very often."[5] Moreover, he penned a barrage of letters over the years, so many that he had "lost track of the amount" but it was enough that "one could write a book, just from putting the letters together."

Counsel for the plaintiff began to read these letters into the record, the purpose being to establish the evidence for the allegations in Joe's Statement of Claim. After reading a number of letters to various politicians, Shumiatcher was interrupted by his learned friend, who questioned whether all this was necessary. Justice Matheson seconded the question. Well, replied Shumiatcher, for the sake of the media and others who had an interest in the letters, he thought that this was the best way to proceed.

Surely members of the press could look the letters up themselves, were they interested, the justice responded. The tenor was no doubt the same in all the missives. "May I use a little discretion?" asked Shumiatcher, adding that if "there is a choice line or two I would like to read to Your Lordship, I trust you will allow me to do that, My Lord."

"This is on the assumption that I can't read it myself?" gently questioned Justice Matheson.

"Not a bit, no sir, indeed no."

Shumiatcher continued, entering the letters Joe had sent to politicians such as Minister of Justice Otto Lang, Conservative leader Robert Stanfield, Prime Minister Pierre Trudeau, Finance Minister John Turner, as well as correspondence relating to Joe's decision not to file his taxes. Correspondence with the Canadian Medical Association was also entered as an exhibit.

Was there any response, asked Shumiatcher, any change to Section 251 of the Criminal Code as a result of all the letters Joe had written?

"No," replied Joe, "...after years of agitating, advocating, writing and arm-twisting, there wasn't even a hint of any possibility of any change either provincially or federally and that is why we are in court today. There was obviously not going to be any resolution through the political process."[6]

"You started out trying to work through the cabinet and then when you resigned, you wrote letters to officials, federally and provincially, and then you demonstrated, and then you went to jail and now, I see, that there is a letter here dated August 18, 1977, addressed by you to the Office of the Public Trustee in Winnipeg."[7]

This was one of Joe's final attempts, before joining up with Shumiatcher, to somehow get the matter of the abortion law before the courts. His lawyers at that time[8] had charged that the public trustee, the "guardian ad litem of the infants of this province," had a duty to challenge those provisions of the Criminal Code, which purport "to authorize in certain instances the carrying out of an assault upon the person of an unborn infant." The public trustee replied that he had no jurisdiction to launch such a challenge on behalf of unborn children, although "I am generally in concurrence with the views expressed in your letter."[9]

Joe's lawyers then sent the same request to Howard Pawley, attorney-general of Manitoba, whose pithy response was entered as evidence: "I do not propose to take the proceeding which you envision."[10]

They sought redress at the federal level. A letter was dispatched to the deputy attorney-general of Canada, suggesting that a Therapeutic Abortion Committee contravened the Criminal Code and the Canadian Bill of Rights. The only response they received from Mr. Roger Tassé was a request to be "apprised of any proceedings" Joe and his lawyers might take.

Shortly after this, Joe met with Shumiatcher and their plans were conceived, which later gave birth to the current proceeding. Joe also testified to his travails with Revenue Canada, which resulted in incarceration for the better part of 1979.[11]

Sojonky was remarkably brief in cross-examination, limiting himself to eight questions, the majority of which were directed towards establishing where Joe's business was located and what his tax-paying status was. Did he pay income tax, asked the Crown lawyer. "I personally do not pay taxes," but the family business, incorporated in 1977, paid all its taxes. As president of Borowski Health Foods, he did not take a salary and therefore did not need to pay any taxes.

As his penultimate question, Mr. Sojonky produced a non sequitur. "Why," he asked, "do you feel that Planned Parenthood Association is anti-life?"

Joe had read its literature and knew the organization in the States ran 81 abortion clinics, "and the only reason they are not doing it in Canada is simply because it is still illegal...they are in the forefront for pushing for liberalization of abortion."[12]

"Now, you believe abortion is murder, Mr. Borowski, correct?"

"Yes, I do."

With that, Joe Borowski left the stand and the Court adjourned for the day.

Notes
Chapter 15
The trial continues

[1] Ibid, *Trial for life*, p. 255.
[2] Ibid.
[3] Ibid. p. 259.
[4] Ibid. p. 261.
[5] Ibid. p. 265.
[6] Ibid. p. 272.
[7] Ibid. p. 276.
[8] Messrs. Christie, De Graves and MacKay of Winnipeg.
[9] Ibid. pp. 277-278.
[10] Ibid. p. 279.
[11] Ibid. p. 280.
[12] Ibid. p. 281.

Chapter 16

When does life begin?

*"I'm not speaking about my personal belief,
I'm speaking about facts."*
Dr. Jerome Lejeune

SPECTATORS WHO GATHERED IN THE COURTROOM THE NEXT DAY GAVE voice to an audible buzz when Shumiatcher called his next witness. It was the esteemed geneticist, Dr. Jerome Lejeune.[1] The world-renowned French scientist had discovered the cause of Down's syndrome—an extra chromosome in the DNA of those afflicted. This irregularity "disturb a little their ability and their mental capacity," explained the elegant geneticist, in his slightly imperfect English.

"It was the first abnormality in man to be related to a chromosomal aberration and it was, in fact, the start of a new chapter of human pathology," Lejeune elaborated. He and his team subsequently discovered over a quarter of the hundreds of syndromes related to chromosomal irregularities.

Lejeune, a professor of fundamental genetics at the René Descartes University, an adjunct of the University of Paris, also worked at the Sick Children's Hospital in Paris, the oldest such hospital in the world. There, he was in charge of the "consultation for the abnormal children, essentially for mentally retarded children due to genetic causes; and our consultation of those abnormal children is now the biggest of the world. We have more than three thousand children suffering from a chromosomal disease that we treat and we follow."

He was a member of a number of scientific academies, including the Pontifical Academy, and the recipient of several awards, among these, the Kennedy Award, which he received from the late president himself just scant months before Kennedy was assassinated.

Sporting a meticulously trimmed moustache and possessing a Gallic eloquence that made the previous witnesses appear almost taciturn by comparison, Prof. Lejeune explained to the Court that the genetic makeup possessed by all living matter is what gives such matter "the incentive, the direction and the possibility of developing itself according [to] so to speak, a printed pattern." Genetic makeup, the biological fundamentals of life, determines that "a cat will develop as a cat, a carrot as a carrot, an elephant as an elephant."

Genetic information "is written as a DNA according to a special code, just in the same way that the whole symphony can be translated into code by small chains of magnetics on the tape." Lejeune likened the chromosome to a "mini-cassette" in which the long strands of DNA are wound and coiled. Applying this analogy to the beginning of human life, Lejeune testified that when the 23 chromosomes from the sperm and the 23 from the ovum unite at fecundation, the fertilized egg becomes "the tape recorder, so to speak... The very moment that the mechanism is triggered, what is played is a new human life."

The 46 chromosomes of the newly conceived human life carry a "new constellation of genes which has never been produced and will never be reproduced again as such, for very simple statistical consideration, because the number of combinations is many orders of magnitudes greater than the number of human beings which have ever lived on this earth,"[2] thus, the new human being is "perfectly unique for his genetic endowment."[3] This endowment determines the colour of the eyes, the skin, and the hair, the "form of the nose, the form of the ears, and even it spells out the weak and the strong—the strongness, if I can say so—of the person."[4]

The last 12 years had witnessed a breakthrough in genetic

research, Lejeune told the Court. It was now possible to recognize various species by detailed mapping of the chromosomes.

Had this knowledge changed "the perception of life insofar as scientist are concerned, that is to say, as to the nature of life?" asked Shumiatcher.

It was more that the knowledge "confirmed all the fundamentals of life which were already known before," Lejeune testified. Scientist and philosopher René Descartes had posited, on purely logical grounds—in the absence of the existence of a half-man, half-animal creature—that "there must be laws written on the matter which define the species."

"You have methods of reasoning, you are sure of the logic," Lejeune observed, "but if you can look at it on a methodological ground, you are now very safe...So the reality was known, but since, I would say, the last fifteen, twelve years, the amount of demonstration is beyond any possible doubt."[5]

"Have there been," questioned Shumiatcher, "any new perceptions developed as to the beginning of life" as a result of this research?

"I don't think, My Lord, it has been new," was the response. It was always known intuitively; fifty years ago, no scientist questioned that what was growing in the womb was anything but a human being. In the last 20 years, however, a "very curious phenomenon...has occurred in the general perception of science." It appeared that this "inborn feeling of life was not agreeable to the people who wanted to make a grey zone around the beginning of life, so that you could eventually dispute what kind of thing was growing there."

The result is "an obscurity suddenly invading not science, but the expression of science and its perception by non-scientists that maybe we did not know really what was going on in the beginning. And that is very interesting...because it's purely psychological. It has nothing to do with the knowledge that we have severally about what are the fundamentals of life."[6]

Lejeune traced the development of the tiny human in the womb, referring to the photographs of *Life* magazine. With ultrasound it was observed that the four-month-old baby jumped at unexpected noise.[7] Two months after conception, "nature has provided already a filling on the upper lip because the building of the nervous system is made so that everything which is needed first is built first." What a newborn baby needed to do was to be able to suckle; the "innervation of the lips, of the tongue and of the muscle there" developed very early, and "that's the reason why at three months of age [the baby] begins to suck its thumb because he has already the neurological mechanism of suckling long before it is needed."

At an earlier age, 11 weeks after conception, the baby could be seen dancing in the womb. At that age, the baby's body contains a lot of water, so he "has relatively the same buoyancy as the fluid" in the amniotic sac and is not bound by gravity. "And then he has a slowness and a gentleness of movement that you cannot realize on another part of the earth, like a baby playing on a trampoline, so to speak, but he does it in a very elegant and very easy manner." To see a "trampoline-dance" by the baby, "full of youth and full of joy" was "a very refreshing input of science." But knowledge of the unborn child had been known by the "heart, the deep feeling of the mothers knew that, so to speak, intuitively," long before science made its contribution. Every country in its folklore had the story of Tom Thumb, commented Lejeune.

During our "obscure life" in the womb "we have enjoyed kinds of pleasures that we do not find when we are grown up" except in special situations—one of these, Lejeune said, would be a discothèque.

There, "you go underground, and you come under a vaulted shelter, where is a red, very dim light. The atmosphere is hot, sweaty and there are people there slowly moving or very rapidly jumping, and there is a terrible noise inside, a very strong noise which beats at around sixty per minute, which is a counter-bass and you feel that your chest is moved by the beating of the counter-bass." Heard against that sound was the "very rapid cadence of the maracas, which are around a hundred and fifty, a hundred and seventy, and which makes your head vibrate."

It might seem surprising that people actually like this scene—but they do.

"It's because, in a sense, they unconsciously remember there has been a time in which they were in a vaulted shelter, with a very dim red light, and there was again this very primitive music. One was the reassuring hammering of the heart of the mother around sixty, seventy [beats] per minute, and the other was the beginning of the career of their own heart, who is running at a hundred and fifty, hundred seventy.

"And if we look inside the uterus," continued Dr. Lejeune to his attentive listeners, "we can see that the thoracic cage of the baby is expanding and compressed by each hammering of the heart of the mother...and the head of the baby is vibrating at the cadence of his own heart."

It was not surprising to the biologist that the most primitive music "is always made with two rhythms: one big, low...one, and one high-pitched, rapid one, because it's a symphony of two hearts which is the earliest symphony any human here has heard, that everyone of us has heard."

He was not making use of "a kind of pseudo-poetry" in saying this, Lejeune testified, but "it's because it's deeply rooted in the human nature to feel that babies in the womb are really babies and we have still that memory, we grown-ups."

"That's a beautiful story," commented a rapt Shumiatcher.

"It's a true story," responded the witness. "It's not a story, it's nature."[8]

Lejeune gave the Court a detailed explanation of in vitro fertilization, mentioning Drs. Edwards and Steptoe, who were the first to engineer the conception and birth of "test-tube" babies. The British doctors successfully implanted a human embryo, conceived by the union of sperm and ovum in a petri dish, into the womb of Mrs. Brown. It was with the confidence that what they were implanting in her uterus was not a tumour or ordinary tissue, but could not be anything but "incredibly young, tiny human beings" that they proceeded.

"And nine months later, it was the very same little Louise Brown which came to the light because they had seen her when she was the smallest, tiny being any human can be," Lejeune said. "I would say that the *in vitro* fertilization has been the experimental demonstration that the life of tiny Louise Brown had begun at fecundation. And it is beyond any mystical, any metaphysical, any philosophical contention—that is, we have here the experimental demonstration in our species that human life and this very particular Louise life had begun at fecundation."[9] The technique also revealed, the doctor continued, "the very incredible and stupendous tenacity of the early human being to live" because at this point, the tiny life was a cluster of cells resembling a berry and enclosed in a protective sac (*zona pellucida*) and was only one millimeter and a half in diameter. Yet, "it can withstand a very enormous amount of mistreatment and still be alive and still continue its own destiny."[10]

"We are fast approaching 1984," remarked Shumiatcher, "and the wonderful world of George Orwell and Aldous Huxley and his *Brave New World*. What is there for us, or what can we learn from Huxley's imaginary world of tomorrow that would be relevant to the subject we've been discussing today?"

Admittedly, responded Lejeune, poets and writers see science better than scientists "because they see it from outside and so they see it coming" while the scientist, preoccupied with his research, can miss the greater implications of his discoveries. Huxley had a deep understanding of human nature, and offered profound insight in *Brave New World*, in which all human beings were created in test tubes, sex was only for recreation, and, the word that was banned from all literature and considered obscene in conversation was "mother."

"If this link between one generation and the next is broken," observed Lejeune, "then you are breaking really one of the fundamentals, not only of the society, but of the human feeling by itself."

"I'm sorry to speak about literature; I'm a geneticist," he added, but even more profound insights than that of Aldous Huxley are contained in the works of Wolfgang von Goethe, particularly in Dr. Faust. The first story of the doctor's damnation concerned "the story of the beloved—seduced, pregnant and...abandoned," recounted the witness. The second Faust built a technological empire and peopled it with small beings, after creating a "*homunculus*" in a test tube. Losing his mind, he destroyed his empire save for the small cabin where dwelled Philemon and Baucis, "the paragon of human love," who were finally destroyed, at Faust's request, by the devil Mephistopheles. "At that moment, sorrow invaded the heart of the doctor and then he died.

"I do believe...the poet is telling us much more than science can describe. That is, if we destroy this respect for our own progeny, we will destroy also what is the most precious part of our life, which is simply love."[11]

The deep subjects under discussion may have defied the judgment of King Solomon, commented Shumiatcher. Would his wisdom have some bearing on this case?

At this point, the Crown lawyer interrupted. "My Lord, I find this a fascinating expert witness, but I think we'd all agree, and as the witness—"

"He's qualified as a geneticist, Dr. Shumiatcher," concurred the justice.

Sojonky pressed his point: it was interesting that through the expert witness, Shumiatcher was indicating the issue before the Court "is one not only of science, but of philosophy and poetry and so on."

"I think they're all inseparable," countered the counsel for the plaintiff, "and if we lose our poetry and if we lose our sensitivity and our philosophy, we're really losing the whole basis of law."

Later Edward Sojonky would try and puncture, if he could, any holes in the remarkable and far-ranging testimony of this learned and humble witness. The grilling, which carried over to the next morning, turned out to be, according to one eye-witness, the "most combative cross-examination of the entire trial."[12]

"Dr. Lejeune, what is your religion?" was the Crown lawyer's first question.

"Is that question relevant, My Lord?" the witness asked Justice Matheson, who replied, "It was asked of a previous expert witness."

"Very well," replied Lejeune, "I'm Roman Catholic."

And therefore, personally opposed to doctors performing abortions, continued Sojonky.

"I am opposed to any abortions," came the reply, "not about only doctors."

Even if the mother's life was in danger?

The baby's life must be preserved by all means because "he is a member of our species." If the life of the mother were in jeopardy, the duty of a doctor "is to try to save both lives...and that is what medicine is doing now. And I would say that in our lifeboat of medicine...and I would say bluntly, in every foreseeable case, we have a lifeboat with two places: one for the mother and one for the child."

"I'm going to repeat the question," said the Crown lawyer, "because I don't think I got an answer. Now, assuming that the mother's or the woman's life is in danger, would you—personally—would you feel that an abortion would be appropriate?"

"I would, My Lord, fight the danger. I would not fight against the baby," answered Lejeune.

"And if the mother's life could not be saved?" Sojonky persisted.

"I don't see any actual case in which we could say that actually, sir."

"There would be no cases in this world—"

"I'm not an obstetrician, I am a geneticist," stated Lejeune; his good friend, however, was in charge of the biggest delivery hospital in Paris, and had "presided over fifty thousand child births…. In no case was he forced to make an abortion in order to save the life of the mother; that was his own testimony."

What if the pregnant woman's psychiatric or mental health were in danger? Would it be Lejeune's personal belief that an abortion was not justified in this case?

"I'm not speaking about my personal belief," retorted Lejeune, "I'm speaking about facts."

"But I'm asking for your personal belief, Doctor," pressed the counsel for the defendants.[13]

"But it's not a matter of belief," returned the witness. "It's a question of behaving, as a doctor, in front of the facts." In the case of psychiatric disorders, such as schizophrenia or severe depression, he did not know of cases where the state of the mother worsened because of pregnancy. He was aware that among mothers suffering from such disorders, some had had abortions and others had not, but there was "no evidence whatsoever" that a pregnancy carried to term under such circumstances was "really damaging" more than an abortion.[14]

When asked to confirm that abortion was legal in his own country, Lejeune had used the phrase "kill the baby." Questioned Sojonky: Was that because he believed abortion was murder? The "child *in utero* is a human being to the best of the scientific knowledge we have," responded Lejeune. "And I would affirm definitely that deliberate, artificial abortion is a homicide. Whether it will be called a murder, that's the opinion of the Court. It's not any longer the opinion of the biologist."

Joe Borowski:
A Pictorial History

Photos on pages P1–P13, P20, P27-28: Courtesy of Jean Borowski
Photos on pages P14–P25, P29–P31: Campaign Life Coalition

Family Portrait

Joe with his family. From left, back row: Mom (Bernice), holding
baby brother Wallace, Dad (Joe Sr.), middle row Frank, Walter,
Joe, Ike (Isaac). Front: sisters Mary, Terry (Matilda) and Helen.
Joe had two other sisters, Lillian and Irene, not pictured here.
The Borowskis had met and married in Bialystok, Poland. For
the first seven years of their married life it was their sorrow to
remain childless, but once Isaac and then Frank were born,
Joseph and Bernice began to think about opportunities for their
children. Ambition for their children compelled the Borowskis
to emmigrate to Western Canada in 1930.

Joe As A Teenager

Joe Borowski had struck out on his own at the age of 14, working in bush camps across Canada
He quit school after Grade 6. "Rather than try and be the fourth kid, little kid...he wanted to go and try his hand at life," said his sister Mary.

Working Man

In his later years as a budding politician Joe became known as "Lunchpail Joe" because he never lost touch with his working class background.

Joe In His Twenties.

Said Jean about Joe at this time, "I didn't think much of Joe"... "I always liked the darker guys, you know, black hair and brown eyes, and he had green eyes... After, I thought he was real handsome, but at the time I thought, 'He reminds me of a spoilt brat'."

"This fellow also had a curl that hung down on his forehead that he kept brushing away"; Jean suspected he was trying to draw attention to his locks. She discovered later that Joe was conscious of that curl and hated it.

Joe And Jean During Their Engagement

Jean's father said of Joe: "A good man is hard to find. It's like finding a diamond in the sand."
"He's going to be a good man, [He] looks like a good man."

Joe and Jean relaxing in the great outdoors.

Father And Son

Joe and his dad, Joe Sr., take a break to check quality while making a batch of "moonshine" for the celebration of Joe's upcoming wedding to Jean Zelinski.

The Wedding

Joe Borowski married Jean Zelinski on August 20, 1952. Joe was 19 and Jean was 20.

Inco Days

Joe and brother Wallace had to sleep in tents during their early days of working for Inco in Thompson, Manitoba.

Debbie, Joe and Karen during the Thompson days. Jean and the girls moved to Thompson permanently in June 1961 after living in a trailer in Saskatchewan.

Joe as a hardrock miner at the Inco Thompson site in 1960's.

Inset: In the summer of 1981, Ed Schreyer, the Governor General of Canada, met with First Nations communities at the grounds of the Nickel Days Festival. The Nickel Days Festival is an annual event which takes place in Thompson, Manitoba in recognition of the large role that mining plays in the community.

Photos: Government of Canada Archives

JOE BOROWSKI

A MAN FOR THE NORTH

IN MANITOBA'S LEGISLATURE

YOU KNOW WHEN HE SAYS SOMETHING HE MEANS IT

Joe Borowski your New Democrat in this by-election is well known as a champion of the working man in Northern Manitoba. He has spoken out against our low Minimum wage, which keeps all Manitoba's wages low. He went to Winnipeg twice and his voice was heard. We now have a town council and he helped expose the truth of the South Indian Lake flooding. "YOU KNOW WHEN HE SAYS SOMETHING HE MEANS IT."

JOE BOROWSKI AND FELLOW COMMUNITY LEADERS DISCUSS THE PROBLEMS OF THOMPSON.

★ ★ ★ ★ ★ ★ ★ ★
WANTS ACTION NOW

JOE BOROWSKI AND A NORTHERN SCHOOL TEACHER DISCUSS THE ADVANTAGES OF HAVING A JUNIOR COLLEGE IN NORTHERN MANITOBA

★ ★ ★ ★ ★ ★ ★ ★

VOTE

BOROWSKI, [X]

BOROWSKI N.D.P.
CAMPAIGN HEADQUARTERS

JOE BOROWSKI HAS EXPERIENCE AND KNOWS NORTHERN MANITOBA

*LOOK AT HIS CREDENTIALS:

* 11 YEARS RESIDENT IN THOMPSON
*UNDERGROUND FOR 6 YEARS WITH

HARRISON AND INCO.

*FORMER VICE-PRESIDENT OF LOCAL 6166.

*ESTABLISHED AND RUNS A SUCCESSFUL

BUSINESS IN THOMPSON.

* MEMBER OF LOCAL "PRIVY" COUNCIL.

*MEMBER - TV FOR THOMPSON

COMMITTEE.

*PRESENTED BRIEF TO COUNCIL RE-

QUESTING ESTABLISHMENT OF A TRAILER

COURT, WHICH WE NOW HAVE.

Joe Borowski with his wife Jean, and daughters: Debbie 15, Karen 12, and Sandy 8.
Joe's family are also involved in their community. Jean, as president of her bowling league, Debbie, as a Sunday school teacher, and Karen as a member of the Girl Guides.

CHURCHILL, GILLAM, LYNN LAKE, SNOW LAKE.

Joe lives in Thompson but he knows your community and during the campaign he will try to meet as many of the residents as possible by calling at their homes and discussing their ideas and needs. Joe will be back after the election visiting all the major communities to report and listen.

PERSONAL APPROACH

The voters in the north are responding to the personal approach of Joe and Jean Borowski as they attempt to contact as many persons as possible to tell them where Mr. Borowski stands and get the resident's ideas.

MR. HORACE COCKERELL of Lynn Lake said, "It's about time a politician came to listen to people; this time I'm voting for Mr. Borowski".

ROAD TO LYNN LAKE

Communication and transportation in the north are two of the biggest and costliest problems for its people. As a first step to improve this situation JOE BOROWSKI will fight in the legislature to speed up the construction of the road linking Lynn Lake, one of the older, larger communities with the provincial highway system.

SOUTH INDIAN LAKE FLOODING AFFECTS CHURCHILL AND THOMPSON ALSO

JOE BOROWSKI, while at the Winnipeg hearings discovered many facts hidden from Northern Residents.

DID YOU KNOW:

90% of Churchill's water supply will be cut off just when the Federal Gov't. promised water and sewers.
Thompson's water will be polluted by debris and algae from flooded South Indian Lake.
650 SELF SUPPORTING Indians will be uprooted and moved to an area where there may be no means of livelihood.

CRACKED WINDSHIELDS?

Windshields are expensive and the only way to protect your car is to have properly paved highways. Joe Borowski will strive to have our roads paved.

JOE BOROWSKI WENT TO WINNIPEG

He was the only candidate who attended the Hydro hearings. When Joe discovered the effects of the flooding on Thompson and Churchill as well as several Indian communities he dropped his campaign to fly to Winnipeg to speak out for your area, and as the Winnipeg papers show - his voice was heard throughout Manitoba.

Campaigning

Who best to run for the NDP but the well-known champion of the working class, Joe Borowski?

Above, Joe's campaign flyer for the February 1969 by-election in Thompson.

Escorting Royalty

Joe escorts Queen Elizabeth on a tour of the Thompson mine when she visited Canada in 1970. Joe was Minister of Highways for Manitoba at the time.

All Grown Up

As Joe and Jean's daughters grew into womanhood their father became more and more involved in the pro-life movement. From left, Sandra, Karen and Debbie in 1977.

Roman Holiday

Above, During a visit to Rome in 1983, Joe finally meets one of his heroes, Mother Teresa.

Below, Pope John Paul II presented Joe with a papal rosary after his audience with him during the 1983 trip.

Health Food Guru

Above, Borowski's Health Food Store, was his pride and joy, and served as the hub from which Joe reached out in his pro-life activities. Here he is seen serving a customer

Left, Joe checks his stock.

Below, outside the store during the Referendum for Life in 1992.

Joe Borowski was determined to "close up shop" on Henry Morgentaler. Joe prayed at the door, spoke to the media and was even arrested for his acts.

Above, from May 1 to July 19, 1981 Joe embarked on the "Fast for Life" to advance the cause of protection for the unborn.

Below, Paul Dalby, correspondent for CBC News, interviews Joe Borowski as he takes the "Fast for Life" on the road.

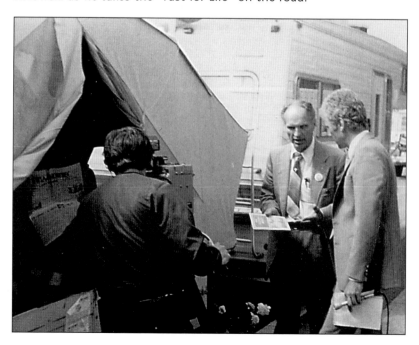

Joe took every opportunity to promote the pro-life message during the fast.

Above left, Joe gives a talk at Campaign Life Coalition.

Above right, a pensive looking Joe ponders the battle ahead.

Below, a feisty Joe answers questions at another conference.

Taking The Battle To The Streets

Right, Joe, seen here with Paul and Luke Jalsevac, joins in the 1987 picket protesting the treatment of Constable David Packer, a policeman that refused to guard Morgentaler's illegal abortuary in Toronto.

Below, Joe encourages picketers in a 1985 demonstration outside a hospital that commits abortions in Kingston, Ontario

Co-workers In The Cause

Above, In Toronto with Jim Hughes, National President of Campaign Life Coalition.

Below, In P.E.I. with pro-life priest and author Fr. Ted Colleton at a National Conference.

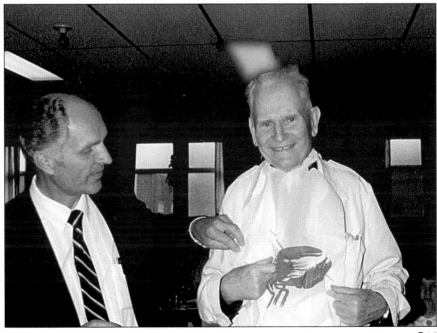

Above, Jean and Joe pose with, from left, Sara Mullally, Denise Hughes and Emily McLuhan.

Below, Joe with activist Margaret Purcell of Saskatchewan.

Above, Joe takes time out to sing God's praises with Kingston Archbishop Francis Spence, Fr. Carl Clemens and Bishop Eugène Philippe LaRocque of Cornwall Ontario.

Below, Joe with pro-life leaders at a Human Life International dinner in Ottawa October, 1987. From left attending were, Jean and Joe, Dr. Gus Mitges M.P., H.L.I. founder Rev. Paul Marx, Rev Archbishop Angelo Palmas, Papal Nuncio to Canada, and Sr. Lucille Durocher.

Above, Joe, Fr. Bernard MacDonald, Michel Arsenault and Larry Henderson at a 1983 Alliance for Life Convention in Moncton, New Brunswick.

Below, Joe with American activist Joan Andrews at a Human Life International conference in 1988. At that time Joan had served more than two years in prison for her work in the American "Rescue" movement.

Awards Given, Awards Received

Above, Joe, second left, presents pro-life awards to Larry Henderson, editor of *The Catholic Register*, Fr. Alphonse De Valk, at that time editor of *The Interim* and Jim Hughes, National President of Campaign Life Coalition.

Left, Governor General Ed Schreyer, Joe, and Archishop Leonard Wall socialize during the award celebration.

On January 9, 1996, Joe received one of the the highest honours the Vatican can bestow on a layman, the *Pro Ecclesia Et Pontifice* (For Church and Pontiff) medal. "When I first found out about it, I joked that it seems to me they only give this award to people who are very old or who are about to die," Joe told reporters.

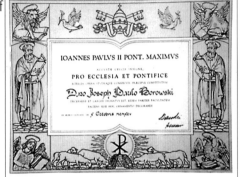

Right, the certificate that accompanied Joe's Papal award.

Below, from left, Fr. Pat Morand and Archbishop Leonard Wall of Winnipeg, congratulate Joe after his winning the Papal award.

"Trial for Life"

Dr. Bernard Nathanson, above, was a notorious abortionist until he came to the realization that the fetus was a human being from the time of conception. He is now an activist on behalf of the unborn.

Below, the late Dr Jerome Lejeune, the geneticist who discovered the cause of Down Syndrome.

Both of these doctors, experts in their fields, testified at the 1983 "Trial for Life" on behalf of Joe Borowski.

Down Time

Joe loved Golf. He even consructed a nine hole course on his property.

Above Joe poses with, from left, Peter Johnson, *Interim* columnist Frank Kennedy and Steve Johnson.

Left, Joe poses with Ray Holmes, of Derrydale Golf Course in June 1987.

Below, Joe even managed to get in a round on his visit to New Zealand in 1984.

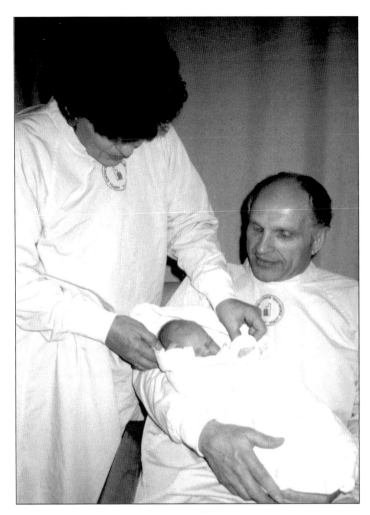

Proud Grandfather

Joe doted on his grandchildren as much as his own children.

Above, Jean and Joe shortly after the birth of their first granddaughter, Jenny.

Left, Joe "horses around" with grandchildren Jenny and Lee.

Above, the family celebrates a birthday. From left, Archie and Karen with Lee and proud grandparents Jean and Joe in 1986.

Right, Joe enjoys a quiet moment with Aaron, Lee and Jenny in 1991.

Joe Borowski's Final Journey

Pall bearers at Joe's funeral included former Manitoba Premier and Governor General of Canada, Rt. Hon. Ed Schreyer, (second left front row), CLC National President Jim Hughes, Ernest Wehrle, Robert MacKulski, Arthur Kimery, Niel Slykerman, John Puchniak and Dr. Matthew Buckley.

Below, Former Governor General of Canada Ed Schreyer delivers the eulogy at Joe's funeral.

Above, Joe Borowski is interred in St. Mary's cemetary in Wynyard Saskatchewan.

Joe's good friend Fr. Patrick Morand donated a memorial to Joe Borowski's struggle on behalf of the unborn. It is located at St. Vital parish in Winnipeg, Manitoba.

Below Jean and grandson Aaron and Fr. Morand.

Above, from left, Joe's grandson Lee, Jean, Debbie, Karen, grandson Aaron, grandaughter Jenny, and Sandra.

"A voice is heard in Ramah, mourning, and great weeping, Rachel weeping for her children; and refusing to be comforted. Because her children are no more. (Jer 31:15)

Painter and writer William Kurelek (1927-1977), above right, was born in Alberta of Ukrainian heritage, and grew upon farms in that province and in Manitoba. Bill was inspired by the dedication of Joe Borowski.

Kurelek gained an international reputation and by the time of his death was one of the most successful Canadian artists of his generation, and himself an outstanding defender of the unborn.

Sojonky tried a number of tactics to undermine Lejeune's testimony. In particular, he produced testimonies of geneticists whose views were at variance with their French colleague's. For these medical opinions, Sojonky relied on transcripts from the 1981 hearings of the American Senate Subcommittee on the "Human Life Bill." At those hearings, at which Lejeune himself had testified, one geneticist had held that there was no simple answer as to when human life begins, and further stated that the fertilized egg is a living cell with the "potential" for human life.

Despite the Crown lawyer's efforts, Lejeune remained unperturbed. He observed only that the statement quoted by Sojonky was, "a very bewildering statement, that if a human geneticist cannot tell if human life does exist…. it meant he does not know what a human being is. He does not know that a species is existing, and I cannot agree with that statement."[15]

As for the question of "actual" or "potential" life, Lejeune stated bluntly, "I don't know what is a potential life."

Did Lejeune believe that the question of when life begins was not a religious issue?

If, the witness responded, God forbid, the Pope ever allowed abortion, "I would stop being a Catholic for scientific reasons, because no moral authority can make me believe that discarding an early human being is not discarding a human being. Now, you have what I feel."

Was "when life begins" a philosophical or ethical question?

The philosopher, the ethicist, the religious person, all must have the facts, Lejeune said.

But even the witness has been quoted as saying "scientific arguments are of little help in ethical issues," accused Sojonky.[16]

Lejeune clarified: the issue under discussion was not when life begins but "whether humanity must respect every member of our kin. And I said to that, biology can only tell us this yellow man is a member of your kin, this white man is a member of your kin, this tiny human being is a member of your kin, but biology cannot tell you, you have to respect them. That is the moral, that's the ethics who has to tell us that; but first we have to know whether the man in question is really a member of our kin, and that is scientific."

When Sojonky continued to use testimony from the U.S. Senate hearings in an attempt to refute Lejeune's statements, Morris Shumiatcher had had enough. He erupted into objections: it was unclear who these so-called "experts" were. Sojonky could not, in this roundabout way "seek to establish another authority taking a different view."

Justice Matheson reassured the excited Q.C. that, while the Crown lawyer could present the views of other scientists, these would not be considered by the Court as the testimony of expert witnesses: "What Mr. Sojonky says is not evidence, Dr. Shumiatcher."

A particularly robust exchange took place between Sojonky and Lejeune over the statements of a Dr. Lewis Thomas on the subject of "personhood." Thomas had stated that "science can tell us nothing about the personhood of a cell." Not only that, he quoted a resolution by the National Academy of Sciences which declared that, "Defining the time at which the developing embryo becomes a person must remain a matter of moral or religious value."[17]

"I would stress," Lejeune responded, "I have never talked about person or personhood. I have talked about human being and I would say that a human being is there—and I will repeat—when all the genetic information necessary and sufficient is there. That is right from the beginning."

Then Lejeune would say the human embryo was a human being, asked Sojonky.

There's no doubt, replied the geneticist.

But "you wouldn't go so far as to say it was a person?"

"In the ordinary language, I would not use that word," said Lejeune. "Maybe it's because my English is poor, but I guess most of the people do not talk about the baby as a person...."

"But human being is a term used in the common language as well—"

"Very true," broke in the witness. "But a schoolboy is a human being, a soldier is a human being, an old man is a human being, a little girl, an old lady, and a human embryo; all of them are human beings."

Sojonky continued. The living cell, the product of fertilization of the human egg by human sperm, would he describe that as a human being?

"It's not my will that this cell is dividing and producing the form that everyone can recognize. That's not my postulate. It's what the cell does," the witness exclaimed.

"Well, you describe that cell as a human being?" persisted Sojonky.

"That cell is a being, this being is human, then it is a human being."

"Now, is that a genetic definition?"

"I guess it's the best genetic definition we have. If you have a better one—"

What about, continued Sojonky, the case of human *in vitro* fertilization. "You would say that cell in the glass is a human being?"

"I would because it is," firmly replied Dr. Lejeune. "Now, My Lord, may I make a personal statement? That is, it's very comprehensible that many people have difficulties to really understand that thing which is close to a miracle, but which is really true; that at the very beginning, all the properties which will later be expressed as someone, a member of our species, are really reduced to that extraordinary, simple expression. It's difficult to believe, but that is the basics of genetic science."

If the "product *in vitro*" were destroyed, would that then be an abortion, asked Sojonky.

"I would not call it an abortion," answered the geneticist, "It's not in a body, then it can't be an abortion."

"How would you describe it?"

"As a tiny homicide, killing a human being."

"As a tiny homicide?"

"A homicide on a tiny human being," repeated the witness.

"Thank you, Dr. Lejeune. I have no further questions."[18]

Notes
Chapter 16
When does life begin?

[1] Op. Cit., Tahn, p.26.

[2] Op. Cit., *Trial for Life*, p. 288.

[3] Ibid. p. 289.

[4] Ibid. p. 287.

[5] Ibid. p. 291.

[6] Ibid. p. 292.

[7] Ibid. p. 298.

[8] Ibid. pp. 303-306.

[9] Ibid. p. 313.

[10] Ibid. p.314.

[11] Ibid. p. 317.

[12] Op. Cit., Tahn, p.28.

[13] Ibid. p.323.

[14] Ibid. p. 324.

[15] Ibid. p. 328.

[16] Lejeune had made this statement at The Allen Award address, as quoted by Dr. Rosenberg, Ibid. p. 336.

[17] Op. Cit., *Trial for Life*, p. 345.

[18] Ibid. p. 350.

Chapter 17

"The butcher of Amsterdam Avenue"

"…when I became immersed in the study of fetology…it became unmistakably clear to me that the person inside the uterus was a human being…"

Dr. Bernard Nathanson

ONE OF THE MORE DRAMATIC TESTIMONIES DURING THE BOROWSKI trial was that of Dr. Bernard Nathanson, an American obstetrician/gynecologist once known as "the Butcher of Amsterdam Avenue"—not only because of the number of abortions he performed, but because of his zeal in promoting abortion on demand in his native country.

But the Bernard Nathanson who testified for the plaintiff in May of 1983 had long ago laid aside the abortionist's weapons and was publicly denouncing his former occupation. He was now assistant clinical professor of Obstetrics and Gynecology at Cornell University Medical College, as well as a teacher at the Columbia University's medical school.[1]

Responding to the questions of Morris Shumiatcher, the well-dressed, bespectacled obstetrician related how, in 1968, he co-founded, with feminist author and activist Betty Friedan, the National Abortion Rights Action League (NARAL), which was the "first pro-abortion political activist group in the United States, or indeed, to my knowledge, in the world."

"[W]e devised a great many tactics which were ultimately successful in overturning the [abortion] law in New York State and other states, and finally contributory to the *Roe v. Wade* decision in the United States Supreme Court," Nathanson told the Court. "In that regard, I did in fact organize and carry out demonstrations, press conferences, and other media-grabbing devices which were enormously successful in mobilizing the media to our cause."[2]

From 1971 to late 1972, Nathanson was also director of the Center for Reproductive and Sexual Health in New York City. The name was a "euphemism," and "an Orwellian appellation," the witness said; the centre "was not in fact interested in reproductive health, it was primarily interested in destroying the unborn child." It was, in reality, an abortion clinic, the first in the United States and the largest in the "western world," with 35 doctors doing abortions every day of the year. "During my hegemony there," stated Nathanson, "we accomplished 60,000 abortions."

Abortions were performed at the clinic only on women who were less than 12 weeks pregnant; after this time, the maternal complication rate greatly increased. Nathanson worked on refining the technique for the saline solution abortion, to deal with later pregnancies. This method consisted of injecting a salt solution into the womb, following which, the mother would go into premaure labour and would deliver "a macerated, scorched, unborn child."

Nathanson told the Court that until the passage of New York's liberal abortion law in July 1970, he and his cohorts relied on a "sham" in which friendly psychiatrists would certify that a woman was suicidal because of her pregnancy and so the abortion was approved. These "fictitious" letters backed up 99 percent of abortions.

Nathanson derided the therapeutic abortion committee system in New York as "ludicrous and laughable." The TACs took no notice of the unborn child. He then described to the Court his own revelations in that regard. The science of fetology was just emerging in the early seventies, and the technical advances that allowed for a "systematic observation" of the child in the womb contributed to an explosion of knowledge about the development of intrauterine life.

"I suppose a historical irony is that the same year that the *Roe v. Wade* decision was handed down in the United States Supreme Court, fetology emerged as a full-fledged medical specialty, having within it, I suppose, the seeds of the destruction of that decision, or at least of permissive abortion in America."[3]

The beginning of a human life was now "clearly definable," Nathanson testified. It was analogous to the "starting of a fire" which begins as one spark. "[T]his biological fire we call life, begins with that spark that is struck when the egg and the sperm unite, and it ends at death."

"And throughout that period of time, do you regard that fertilized egg or ovum fertilized by a sperm as being an individual human life?" asked Shumiatcher.

"Yes, it is an individual human life, an unborn child," replied Nathanson.[4] "We know from the recent work in *in vitro* fertilization exactly when the spark is struck.... We have done it ourselves. We are no longer back in the Ice Age when fire mystified us."

Science does not judge what a human being is, based on appearance or "external contours," observed the witness. The "essence of the human being is, or resides in its genetic structure, which is peculiar only to human beings." Following the conception of a new human life, there is a continuum of growth and development.

His reasons for abandoning, in the words of Shumiatcher, "the practise of aborting babies to take up the practise of saving them" were "purely secular"—he had no religious beliefs, emphasized Nathanson. When he so assiduously promoted unrestrained abortion in the mid to late 1960s, it was because in his mind "abortion on demand seemed to be necessary for women trapped in a difficult social situation, an unplanned pregnancy."

Moreover, there was "no countervailing moral force in the balance,... Nothing of value... was being destroyed." Subsequently, as chief of obstetrics at St. Luke's Hospital at Columbia University, he established one of the first fetology units in the northeastern United States.

"When I became immersed in the study of fetology...it became unmistakably clear to me that the person inside the uterus was a human being, indistinguishable from any of us, validated by all these new technologies," Nathanson said. The "continued

destruction of this person was impermissible in my ethical framework." That framework was the Golden Rule: do unto others as
you would have them do unto you.[5]

In describing the physiology of pregnancy, Nathanson
explained that, because the baby was a unique individual, the
mother's white blood cells—"trained to recognize self from non-
self"—would attempt to "mount an attack to expel the intruder."
That attack "fails in most instances, since the unborn child has,
through the eons, developed very efficient protective mechanisms, an immune sanctuary, as it were." Nevertheless, the
attempted attack proved that "the unborn child is not part of the
mother's body...and at the very most one can only say that the
unborn child is an uneasy tenant."[6]

As had Sir Liley and Dr. Jerome Lejeune before him, Nathanson
gave details of the development of intrauterine life. He noted that,
as well as evident sensitivity to sound and light, the unborn baby
unquestionably feels pain.

"I myself, and many others who have done late saline abortions
have occasionally stuck by accident the unborn child with a needle, and watched it jump away from the needle. In fact, we've
watched it move away from the needle even when it wasn't stuck,
indicating that it perhaps has some sense of impending disaster,"
the doctor related.[7]

"Did this bother you?" asked Shumiatcher.

"At the time it did not," came the response. "It was—I remarked
upon it but it did not—clearly did not deter me from carrying out
the abortion."

Shumiatcher went through various arguments to defend abortion, all of which Nathanson refuted. To the assertion that life
must exist independently, Nathanson noted that newborn infants
require care. "None of us exist independently." To the notion of
viability the doctor pointed out that the concept is so "slippery"
that it has little validity. With the advances in medical technology,
a baby born prematurely would be "viable" at a much younger age
than when he was studying obstetrics.[8]

Did Nathanson invent the term "therapeutic abortion"?

"No, I didn't invent it," answered the witness, "I must say that I
popularized it." He added thoughtfully: "It is doubtful that there
is in fact such an entity as a therapeutic abortion any longer.
Women do not kill themselves and never have as a result of being

pregnant."[9]

What about "socio-economic factors," questioned the counsel for the plaintiff; had an impoverished woman, for instance, ever had her "condition alleviated by abortion?"

"No," said Nathanson, "I think that the unplanned pregnancy is a social problem, and as a social problem, it requires social solutions. I don't believe that civilized humanity should promote the solution of social problems with surgical holocausts."

What about the "unwanted child" that one heard about?

"We don't really have unwanted children," responded the witness. "We have children who are unwanted by their parents" but there are from a half to a million couples "who are frantically applying for children" in the United States "at any given time."[10]

What about the term "potential life"—did it have a meaning?

"The phrase is a relic of pre-fetology days," said the witness dismissively. "We do not operate on potential human beings; we do not diagnose illness in potential human beings; we don't have any potential patients, we have patients, we have people. We are dealing with concrete—with real people here, whether they are imprisoned in a uterus for nine months, or out in a prison somewhere in upstate New York or away from society's view, is irrelevant. The reality is these are people and patients and human beings."[11]

Shumiatcher asked the witness what he thought of abortion in the case of a child conceived as the result of rape. While this is "the most painful case in the abortion arena," responded Nathanson, it must be said that "abortion is an act of violence, it is the destruction of a human being as we know it, and to compound one act of violence, (i.e., rape) with another, abortion, does not eradicate the stigma and the experience, the humiliating memory of the rape."[12]

The child "created in the act of rape is an unfortunate victim in a sense, but certainly should not have its life stigmatized or ultimately destroyed because of the circumstances of its creation." It's likely that "many of us even in this room were created in circumstances other than perfect."[13] The same would hold true for children conceived as a result of incest.

It was not religious conviction that motivated him to stop performing abortions, Nathanson said. It was only when, through the advances in fetology, he became convinced that the woman was carrying in her womb a unique human, that abortion became, for him "ethically impermissible as a social solution."[14]

Sojonky rose to cross-examine. Did Nathanson, then, mean to say he was an atheist?

"That's correct," answered the witness.

And before that, was he raised in the Jewish faith?

In the Jewish tradition, qualified Nathanson: "I was not a practitioner of the Jewish faith."

In his testimony to the U.S. Senate hearings in 1981, the hearings for the Human Life Bill, Nathanson had used the words "fetal life" and fetuses, Sojonky observed. Yet, two years later "you speak of the unborn child." Why the change?

The developments in fetology had been such that even within two years, Nathanson replied, his views had become "more insistently pro-life and more egregiously anti-abortion, and have allowed the fetus to emerge more clearly as in fact the unborn child."[15]

"You're now a pro-lifer, in common parlance?" asked Sojonky.

He was not in any organizational sense, no, answered Nathanson. "I am my own person in this issue; I am simply...against the casual and cavalier destruction of human lives."

Nathanson was against the destruction of "fetal life unless the mother's life is at stake?" asked the Crown lawyer.

"Well, I believe, respectfully, I said, unless the mother's physical life is in imminent and clear jeopardy."

In Nathanson's morning testimony, he had used the term "human being," remarked Sojonky. "Is your definition of human life a medical definition?"

While no one could "quantify or describe human life with Euclidean certitude," there are "certain biological criteria. We also have an intuitive sense as to who and what is human and what is not." There was, perhaps, a "semantic failure, that we don't really have, I suppose, that appropriate or apposite word for that quality which is common to and embraces the entire human community." It was clear, however, that the "entity within the uterus for nine" months was a member of the human community.

Was it necessary to look to theology and philosophy and ethics to define human life, asked Sojonky.

It may well be, conceded Nathanson, but those philosophers and theologians had to observe, in their definition of what is human, the "biological landmarks and guidelines and sign-posts which are common to all human beings." If they failed to do so, their definition would not be valid.

But the view given by Nathanson, that the "living cell" present after conception is a human life, that is a "personal view," Sojonky argued.

No, the witness countered: "This is a view as a scientist, as one who, modestly, has had more experience and wider experience with abortion than perhaps anyone on this continent, both in the political and in the medical area."

"And you went through quite an amazing transformation?" queried the Crown lawyer.

"Not really. It was not a sudden epiphany," Nathanson replied.

"Is the living cell just subsequent to conception, is that a baby?"

"Which living cell are you referring to?" asked the puzzled witness.

"The living cell that exists two days after conception...is that a baby?"

"Yes. It's an unborn child, a human being."

"And it's a baby?" persisted Mr. Sojonky.

"Baby, if you like."

"I'm asking you."

"Yes, it's a baby."[16]

"And of course," continued the Crown lawyer, "you would want to say it's a human being?"

"Certainly."

"And a person?"

"Yes."

"And when you say it's a person, is that a medical opinion?"

"Again, we are involved in semantic failures here," the witness said, "A person—it may be a medical opinion, it may also be a sociological opinion. In my view, as I used it, it's a medical opinion."[17]

There are some scientists who would admit there is a living human cell, but not a human being, Sojonky said.

"There are," rejoined Dr. Nathanson, "people who belong to the Flat Earth Society, counselor."

But there was dissension on this point?

"If you say so."

"Well, I'm suggesting to you that there is?"

"I defer to you on this."

"There is dissension?"

"I am not aware of any significant dissension."

"Not aware of any significant dissention, but it exists?"

"I think you're arguing with me, and I don't know how to respond," the exasperated doctor replied.

"Well, My Lord," Sojonky turned to Justice Matheson and quipped, "the witness has an aversion to any dissention akin to that of the devil for holy water."[18]

The Crown lawyer then returned to the testimony of Dr. Rosenberg, at the hearings on the American Human Life bill which he had formerly brought to the attention of Lejeune. The views of Rosenberg, observed the witness, were "more political ideology than sound science…I cannot imagine anyone denying when life begins any more than I can imagine someone denying when life ends."

But there was controversy as to when life ends, was there not?

Perhaps the microsecond when someone had died might be disputed in some cases, but "I don't think anyone is in serious doubt as to whether all those people lying in cemeteries are dead or not."

What about the people not in cemeteries, pressed the combative Crown lawyer.

"Well, I for one think I'm alive, but again—you're beating me down."

Back to when life begins: there were members of the medical community who would not call the living cell at conception "a human being," and therefore, Nathanson would disagree with them, would he not, asked Sojonky.

"In a general sense, of course I would." answered Nathanson. "The question is rather Pickwickian and nebulous…what you are describing is politics, not science."

Sojonky cited the testimony of a Dr. Joseph Boyle, who asserted that the time when the "qualities of a human person attach to a fetus cannot be stated as a settled scientific matter." Did Nathanson disagree with Boyle?

Yes, answered the witness: "Doc Boyle was enunciating politics again more than medicine," as he was the president of the board of the American Medical Association, and that august body had endorsed permissive abortion as its policy since 1970.

The dogged Sojonky returned to the question of what maternal conditions could be worsened by pregnancy, mentioning cardio-vascular disease and infectious diseases. Nathanson conceded that it was theoretically possible such a condition might result in the death of the mother. However, in actual fact, the efficiency of medical science was such that there were "vanishingly few" conditions that would "necessitate the termination of pregnancy."

Questioned as to whether the mental health of a woman could be affected by the continuation of a pregnancy, Nathanson said that it could be affected one way or the other.

Shumiatcher rose to re-examine the witness, picking up where Sojonky had left off. Had Dr. Nathanson found that any of his patients had been "affected adversely mentally as a result of pregnancy and childbirth?"

"There's no doubt that any of us who have had children can verify this: life becomes more complicated, more difficult and perhaps fuller and happier with pregnancy and children. That's part of life," answered the witness. But parents do not destroy their children when they present problems. "I don't think that this is properly a medical or scientific issue, this is an existential issue," and "is not appropriate in a consideration of the ethical permissiveness of abortion."

"Are you of the opinion," queried Shumiatcher, "that a resolution of a group of men...as to the time that an unborn child becomes a human being can determine that issue?"

"I think the time is long past now when the determination of this issue requires an opinion," Nathanson said. "It is now an observable fact, we do it, we create life now.... There is no longer any proper place for opinion. The rest is politics."

The last person to question the famous obstetrician was Justice Matheson. If abortion were legal only in the case expressed by Nathanson—when the mother's life was in imminent jeopardy—would that definition "very quickly become an anachronism" as such situations exist only theoretically?

Medicine, responded the witness, "is moving so rapidly in so many directions that I would reserve the theoretical exception, I would not rule it out."

But would the result be no abortions in practise, as there would be no practical circumstances that justified it?

Those circumstances were "vanishingly small," repeated Nathanson. "Twenty years ago, it is true, we had a number of medical situations in which the mother's life was imminently threatened by the pregnancy, but today that list has shrunk to, as I say, almost a theoretical objection."[19]

With that, the testimony of Dr. Nathanson was complete.

Notes
Chapter 17
"The butcher of Amsterdam Avenue"

[1] Op. Cit. *Trial for Life*, p. 384.

[2] Ibid.p. 387

[3] Ibid. p. 394.

[4] Ibid. p. 396.

[5] Ibid. p. 422.

[6] Ibid. p. 402.

[7] Ibid. p. 398.

[8] Ibid. p. 401.

[9] As part of the strategy to obtain permissive abortion, Nathanson attempted to get the statistics on "the number of women who had killed themselves because they were pregnant." However, the medical examiner for New York City "was unable to give us even one case, one case, where a woman had clearly committed suicide because she was pregnant—this was New York City—so we were chagrined and never, of course, publicized that finding," he told the Court. To do so would have "invalidated our efforts in the late '60s to carry out abortions on a psychiatric basis." (Ibid. p. 409.)

[10] Ibid.

[11] Ibid. p. 413.

[12] Ibid. p. 418.

[13] Ibid. p. 419.

[14] Ibid. p. 418.

[15] Ibid. p. 423.

[16] Ibid. p. 426.

[17] Ibid. p. 427.

[18] Ibid. p. 428.

[19] Ibid. p. 437.

Chapter 18

The ethicist

"...each of us may say and none of us may
deny that I am the fetus that was.
There has never been a time when I was
not that same individual item of humanity."
Dr. Harley Smyth

D R. HARLEY SMYTH, A NEUROSURGEON AT TORONTO'S WELLESLEY Hospital, was called as a witness for the plaintiff on May 18. He had studied as a Rhodes Scholar at Oxford University for four years, then returned to Canada to complete his clinical training in Toronto. As well as his medical specialty, Smyth wrote and spoke extensively on medical ethics, a subject that, he told the Court, "is a very active part of the practise of a neurosurgeon." He was therefore accepted as an expert in the fields of both neurosurgery and medical ethics.

In his testimony, Smyth related some instances where a pregnant woman came into his care for neurological problems. There was no difficulty in recognizing that there were two patients under his care, mother and baby; such has been "the long and running tradition of medical practise."[1] The traditional classical medical ethic, expressed in the maxim: 'first, do no harm', has always precluded "the taking of the life of an unborn child," explained

Smyth, "except traditionally in circumstances where the continuation of the pregnancy constituted a positive threat to the life of the mother, and so in a proportional way life has been balanced against life—not life against health, or life against contemplated well-being, but life only when a life was at stake. That is simply traditional classical obstetrics up until 1969 in this country."

Smyth recounted the story of a family friend, who confided to him, at the age of 91, what had occurred when she was pregnant in 1926. She had gone from 126 pounds to 67 by the midterm of her pregnancy, as a result of *hyperenesis gravidarum*, or "the intractable vomiting of pregnancy."

"She was literally dying of malnutrition at that point, and all the nutritive attempts by her physician at that time had failed," Smyth testified. What in his day would have been solved readily by deep tube feeding and other techniques, was in this 57-year-old case resolved when the obstetrician decided to abort the unborn child. "I believe firmly, as she did, that her life was saved by ending her pregnancy at that point."

Such an outcome was regarded as "genuinely tragic" but "I don't think that there was ever any doubt or culpability on the part of the physician who acted in good faith when medical necessity was so clearly proven, so much a matter of life and death in the mother's case, and I don't think that there was an ultimate difficulty in justifying the fortunately rare instances in which it was a clear necessity."[2]

"One has met many such patients of an older age group whose lives were saved only by the ending of their pregnancy. There are poignant examples of this still alive amongst us today, women who are—who can testify as to the experience and its necessity, and the remarkable thing is that, arriving in the same decade as the practical disappearance of the last necessity, came this change in the circumstances under which the decision may be made."

"What you're saying," asked Shumiatcher, "is when it became possible to save more young lives, the will or the penchant to destroy them increased?"

"It certainly seems one of the most outstanding ironies of our time."[3]

Physicians, Smyth told the attentive Court, have for almost "three millennia" been "classical moralists" insofar as they have upheld, as formulated by the Geneva Convention, that theirs is the duty to protect human life from conception until death.

The physician had always had a "covenant relationship" with the individual who "has made a claim on one's care." That relationship "bore no relation to the weakness or the frailty or the articulateness or the ability of the patient to state this claim, but was based in the mere recognition of... itemized individual human life."[4]

There are some, remarked Shumiatcher, who would not recognize the individual as such until he or she can speak.

No doubt, responded the witness, there are "many scales on which the membership in the species might be measured, but I don't think there has been any difficulty here or elsewhere or in the literature establishing the humanity of the unborn offspring of man.... I don't think there's any difficulty in establishing its genetic foundations as a totally unique item of human life."

The difficulty was not scientific or based on "confusion or uncertainty or ambiguity of biological data." The difficulty "seems to arise in acknowledging the human claim that the unborn child has upon our care."

When does that claim begin, asked Shumiatcher.

It begins "as soon as the evidence of the...individual's presence is available," said Smyth. "It has been said that an individual is an individual when he or she casts a shadow. We saw that a twenty-one millimeter individual clearly casts a shadow."

"Why are you so certain that the individual that casts the shadow is a human being?"

"I suppose probably the evidence for that is present in all of us here, that—that each of us may say, and none of us may deny, that I am the fetus that was. There was a time when I couldn't walk and a time when I couldn't speak and a time when I couldn't articulate my claim upon you as my brother, but there has never been a time when I was not the same individual."

If this claim were not recognized, the consequences would be far-reaching for the entire nation. When an abortion was permitted for non-medical reasons and carried out by a doctor, the latter became "the technical extension of the will of an individual" and the consequences to the profession were grave indeed, Smyth told the Court.

This practise "introduces into the life of a hitherto unitary function of the physician a divided purpose, and a necessary diminution in the evaluation of a single human life."[5]

Moreover, "if one member of a species can arrive at a private contractual arrangement with another member of the species to end the life of a third member, then that is a generality which is an important precedent, and is not different logically or ethically or even technically from infanticide."[6]

For centuries, he testified, physicians had accepted the right to life as "self-evident." That had changed. "There's evident pressure to change those grounds and to suggest that humanity is something that is subject to measurement." This startling view was very widespread: the witness cited an Anglican task force that concluded that, when faced with infants with multiple disabilities, "the most humane thing was to consider them inhuman."

Smyth went on: "I think that reverence for life is a—very much a motivating factor in the lives of many young students who begin to study medicine. I think it is an element that is very strongly developed in many of them, and an element which one has to believe, has had a great part in their—sorting out their vocation."

However, this reverence for life had been eroded and replaced with a "defensive cynicism" in these students, precisely because of "the political reality of mass elective feticide for non-medical reasons," testified the ethicist. "The sheer weight of this political event in the life of our country is something with which…the current generation of medical students has grown up. They cannot remember the day before 1969 when this was not the case."

He told of a conversation he overheard, between a young resident in obstetrics who mentioned to his junior colleague that his wife had suffered a miscarriage. After his colleague offered condolences, he said, "Well, yes, I suppose, but it's really not possible to get very excited about that sort of thing these days." He was, in fact, scrubbing up to perform abortions.

"It's just a story," the witness concluded, "but it's a story which seems to disclose a certain sense of the loss of respect for life, or a loss of the joy of life, or a loss of the expectancy of life, that perhaps has had to form a necessary part of their accommodation to their work. I don't know."[7]

The ethicist had written elsewhere, Shumiatcher noted, that "medicine now adopts the economic model, where the only rule is that the customer is always right." Would that be "contrary to the traditional role of the physician?"

It would be, answered the witness. The physician's "professional judgment is given to the patient and the patient's request is secondary to the actual exigencies and the facts of the situation, the medical facts. That has been the principle on which unnecessary surgery is avoided." In the "economic model" the "covenant relationship had been altered" and the "principle of customer and merchant might replace it."

In discussing this development, it must be noted that the practise of seeking a second opinion was valid, and that the medical profession was becoming more sensitive to "paternalism." But even though "there is a desirable increase of sensitivity and communication between doctor and patient" this "should nevertheless not alter the medical facts on which judgments should be based."[8]

Shumiatcher turned to semantics. Would Smyth comment on the term "therapeutic abortion"?

In the classical sense, replied the doctor, such an abortion "is conducted as part of therapy for an abnormal condition." However, in the case of the many abortions done for non-medical reasons, the diagnosis given was "reactive depression of pregnancy," a psychiatric condition which was quite rare. "[W]e are asked to believe by this use of language that a formerly rare condition has now become of epidemic proportions" noted Smyth. This has led to "a kind of cynicism."

"…[T]his use of medical language is false and misleading. And so the abortion that is being conducted for clearly non-medical reasons is not therapeutic because it does not treat any disease, remove any abnormal tissue, or cure any symptoms in the vast majority of cases, and so it continues to be a source of systematic misuse of language."[9]

Smyth told the tragic story of a young married woman, pregnant with her second child and happy to be so, who was advised by her obstetrician to abort the baby because she had suffered severe sciatic pains during labour with her first child. Because the opinion was expressed so strongly, she and her husband concluded that the doctor knew best and she did, in fact, have an abortion.

When the neurosurgeon saw her some weeks later, she was unable to walk, having lost feeling in her legs. Nevertheless, the loss of sensation she suffered did not "correspond to the organization of the nervous system, but corresponded to the patient's view of her legs, so that the sensory loss was what practical psychiatrists would have called 'hysterical sensory loss'."[10]

When he explained to the couple that there was no evidence of spinal cord damage, the husband questioned, what then was the problem. "Then I asked, 'What would you think about being paralyzed by grief?' And at this point, neither of them said anything but the woman spontaneously burst into tears and cried for a good long time in the office, and both immediately understood the meaning of that response of hers, and in fact, she walked out of the office."

Smyth was concerned enough about this case to look up the record of the abortion, and it revealed that the diagnosis was "reactive depression of pregnancy." It was clear that the Therapeutic Abortion Committee had not been advised why the obstetrician had referred her in the first place. Nor was there any documentation as to why she had the sciatic pain during her first labour, nor evidence to show that she had been examined since, nor had she suffered any pain since that time.

Had there been more consultation, it was very likely a psychiatrist would have found a "psychological contraindication to an abortion."[11]

The phrase "reactive depression of pregnancy" was not generally "heard from psychiatrists." In fact, the witness said, the senior psychiatrist at his hospital "has stated it as his view that there are no psychiatric indications for abortion, but that his role is confined to defining where there may be a psychiatric contraindication to abortion."

Sojonky swung into action. In this case, the Crown lawyer kept his cross-examination brief, and principally confined to the issue of what circumstances would warrant a truly "therapeutic" abortion.

"Your view, Dr. Smyth, I take it, is that a therapeutic abortion would be permissible if the woman's life is in danger, medically endangered?"

"That has been the classical view of obstetrics for a century and a half," responded the witness, adding that this view was held by a majority of physicians.

"And in the view of the majority of physicians, including yourself, an abortion would be permissible given that set of circumstances, the woman's health would be endangered?"

"Well, you've moved from life to health in your question."

"You would concede," persisted the Crown lawyer, "that a woman's health may well be endangered temporarily or permanently as a result of pregnancy?"

"Not in an unqualified way, no, I don't think I could," came the reply. "If it is mental health that we are talking about, we are hard put to find objective records from psychiatric case reports of an illness which is identifiable with pregnancy, or continues after pregnancy in an indefinite way, in a way that would be to any permanent disability. No, I—I'm not aware of those situations."

But, given that the word "health" is not defined in the Criminal Code, then the case must be that either by committee or individual physicians "do consider whether a woman's health is in danger?"

"I wish I could be certain that it were so," Smyth answered. However, his own testimony revealed a situation "where a referral was made for medical reasons, and the medical reason was completely neglected by the committee." It was just such incidents that made him very uncertain that "justice is done. I wish that it were so, but I cannot assure you that it is so."

"I'm not actually asking for assurance," rejoined Sojonky, only for a concession "that good men and women, medical doctors in Canada, do decide that a woman's health might well be endangered because of pregnancy?"

"Well, I can't answer further on that."

Under the law, questioned the Crown lawyer, "in the application of Section 251, doctors must make medical decisions" must they not?

They ought to make medical decisions, countered the witness, "but one has reason to believe that they are often not decisions of medical substance."

Was it Smyth's belief that there were abortions performed at the Wellesley Hospital that were not therapeutic abortions, asked Sojonky.

Yes, answered Smyth, and if the therapeutic abortion committee members "agree not to tell the truth in language diagnostically, not to tell diagnostic truth, there is no guarantee that the decisions they have made are truthful either."

Sojonky doggedly returned to "health." Would not abortion be permissible if the mother's health were in danger?

"If we are going to engage that question finally," carefully explained the witness, "we would first have to agree to accept that health was a value equivalent to the value placed upon another single human life." In other words, society would have to "decide together that the health of its individual and articulate members was equal in value to the very existence of otherwise healthy but inarticulate members. I'm not persuaded that as a society, we have made that equation yet, and I don't think the law under which we are functioning has sanctioned that equation."[12]

When Sojonky was done, Justice Matheson had his own questions. The woman who suffered intractable vomiting, he queried, was that not a danger to her health at the same time as it was considered a danger to her life?

It must have been, answered Smyth.

In the Criminal Code, continued the justice, the words "life" and "health" were used disjunctively. "Is that what the problem is?"

"Perhaps," came the response, "I think that any illness that is deemed terminal can be said *pari passu* to be affecting the person's health, and certainly their future health, but my understanding of the Criminal Code section is that they are used severally, or separately."

"And therefore are looked at separately? As two different types of things, in medical terms?"

"Yes."[13]

Notes
Chapter 18
The ethicist

[1] Ibid. p. 477.
[2] Ibid. pp. 484-485.
[3] Ibid. p. 484.
[4] Ibid. p. 483.
[5] Ibid.
[6] Ibid. p. 487.
[7] Ibid. p. 505.
[8] Ibid. pp. 506-507.
[9] Ibid. p. 490.
[10] Ibid. p. 501.
[11] Ibid. p. 502.
[12] Ibid. p. 513.
[13] Ibid. p. 526.

Chapter 19

The family doctor

"...usually when a pregnancy would occur
in an incestuous relationship, it's been a repeated event,
and that needs a lot of treatment, a lot of support,
and a lot of talking about,
and I don't think that by adding
a further trauma of an abortion to this,
is really good medical care."
Dr. John Donovan Brown

ONE OF THE LAST WITNESSES SUMMONED FOR THE PLAINTIFF WAS IRISH doctor John Donovan Brown, who had a family practise in Regina at the time. Brown, an Orange Presbyterian, received his degrees in medicine, surgery and obstetrics in Belfast. He had, before coming to Canada, been administrator of a 300-bed hospital in Kenya, which served a district of about 4,000 square miles and a population of about a half million.

When he arrived in Regina, Brown opened a family practise, which at the time of his court appearance had grown to include four colleagues. He was a physician for the Saskatchewan Rough Riders football team, and assistant clinical professor in the Department of Family Medicine at the University of Saskatchewan.

Brown also happened to be the "noontime running mate" of

Morris Shumiatcher and during the course of those excursions, the latter opened the eyes of the former "to the facts of pre-natal life."[1] That both Dr. Brown and Dr. Shumiatcher were faithful to these midday exertions was demonstrated during the trial, when proceedings were slightly delayed by the tardy appearance of the counsel for the plaintiff.

Accepted an expert in family medicine, Brown described for the Court the general medical care for a pregnant woman, beginning from the time the patient's first appointment onwards through the pregnancy. He explained how he would chart the information gained about the unborn child, the expected time of delivery, how he routinely sent expectant mothers for ultrasound to accurately pinpoint the baby's age. Generally, what the mother "wants to know most is when the baby is going to arrive."[2]

Among other things, Brown and his colleagues had the use of a Doppler fetal stethoscope in their office, with which they could detect the baby's heartbeat. "We can pick them up regularly at nine weeks," he observed, "and this is another rather exciting event for the mother to hear the child's heart." Moreover, in keeping with the tradition of family practise, the father and siblings, if any, are also "invited along to hear the baby's heart from time to time."

This had provided "a totally new dimension for the fathers, who, I find, are very excited about this, it now lets them in to participate in the pregnancy, which at one time they were excluded from," he testified. The mother, who formerly would be aware of the baby moving at the time traditionally known as "quickening," (at about 20 weeks) was now, through the Doppler stethoscope, assured much earlier that her baby was healthy.

"Now, have you ever had a woman come and see you and say she wished an abortion?"

Yes, responded the witness. Frequently, the idea was not entirely the mother's, but she was under "great pressures from other quarters"—her mother, boyfriend, husband or "some outside family pressures."[3] His advice to such mothers was that in his medical opinion, "it would be a better and more healthy thing to go through with the pregnancy, and to then rethink their problem, than to have an abortion."

A normal pregnancy was much healthier than an abortion, which "is a surgical procedure and requires an anesthetic. There are the risks of damage to the womb; there are the risks of hemorrhage; there are risks of the introduction of infection into the womb. These, of course, are immediate dangers, but there is also the danger of, further down the road, damage to the fallopian tubes following infection, so that subsequent pregnancies may be harder to achieve."

If the patient remains "bound and determined" to procure an abortion, then Brown tells her to find another doctor "amenable to their ideas.... But I also reassure them that subsequently to that, if they do that, I'm still very willing to look after them as patients."[4]

When that happened, what effect, in his experience, did the abortion have on the mental health of the patient, queried Shumiatcher.

The patient would suffer great feelings of guilt, testified the witness: "I personally do not feel that their mental health has been improved by going through a therapeutic abortion. I very well remember one case of a patient who was dying from cancer, it was breast cancer, actually, and on her deathbed really, she told me that she felt that this was God's punishment again, for her having had a therapeutic abortion many, many, many years ago, which I knew nothing about."[5]

The family, too, suffered the effects of the abortion, insofar as those "who have had these procedures, seem to have less respect for the life of their children." He had situations where "child beatings" occurred in families with a history of abortion, Brown told the Court.

Was there any likelihood of a mother losing her life as a result of a pregnancy, asked the counsel for the plaintiff. "I certainly can't think of anything or any time that that would arise, with the facilities that we have in Regina, and certainly in the length of time that I've been practicing here, I haven't come across a case," replied Brown.[6]

"A normal pregnancy is not a disease, a normal pregnancy is, you know, certainly a healthy experience." But because of a slight risk for mother and baby during delivery, or the possibility of an unanticipated complication, it was typical in Canada that women have their babies in hospital. In his native Ireland, Brown related, midwives traditionally attended births; in Kenya, women generally bore their children at home.[7]

Shumiatcher asked the family physician about the use of the terms "embryo", "fetus", "baby" and so on: what was the significance of these terms?

While "embryo" and "fetus" were scientific terms, a family doctor would, when communicating with his patient, tend not to use such appellations. "I feel that a woman would be rather indignant if I asked her would she like to hear her embryo's heart," Brown explained. "The purely medical terms have no greater or less meaning than 'infant' or 'child'. In fact, the long accepted English term for a pregnant woman, which is used to describe the Mother of God in the Gospel of Matthew, is 'with child.'"

The reality of the various labels attached to the unborn child in this case, was that "if you don't want to consider something as belonging to the species, you can always sort of cloud this over by giving it a rather odd name." The normal word to use for the unborn baby was child. "However, if you want to say this is not a child, you can say it's an embryo or it's a fetus. In other words, it's not human. The implication is there when you use a scientific term, that it's not human."[8]

Would Brown care to comment on the issue of a pregnancy resulting from rape; had he dealt with this difficult situation in his practise? While he had not, Brown testified that "one cannot destroy a life, simply because of the way in which it began, and my view is that the pregnancy should go ahead, with every care taken to support the mother, because the rape is the main trauma in this case."

Pregnancy as a result of incest probably occurred "with a greater amount of frequency than, even as a family physician, we are aware of." But the same principle would apply, Brown said, as for rape. "There is no medical or genetic reason to assume that an incestuous pregnancy is any less a human being. As a matter of fact, the Egyptian dynasties were run entirely on an incestuous relationship. The Ptolemies were all brother/sister, and obviously genetically very successful."[9] With incest, "we are dealing with someone who has probably been scarred very dramatically by the relationship, and that is what needs treatment, the scars of the incestuous relationship, rather than the pregnancy. It's not likely to occur the first time. So, usually when a pregnancy would occur in an incestuous relationship, it's been a repeated event, and that needs a lot of treatment, a lot of support, and a lot of talking about, and I don't think that by adding a further trauma of an abortion to this, is really good medical care."[10]

At this juncture, a woman spectator leaped to her feet and made a noticeably agitated exit, slamming the door behind her. The press made much of her departure.[11]

Whether this dramatic moment affected Morris Shumiatcher can only be conjectured, but it seemed as though the advocate was not in his best form—or perhaps it was his best form. A certain recurring piquancy characterized his examination of this witness. It was the eighth day of the trial, and the patience of Sojonky at the sometimes theatrical flights of his famous adversary was wearing thin. Did Shumiatcher notice? Was he moved to provoke?

He attempted to have Brown comment on fellow Irishman Jonathan Swift's satire, *A Modest Proposal*. When Sojonky objected, Shumiatcher countered that he had hoped for a "literary uplift for my learned friend…well, some people just won't have culture thrust upon them."

"I thought," pointedly rejoined Sojonky, "you were doing it for the benefit of His Lordship, and not for me. Maybe I misunderstood."

"His Lordship didn't object; His Lordship was all ears."

"Except," Sojonky had the last word, "His Lordship has sustained my objection."[12] Shumiatcher asked the witness if an abortion performed on an unborn child conceived as the result of an incestuous relationship "would be to punish the child for a sin to which he was no party?"

The Crown attorney was instantly on his feet.

"I think the question is improper," he stated flatly.

Shumiatcher resumed his questioning.

"Dr. Brown, have you considered at what point the unborn child has acquired the right to life, to continue his existence?"

"From the moment of the beginning of that child's existence," came the answer.

"Which would be when?"

"At conception."

Would it be Brown's view, continued the Q.C., "that an abortion in the family is beneficial to the family, in the relationship of its members, one to the other?"[13]

"In my view, and in my own family practise, I don't know any-where where an abortion could have been considered to be ben-eficial."

Shumiatcher questioned the witness about his medical practise. Had he ever had a patient walk in and demand the removal of one of his limbs? As a matter of fact, Brown testified, he had had a patient do exactly that. A man had asked the doctor to cut off his penis: "He had decided that this was of no further use to him and had taken a dislike to it, and he wanted it amputated."[14] Brown realized the man suffered from schizophrenia and, obviously, did not carry out his wishes. Parenthetically, the man returned some-time later without his teeth, having managed to "inveigle" a den-tist into pulling them.

Similarly, if a pregnant woman came into the doctor's office and "she says, cure me, get rid of it," Shumiatcher asked, "What would you do and what would you not do?"

In such a situation "one would not amputate the pregnancy," Brown said, as such a condition "is not an illness and...it will take care of itself." The physician would provide care and treatment for the patient as required.[15]

Counsel for the plaintiff also touched briefly on the idea that a human being, to be considered such, must be capable of inde-pendent existence. Brown observed that in many cases, a patient was "anything but independent" and required technological assis-tance, or anesthesia during surgery, but was still considered a human being. He cited the case of a patient who was "entirely dependent on a mechanical heart; he was still very much a human being, and he was treated as such."[16]

Shumiatcher read from five textbooks on embryology, as well as two other authoritative tomes, including the *Encyclopedia Britannica*. All these texts, without exception, asserted that a new life begins at the moment of conception. All these statements the witness agreed to unequivocally. With this, Shumiatcher's exami-nation of Brown was complete.

Sojonky cross-examined. Dr. Brown had mentioned in his testi-mony that abortions after 20 weeks gestation were frowned on. Would it be fair to say, the Crown lawyer said, that before 20 weeks, abortions were safe?

"I think abortions are dangerous both before and after 20 weeks. I think that those people who carry out abortions say that after 12 weeks they become more hazardous."

But, pressed Sojonky, a previous witness, Bernard Nathanson, had appeared to indicate that he considered abortions done before twelve weeks to be "quite a safe procedure."

"I don't consider any surgical operation to be a safe procedure," countered Brown.

"So, you disagree with Dr. Nathanson?"

"Yes."

Sojonky's cross-examination came quickly to a close, and Justice Matheson turned to the witness. Some surgery was more dangerous than others, asserted Brown, but it was his contention that "all surgery has a risk."

"You are not necessarily saying unsafe is the same as dangerous?" contered the judge.

"No," answered Dr. Brown.

With that, the witness was dismissed.

Notes
Chapter 19
The family doctor

[1] Op. Cit., "I set before you life and death" Shumiatcher, p. 1.
[2] Op. Cit., *Trial for Life*, p. 531.
[3] Ibid. p. 536.
[4] Ibid. p. 537.
[5] Ibid. p. 538.
[6] Ibid. p. 539.
[7] Ibid. p. 540.
[8] Ibid. p. 547.
[9] Ibid. p. 553.
[10] Ibid.
[11] "MD'S testimony upsets woman at abortion trial," Pat McNenly, *Toronto Star*, May 20, 1983, p. A9.
[12] Op. Cit., *Trial for Life*, p. 542.
[13] Ibid. p. 555.
[14] Ibid. p. 558.
[15] Ibid. p. 557.
[16] Ibid. p. 558.

Chapter 20

Of moles, ultrasound
and abortion committees

"If we have a mole, we evacuate the mole.
If inadvertently we run into these one-in-several-thousand cases
where there is a still-living baby in there, there's no way of knowing
it at this early stage that we're talking about."
Dr. Patrick Beirne

D R. PATRICK BEIRNE, ORIGINALLY OF GALWAY, WEST IRELAND, WAS
summoned to the court on May 17, and qualified as an
expert in obstetrics and gynecology, with additional expertise in the use of ultrasound. Beirne, at the time of the trial, was a
full professor at the University of Toronto in obstetrics and gynecology, and a member of the staff at St. Michael's Hospital. He had
been the first practitioner in obstetrics to start work in ultrasound
in Canada, in late 1967.

In his post-graduate work, he had studied for a year at Cornell
University in New York, where one of his professors was Dr.
Bernard Nathanson.[1]

While the bulk of Beirne's testimony concerned a very detailed
description of the technical aspects of ultrasound, he initially clarified some obstetrical issues that had arisen in former testimony.
Beirne explained the situation that arises when a mother has Rh

negative blood and the baby Rh positive.

In the normal course of events, the baby's and mother's blood circulation were separate, but sometimes there was cross-over of blood because of "little minute breaches, breaks, in the baby's blood vessels." When the Rh positive cells passed into the mother's blood stream, her immune system would manufacture antibodies to attack these cells.

The danger arose when these antibodies "move back into the baby's circulation," explained Beirne. They would attack the baby's Rh positive blood cells; as a result, the baby developed anemia, which could prove lethal. These were the cases where an intrauterine blood transfusion, a technique developed by Dr. Liley, might be necessary.[2] This situation provided further proof, if needed, of the fact that the mother and baby were separate individuals, possessing, in this case, incompatible blood types.

Beirne then described another intrauterine hazard for the child, which was always lethal. It had been the subject of a brief exchange between Nathanson and Sojonky when the former occupied the witness stand, but, Beirne remarked, the testimony could have left the layman confused. The subject discussed was the occurrence of a "mole." At a very early stage in the development of the life of the unborn child, at about 16 or so cells, there occurs a division in which a number of these cells begin to form the placenta. The placenta is an organ of the baby necessary only for his or her time of growth in the womb.[3]

It can happen that the afterbirth, or placenta cells, become cancerous, testified the obstetrician. When the "uncontrolled, purposeless growth" of these cells occurred, it was a mole.

The presence of a mole "is not compatible with continuing intrauterine existence" and if it were not excised, it would likely prove fatal to the mother, Beirne explained. There is no option in this situation but to "evacuate the uterus."

"Is that in the profession regarded as an abortion?" asked Shumiatcher.

"No."

"Why not?"

"Well, on rare occasions, it may be," replied Beirne. He explained that "almost inevitably and almost invariably" the unborn child is dead before the uterus is cleared. However, there may be a case where the cancerous growth began later in pregnancy, so the baby is still alive "at the time of the evacuation."

"Under those circumstances, has the baby survived?"

"No, sir," testified the physician.[4]

"Would that be tantamount to what is a spontaneous abortion, or would abortion be appropriate at all?" asked Shumiatcher.

A long pause followed, and the counsel for the plaintiff was puzzled. "Sorry, I didn't hear your answer?"

"I didn't answer," came the reply. Finally, Beirne said: "It wouldn't be appropriate... If we have a mole, we evacuate the mole. If inadvertently we run into these one-in-several-thousand cases where there is a still-living baby in there, there's no way of knowing it at this early stage that we're talking about." One could state that "an abortion happens, if you like, or we cause an abortion simultaneous with our evacuation of this tumorous tissue."

Were there other situations where "it would be justified to evacuate the unborn child?" "To do an abortion, are you asking me?"

"Yes, in effect?"

In medicine, testified the witness, "there's no such thing as 100 per cent" and such cases could arise—in theory. But "I have never run across a case," Beirne said.[5]

He then testified regarding ultrasound, or "ultra high frequency sound." The sound people hear around them is at a frequency of 16,000 to 20,000 cycles per second; at the "ultrasound range," the cycles are a million per second. At this frequency, "the properties and characteristics of sound are quite different." It is unidirectional, and therefore can be "beamed very much like a searchlight." It is not "propagated in air or gaseous medium" but "requires a liquid medium."[6]

Ultrasound is produced by rocks or crystals, either naturally occurring or man-made, with piezoelectric, or "pressure electricity" properties. When these "are electrically charged, they will vibrate at an extremely rapid rate, and conversely, if they are made to vibrate, they generate an electrical charge."

One per cent of the time the crystal, when it is electrically charged and sending out its beep, acts as a transmitter, "then it spends 99 times as long listening and it will receive back echoes." The intervals of time are millionths of a second. When hit by an echo, the crystal generates an electric charge, and "these things are electronically displayed on a television screen."[7]

That is the principle of ultrasound, Beirne told the Court; as to how "these electronics change these facts into a visual image, I don't want to be quizzed on that." However, he did describe how the body, 98 per cent water, "is a good conductor of ultrasound—except for those areas, such as the lungs, which contain gas." He elaborated on the "acoustical impedance" of various structures in the body, bone, fat, muscle, and described how those that were denser, such as bone, gave back a stronger echo which resulted in a clearer picture.[8]

An obstetrician would beam the ultrasound and scan the uterus, and interpret the images obtained. Beirne illustrated this with a series of ultrasound images, reproduced on video tape, which he had taken at regular intervals during one woman's pregnancy, thus charting the course of the development of her unborn child.[9]

He also had a tape of the heartbeat of a child in the womb, picked up with a "Dopp phone," which, he explained, was based on ultrasound but designed to detect motion only. The baby whose heart he recorded was eleven-and-a-half weeks old, but equipment existed that was capable of recording a heartbeat of an unborn baby six to seven weeks after conception.[10]

Shumiatcher referred to *Williams' Obstetrics*. The textbook was widely used in North America, said Beirne. It asserted, he read, that as a consequence of the increased knowledge of fetal development, "the fetus has acquired the status of a patient, who should be given the same care by the physician that we have long given the pregnant woman."[11]

In cross-examination, Beirne testified that he was Catholic, and totally opposed to abortion. Sojonky asked him if there were doctors who performed abortions because they believed the life or health of the mother was endangered. The witness was doubtful. When he had discussed the matter with his colleagues, "they admit very freely that the vast majority [of abortions] are done because the mother does not want to be pregnant, virtually on demand."[12]

The doctor had asked the heads of seven teaching hospitals how many women were turned down in their request for an induced abortion—the answer was zero.

The detection of an abnormality *in utero* was no justification for ending the life of the baby, Beirne testified. If a baby with spina bifida, which could be treated, was destroyed at four or five months gestation, "why not eliminate them later on when they're born? I would much prefer to see efforts made to treat them."[13]

Justice Matheson also had questions for the witness. If all doctors agreed that abortion would be permissible only if the continuation of the pregnancy could result in the death of the mother, "would it be fair to say there would then be no abortions? Except in theory?"

"Yes," came the reply. But, added Beirne, "society would have to accept the less than perfect baby, or handicapped—"

"Oh yes," interjected the justice, "I'm talking solely about the—"

"But we are eliminating some of them before birth."

"—the ground…the only ground being that the termination was necessary to prevent the death of the mother," clarified Justice Matheson.

"Death of the mother," repeated Beirne. "No need for abortions in my opinion."[14]

The same day yet another expert in ultrasound testified on the plaintiff's behalf, a Dr. Robert Kudel, a Saskatchewan-born and trained medical doctor with a specialty in diagnostic radiology. He had been practising diagnostic ultrasound since 1977, Kudel told the Court, and it was of this, as well as radiology, that his office and hospital practise consisted.

He and his colleagues also traveled to hospitals in surrounding Saskatchewan towns to provide "radiological and ultrasound services."[15]

The young doctor of medicine distinguished himself by receiving the admonition not once, twice, but three times from the elderly doctor of law, Morris Shumiatcher, to speak slowly. Think of the court reporter, implored the Q.C. Think of the rest of us, he added.

The nimble-tongued Kudel tried to slow down as he explained the purposes of ultrasound. These were varied, but in the field of obstetrics, were generally contained to ascertaining if the baby were living, the age of the baby, the position of the baby *in utero*, and the location of the placenta. When abnormalities were detected, ultrasound was the means to monitor the unborn child's progress.[16]

The witness led the Court through a description of real-time ultrasound, in which static scans were transmitted in such rapid succession that they produced, in effect, a moving picture on the screen. He screened some examples of these for the benefit of the Court, pointing out the various physical attributes and activities of the unborn children so revealed.

The videos included a baby 16 weeks gestation, shown sucking his thumb. The youngest of the group was a baby of 8-and-a-half weeks of age, and his heart, head and abdomen could be detected as he lay on his back, "flexing its neck," Kudel pointed out.

Added to these video exhibits were two photographs "very precious to me," admitted the witness at the conclusion of his testimony. These were an ultrasound image of his son, taken when he was between three to four weeks gestation, and appeared as "that little white dot surrounded by black" which was in fact "the gestational sac" in which the tiny fellow resided. Also visible on the image was his mother's bladder and uterus, and a darker area Dr. Kudel described as "an implantation bleed" which was not of significance to the pregnancy.

The next photograph was of his son two years later, to demonstrate the amazing development from tiny dot to winsome tot— the same individual human being as in the first image, only older.

The Crown lawyer's cross-examination was the epitome of terseness. In short order, he established that Kudel was a Catholic, absolutely opposed to abortion and was, of course, familiar with the term "fetal life."

"And would you agree with me that 'baby' is a term, is a lay term for infant?"

"A baby to me is," countered Kudel, "this individual that I am seeing there. You're just putting a name on it, whether it's a baby or whether it's a fetus, but to me these are all individual human beings."

"But a baby, in the medical dictionary, could be a lay term for infant?" persisted Sojonky.

"That's correct," responded Kudel.

With that, the witness was dismissed.

Next on the stand was Dr. Heather Morris, "a spritely, dark-haired sparrow of a woman,"[17] who received her medical training in England and Scotland. A founding member of Canadian Physicians for Life,[18] Morris, at the time of the trial, had been practising as an obstetrician and gynecologist in Toronto for ten years.[19] She was a member of the staff of Women's College Hospital in that city.

Morris recounted her various activities in the field of family planning; for 12 years, she had taught a course on marriage counseling at the Catholic Information Centre, until, she quipped, "they finally decided to get a Jew off their lecturing—"

"You are Jewish, are you?" interrupted Shumiatcher. "I see."

Morris also taught graduates and postgraduates at Women's College in the field of obstetrics and gynecology, and had taught a course in Brazil to doctors there under the auspices of the Scarborough Foreign Mission Society.[20]

The three types of high risk pregnancies she typically dealt with included mothers with a "bad obstetric history", that is, having lost one or more previous babies before birth; mothers who had health problems such as diabetes or heart condition which made the pregnancy more difficult, and mothers who early in the pregnancy had indications that either they or the child *in utero* had some irregularity or abnormality which warranted close monitoring.[21]

Under questioning from Shumiatcher, the witness related her experiences on the therapeutic abortion committee at Women's College Hospital, called the Judicial Committee. She was a member of the committee for a month. It was "a very frustrating experience" and demonstrated an "almost schizophrenic" thinking in her colleagues, who under different circumstances "show enormous concern for the contents of the uterus of a pregnant woman, namely for the developing embryo or fetus."

It struck Morris as ironic that this committee sat on the same floor "as our neonatal intensive care unit where thousands and thousands of dollars are spent trying to save the lives of babies very little older, in terms of time from conception, than these that were destroyed, or whose destruction was being sanctioned with such relatively little thought." She volunteered to sit on the committee because she hoped to "exert some influence so that the distressed women perhaps get what I feel is probably more reaching and ongoing help for their problems, and also try and save the lives of their healthy, or presumably healthy, unborn children."[22] What happened, however, was that she was the minority opinion in all cases, and overruled by the other two physicians. Not one of the applicants seeking an induced abortion was denied, yet, in her opinion, not one of these abortions was justified.[23]

The committee met one hour a week, at which time the members would consider 12 to 15 applications. There was generally an oral presentation by the obstetrician of the woman seeking the abortion. Because of time restraints, often the abortion would be in fact sanctioned before the reporting of the case was completed.

During the month she sat on the committee, all the abortions were granted for "socio-economic reasons," Morris told the Court. "In fact, in the time that I was on the committee, there was no instance in which a serious physical threat to the health of the mother was ever demonstrated, and I can't recall any patient with a diagnosis of psychological or emotional illness being sick enough to even have been referred to a psychiatrist."

Socio-economic factors "were not legitimate reasons for terminating a pregnancy," the witness testified. "When I challenged the other committee members, the response was that the social or economic situation was such that the woman was depressed and, therefore, this was a threat to her health."[24] This view she strongly opposed.

"What was it that moved you to reject these applications, Dr. Morris?"

"I am aware from all my clinical training, my medical school training, that a human life starts at conception, and I think we have to have an extraordinarily good reason for taking a human life, no matter how young, how old," responded the physician. "There may be some very good reasons, but certainly in my time on that committee, I was never presented with one that I even needed to consider for more than a few moments, because there was really no situation in which the unborn child, the fetus, was threatening, genuinely threatening the life of the mother."

What about the health of the mother, asked Shumiatcher: was that ever threatened?

Such was never demonstrated, came the reply. Certainly "temporary emotional distress and perhaps financial distress, these were very real" and the women whose cases the committee considered often "needed a great deal of help and support in these areas." But no threat to health was ever sufficient as to justify taking the life of the unborn child.[25]

Was the question of whether the unborn child should be considered ever raised?

"No."[26]

Morris then described her practise. On a typical day, she would see perhaps 50 patients. She was always struck by the fact that the woman was conscious from the moment she realized she was pregnant that she was carrying another person, and that her actions, such as smoking or drinking, could well have a detrimental effect on the development of that child in her womb.[27]

Moreover, new mothers always refer to the baby *in utero* as a baby: "I think in seventeen years, I've had one person, one patient asking me how the fetus was," Morris observed.

While some situations may present more difficulties than others, given the state of medical technology, it was, in her experience, always possible to assure both mother and baby kept in good health throughout the pregnancy. "I can't recall, in my own specialty practise in seventeen years, a time in which we have had to sacrifice the baby because of the mother's life being at stake. I think it does occur," Morris testified, "but it fortunately has not been my experience."[28]

When her patients requested an abortion, she tried to ascertain the reason why, and what alternative assistance could be provided. "[Q]uite honestly, I think abortion is a request for help" and when alternatives were offered some women decided against abortion. Teen-agers are susceptible to "low self-esteem," and it was worthwhile to "suggest to them that they are perhaps better people than they believe; that by doing what is perhaps the most unselfish thing in their lives; namely, allowing that baby to grow and develop, that this is a very maturing" event.

Morris made it clear to patients who still wished to have an abortion that she would not assist them in any way, but remained willing to help them in other areas.[29]

How did the changes in the Criminal Code in 1969 affect her practise, Shumiatcher asked the doctor. The law did not change the facts of life before birth; in fact, these were even more clearly in evidence than previously, Morris told the Court. What had altered was "the morality of killing the developing baby." There was no reason for her to change her attitude or practise.

As far as medical indications for abortion, she could think only of cancer of the cervix discovered early in a pregnancy, and in this instance, "the abortion would be carried out almost as a coincidental happening."[30]

Shumiatcher sat down and Sojonky rose to cross-examine.

Dr. Morris was a member of the pro-life group, Canadian Physicians for Life. What was her view of "so-called pro-choice groups," the lawyer for the Crown wanted to know.

"I don't think of them as pro-choice groups," came the reply. "I think of individual people who are misguided...[and] are not willing to allow the unborn to have a choice for life"—despite their claim to being "pro-choice."

"Why do you feel they are misguided?" queried Sojonky.

"Because I think if many of them really understood that this is a human being, that many of them would not really wish to be involved in a situation that would deny life to any human being. ...And I think they are misguided because they have to deny to themselves the humanity of the unborn child."

But some Canadian citizens took the view that the unborn child was not a human being, countered Sojonky.

"I would agree with you that there are Canadians who accept this view. I would not agree that they are right." When it came to fellow physicians, while she could not speak for doctors "en masse" she has discussed the matter with her colleagues and "some of them will say to me, yes, I know it is a human life; I think that human life is of less value than the distress of the adult patient I see before me."[31]

Sojonky referred to pregnancy that resulted from an incestuous relationship. Would an abortion be justified in such circumstances?

She would try to see the whole family, as undoubtedly "there is considerable disorder in the family," replied Morris. The intervention of psychiatrists and social workers would be "much, much more constructive" than an abortion. "After all, in that family the people that are probably most diseased, are the male who impregnated the young girl, and the girl who has been made emotionally disturbed by the home environment that resulted in the incest. The only healthy one in the trio is the unborn child. That would not be the one that I would seek to eliminate."[32]

There also was no evidence to show that severe psychiatric disorders were improved by an abortion. She would "not terminate the life of a baby for temporary or minor emotional or mental health disturbance. On my scale, those don't weigh well."[33]

Sojonky took up the definition of "health"—Morris was aware that the word was not defined in the Criminal Code? No doubt there existed "a real diversity of opinion of medical doctors in Canada" as to the definition of health?

Such was the case, Morris concurred. In fact, she wryly noted, doctors could use the word differently depending on context, as could lay persons: individuals "who might wish to say that they were unhealthy when requesting an abortion, would be the first to say that they were totally healthy when seeking life insurance."[34]

The Crown lawyer then defined a therapeutic abortion as "an abortion that's induced because of a woman's poor health."

This was not a definition Morris could recall but, the witness responded, she was willing to concede that it was a possible definition. It would then follow that, in her view, "a therapeutic abortion should only be performed when the woman's life is endangered or when the woman's health is endangered?"

"My view," replied Morris, "is that an abortion, an induced abortion, terminates the life of a young human being and therefore...that this should only be performed if the mother's life is at stake."[35] If the mother's health was the issue, "there are alternative methods of preserving the woman's health and treating her disease." However, it was true that a woman's health could be "temporarily distressed" by pregnancy, and her medical condition "aggravated." The fact was that "any normal pregnancy may endanger the woman's health, yes. Pregnancy accidents do occur in any pregnancy, unpredictable, totally unpredictable."[36]

Justice Matheson, too, had a question for the witness.

"You said at Women's College Hospital, disaster means the loss of a baby?"

"No, perhaps I should turn that around to say the loss of a baby is a disaster."

"What would you term the loss of a mother?" queried the justice.

"A disaster."

"That's all," concluded the judge.

Notes
Chapter 20
Of moles, ultrasound and abortion committees

[1] Ibid. p. 438.
[2] Ibid. p. 440.
[3] Ibid. p. 441.
[4] Ibid. p. 442.
[5] Ibid. p. 443.
[6] Ibid. p. 444.
[7] Ibid. p. 445.
[8] Ibid. p. 446.
[9] Ibid. p. 450.
[10] Ibid. p. 453.
[11] Ibid. p. 454.
[12] Ibid, p. 458
[13] Ibid. p. 459.
[14] Ibid. p. 463.
[15] Ibid. pp. 464-465.
[16] Ibid. p. 468.
[17] Op. Cit, Tahn, p. 17.
[18] Ibid. Op. Cit, *Trial for Life* p. 594.
[19] Ibid. p. 566.
[20] Ibid.
[21] Ibid. p. 569.
[22] Ibid. p. 576.
[23] Ibid. p. 575.
[24] Ibid. p. 573.
[25] Ibid. p. 575.
[26] Ibid. p. 576.
[27] Ibid. p. 580.
[28] Ibid. p. 585.
[29] Ibid. p. 587.
[30] Ibid. p. 590.
[31] Ibid. p. 595.
[32] Ibid. p. 598.
[33] Ibid.
[34] Ibid. p. 599.
[35] Ibid. pp. 596-597.
[36] Ibid. p. 597.

Chapter 21

The evidence mounts

"I've argued that point from the day it was called
therapeutic because it's certainly
not therapeutic to the baby and
I don't think it's therapeutic to the mother."
Dr. Alfred Eistetter

D R. ALFRED EISTETTER WAS BORN AND RAISED IN SASKATCHEWAN BUT his travels in pursuit of his medical studies and career rivalled those of Gulliver. After obtaining his medical degree at the University of Western Ontario, and subsequently earning various degrees in Great Britain and Canada, "I did general surgery in the state of Iowa, pathology in London, England, obstetrics and gynecology in Oxford, England, and internal medicine at Saskatoon, Saskatchewan."[1]

When he took the stand in May 1983, Eistetter had been practising for 28 years, having specialized in obstetrics and gynecology for 21, and it was as an expert witness in this field that he was presented to the Court.

He testified about his years in post-graduate work in obstetrics at the Radcliffe Infirmary at Oxford University, where he and another colleague looked after 4,000 to 4,500 high risk pregnancies a year, those considered "unsafe for home deliveries." At the time, home deliveries constituted 70 per cent of the births in Britain, he estimated.

During his two-and-a-half years there, Eistetter said, he had under his care women suffering from heart disease, diabetes, various kinds of cancers and toxemias, yet, he did not perform any abortions. In fact, that option was not even considered.[2]

"Why was that?"

It was due, likely, to the influence of Sir John Stallworthy, a "world-renowned" obstetrician and head of the department at Oxford, who taught "that a pregnancy should never be jeopardized because of the health of the mother." It helped that pregnant women typically were young and healthy—other than the effects of the disease that made their pregnancy a risk.

The "patients were admitted to hospital with a view to treating their concomitant disease, carrying the pregnancy to term, delivering the baby, and continuing with the treatment of the mother, if indicated, when she was confined," Eistetter testified.[3]

What did the phrase "therapeutic abortion" mean to Eistetter, asked the lawyer.

"I've argued that point from the day it was called therapeutic because," responded the witness, "it's certainly not therapeutic to the baby and I don't think it's therapeutic to the mother." Therapeutic, he added, "means treatment."

Why was it not so for the mother?

His answer was based on his experience as medical director of Martha House, a residence for unmarried mothers, Eistetter told the Court. "And we've had a lot of counselling on girls who had been there more than once, some of whom had abortions before, and I've seen a lot of patients who've had abortions carried out before, and so many of them have said, 'We would rather not have gone through that experience.'"

Women would be just as traumatized and suffer just as many ill-effects from an abortion even if it were done because the conception occurred as a result of rape, the doctor testified.[4]

Eistetter told the Court that he had never had a maternal death in all his time of practise. There had been infant deaths but with the medical improvements, these were less frequent than when he first started practising. "Children die in the obstetrical process because of a multiplicity of diseases...of the placenta" and "because of the mechanics of delivery." There was also the possibility of "abnormality in the position of the placenta, abnormality in the position of the cord and sometimes gross abnormality of the baby...certainly, we do deliver dead babies."

However, he had never come across a situation where the baby's disease had put the mother's health in jeopardy, although the reverse could happen. "Generally speaking, the healthier the mother, the healthier the baby."

"In your experience, Doctor," asked the Q.C., "how often does a mother have a psychological or a psychiatric problem that has been caused or worsened by pregnancy?"[5]

This was not "a significant problem" in his practise, Eistetter said. Psychological stresses typically related to either marital problems, or to the social stigma attached to bearing a child without the benefit of marriage. The latter had practically ceased to be an issue, he acknowledged, as pregnancy outside marriage, along with common-law marriage, had become in the last 10 years much more acceptable. Even when the situation was frowned on, the psychological burden did not seem onerous. Many of the mothers at Martha House, he testified, who remained there during their pregnancy and carried their babies to term, in retrospect "felt they learned something, they felt that they perhaps became a better person."[6] ..."We have nothing but unmitigated compassion for those people because they feel they were damned by getting pregnant and they're damned by stopping it."[7]

Had he ever had "an experience where a patient of yours, after she has delivered her child, expressed the view to you that she wished she never were a mother?"

"Yes," the witness replied, "We've had a few of those" but the regret typically lasted only a short period of time and occurred "at a time of marital instability."

Now it was time for Sojonky to cross-examine. The counsel for the defendant rose and referred to his notes. His line of questioning followed familiar paths he had blazed on previous occasions during this lengthy trial.

Did Eistetter believe that abortion was wrong? Yes, "that's my belief as a physician and as an obstetrician."

"It's your personal belief as well?"

"That's correct."

The witness stated, in response to further questioning by Sojonky, that he would not agree to an abortion of a child conceived in an incestuous relationship. But, Sojonky persisted, he must agree that his colleagues in Canada would take the view that such a pregnancy would affect the mother's life or health? And therefore, the implication was, that abortion would be justified.

"Their opinion would be their own, yes."

"And it would be a medical opinion?"

"It may be."

"Well, why do you say it may be?" quizzed Sojonky. "If it's not a medical opinion, what other—"

"There is a lot of medical doubt as to whether an incestuous relationship is going to terminate in a baby which is going to be abnormal," countered the witness, "which is the most common reason for doing it."[8]

Could there be an adverse effect on a woman as a result of pregnancy, asked Sojonky, referring to Eistetter's previous testimony.

"What is an adverse effect?" countered the witness.

"Well, I don't know. You used the words. Perhaps you could assist me."

"You'll have to rephrase your question," came the helpful suggestion.

"Well, you indicated that you didn't think that there were any adverse effects of pregnancy or words to that effect?"

"Yes, that's right."

"Now, there could be an adverse effect, is my question to you?"

"Oh, yes, certainly."

"And it would be the mother who would be affected, of course?"

"That's correct."[9]

When Sojonky sat down, Shumiatcher rose to clarify those points over which the Crown lawyer, through his cross-examination, had thrown a veil of obscurity.

His learned colleague had posed the question about the adverse effect of pregnancy on a mother. "Now, do you think that there is a difference between a pregnancy having an adverse effect on the health of a woman on one hand, and a pregnancy that would be likely to endanger her health on the other?"

"Yes, I think there is a very significant difference between the two suggestions," responded Eistetter. While psychiatric, psychological and sociological problems do exist, the proper response "is to treat those problems and not to treat them by creating another problem. This is really the answer I hoped to give him."

Answering a further question by Shumiatcher, the witness testified that he could not think of any circumstance that would jeopardize the mother's health, not in 1983. "It is our philosophy as physicians and as obstetricians to treat the diseases, be they psychological, be they psychiatric, be they medical, treat them and let the pregnancy look after itself. It will look after itself."[10]

The Borowski action, it will be recalled, requested an injunction prohibiting the use of public funds in providing abortions, a request that emanated logically from the contention that the abortion provisions of the Criminal Code were nullified by the right to life guaranteed in the Charter of Rights. If the Court granted the latter, it must so grant the former.

Thus the Borowski legal team summoned three witnesses to give evidence regarding the intricacies of federal and provincial funding for health care, and more specifically, of abortions. These men testified at various points in the trial, and one in particular gave explanations of a system of such labyrinthine complexity that the Crown lawyer was moved to apply the remedy of humour.

"I think, My Lord," quipped the normally somber Sojonky, "I'd like to get back to the question of when life begins after hearing that evidence."

"It's simple," broke in the irrepressible Shumiatcher.[11]

The testimony so qualified by the doctor of law was that of Don Rowlatt. By the time he testified, the trial was into its fifth day. It was Friday, May 13, and outside, protesters had gathered for their daily picket. Inside, the number of spectators had thinned out considerably since the departure of the luminous Dr. Lejeune.

It was Brad Hunter, Shumiatcher's junior assistant, who questioned Rowlatt, Director of Taxation and Economic Policy for the Saskatchewan government. To him fell the onerous task of explaining the statutes and mechanisms through which the federal and provincial governments coordinate their expenditures.

The provincial entitlement was established by the Federal-Provincial Fiscal Arrangements and Established Programs Financing Act, and the federal contribution was then subsequently calculated within this Act, Rowlatt explained.

The difference between the province's entitlement and what it actually received in federal contributions was accounted for by a tax policy that came into effect in 1977. The federal government reduced its cash contributions, but also reduced personal and corporate income tax, thereby permitting the provinces to top up the shortfall by increasing its own taxes. The taxpayer would, theoretically, not notice a thing.

The contributions were allocated to medical care, hospital insurance and post-secondary education. Contributions to the first two categories were paid out to the provinces by the federal Minister of Health and "subject to the conditions and all aspects of the Hospital Insurance and Diagnostic Services Act, and the Medical Care Act," the witness explained.[12]

"Could these payments be withheld by the Government of Canada or the Minister of Health?" asked Hunter.

The conditions in the two statutes he cited did indeed, said Rowlatt, "contemplate the termination of the cash contribution if the conditions are not achieved."

These contributions from the federal government, in the case of his province, poured directly into an entity with the enticing name of the Consolidated Revenue Fund, but the flow was not measured to fill exactly this capacious bucket.[13] The entitlement for a fiscal year and "ultimate cash flows" were re-estimated a number of times and "flow over a number of years," so the money to which the province was entitled in a given fiscal year, it would have "received in one fiscal year or another."[14]

Sojonky had a few questions for the witness. Would it be fair to say that, outside certain broad requirements being met, the federal government does not audit to determine if money was expended for medicare, and did not earmark funds for such purposes?

That was indeed the case, concurred the witness. So, continued Sojonky, since medical care and health insurance had to be paid for somehow, the province "puts in dollars and you add the federal contribution, and if monies can be saved in certain areas, well, more power to Sakstachewan, is that correct?"

"If I may question the order in which you had the money going in, I couldn't agree with the way you describe it," admonished Rowlatt. "In effect, what happens is the federal government provides a contribution to the province, the province allocates money to the medical care or hospital insurance programs."

But there was no allocation of funds for specific purposes in the health care field, and no funds established for "the establishment and maintenance of therapeutic abortion committees, I think that's quite clear?" Rowlatt did not know of any other financing other than the "broadly defined category of insured services"; what that encompassed, he did not know.[15]

Also testifying on the mechanisms for the funding of abortion were Donald Cameron and Darryl Thompson. They were the assistant executive director of the Saskatchewan Hospital Services Plan and director of the statistics branch with the Medical Care Insurance Commission, respectively.

Cameron told the Court that the Saskatchewan Hospital Services Plan provided funding for services considered medically necessary. He verified that in 1982-83 the province of Saskatchewan had paid for 1,616 Code 635 procedures, which in the ICD-9 system—that is, the International Classification of Diseases, a classification system developed by the World Health Organization—stood for "therapeutic abortions done on an out-patient basis."[16] However, that figure was based only on the information they received and coded, Cameron explained. As the hospitals were not obliged to submit this information, the figures could well be incomplete.[17]

The witness also corroborated the testimony of Rowlatt when he explained that the amount paid for an outpatient abortion (where the mother did not remain in hospital overnight) was taken from the Consolidated Revenue Fund. The amount at the time was $180, the standard day surgery rate.[18]

The second witness, Darryl Thompson, testified that in the year 1981-82, the Medical Care Insurance Commission (MCIC) paid out $116,000 to cover the fees for 1,521 abortions done in Saskatchewan hospitals that year. He also testified that the province covered the cost of 48 out-of-province abortions in the same year, the total cost of which was $3,837[19]

Thompson said that the MCIC did not verify if the abortions were actually done but based their figures on the claims submitted by physicians.[20]

Hunter questioned the witness concerning the total cost of an abortion. Thompson agreed that the "potential" or "estimated" cost of a "therapeutic abortion" could total $399, which would include the hospital fee of $180, the obstetrical consultation of

$37, psychiatric consulation of $69, general practitioner consultation of $31, and the obstetrician fee, for the actual abortion, of $82.[21]

Thompson verified that the MCIC, which administered insured medical services, paid monies to either the doctor or the designated beneficiary out of the Consolidated Revenue Fund.

Edward Sojonky had no questions for either witness.

Notes
Chapter 21
The evidence mounts

[1] Ibid. p. 364.
[2] Ibid. p. 365-366.
[3] Ibid. p. 366.
[4] Ibid. p. 372.
[5] Ibid. p. 376.
[6] Ibid. p. 377.
[7] Ibid. p. 371.
[8] Ibid. p. 379.
[9] Ibid. p. 381.
[10] Ibid. p. 382-383.
[11] Ibid. p. 361.
[12] Ibid. p. 357.
[13] Ibid. p. 357.
[14] Ibid. p. 359.
[15] Ibid. pp. 362-363
[16] Ibid. pp. 518-520.
[17] Ibid. p. 520.
[18] Ibid. p. 521.
[19] Ibid. pp. 524-525.
[20] Ibid. p. 525.
[21] Ibid. p. 526.

Chapter 22

Trial by media

"Here's a man who worships in a painted shrine
in his backyard and decks his body with special amulets
to save him from the fires of hell."
Michele Landsberg[1]

"I would describe [the media] as being arrogant,
vindictive, paranoid, tending to attack
anyone who opposes them."
Joe Borowski [2]

AFTER TWO FULL WEEKS OF TESTIMONY BY WITNESSES ON BEHALF OF THE plaintiff, Joe Borowski, it was the defendants' turn to call witnesses.

However, in a move that amazed his adversaries and infuriated abortion advocates, Crown lawyer Edward Sojonky announced that he would call no witnesses, introduce no *viva voce* evidence. It was the position of the attorney-general, he told Justice Matheson, "that any medical evidence relating to the unborn and the various developmental stages of the unborn, was not particularly relevant or germane. Now, I should add that much of the medical evidence, I suggest, is not in dispute, and perhaps it's fair to say it has not been in dispute, nor has the attorney-general, I submit, ever suggested that it was in dispute."[3] Sojonky filed only the *Badgley Report* of January 1977, and the 1980 Statistics Canada report on therapeutic abortions, as evidence.[4 5]

Joe Borowski was taken aback by this turn of events. "The federal government has a huge budget, there's not a shortage of funds like we had to face," he told reporters. "They seem to be folding up their tents."[6]

Abortion advocates took the Crown's move to mean that the government didn't care. The Canadian Abortion Rights Action League (CARAL), "shocked" at what happened, chastised federal Justice Minister Mark MacGuigan. "The final day of the trial in Regina confirmed our worst fears," read a telegram to the Minister signed by CARAL president, Norma Scarborough. "Even Joe Borowski stated that he was astounded that the government called no witnesses."[7]

Some weeks earlier, Scarborough had herself hired lawyer Morris Manning to mount a CARAL challenge to Section 251. The group claimed that the abortion law provisions were contrary to the Charter of Rights, and contravened women's right to "liberty and security of the person" as guaranteed under Section 7. CARAL did this in answer to Joe Borowski's lawsuit.[8]

Scarborough was front row and center at the Borowski trial, having taken a vacation from her job as an executive secretary at a suburban Toronto high school.[9] Her harrowing hours there were relayed sympathetically to the public by *Toronto Star* columnist and wife of Ontario NDP leader Stephen Lewis, Michele Landsberg, who quoted the CARAL president: "I had no idea how depressing it would be. I left in tears after listening to all these men—judges, lawyers, witnesses—jousting and game-playing about the most personal things in a woman's life, while we women sat by helplessly."

Landsberg was noteworthy among the press for her screeds against Joe. Calling him "Holy Joe" and deriding his Catholicism, she heaped scorn on "this whole cult of worship of fertilized eggs" and the "lunatic spectacle in Regina."[10]

Not all feminists were as hostile to Joe as was Landsberg. Interestingly enough, in the fall of 1974, Joe squared off against Germaine Greer, a well-known advocate of women's rights and author of the *The Female Eunuch*, on a CBC current affairs program. While Greer disagreed with Joe's convictions and philosophy, when asked by the host what she thought of the man himself, she replied, "I rather like Joe." It could be surmised that Joe's sincerity and obvious lack of guile were instrumental in disarming the Australian writer, academic and career feminist.

Pro-life lawyer Gwen Landolt, when commenting on the Borowski trial in an article, called the press coverage "super, superb." Others were not so sure, among them Joe himself, who as usual was candid about his disgust. The *Toronto Star* and *Sun* "were at their worst in 1983 when I was arguing my court challenge," he admitted years later. "The attacks reached a new low when they personally attacked me because I had the gall to challenge their sacred abortion law. I'm not going to repeat the garbage they threw at me. Perhaps those that suffered most were my family." It was one thing to go after a politician or capitalist fat cat, but another matter to attack "a political has-been and average Joe like me."

The media's "empty claim" that people have a right to know "has never been at the heart of reporting and honest journalism. In fact, profit, circulation and rating figures are the crude and obscene yardstick used to justify the headlines, stories and attacks on defenceless individuals," Joe charged. "But what the powerful and monopolistic media lack most is tolerance, compassion, understanding and a heart and soul."

He advised newsmen to heed the message of Pope John Paul II, who observed that they "contribute to the operation of justice in giving voice to the voiceless." There was no one more "voiceless" than the unborn child.

A survey conducted by historian Alphonse de Valk concluded that, despite the initial fanfare, Joe's trial was "poorly reported." Newsmen showed "more interest in side issues than in analyzing the significance of the testimony presented." The testimony of the nine expert witnesses barely saw the light of day, with most papers reporting on "no more than three or four" of these. Only the *Regina Leader-Post* carried daily reports; that paper, along with *The Toronto Star*, had the best coverage, he assessed.

Canada's self-described "paper of record" could fairly be said to have had the worst coverage of all. Richard Cleroux, reporter for the *Globe and Mail*, disappeared after filing a report on the first day of the trial. The *Globe*, which had promoted abortion on demand since the 1970s, subsequently printed only two more stories: one when Sojonky did not call any witnesses, and one to announce the trial was over.[11]

De Valk found it curious that, while at least a dozen reporters were present for the trial, the majority of daily papers relied on *Canadian Press* reports, which he noted were generally lacking. These repeated "*ad nauseum*, facts already known or irrelevant, such as the origins of the trial, the colour of Mr. Borowski's suit, and above all, what the right to abortion activists were saying or doing outside the courtroom." On four occasions the news bureau released two dispatches, one on the trial, and one on the views and activities of abortion advocates. When this occurred, a number of papers printed only the latter report.[12]

Certainly the complaints of the right-to-abort contingent were well amplified in the press. Evanna Simpson, spokesperson for the Pro-Choice Coalition, expressed outrage that "a singular moral viewpoint [was] threatening to impose itself on the rest of society." She, too, objected to the fact that "a small number of men are putting the women of Canada on trial. People who never experience pregnancy want to decide when pregnancy should take place."[13] [14]

Joe was quizzed on this matter by reporters from the *Prairie Messenger*, Saskatchewan's Catholic weekly, published by the Benedictine monks of Munster. Had he "ever been close to someone faced with an unwanted pregnancy?" Eileen Saunders and Heather Meagher wanted to know.

"Sure," Joe replied. "When I was in the government, we had an open door policy and this attracted all kinds of kooks with inventions they wanted to get on the market, but we also had women with problems, and we directed them to where they could get help. In the past five years, I've come into contact with many more women through speaking."

Had anyone close to him ever been in that situation? "Thank God, no," said Joe. "No brothers, sisters have been involved like that. But I know we'll always have unwanted pregnancies with the kind of moral climate we live in—shack-ups and premarital sex. These are the building blocks of abortion and we are going to need more and more facilities to look after them—both private and government. It's not good enough to give high and holy speeches—you mustn't do that. Words are cheap. Mother Teresa says, 'Don't kill that child—give it it me.' Money is needed and I'm not asking pro-lifers to put families on welfare. But we have to give what we can to help these women—even though much comes about because of sexual irresponsibility."

"Why wouldn't God choose a woman to lead this movement in this time of women's rising influence?" asked one of the reporters. "He did," came Joe's prompt reply, "Mother Teresa. Next to the Pope, she is the most outspoken advocate of pro-life. I quote her often. She says, 'Abortion not only destroys the child but destroys the conscience of all involved.' She doesn't tire of talking about it. And there are other women, like my wife, but the press doesn't tell about them."[15]

On May 25, the flamboyant Morris Shumiatcher rose to make his final summation. While interest and attendance had waxed and waned as the days passed, that Wednesday it was standing room only in the second-floor courtroom[16] as the renowned Queen's Counsel, hunched over a black-and-orange wood podium five metres in front of Justice Matheson, argued the case for the unborn child on behalf of an attentive Joe Borowski.[17] A mother holding a baby in her arms was among the dozens who patiently stood in the aisles, while additional "curious onlookers were forced to peer through peepholes to catch a glimpse of the historic proceedings."[18]

Outside, in the bracing air of an unseasonably cool May, pro-life supporters showed up for the first time to rally for Joe. The presence of about 300 pro-lifers engaged in a "prayer walk" in front of the Victoria Avenue courthouse bumped the usual group of right-to-abortion demonstrators, who had maintained a noon-hour picket throughout the trial, to an unaccustomed position across the street. This state of affairs put the collective nose of the ad hoc collective, Citizens for Reproductive Rights, out of joint, and added further to their already frequently expressed disgruntlement.[19]

In court, Shumiatcher wove disparate strands of testimony together into a coherent tapestry. He spoke for seven hours over the next day-and-a-half, and while much of his argument was eloquent, enough of it was deemed to be "technical and legalistic" to the point that spectators "drifted away."[20]

"Our first position is simply this," began the grey-bearded advocate, "that 'everyone' as it appears in the Charter, includes the unborn child living within the body of his mother...To destroy an innocent child capriciously is contrary to the substantive principles of fundamental justice that Section 7 of the Charter speaks of."

The plaintiff's second position was that "if an abortion committee is to exist at all" then the members must consider the unborn child as well as the mother. The Criminal Code "is silent concerning the life and health of the unborn child. If that child is someone, anyone, it is our position that he, like his mother, must be considered before it is decided to destroy him. His life and health, like the life and health of his mother, also has significance. He's not so small; he's not so inconsequential that the Canadian Charter of Rights and Freedoms and the Bill of Rights have ignored or forgotten him."

Without "constitutional and statutory guarantees to the unborn child, subsections 4, 5 and 6 of Section 251 of the Code create a punishment without a crime, and a death without a trial."[21]

The government took far greater care in providing statutory safeguards to privacy when it drafted legislation regarding wiretaps, than when it constructed the exculpatory sections of 251, which Shumiatcher excoriated as "shoddy, thoughtless legislation." When one considered that the three medical doctors on the therapeutic abortion committee "don't have to have any qualifications of a judicial or quasi-judicial nature at all to decide whether the unborn child is to live or to die" it becomes apparent that the unborn child could be described, Shumiatcher said, in the lines of a "little quatrain" he had composed:[22]

"We are the little nobodies,
Not dog nor fowl nor cat
We cannot meow or bark or cry
De minimus lex non curat.[23]

"The law," he continued, "certainly under 251, takes no cognizance of the unborn, and they are treated like trifles. But that was before ultrasound, before we could see who and what they were and watch them live their intrauterine life."[24]

Justice Matheson questioned whether the disputed subsections of Section 251 were "intended, at the very least, to cover a situation where a mother had cancer of the cervix which was diagnosed very early in the pregnancy, and without that exception, might not someone who treated her, with the unfortunate results to the fetus, be faced with a charge under 251 (1)?"

Shumiatcher's first response was that the law should provide for a judicial body to determine whether the pregnancy would endanger the life of the mother. "Well, why should judges second-guess medical practitioners?" countered Matheson.

"For the same reason we have sitting on the Bench of this Court today, a judicial officer who is a judge, and not a medical practitioner," replied Shumiatcher. "These are matters of life and death."

A judicial process might take too long to be of any practical use to the mother in such a case, the judge observed. Celerity, rejoined Shumiatcher, "is not necessarily a quality wanting in the law." Injunctions, for example, could be obtained "in a matter of hours." More to the point, the parliamentarians who drafted this law "placed nothing in the legislation…to provide any defence or safeguard for the unborn child."

"Well, no," conceded Justice Matheson, "I understand that."[25]

The "test of the threat or danger to a woman's life which would justify an abortion," Shumiatcher elaborated, would be that "since it is the child's life that is forfeited in abortion, to claim that life, it must be clear that without it, the life of the mother would be lost." That case could apply in the circumstance of cancer of the cervix, and then, it would not be an abortion as defined in the Criminal Code.

"After all, we are dealing here with criminal law, and we're dealing here with serious offences. *Mens rea* lies at the root of these offences. And so in every case, one must ask the question: what is the intention of the procedure?"[26]

If the intent were to destroy the child in the womb, the act would be an abortion. But if the intent "be to treat the disease or the abnormal condition and preserve the life of the mother…and the incidental effect thereof would be to remove the pregnancy, that is not an abortion."[27]

A significant exchange occurred when the lawyer brought up Section 206 of the Criminal Code, which stated that, "a child becomes a human being within the meaning of this Act when it has completely proceeded, in a living state, from the body of its mother."

"You don't take any issue with that definition?" queried the judge.

"Well, the definition is there," replied Shumiatcher.

But the Code was "talking about a human being coming into existence at a prescribed time," persisted Justice Matheson. "Now, insofar as the Charter is concerned, is it possible to be within the group of everyone and not be a human being?"

"I doubt it, My Lord," joked the Q.C., "unless you want to be E.T."

"Well, the Code says that when a child becomes a human being."

Shumiatcher paused. "Well, it's a—yes, as a matter of fact, My Lord, I think I should consider that. I think Your Lordship is right. It should be considered. I would like to give it a little consideration."

Possibly he could speak to the matter further, the lawyer then suggested.[28] Shumiatcher did not return in great detail to this point, however, mentioning only Section 206 in passing the next day, and then only to say that the Section "certainly recognized that the unborn human is a child, and a child assuredly is someone, and someone undoubtedly is a particular of everyone. It is everyone that the Charter protects."[29]

He did provide an oblique reply to Matheson's comments when he assembled an impressive array of cases to demonstrate the protection that the law had provided to the child in the womb. In particular, a ruling based on Section 203, which deals with death by criminal negligence, spoke to the very issue. The 1979 Marsh decision concerned an unlicensed physician whose negligence caused a baby to die just prior to delivery. The judge noted at that time that the "essential nature" of the unborn child "is not changed by the fact of birth." If criminal negligence causing death of a child after delivery "is an indictable offence," wrote the judge, then to hold that "similar negligence causing death immediately before delivery is not criminal, is not a conclusion that accords well with the concept that the State has a duty to protect unborn children and to preserve their opportunities to be born and to enjoy the rights and obligations normally incidental to the status of humankind."

The injuries inflicted upon the unborn child in this case prevented it from surviving "the short but perilous passage from its mother's womb to the greater world, and thereby to achieve full status as a human being. For the purposes of this ruling, I find that a full-term child is a person within the meaning of Section 203 of the Criminal Code notwithstanding that it remains unborn."[30]

This case formed part of the "technical and legalistic" sections of Shumiatcher's argument that dispersed the eager crowd, and which included further citations of case law and tradition supporting the right to life of the unborn child. The lawyer quoted William Blackstone, the famed British legal authority from the 18th century, to buttress his contention that "law favours life, and under the law no one may be deprived of life save for just cause."[31] According to Blackstone's *Commentaries on the Laws of England*, "life is the immediate gift of God, a right inherent by nature in every individual, and it begins in contemplation of law as soon as an infant is able to stir in the mother's womb."[32] He further wrote that "an infant *en ventre de sa mère*, or in the mother's womb, is supposed in law to be born for many purposes" which would include having a legacy, a guardian, and an estate "limited to its use."[33]

Shumiatcher also cited the 1959 United Nations' Declaration on the Rights of the Child, which stated that the child should have "appropriate legal protection before as well as after birth" and "adequate prenatal and postnatal care" among other rights. This, the lawyer asserted, indicated that there was international recognition that "the child is anyone...that he is somebody and a very important somebody in the family and in our society, as well as, of course, for himself."[34]

As far as case law in Canada, Shumiatcher emphasized a 1933 decision of the Supreme Court that "upheld the right of a child to sue for injuries suffered while in the womb."[35] He pointed to a 1919 case in which the unborn child was included among the class of children entitled to receive benefits from a will.[36]

More recent cases included a 1979 injunction proceeding by a father in Nova Scotia to prevent the abortion of his child; a family court in that province appointed a guardian to act for the child in the womb.[37]

The case of a Kenora, Ontario child who was apprehended at birth by the Children's Aid Society, demonstrated that the unborn child was entitled to protection. The judge ruled that abuse had taken place in the womb; the mother was an alcoholic and had previously given birth to two children who suffered from fetal alcohol syndrome.[38] A similar ruling was made regarding a child born addicted to methadone to a woman who, during her pregnancy, had been taking this drug as a substitute for heroin, to which she was addicted. In this case, the Supreme Court ruled that "the child had been abused while unborn and therefore, was a child in need of protection at the time of birth."

Shumiatcher spent considerable time arguing that the Charter, unlike the Bill of Rights which it superseded, encompassed a notion of fundamental justice that touched the very substance of the law, not just procedural matters.[39] This was significant because, if the fundamental justice referred to in the Charter was substantive justice, then legislation that was judged to contravene fundamental justice could be declared ultra vires, or without force—invalid.

Therefore, Joe Borowski's lawyer took pains to persuade Justice Matheson that this was indeed the case when the present law permitting abortion was held up to the scrutiny of Section 7 of the Charter. Fundamental justice required that "you can't capriciously kill an unborn child for no reason at all, any more than you can hang a man for no reason or little reason or capriciously." Moreover, "you can't pass a law doing those things, because that's the substantive part of the phrase 'fundamental justice'."[40]

The therapeutic abortion committee, as governed by subsections 4, 5, and 6 of Section 251, "provide none of the requisites of fundamental justice, of due process for the protection of the unborn child... In light of the child's future, the committee should be required, indeed is, I submit, required under the Charter now, to examine into the state of the child and, of course, the condition of the mother and the needs of each of them."[41]

Finally, Shumiatcher brought up the famous "Persons" case of 1929,[42] in which the Supreme Court of Canada declared that women were not persons. The Court made this momentous discovery in response to a petition by Henrietta Muir Edwards and four other women, who were lobbying for women to be members of the Senate. The BNA Act required that members of the Senate be "persons" under the law. When the Supreme Court ruled that, for the purposes of the Act, women were not legal persons, Muir *et al.* appealed to the Judicial Committee of the Privy Council in England, then the supreme authority over the Dominion of Canada.[43]

Lord Sankey of the Privy Council ruled that women indeed were persons and elucidated his principle of constitutional interpretation. "The British North America Act planted in Canada a living tree, capable of growth and expansion within its natural limits." He and his fellow Lords did not consider it their duty to constrain the Act "by a narrow and technical construction," the peer observed, but "to give it a large and liberal interpretation."[44]

Shumiatcher besought the judge presiding over the Borowski trial to "give to the word 'everyone' the amplitude of interpretation that Lord Sankey visualized in 1929." Thus, it would follow that the word "everyone" in Section 7 of the Charter would include the child in the womb.

Concluding with a flourish, the able advocate emphasized that "the timing of this trial raises two great ironies, which must not escape us...First, more abortions are being performed at the very time that there is no need for them." Secondly, to carry out these abortions, "society has unsheathed the sword of the magistrate and handed it over to untutored people at the very time in which the Constitution requires that these matters be dealt with according to the principles of fundamental justice.

"The first act has taken the lives of myriads of innocent children, and the second act has stripped them of all hope of defending their lives."[45]

In the clear Saskatchewan sky, high about the two-story concrete building on Victoria Avenue, a 20-foot yellow blimp serenely drifted, carrying the message, "We're with you all the way, Joe."[46] Down in the second-floor courthouse, Edward Sojonky had sat patiently, one metre to the left of his learned friend, during the latter's seven-hour summation, breaking his impassive stance only occasionally to rapidly take notes.[47]

Now, the dark-haired counsel for the defendant, 20 years Shumiatcher's junior, rose to argue the Crown's case. While Shumiatcher had remained riveted to the podium, reading from a typewritten text, the lanky Sojonky strode back and forth in front of the judge's bench, often using his hands to emphasize a point.[48]

The defendants did not dispute the "medical and physiological facts respecting the growth and development of the unborn." But whether "a person can be said to exist from conception…is not a medical matter. When one speaks of 'human beings' or 'person', 'everyone', one is using words which carry a signification that goes beyond medicine and biology."[49]

Sojonky asserted that the word "everyone" in the Charter was a substitute for "person" or "individual" in the Bill of Rights.[50] In determining the meaning of the word "everyone" in Section 7, Sojonky argued that it was necessary to look at "the state of the law" before the Charter. And "clearly the unborn were never recognized as persons having enforceable legal rights."[51]

Any rights granted to the child *in utero* were "conditional upon subsequent birth"—such as actions laid on behalf of a child for injuries suffered *en ventre sa mère*. Sojonky cited the *Dehler* case to back up his contention that "the law has selected birth as the point at which the fetus becomes a person with full and independent rights."[52]

But the judgment in that case, interjected Justice Matheson, was based on the Criminal Code. Now, there was a "supervening law," he said: "Can the Criminal Code distinguish between human beings without heed to Section 7 of the Charter of Rights?" The Charter, Sojonky responded, "is by virtue of its own sections, perhaps a different law and a supreme law, I'll concede that."

To start with an inferior law—the Criminal Code—and move to the Charter was "putting the cart before the horse" was it not, further questioned Matheson. "Is it not necessary to determine what is meant by 'everyone' and then look at the Criminal Code to see if something in the Criminal Code detracts from those?"[53]

"My Lord, with respect, I think not," said the undaunted Crown lawyer. Only if an "inconsistency" emerged would it be necessary to strike down a provision as unconstitutional. It was evident that the framers of the Charter "would not have placed a provision such as Section 7" in the Charter, if they thought it would conflict with Section 251 of the Criminal Code.[54] In fact, "my submission would be that Parliament did not intend by the simple use of the word 'everyone' to change the law at all."[55] The Charter, added Sojonky, "in my respectful position, is not akin to the Ten Commandments. It's not the voice of God, it's the voice of

Parliament. It was drafted, in effect, by people. These legislators had intention, Parliament clearly had intention, and they had meanings and intention in mind."[56][57]

Sojonky hammered away at Shumiatcher's contention that the unborn child did not receive substantive justice, and that the therapeutic abortion committees should, at the very least, consider the rights of the unborn child. The TAC was not a legal body, Sojonky flatly stated. "There are only medical decisions that must be taken, and that's the end of it. And who better…to make those medical decisions, to make a medical opinion than the doctors?"[58]

In the course of this argument, Sojonky had a curious exchange with Justice Matheson. "If one concludes that an unborn child is part of 'everyone',," the latter asked, "do you think the non-legal process that you've described is in accordance with fundamental justice?"[59]

After some hesitation, Sojonky admitted that, if "everyone" was found to include the unborn child, then "certain procedural safeguards would be appropriate."

"Well, am I to assume then," continued Justice Matheson, "when you're emphasizing that the therapeutic abortion committee is not a legal process, that you're conceding that this procedure does not follow the principles of fundamental justice?"

"It does not have to," swiftly responded the Crown lawyer. "It does not have to follow any such procedure, given the words used in 251."[60] The Code only required a medical diagnosis to be made and an opinion given "that would meet the requirements of the exempting provisions of 251."

"Take it one step further," persisted the justice. "If, for example, you have a three-year-old child whose activities are such that the mother is in imminent danger of both a mental and physical breakdown and medical opinions so certify that, does that justify terminating the life of the child?"

"Not at all," Sojonky replied; in that case, the mother would be charged with homicide, "and she would be the one receiving the fair trial." If one were contemplating taking the life of a three-year-old child, Parliament "would want to ensure that there were, in that situation, some procedural safeguards, yes."

"Well then, do I gather that you say because the child is unborn, it doesn't require these procedural safeguards?"

"That's correct, yes."[61]

The Crown counsel spent some time in his four-hour summation in detailing what effect Section 1 of the Charter could be said to have on the matter before the Court. (That Section, it will be recalled, guarantees the rights and freedoms of the Charter, subject only to those limitations that are held as reasonable in a free and democratic society.)

"Now, it's clear that the pregnant woman has rights, as conceded, and a pregnant woman has a right under sections such as Section 7," he argued. "Now, in considering Section 1, those rights of the woman must be balanced against those accorded to the unborn, again all the while based on the premise and the assumption that we, in fact, do have competing interests or rights."[62]

Therefore, Section 251 was reasonable, as it sought, Sojonky claimed, to "achieve a balance between respect and protection for the life of the unborn...and the interests of the pregnant woman. And I would submit further that the life of the unborn cannot be regarded in isolation and it's inextricably connected with the life and health of the pregnant woman."[63]

Justice Matheson engaged the lawyer. Was he saying that Section 251 of the Criminal Code "in total is a reasonable limit prescribed by law and can be demonstrably justified in a free and democratic society?"

"Exactly, exactly."And if the abortion provisions of Section 251 were struck down, added Sojonky, it would "force the women in Canada to go full term. There's just no doubt about it. It's as simple as that. Force all the women to go full term...Abortion would not be permissible in Canada under any circumstances. And that, My Lord, would be a disastrous consequence."[64]

Once again all eyes in the courtroom turned to the venerable doctor of law, Morris Shumiatcher, as he rose for his final rebuttal. As was his habit, the man who had initiated the momentous proceedings sat behind his advocate, attentive to every utterance. Joe Borowski was on the periphery in this arena, where Shumiatcher, who evidently relished the verbal and intellectual parry and thrust of the trial, had thrived for decades.

"May it please Your Lordship," he now began, "my learned friend, Mr. Sojonky, ended on a terribly somber note, I thought."

Moreover, the Crown counsel's contention was "not correct": should the abortion provisions of Section 251 be struck down as contravening the Charter, the law would revert to pre-1969 conditions. Then, decisions were made on a case-by-case basis as to whether or not an abortion was medically necessary.

While Sojonky contended that it was not the intention of Parliament to promote abortion when it passed the abortion provisions of Section 251, Shumiatcher was not so sure. "It may not have been the intention, although that is questionable, but the result has been precisely that." After 1969, the abortion rate increased to the point that "since 1972 the births in this country are not keeping up on a *pro rata* basis with the deaths. We are depopulating our nation.[65] And, My Lord, I don't know how you can have a free and democratic society under those circumstances; indeed, I don't know how you can have any society where you're killing off the great potential for good of a nation."

Shumiatcher had his own curious exchange with Justice Matheson. Based on a hypothetical situation, said the judge, if there were a therapeutic abortion committee consisting of Drs. Beirne, Smyth and Morris, "what do you think the result would be in view of their testimony?"

"[I]n this country we have a rule of law or by law, and that's affirmed in the Charter, and not of men. It's true men must sit on a board, a court, in a cabinet and so on, but it seems to me that ...it wouldn't be enough under the legislation as it now stands to appoint the Archangel Gabriel," replied Shumiatcher. Having "high-minded persons, sensitive and knowledgeable people on such a committee is *sine qua non*. I don't think that is enough. I think the safeguards must be built into the law."[66]

But, asked Justice Matheson, why do not doctors state, as the witnesses produced by Shumiatcher undoubtedly would, that the woman's pregnancy "will not endanger her life?"[67]

"Oh, because, I think, the reason is very, very simple," came the response. "I think it's part of the whole consumerism concept of our society...The customer is always right. If you want it, you can have it...And it's part and parcel of the casual relationship that we have towards the most important values in society, traditionally we have had in society, that little kids don't count."[68]

Justice Matheson still seemed dissatisfied. If the provisions were "strictly interpreted, and not in the sense that you've been talking about where consumerism seems to prevail, what the consumer wants the consumer gets, would the number not then drop substantially, the number of abortions?"

"Well, it—I don't know. I can't say, because at least if there were present, those guidelines—"

"Well, I'm just going on the basis of these witnesses. They could think of very few instances when an abortion would be necessary under these terms. That's really what I'm getting at," the judge said.

"I don't want to be taken to accept the position that this pact is operating as is simply because there has been…a cavalier attitude by the medical profession in carrying this out…I'm not taking that position…I wish to make that very, very clear," responded Shumiatcher "I am—I think that the doctors look at this and they say, well, what's the minimum we have to do? They're busy people. And that's what they've done, the minimum they had to do."[69]

After that uneasy exchange, Shumiatcher went on to rebut Sojonky's arguments. Shumiatcher took issue with Sojonky's claim that the law struck a "necessary" balance between the supposedly competing rights of the mother and child *in utero*. "I'm puzzled over that. While that sounds very nice, where is the balance?" The unborn "isn't even mentioned" in the disputed subsections of Section 251.

As for the contention by the Crown that abortion was only a medical matter, and therefore no due process needs to be followed, "that was a shocker to me," Shumiatcher told the judge.[70]

To regard it as merely a medical matter was just an attempt to "salve our conscience about what's really happening under these terms." The doctors may say the abortion was required for health reasons but the evidence proved that "the vast majority of the abortions are carried out for socio-economic reasons."[71]

Shumiatcher also repudiated Sojonky's claim that the abortion provisions in the Criminal Code were a reasonable limitation as justified in a free and democratic society, as sanctioned by Section 1 of the Charter. Pointing out that Sojonky had not brought in a single witness "to say why it is necessary to take this life away" Shumiatcher observed trenchantly that in an abortion, life was denied, not limited. "How can you limit life? How? You either have it or you haven't it."

At last, it was over. Thirteen days of testimony and arguments ended in the early afternoon on Friday, May 27. There were no demonstrators from either side in evidence as the courtroom on the second floor of Victoria Avenue emptied out.[72] Only the yellow blimp with its "pro-Joe" message gave testimony to the events below.

Justice William Matheson was expected to take his time deliberating the wealth of testimony and the complex constitutional arguments and issues, and he himself concurred with this widespread opinion. "Needless to say, I reserve decision," he told the Court, after ruling, in the view of one commentator, "quietly and firmly over the most sensational trial here since Louis Riel was sentenced to hang for treason nearly a century ago."[73]

A buoyant and smiling Joe Borowski stood on the steps of the courthouse, and radiated confidence after this effort, the culmination of his years of struggle, came to a close. "I feel great. I liked the tone and the direction the trial took, and the attitude of the trial judge. He certainly gave us every opportunity to present our facts."

Nevertheless, he was more than ready to make the seven-hour drive back to Winnipeg to his wife and daughters. "I plan to go home to Winnipeg and put out a serious brushfire in our backyard," he announced to reporters. "That is Dr. Henry Morgentaler's abortion clinic."[74]

Notes
Chapter 22
Trial by media

[1] *Toronto Star*, May 23, 1983.

[2] "Borowski fights back," *Toronto Star*, August 2, 1988.

[3] Op. Cit., *Trial for Life*, p. 602.

[4] The *Badgley Report* was released in 1977 and contained the findings of the Committee on the Operation of the Abortion Law, a committee headed by Robin F. Badgley, a medical sociologist from Toronto. His colleagues were Marion Powell, director of the Bay Street Birth Control Clinic in Toronto, and Denyse Fortin Caron. The committee, formed in 1975 under the federal Liberal Justice Minister, Ron Basford, was directed to review and report on whether the procedures provided for in the Criminal Code (i.e. subsections 4 to 7 of Section 251) were "operating equitably across Canada." After much investigation, the committee concluded that there was "wide variation" in the ease of obtaining abortions across Canada. The therapeutic abortion committees (TACs) were shown to have rubber-stamped applications without further examination, a point which certain abortion supporters had denied consistently. The Badgley Report also revealed that in the first year abortion was permitted by law (1970), 11,152 abortions were performed. By 1974 that already high figure had risen to 48,136 and the Report noted that a decline in the birth rate was now in evidence.

[5] Sojonky also attempted to file the document that he had freely utilized in his cross-examinations, the hearings of the American Senate on the "pro-life amendment,"(formally titled: *Hearings before the subcommittee on the separation of powers of the committee on the judiciary, United States Senate, 97th Congress*) but Justice Matheson would have none of it. The transcripts were ruled inadmissible because they were from a foreign jurisdiction—a decision a "shaken Sojonky" had to accept. (Op. Cit., Morton p. 148.)

[6] "Borowski 'astounded' at Crown's stance," *Star-Phoenix*, May 21, 1983.

[7] "Pro-abortion group raps Justice Minister," *Vancouver Sun*, May 31, 1983, p. A12.

[8] "Abortion rights league to launch own challenge," Ron Petrie, *Leader-Post*, May 6, 1983, p. A3.

[9] "Pro-choice president says case anti-woman," *Toronto Star*, May 17, 1983, p. B1.

[10] "Lunatic spectacle in Regina," *Toronto Star*, May 12, 1983.

[11] Alphonse de Valk, *Joseph Borowski and the Trial of the Century* (Edmonton: Life Ethics Centre, 1983), p. 1.

[12] Ibid., pp. 1-3.

[13] "Demonstration planned to oppose court challenge," *Leader-Post*, May 6, 1983, p. A3.

[14] Gwen Landolt points out that these pro-abortionists were known for "strategically not mentioning that it was men who brought in this infamous abortion law in 1969 and that it is mainly men who are sitting on the rubber-stamp therapeutic abortion committees. Abortion, of course, is not a male-female ques-

tion, rather it is a matter of human rights and justice and no sex has a monopoly on this." (*Toronto Right to Life News*, July 1983, p 4.)

15 *Prairie Messenger*, May 22, 1983.

16 "Abortion 'cruel punishment' lawyer tells packed court," Pat McNenly, *Toronto Star*, May 26, 1983, p. A14.

17 "Borowski ready to fight another battle," *The Edmonton Journal*, May 28, 1983.

18 Op. Cit., McNenly.

19 "Prayer walk helped by pro-life supporters outside courthouse," Lyn Hynes, *Leader-Post*, May 26, 1983.

20 Op cit., McNenly.

21 Trial transcripts. pp. 611-612.

22 Ibid. p. 627.

23 (The law takes no account of trifles.)

24 Ibid. p. 628.

25 Ibid. p. 686.

26 Ibid. p. 691.

27 Ibid. p. 692.

28 Ibid. p. 678.

29 Ibid. p. 683.

30 Op. Cit., *Trial for Life*, p. 700.

31 Op. Cit. "Abortion 'cruel punishment,' Pat McNenly.

32 Op. Cit., *Trial for Life*, p. 648.

33 Ibid. pp. 648-649.

34 Ibid. p. 652.

35 Ibid. p. 656. reference to *Montreal Tramways Co. v. Leveille*.

36 Ibid. p. 670.

37 Ibid. p. 671. reference to *Sims and H.*

38 Ibid. p. 675, reference to *Superintendent of Family and Child Services v. M and O.*

39 It was this very point that Svend Robinson had brought up with the Joint Committee. (See: Chapter 12, p. 158.)

40 Ibid. p.703.

41 Ibid. p. 704.

42 *Henrietta Muir Edwards v. The Attorney-General of Canada*.

43 Op. Cit., Morton, p. 136.

44 Op. Cit., *Trial for Life*, pp. 718-719.

45 Ibid. p. 720.

46 *Toronto Star*, Pat McNenly, May 28, 1983.

47 "Canada's abortion legislation called 'thoughtless, shoddy'," *Star-Phoenix*, May 26, 1983.

48 "Abortion case summations under way," *Star-Phoenix*, May 27, 1983, p. 3.

49 Op. Cit., *Trial for Life*, pp. 746-747.

50 "Lawyer says rights are conditional upon birth," *Leader-Post*, May 27, 1983, p. A4

52 Ibid. p. 750. In April 1977, Ottawa Queen's Counsel David Dehler launched a class action suit on behalf of the unborn child, with himself as plaintiff in a representative capacity, against the Ottawa Civic and Riverside Hospitals. Dehler had, on five previous occasions, sought an injunction to stop an abortion from taking place, in each case acting on behalf of the father of the unborn child—

two children were saved through his efforts. He then decided, rather than dealing with injunctions on an ad hoc basis, to file a lawsuit under the Civil Rules of Practice. Dehler sought a permanent injunction that would prohibit all hospital personnel from performing abortions, and a declaration from the Court that unborn children "are entitled to equality before the law and full protection of the law" (p.24). Dehler's case was dismissed before trial by Justice Sydney Robins of the Ontario Supreme Court, who released his reasons for judgment on September 5, 1979, a year to the day after Morris Shumiatcher filed the Borowski lawsuit at Regina's Court of Queen's Bench. In order to dismiss the case so summarily, the judge had to accept Dehler's "allegations"—that the unborn child is a human being from the moment of conception—as fact. This Robins did, noting that these facts "must be assumed to be true or at least capable of being proven" for the purposes of the matter before the Court. But "accepting as fact the conclusion the plaintiff seeks to establish by testimony at trial, that is that a fetus is a human being from conception," he wrote, "the legal result obtained remains the same. The fetus is not recognized in law as a person in the full legal sense... The cases here and elsewhere demonstrate that the law has selected birth as the point at which the fetus becomes a person with full and independent rights." (p. 171). Dehler could not represent children *in utero* nor launch a class action suit on their behalf for the simple reason that these children were not persons recognized by the law, and a representative "cannot confer on those he represents status or rights which the law does not otherwise accord them." Justice Robins cited the 1975 Supreme Court *Morgentaler* decision, which concluded that while Parliament regarded the "procurement of an abortion as a serious crime," it also had the authority to set the terms and conditions under which abortion was permissible. "The wisdom and policy of the legislation are matters belonging to Parliament and it is not for the judiciary to intrude into the proper province of the legislations." (p. 161) Dehler appealed the ruling, which he described as "legally untenable" and a "break with the law," which hitherto had consistently held that the child *en ventre sa mère* had rights and was a human being unique from his mother. He referred to Prosser on Torts, who wrote in 1964 that "medical authority has long since recognized that the child is in existence from the moment of conception, and for many purposes its existence is recognized by the law...the unborn child in the path of an automobile is as much a person in the street as the mother." (p. 145.) Dehler argued that rights which can be exercised only after birth still exist *prior* to birth, such as the right to inheritance, and the right to seek damages for prenatal injuries. (p. 142.) The Ontario Court of Appeal upheld Robins' ruling. Dehler then sought leave to appeal the case to the Supreme Court, and in January 1981 he argued his motion for an hour and a half before a panel of three Supreme Court justices: Bora Laskin, Willard Estey and William McIntyre. After a few weeks, the panel ruled that leave to appeal was denied. They gave no reasons. (From an interview with David Dehler, August 2003, and from his book *The new Canadian ethic: kill our unborn Canadians*, (Ottawa: Kanda Publishing, 1980), all page numbers are from this reference.)

[53] Ibid. p. 751.
[54] Ibid. p. 752.

[55] Ibid. p. 761.

[56] Ibid. p. 780.

[57] To support this assertion, Sojonky quoted from the Joint Committee on the Charter, Crombie and Prime Minister Trudeau. (Ibid. p. 780.) (See Chapter 27, note 35.)

[58] Ibid. p. 730.

[59] Ibid. p. 736.

[60] Ibid.

[61] Ibid. p. 737.

[62] Ibid. p. 771.

[63] Ibid. pp. 775-776.

[64] Ibid. pp. 781-782.

[65] Ibid. p. 784.

[66] Ibid. p. 785.

[67] Matheson neglected to note that the provisions included "health and life."

[68] Ibid. p. 789.

[69] Ibid. p. 790.

[70] Ibid. p. 800.

[71] Ibid. p. 804.

[72] "Abortion case quietly adjourns as judge reserves decision," Lyn Hynes, *Leader-Post*, May 28, 1983, p. A3.

[73] "Judge delays abortion verdict," Pat McNenly, *Toronto Star*, May 28, 1983 p. B8.

[74] "Borowski ready to fight another battle," *The Edmonton Journal*, May 28, 1983, p. H7.

Chapter 23

Last stand on Corydon Avenue

"If we can't stop an illegal clinic, how are we
going to stop abortions in hospitals?
It's like Custer's last stand. Either I'm Custer or he's Custer."
Joe Borowski[1]

WHEN HENRY MORGENTALER SAID HE WOULD OPEN AN ABORTION clinic in Winnipeg as well as Toronto, he didn't say if his decision was motivated by a desire to provoke Joe Borowski. Nevertheless, Joe was quick to publicly denounce the notorious abortion doctor.

They met, and fought, on Peter Warren's CJOB open-line radio show. "I make a commitment that that butcher shop will never open in this province," declared Joe. "You are insulting me," Morgentaler sniffed, and remonstrated Joe for his "gutter language."[2]

Warren, a professional boxer in his youth and an accredited boxing judge in his mature years, recalled that "tense" afternoon. "When I had the two of them in the studio, I was not only a judge, I was a bloody referee...there were almost punches thrown."

Who was the more belligerent of the two? "Both of them were as bad as each."[3] But it was good radio.

Provoking Joe Borowski aside, in choosing Winnipeg, Morgentaler was banking on the chance that Manitoba's NDP government would turn a blind eye to his illegal activities.

Things did not go exactly as he had hoped. Manitoba's attorney-general, Roland Penner, turned down Morgentaler's request in the fall of 1982, that the province use its authority to block any prosecution of his clinic. Penner informed the abortionist by return letter that "I have a duty as the chief law enforcement officer of the Crown and the province to act in a way which relatively (to the extent that this can be done) is free from political considerations." He would leave the matter where it properly belonged, to the court.[4]

Relations between Penner and Morgentaler deteriorated further in January 1983 in the wake of a public debate at the University of Winnipeg between the latter and Joe Borowski. Joe was in good form despite his admitted nervousness. (Anna Desilets recalled popping in to wish him luck shortly before the debate began. "Butterflies, Joe?" she asked. He grinned weakly, "No, elephants!") Joe told the crowd of 1,600 that Morgentaler was "a shrewd businessman who has made between $3 million and $4 million. He wants to open a clinic here so he can make a killing. Pardon the pun." He accused the doctor of running establishments "probably half as clean as a vet's clinic,"[5] and pointed out the falsity of the claim of maternal deaths to back street abortions. Rather than "thousands or tens of thousands of women" who reportedly died annually from botched abortions, the real number was "eight before the changes in the laws and six after."[6]

Morgentaler dropped a bombshell that night: "I recently performed an abortion on the girlfriend of a son of an attorney-general in one of the provinces (where) I plan to establish a clinic. The son promised to tell his father not to prosecute." Shortly afterward, the auditorium was evacuated because of the threat of a bomb of another sort.

Penner reacted in anger, publicly rebuking Morgentaler for his unethical and "shamefully exploitive" revelations. People may conclude that he was the unnamed politician, but "it wasn't this attorney-general. I find this kind of maneuvering intolerable."[7]

Morgentaler pushed ahead with his illegal operation. Delaying tactics cannily employed by pro-life groups were relentlessly overcome as, on every level, politicians capitulated. Still, pro-lifers fought every inch of ground. Hundreds of spectators crammed the chambers in March as the Winnipeg City Council debated whether or not to uphold a building permit that had been granted to renovate the house on Corydon. Two hours of presentations from both sides were heard before the councilors voted 4-2 to allow the permit, saying there was no valid reason to deny it, and throwing responsibility to the attorney-general and the courts.[8]

Next, an occupancy permit was finally granted after Morgentaler's lawyer Greg Brodsky took the matter to court May 5, arguing before the Court of Queen's Bench that the clinic met building code standards.[9] "The city will do its duty," he trumpeted to the press. "The City of Winnipeg is a law-abiding citizen…(and) it has no reason not to grant the occupancy permit."[10]

On May 11, Morgentaler admitted in the press that abortions had been and were being done at the clinic. Now Penner faced criticism from pro-lifers, among them Joe Borowski, who from his trial in Regina, blasted the attorney-general for not raiding the illegal establishment. "For the chief law officer to have a crime of manslaughter reported to him and not take action is incredible," he exclaimed. Penner was "unfit for office."[11]

When he returned from Regina, Joe warned Penner that pro-lifers would invade his office unless and until he did something. The focus would shift from Corydon Avenue, where a makeshift pro-life headquarters had been set up in a mobile home on a neighbour's lawn, to the legislature, and it would be a welcome change for picketers, who would find the comfort of air-conditioned government offices a refuge from the pitiless rays of the late May sun, observed the practical Joe. "Our people have sore feet and are hot. They're not exactly having a ball out here. I'd prefer to be golfing myself," he ruefully admitted.

Meanwhile, Penner nixed an injunction application brought against the abortion clinic by the Manitoba League for Life. The injunction, filed in mid-May, contained an affidavit by clinic nurse Lynn Crocker, which stated that seven women were booked for abortions for May 7. (She had evidently given the affidavit to city officials in the course of applying for a permit to open.)

When Penner refused to authorize the injunction, citing insufficient evidence, a former attorney-general, Conservative Gerry Mercier, lashed out at him in the House, calling his comments "sleazy and whining." Penner did not budge, called Mercier a "legal and functional illiterate", and remained adamant that "the law will take its course."[12]

Joe's former sometimes adversary in the House, Health Minister Larry Desjardins, also figured in the controversy when the press revealed that at the Morgentaler abortuary, the remains of unborn babies were run through the garburetor and washed down the drain. "We do not consider it a human being," explained Morgentaler. In "very rare conditions...if there's an abnormality" the tissue is sent to a laboratory for a pathology report.[13]

When the story broke, Desjardins initiated enquiries as to whether this gruesome practise contravened Manitoba law, which required that tissue removed during an operation be examined by a pathologist. The Catholic politician also refused to grant the abortuary hospital accreditation; if more abortions were needed, he said, these would be provided "in a hospital setting." In fact, Desjardins was sceptical that any abortions had been performed at the clinic. "There is a lot of noise from Dr. Morgentaler who seems to want to stir up the pot...it is quite obvious he is trying to be mischievous."[14]

But far more serious and grisly events than mischief were, in fact, going on at the house on Corydon Avenue as the police, who had been quietly investigating amid the political posturing, furor and demonstrations, eventually surmised. Spokesman for Winnipeg's finest, Superintendent Herb Stephen, had consistently maintained that the police had "absolutely no authority" to go into the clinic based on insufficient evidence such as Morgentaler's statements. "We have to wait until we get a complaint from someone," he pointed out.[15]

On June 3, 1983, police raided the clinic, and took 12 people, including abortionist Robert Scott of Alexandria, Ontario, downtown for questioning. (Morgentaler was in Montreal.) They were later released, and it was not until June 9 that eight people were charged with conspiracy to procure abortions.[16]

Lawyer Greg Brodsky was upset with the conspiracy charge, insisting that the police "not fool around with any fancy charges."[17] Henry Morgentaler's Toronto lawyer, Morris Manning, was also outraged. "This means the law can't be directly tested in the usual course," he fumed, "as it will be muddied with the whole area of the law of conspiracy."[18]

Naturally the lawyers were upset that the defence of necessity, which had served their notorious client so well in Quebec, had run upon the shoals of the charge of conspiracy. As pointed out by F. L. Morton:

> The crime of conspiracy consists of the intention of two or more people to break the law, plus proof of an agreement actually to carry out the planned illegal action. It would be much more difficult to persuade a jury that the defence of necessity applied to a plot to perform illegal abortions. The success of the defence of necessity rested with presenting a jury with a moving case of a real woman with a real need for an abortion.[19]

Brodsky had been quietly negotiating with the police in preparation for Morgentaler's inevitable and eventual arrest, the lawyer later told writer Morton. Brodsky had made it clear that he expected no "technically tricky defences." He then declared afterward that the conspiracy charge was a mistake: the case had fallen into the hands of a junior Crown attorney who came up with the brilliant idea, which would take care of all alleged perpetrators in one fell swoop, including the absent Morgentaler himself.[20]

Joe Borowski was delighted that the police had taken action, but his main concern was that the clinic not re-open: "Until that matter is disposed of, we are restraining our joy."[21]

That matter was disposed of two weeks later when on June 25 the police raided the white stucco building on Corydon Avenue yet again. Abortuary staff had publicly expressed their intention to keep the illegal establishment going, and this time, police seized the vacuum aspirator used to perform abortions, as well as arresting Robert Scott, four nurses and a receptionist, against whom additional charges of conspiracy to procure an abortion were laid.[22] Henry Morgentaler was hopping mad. The police, he claimed, had "double-crossed" him. His lawyer had reached an agreement with Ed Ogelski, Winnipeg deputy police chief, sputtered the abortionist: "We had a promise that they will not raid. They broke that promise and they double-crossed me. They double-crossed us and they put in danger the lives and health of women in the clinic."[23]

This time, the abortuary in Winnipeg did not re-open. Morgentaler, however, who flew in from Montreal to appear in court on the charges, was preoccupied by the looming court battle in Toronto, where he had also been busy.

When Henry Morgentaler opened his illegal abortion clinic in Toronto, Jim Hughes was 40 years old and had been chairman of Campaign Life Ontario for nearly four years.

The affable entrepreneur had attended an organizational meeting for the new political lobbying group in October 1978—it was, he recalled, probably only his second pro-life meeting. Soon after, Hughes was volunteering full-time for the non-profit group, and subsisting on his savings. "Almost as soon as I got involved, I got really involved. My wife suggested that I give it two years and see what would happen."[24] More than two decades later, the Catholic father of four children was still wholly involved—now as president of Campaign Life Coalition Canada, a national lobbying force with over 150,000 supporters.

Having run a successful business for nine years, Hughes ably piloted the fledgling grassroots movement through its initial growing pains. It was, however, after the entrenchment of the Charter in 1982 that he really came into his own. "Once the Charter came in, a lot of people quit, a lot of people just said, 'Aw, I'm moving to other things,'" he recalled. They feared that judicial activism would run rampant, that politicians "wouldn't have the guts to invoke the notwithstanding clause and on and on and on."

Hughes himself wouldn't brook the defeatist attitude. "I said, 'Wait a minute,' and I took things on in a much larger way, and began hiring other people and trying to expand. We only had 800 people on our mailing list in the early days and then I decided that I was going to try my best to expand that, and it went from 800 to 8,000 in a short period of time."

Despite his sound business sense and whole-hearted commitment, Hughes accepted that he was a novice in the pro-life struggle, especially when measured against such acknowledged giants as Joe Borowski. Joe had 11 years on Jim, and at least seven years' more experience in straining nerve and sinew in the fight against abortion. "He was way above me in terms of his involvement and on the public stage and all that sort of thing, and my feeling was that I had to learn as much as I could from him."

Hughes met the famous Westerner at a Campaign Life forum where Joe was discussing abortion and the law with Ottawa lawyer David Dehler.[25] Not yet involved in the right-to-life movement,

Hughes was perhaps more aware of the issue than other Canadians due to the influence of his parish priest, Father Ted Fournier. Fellow parishioner at Corpus Christi, artist William Kurelek, had also aroused Hughes' sympathy and interest in the plight of the unborn child.

After becoming more than marginally involved in pro-life activism, Jim Hughes began to develop a rapport with Joe Borowski, who regularly came to Toronto on buying jaunts for his health food store. Jim would pick him up at the airport "drive him around, spend time with him, learn as much as I could."

The two men were superficially dissimilar: Hughes, with a *soupçon* of Irish charm not the least bit impaired by hazel eyes and an engaging dimple, was well-spoken to the point of suaveness, adept at backroom negotiations and possessed of a politician's instincts—but, the iron fist in the velvet glove, he never compromised on his convictions. Borowski was known for his bluntness, the diamond in the rough: he held a crowd on the basis of his strength of character and the power of what he had done and sacrificed for his unborn brothers and sisters, rather than by his political finesse.

At times, Jim Hughes was mystified at the bond that developed between himself and Joe, but they became, in the end, true friends. Hughes, however, had few illusions about his mercurial comrade, a man of undeniable, though slight, eccentricity. On more than one occasion, Joe abandoned him temporarily after a disagreement. Hughes and his suitcases were left standing in the snow under the dark and forbidding Winnipeg sky when he refused to accompany his friend to a rally supporting free trade. Joe drove off; Jim hastened to a chilly phone booth, called a cab, and booked into a hotel: no La Salle hospitality that weekend.

Dining out with Joe was also a potentially embarrassing adventure. The duo attended a pro-life conference in Newfoundland. In the land of lobster, Joe perversely hankered after Chinese food, but at the restaurant, he ordered a hot chicken sandwich. When in due course it arrived, he confounded waiter and chef alike by his shock at the gravy and fries. He ordered the waitress to take the dish back to the kitchen to have the chicken scrubbed clean.

Hughes experienced Joe's health rituals first hand—and almost lost his life for his pains, or so the story goes. During one of his stays at La Salle, he accepted Joe's offer of a sauna. He headed for the basement but the Borowskis just laughed; the sauna, they said, was outside.

Down the hill, Jim followed Joe, into the dark night, gingerly treading over the frosty ground in his bare feet, until they reached a sturdy structure by the riverside. After sweating it out for a bit, they emerged, Jim in vain looking for a water pipe for his shower. "Put your hand on my shoulder," offered Joe, and the innocent Hughes was led further down the hill until the ground beneath his feet gave way to icy-cold mud, and frigid water swirled around his ankles.

He lost his balance and fell backwards, only to be completely submerged. Gasping, he rose to his feet to hear Joe's commendation: "Oh Jamesie, that's good! Most people are really timid about rinsing off in the water."

"What is this?" exclaimed Hughes, and Joe laughed.

"It's the river."

"Oh my God!" came Hughes' startled oath. "I could have drowned!" That conviction was in no way mitigated when he contemplated that murky, churning estuary in the light of the next morning; he shivered at the vision of his six-foot corpse swept away, lost forever to human eyes.

Not that evening, but another, Joe gently pulled his friend's arm and whispered, "Jamesie, don't say anything. Look up."

Hughes, standing on Manitoba's prairie, heard the soft wind ruffling the trees, smelled the damp freshness of the clear night air and gazed, fascinated, into the infinite darkness, lit by a billion points of light. "The stars! I mean, unbelievable. These are the heavens."

"Yeah," echoed Joe softly, "the stars." On the distant horizon twinkled, minutely, the lights that were Winnipeg. At that moment, if only for that moment, it seemed as though all of it—the courts, the clinics, and the whole human misery and anguish of abortion—was, like the stars, a billion miles away.

A far cry from the sweetness of prairie night was the muggy, fetid, and exhaust-ridden summer air and clattering streets of Toronto, but that was Jim Hughes' home turf, and it was here that he and his pro-life allies[26] pitted their efforts against Henry

Morgentaler, and his illegal abortuary, in the summer of 1983.

As the summer deepened into fall and the blush of red stole slowly over the maple trees, the battle waged unrelentingly, but as pro-lifers were wont to point out, it was a battle for the hearts and minds of men and women. In Toronto, those minds and hearts were, if figures can be trusted to prove such things, shown to be more callous than elsewhere in Canada: abortions outnumbered live births in that city[27]—figures quoted for 1981, the last year when statistics were available, revealed that 8,313 abortions were done, while live births were recorded at 7,597.

Still and all, Toronto saw the largest pro-life gathering in the history of Canada, when at least 20,000 right-to-life advocates filed silently under 'the crabbing sun' past Henry Morgentaler's clinic on October 1,[28] although one report estimated the crowd at 40,000[29] and still another, 25,000.[30]

While the October wind punished the land 'with fists of turnips', the governments of Ontario and Manitoba administered what looked like, at first glance, a one-two combination against Morgentaler. Ontario's government charged the belligerently defi-ant abortionist, along with Robert Scott and Leslie Smoling, with conspiracy to procure an abortion, after a July raid on his Harbord Street clinic—charges which culminated in a preliminary hearing that November.

In Winnipeg, meanwhile, Morgentaler and his eight alleged co-conspirators faced a preliminary inquiry on October 6, over which Provincial Judge Kris Stefanson presided. The three days of testi-mony by 15 witnesses were notable for the frequent dramatic eruptions of both Greg Brodsky, Morgentaler's lawyer, and Crown attorney Wayne Myshowsky, both of whom often leapt to their feet "like the characters in a Perry Mason drama."[31]

Joe Borowski attended the hearing, and threaded his way through the crowd during morning recess to shake Morgentaler's hand. "I hope you don't mind, but I'm praying for you to see the errors of your ways," he said, as reporters looked on, scribbling comments and furtively noting that the encounter "appeared friendly." Morgentaler shrugged. He didn't mind that, but he did-n't care for the language used to protest his clinic. "Well," rejoined Joe. "You know the old school saying, 'Sticks and stones will break my bones, but names will never hurt me.'"[32]

On Friday afternoon, Judge Stefanson adjourned the hearing

and left with a 530-page black book tucked under his arm—the copies of medical records police gathered during their search of the clinic. "It makes a long weekend," he admitted before he disappeared into the lowering Winnipeg twilight. The decision as to whether the evidence warranted proceeding to trial would, it appeared, be some time in coming.[33]

But scarcely had the doors clicked shut on the Morgentaler hearing, than another decision, long awaited, was released by the Saskatchewan courts.

This time, Joe Borowski received the blow. On October 13, 1983, Justice Matheson dismissed Borowski's claim on behalf of the unborn child. In a 31-page judgment, the judge concluded that the child in the womb was not a person under law, and "not within the scope of the term 'everyone' utilized in the Charter"; therefore, the abortion provisions in the Criminal Code did not contravene the Charter.

The odyssey through the appeal courts was about to begin.

Notes
Chapter 23
Last stand on Corydon Avenue

[1] *Globe and Mail*, May 7, 1983, p. 4.
[2] "Morgentaler plan for clinic causes uproar in Winnipeg," Richard Cleroux, *Globe and Mail*, December 1, 1982.
[3] Interview with Peter Warren, February 2003.
[4] "Abortion clinics to open in Winnipeg, Toronto," *Globe and Mail*, November 1, 1982.
[5] "Bomb scare delays debate on abortion," Richard Cleroux, *Globe and Mail*, January 28, 1983.
[6] "Bomb threat interrupts debate" Catherine Clark, *Winnipeg Sun*, January 28, 1983.
[7] "Morgentaler is criticized by Penner for revealing information on patient," *Globe and Mail*, February 3, 1988, p. 9.
[8] "Morgentaler permit upheld in Winnipeg," *Globe and Mail*, May 26, 1983.
[9] "Abortion clinic gets permit, but opponents won't give up," *Star-Phoenix*, May 6, 1983, p. A8.
[10] "Pro-lifers take positions for abortion clinic battle," Christie McLaren and Doug Speirs, *Winnipeg Free Press*, May 5, 1983, pp. 1 and 4.
[11] "Penner urged to lay charges or quit," Maureen Brosnahan, *Free Press*, May 11, 1983 pp.1 and 4.
[12] "Morgentaler battle rages," *Calgary Herald*, May 18, 1983; "Anti-abortion injunction nixed," *Edmonton Sun*, May 18, 1983, p.26.
[13] "Aborted fetuses washed down drain," Christie McLaren, *Free Press*, May 26, 1983, p. 1.
[14] "Desjardins 'far from convinced' abortions done", Mary Ann FitzGerald and Christie McLaren, *Free Press*, May 27, 1983, p. 3.
[15] "Penner urged to lay charges or quit" Maureen Brosnahan, *Free Press*, May 11, 1983, pp.1 and 4.
[16] Charged were Drs. Robert Scott and Henry Morgentaler, nurses Lynn Crocker, Barbara Burr, Valerie Turnbull and Lynn Hilliard, counselors Patricia Turczak and Marilyn Weizner. ("Charges laid, abortion clinic fate uncertain," Larry Hill and Paul Moloney, *Free Press*, June 10, 1983.)
[17] "Morgentaler warrant cites conspiracy," Christie McLaren, *Free Press*, June 6, 1983, p. 3.
[18] "Morgentaler vows to fight," *Edmonton Journal*, June 10, 1983, p. A3.
[19] Op. Cit., Morton, p. 159.
[20] Op. Cit., Morton, pp. 159-160.
[21] "Morgentaler vows to fight" *Edmonton Journal*, June 10, 1983, p. A3.
[22] "Costs may defeat Morgentaler, lawyer says," Brian Gory, *Globe and Mail*, June 27, 1983, p. 13; "Clinic members refuse bail," *Toronto Sun*, June 27, 1983, p. 26.
[23] "Police double-crossed me: Morgentaler," *Montreal Gazette*, July 16, 1983.
[24] Interview with Jim Hughes, 2002.

[25] See Chapter 22, note 52.

[26] These included Stephen Jalsevac, Paul Dodds and Carl Scharfe of Campaign Life, Laura McArthur of Toronto Right to Life, Gwen Landolt, Martha Crean of the Committee Against Abortion Clinics, Denise Handler, Ken Campbell of Choose Life Canada, and other leaders.

[27] "Abortion outnumber live births in Toronto," *Edmonton Journal*, June 17, 1983, p. A3.

[28] "20,000 anti-abortionists demonstrate in front of Toronto Morgentaler clinic," Michael Tenszen, *Globe and Mail*, October 3, 1983, p. 24.

[29] "Thousands turn out to support, blast issue of abortions," *Ottawa Citizen*, October 3, 1983, p. 2.

[30] "Pro-life rally draws 25,000," Tom Harpur, *Toronto Star*, October 2, 1984, p. A1.

[31] "Judge spends long weekend studying Morgentaler files," Pat McNenly, *Toronto Star*, October 10, 1983, p. A9.

[32] "Tears flow at Morgentaler hearing," Shirley Muir, *Winnipeg Sun*, October 6, 1983.

[33] Op. Cit., "Judge spends long weekend," Pat McNenly.

Chapter 24

Filthy lucre, lucky lawyers

I count on you, O Lord;
it is you, Lord God, who will answer.
I pray: Do not let them mock me,
those who triumph if my foot should slip...
Psalm 38

"We have a tough job to do and
I don't know a nice way to go about it...
The very idea that you should be nice
to the enemy is repugnant to me."
Joe Borowski[1]

IT WAS A FOREGONE CONCLUSION THAT NO MATTER WHAT JUSTICE Matheson decided, his decision would be appealed. That the loser was Joe Borowski, rather than the Crown, put that citizen in the now familiar position of having to come up with the funds necessary to continue on the way of litigation. As Joe pointed out, the government had virtually unlimited funds to subdue or suppress its opposition. He, on the other hand, did not.

However, the story of this modern day Ulysses is a story not only of one man's stubborn perseverance and long-suffering in the face of almost insurmountable odds, but also a tale of quiet heroism—that of the hundreds and hundreds of ordinary and unexceptional Canadians whose contribution to the Borowski trial was entirely extraordinary and exceptional. Generally, pro-life advocates raise large families, and financial support for the costly and lengthy legal battle was an added drain on their already chronically depleted purses. Nevertheless, it was a price they were willing to pay. What was money when measured against the value of human life? Dollars mattered only insofar as they could buy, if possible, the end of the scourge of abortion.

Joe himself had the Midas touch, as attested to by Jim Hughes, who recalled admiringly that Joe could make money "at the drop of a hat, the drop of a dime. I couldn't believe how successful he had been." Joe also lived frugally, and, his daughter Karen observed with some asperity, often expected others to live up to his standard in this regard. But while he put his own personal resources into his pro-life fight, Joe Borowski did not flinch from soliciting donations from like-minded people across the country.

Thus, for years before he finally reached the Regina courthouse, Joe traversed the country, speaking in towns large and small. Sometimes Jean accompanied him, leaving Sandy at the helm of the family business, but often she remained in Winnipeg, running the pro-life shop they had set up adjacent to the health food store.

Joe would, as Campaign Life's Paul Formby recalled, "never pull a punch. Joe would ask people to take out their cheque books and he would say, 'Now, I don't want you to be cheap...remember what this cause is about. I want you to write a cheque out for a lot of money. Just don't think of a hundred, you can think of a thousand, something that you know you can afford, but there's no other worthy cause than this.'

"People loved him," laughed Formby, "because he was so direct. I guess it was that Polish farm background—no frills and right to the heart of the matter."[2]

The other side of the coin was that silver-tongued oratory was regarded—by some—as worth its weight in gold. Morris Shumiatcher, as one of the top lawyers in the land, commanded high fees—a fact that left a slight residue of bitterness with some pro-lifers, including Joe's wife.

The high drama that took place scant 12 weeks before the commencement of the Regina trial and which has now reached the status of legend, concerned this very issue. The fund for the court battle had grown to $100,000 by February of 1983, when Joe was aghast to receive a letter from his lawyer stating that he needed a guarantee of $350,000 to cover costs before he would proceed.[3]

The shocked Joe called a press conference, but the response from reporters was tepid at best. He then turned to Larry Henderson, editor of the Toronto archdiocesan Catholic paper, The *Catholic Register*, who printed an article in his weekly paper, along with an editorial calling for funds. By mid-May, Joe was asking people to stop sending money. "It was like the heavens opened and the rains came down," he told a reporter during the Regina trial. "You can put it in your paper: 'Please, no more donations.'" The needed amount of $350,000 had been surpassed.[4] Among the donors was a Catholic diocese, which gave $10,000 from its Share Life campaign. Other donors included individuals such as Frank Mountain of Ottawa, who sent a letter to 15,000 people and collected $23,000.[5]

Saskatchewan weighed in with the greatest support, with an astounding $15,000 coming from the town of Macklin, which amounted to "$16 for every man, woman and child," calculated the exultant Joe.

He speculated that one reason for the overwhelming response was Henry Morgentaler. "To my way of thinking he is the greatest asset we have, and I hope he keeps going shooting his mouth off in every city in the country. Because he'll get these people off the fence, and we'll have more friends and more soldiers to march with us than we've ever had in our thirteen-year history."[6]

Morgentaler aside, Joe had the money he needed in good time for the Regina courtroom drama. Now, he faced the cost of an appeal. Shumiatcher filed the motion to the Saskatchewan Court of Appeal on November 10, 1983, but it was not until over two years later, in December 1985, that the Court deigned to hear the appeal, and not until a year and four months after that, on April 30, 1987, that the judges would release their ruling. So it was that three and a half years passed before the lawsuit moved through the Saskatchewan Court of Appeal.

Meanwhile, Joe and other pro-life advocates had time to scrutinize the Matheson ruling.

Lawyer Shumiatcher saw much to be thankful for; Justice Matheson had "made the following significant findings of fact:

- "modern biological and genetic studies have verified that the fetus is genetically a separate entity from the time of conception or shortly thereafter;
- "advances in medical procedures have made it possible for a fetus to be treated separate from its mother and, although not sufficiently developed for normal birth, to survive separate from its mother;
- "[p]ermitting a pregnant women to terminate her pregnancy automatically results in the termination of fetal life, which, it seems quite clear, is an existence separate and apart from that of the pregnant woman, even although the fetal life may not be maintainable, during the early stages of pregnancy, independently of the pregnant woman;
- "...a consideration of the factors which might result in a therapeutic abortion being performed necessarily entails a consideration of the fact that if an abortion is deemed justified, the end result cannot be therapeutic for both the pregnant woman and the fetus..."[7]

Joe was philosophical in the matter of his defeat: "We find the judgment is not as bad as it looks. The judge does not challenge a single contention made by our medical experts. He even admits that the unborn child is a separate entity." Matheson had found that "rapid advances in medical science may make it socially desirable that some legal status be extended to fetuses, irrespective of ultimate viability."[8]

The expert witnesses had "proved beyond a shadow of doubt" that the unborn child was a human being. Said Joe: "Now it's up to the courts to clothe it with judicial respect and judicial rights."[9]

He was candid about the status quo, though. "I think the judge is correct in saying there is no legal basis" to declare that the unborn child is protected under the Charter. "That's why it was called a landmark court case. For the first time in the history of Canada we were going to establish a legal basis because it did not exist until this point."[10]

This was precisely the point of contention with Justice Matheson, and why pro-life lawyers and court watchers were not betting heavily on Joe's success. The judge, in his ruling, stated unequivocally that "it is the prerogative of Parliament, and not the courts, to enact whatever legislation may be considered appropriate to extend to the unborn any or all legal rights possessed by living persons."[11]

Shortly before the Regina trial began, the president of Coalition for Life expressed grave reservations about the Borowski lawsuit. "As a lawyer, I think the chances for success are minimal," Leslie Giroday commented to writer Janet Somerville of the *Catholic New Times*.[12] Giroday, who emphasized that she spoke for herself and not her group, was the only one of six lawyers approached by that paper who was willing to comment at that time. Her reasons for apprehension were eerily similar to those expressed by Joe Borowski when he described his quest as a "landmark" court case. "Never in the western world has a court been called on to make a determination of when life begins. Courts have always declined to do this sort of thing. They don't like to get into broad, philosophical, what-is-life issues."

Moreover, Giroday worried that if the court determined that the unborn child was not a person under the law, and therefore was unprotected under the Charter then, "that would make it easier for a pro-choice challenger to come in and get the existing abortion law swept away. Not that I like the present law. But as long as it exists, it at least theoretically protects the unborn except in specific circumstances. The great danger is that we might slip into the American scenario, where abortion is recognized as a right, and pro-lifers are always in the miserable political and legal situation of trying to restrict people's access to what has become a right."[13]

She was also unsure of the wisdom of using the Charter (which Joe himself had protested almost to the point of self-immolation) to defend the unborn child. It was widely accepted that the Charter was a disaster for the child in the womb. "But all of a sudden, here we are flipping over and saying 'the Charter is going to be our salvation.' I think this court effort is premature."

Other commentators were more hopeful, at least in their public utterances. "We support him morally and prayerfully," said Laura McArthur, president of the Right to Life Association of Toronto and Area. "I don't know what his legal chances are, but I wish him well. If he wins, it will be a miracle—but who deserves a miracle more than Joe Borowski?"

Pro-life activists had scarcely had time to absorb the Matheson judgment than yet another legal drama began to take shape, as the saga of Henry Morgentaler versus the state continued.

A week after the Borowski decision, Manitoba provincial court Judge Kris Stefanson ruled that there was sufficient evidence to arraign Morgentaler, Scott and six clinic staff of the Winnipeg abortion clinic on charges of conspiracy to procure the miscarriage of a female person. The alleged conspirators were "probably guilty," said the judge, adding, "A properly instructed jury could probably convict all eight of the accused." (Not surprisingly, the *Globe and Mail* rebuked the judge for his entirely reasonable statement, declaring in an editorial that such comments were "outrageous" and prejudicial to the accused.)[14] He scheduled the trial for November 7.

Morgentaler's Winnipeg lawyer, Greg Brodsky, who had startled prosecutors during the preliminary enquiry when he proclaimed his intention to launch a constitutional challenge to the abortion law on behalf of his client, now reiterated his cunning plan. The challenge would likely take place at the trial or arraignment of the accused, he told reporters: "If the law on which the charge is based is not valid law, there can't be a conviction. If there can't be a conviction, there's no reason for a trial."[15]

But Brodsky was pre-empted in his proposed constitutional attack; the Winnipeg challenge withered on the vine.[16] It was Morris Manning, who, as the Morgentaler relay team of abortion advocates passed the baton back and forth, now began running the race. As the 43-year-old lawyer stepped into a Toronto courtroom on November 21, 1983, to defend his now infamous clients, he also stepped into the glare of the limelight and into the pages of history.

He had fought for that limelight, according to Catherine Dunphy. Brodsky and Manning had "a big quarrel" over who would get "the big trial," Morgentaler told his biographer. However, he and Manning agreed that Toronto was a more suitable venue than the "backwater" Winnipeg, from which to launch a constitutional challenge to the abortion law.[17]

Morris Manning was already well known in Toronto at this point in his career as "the man who cleaned up Yonge Street."

Hired in 1979 as special counsel for the City of Toronto, he managed to close down 50 sex shops and massage parlours. He then successfully defended a homosexual activist charged with keeping a bawdy house, and challenged, on behalf of disgruntled tavern keepers, a Mississauga by-law that required nude dancers to wear G-strings.[18]

Perhaps it was the "discrimination he experienced as a poor Jewish boy in Toronto" that led the burly lawyer to "buck the establishment" occasionally, speculated one reporter.[19] Manning himself, in explaining his career choices, said he was interested in "civil liberties, protecting people's rights": people had a right to walk up Yonge Street unmolested by sex-traders, but should be allowed, if they wanted, to go to strip joints or gay bathhouses.

When it came to abortion, Manning had a personal interest. His wife, Linda Rapson, was a member of Doctors for Repeal of the Abortion Law. He himself was convinced that Section 251 of the Criminal Code was "unfair, discriminatory."[20]

When Henry Morgentaler, Robert Scott, and Leslie Smoling were charged with conspiracy to procure a miscarriage following a July 5 raid of the Harbord Street abortuary, Manning's first move was to file a pre-trial motion to challenge the constitutionality of the abortion law.

Ontario Supreme Court Judge William Parker allowed the motion, leading to what the press referred to as "a trial within a trial." No jury was assembled; Judge Parker alone heard the evidence upon which he would base his decision whether or not to proceed to trial.[21]

Manning claimed that seven sections of the Charter were violated by Section 251 of the Criminal Code, including Section 7, the right to life, liberty and security of persons; Section 2, the right to freedom of thought, belief, opinion and expression; and Section 12, the right not to be subjected to cruel and unusual punishment. To make his case, he called nearly 20 witnesses over what he initially said would be two, but what stretched into three, then four, weeks.

His witnesses consisted of a rogues' gallery of abortion promoters, advocates, and practitioners[22], the combined testimony of whom was nothing more than pro-abortion propaganda, according to the monthly national paper, *The Interim*. "Thus will the Court of Appeal and the Supreme Court of Canada, when they adjudicate this case in subsequent years, be 'informed' on the pro-abortion arguments. Manning, of course, is also no doubt aware of the advantages of the media picking up on this propaganda and of the possibility that it may have an effect on any prospective jurors when the trial takes place," noted a December 1983 editorial.

Squaring off against Manning was federal Crown counsel Arthur Pennington, and his provincial counterpart, Alan Cooper. As Ontario's Crown prosecutor, Cooper had initiated the conspiracy charges against the three co-accused. The Ottawa-based Pennington was there on behalf of federal Liberal Justice Minister Mark MacGuigan, to defend the constitutionality of Section 251 of Canada's Criminal Code.

Pennington made frequent references to the unborn child in his defence of the nation's abortion law, much to Manning's annoyance. Judge Parker allowed the line of questioning to proceed, despite the periodic eruptions from the defence, as occurred when the Crown prosecutor questioned a witness whether an eight-week-old unborn child had primitive organs.

"Yes, but I feel this kind of questioning is very distasteful, Mr. Pennington," responded Minnesota abortionist Jan Hodgson. "I would like very much for you to come and visit me at my clinic and you would see what things are like at these stages."[23]

Pennington was not abashed. "Evidence of the growth of the fetus is very powerful evidence," he told the Court above Manning's objections. The defence "has tried to make this solely a medical issue....there are in fact, much larger issues."[24] But he was more circumspect when questioned by reporters outside of the courthouse. Section 251 was "a balancing by Parliament between the competing claims" of "the potential human life of a fetus and, on the other hand, making exceptions for concerns about the life and health of a mother," he shrugged. "I would not wish to be understood to be going any further than that."

Manning was derisive when informed of his adversary's claims. "It isn't a delicate balance," he snorted. "The legislation deals only with the rights of a woman and her health....The Constitution doesn't guarantee the fetus any rights."[25]

After the defence lawyer had called his last witness, it was 'déjà vu all over again,' as the Crown declined to call any of its own, claiming that Mannning's challenge to the abortion law was "irrelevant" and that the Court had no right to rule on Parliament's legislation. At this juncture, as it was already December 17, Judge Parker elected to adjourn the proceedings until the New Year.

On January 19, 1984, the preliminary hearing resumed, with Morris Manning up to the plate, or in this case, lectern, to present his summation of evidence and oral arguments, which he supported with a staggeringly detailed 13-volume factum. Courtwatchers had commented that the successful lawyer used a "shotgun" approach to the law, using any and all arguments that could prove his case.[26] Now, he turned in the "longest solo argument ever put to a Canadian judge," wrote columnist June Callwood, who described the record-breaking feat:

> After 18 days on his feet, talking steadily morning and afternoon, filling 18 volumes of transcript and nearly a month of court time in a marathon performance that gradually emptied the room of all but five spectators, Morris Manning gathered his black gown around him and sat down, a well-satisfied and exhausted lawyer.[27]

Judge Parker, who, by the same account, listened attentively, took notes and asked questions throughout the long presentation, adjourned the hearing for three weeks. On March 20, 1984, the Crown lawyers argued the case of the state. Federal lawyer Pennington prefaced his more technical arguments with an impassioned plea on behalf of the unborn child—remarks which prompted an exchange of "wry glances" between Morris Manning and his colleague.[28]

The Crown lawyer strongly objected to Manning's submission that the "sole purpose" of Section 251 was "to protect the health of the woman. An obvious purpose is the protection of the developing human life in the womb."[29] Abortion, he argued, "no matter how hard you try to disguise it, involves the deliberate destruction of a developing human life. That separates it from the removal of a wart." Pennington showed Justice Parker illustrations of the developing child in the womb and referred to this as "the miracle of new life."[30]

The Crown counsel disputed Manning's claim that women did not have access to abortion. "My submission is that there hasn't been a single so-called victim called (to testify) from anywhere in the country."[31] It was not up to Parliament to "provide nationwide abortion facilities," nor to guarantee uniform access to abortion.

Given Canada's magnitude and population distribution, the latter expectation was unrealistic, and "to base the constitutionality of federal legislation on this (argument) is unacceptable."[32]

Pennington did concede that the late Bora Laskin, former Chief Justice of the Supreme Court, had, albeit "with appropriate extreme caution...left the door slightly ajar in rejecting ...the invitation to review the substantive wisdom of the otherwise valid legislation" in the 1975 *Morgentaler* decision, in which Laskin (along with Justices Spence and Judson) had dissented from the majority.[33] But he warned against yielding to the temptation to push that door open and to rule on the substance of legislation in the light of the Charter. This would lead to "government of judges" and have dire and far-ranging consequences for Canada.[34]

This theme was taken up by Ontario Crown prosecutor Alan Cooper. To engage in judicial activism would "cause a great deal of unrest and dissatisfaction with our legal system," he argued: to strike down the abortion law would be "an improvident and extravagant excess" and would "Americanize" the Charter. "The Court should not take sides and rent asunder a legislative scheme which is working for most Canadians," he concluded.

By now it was April 5, 1984, and Judge Parker reserved judgment on the motion.

Now that Joe Borowski's time in court was over, he had little to do in that regard but wait for his appeal. Pro-lifers in Winnipeg were chagrined when, while Manning was arguing in a Toronto court, Manitoba's attorney-general decided on December 8 to withdraw the conspiracy charge against the Montreal abortionist and his cohorts, and substitute it with the charge of performing illegal abortions.

As the right-to-life lobby observed, Roland Penner's move amounted to letting Morgentaler off the hook. "There was ample proof that Morgentaler had in fact 'conspired' or agreed to establish an illegal abortion clinic in Winnipeg," pointed out an editorial in the December 1983 edition of *The Interim*. "The chances of a conviction on this charge were excellent."

But Morgentaler himself was not even in Winnipeg when the clinic was raided and charges laid. As for Scott and nurse Lynn

Crocker, also charged with performing an illegal abortion with the conspiracy charge withdrawn, the defence of necessity would now be available, thus decreasing the chance of conviction. Penner's action was "an abuse of power and an interference in the course of justice," a promotion of his personal views on abortion, concluded the *Interim*'s editor. "He is unfit to remain in office."

The only good news for Joe and fellow activists was that the Morgentaler clinic on Corydon Avenue had remained closed since the raid in June of 1983; a welcome respite for pro-life picketers, who also harboured the hope that through the closure many lives would be saved.

Joe, 51 years of age and almost gaunt from his habitual fasting, kept up his speaking and fund-raising, and together with daughter Sandy, ran a successful business. His diet remained idiosyncratic, as did his personal habits, as his daughters recalled. Always susceptible to the cold after his fast, and troubled by poor circulation, he took to wearing pajama bottoms under his slacks, and clipping off the tight band on the top of his socks so it would not impede the flow of blood.

On one occasion—an interview for a Catholic TV broadcast—the camera zoomed away revealingly: "There's Dad, and I swear, the blue pajama bottoms with the navy piping sticking out of the suit, and he had on those weird slipper shoes," Debbie Borowski remembered. "It totally spoiled the image. He looked like, you know, *geek.*"

By this time, Debbie was employed by Manitoba social services. Working shifts as she did, she wouldn't see her family for weeks; it was Joe who reminded her and her sisters of upcoming family events and who kept them all in touch. But he had an aversion to leaving messages on her answering machine. Finally, he hit on a particular line, the punch line of one of his favorite jokes: Two upper class British gentlemen were having a drink at the club. One says, "So sorry, old chap, to hear you buried your wife the other day." Came the reply: "Had to—she was dead, you know."

"So what he would do is, he would leave me a message on the machine, 'Had to, she was dead, you know.' And hang up. That was the message," Debbie chuckled. He couldn't quite bring himself to say, "Hi, this is your Dad, I'm just calling to say hello."

Joe's second daughter, Karen, had in 1980 married an African-American soldier from Alabama and eventually had three sons.

Her husband Archie's skin colour raised eyebrows in some quarters, as well as speculation as to how the patriarch Joe might react. But he had, as his daughters observed, not a racist or prejudiced bone in his body.

The youngest Borowski, Sandra, who of his three children most closely resembled her father, was working at the health food store and had earned a degree in herbology in 1981. Meanwhile, Joe had been studying iridology—the science of diagnosing a patient's maladies by examining his irises. He was fascinated with blood analysis as well, and was gaining expertise in this area, Jean recalled. Her husband would scrutinize blood slides under a microscope and come up with a diagnosis. Joe was able to confer on some of these cases with a world-renowned cancer specialist based in Amsterdam, Sir Hank Oswald, with whom he and Sandy consulted in 1984 when she had some health concerns. She was given a clean bill of health after minor surgery.

The 'smell of mortality' was not unfamiliar to Joe and Jean Borowski. His father had died in 1967 and hers in 1970. Joe's mother, who lived the later years of her life in a Polish retirement residence in Winnipeg, died in November of 1983. Her famous and strong-willed fourth son had visited her faithfully on Sunday afternoons for years.

In the summer of 1984, Joe and Jean prepared for a three-week tour of Australia and New Zealand. They hoped to use the occasion to look up Ed Schreyer, who, following his stint as governor general, had been drafted into Canada's diplomatic corps and was posted as ambassador to Australia.

Shortly before they left, Ontario Supreme Court Judge William Parker handed down his decision on the Morgentaler motion to quash the abortion law. The judge refused to do so, writing in a July 20 ruling that Section 251 was not in conflict with the Charter of Rights. "No unfettered legal right to an abortion can be found in our law, nor can it be said that a right to an abortion is deeply rooted in the traditions or conscience of this country," he pointed out. Thus, Morgentaler, Scott, and Smoling were to proceed to trial on the charge of conspiring to procure a miscarriage. The date set was October 15, 1984. (It will be remembered that in Manitoba, Attorney-General Roland Penner dropped the conspiracy charge, substituting instead the charge of committing illegal abortions.)

As the Borowskis took wing to Down Under, they left behind a country convulsed by abortion. The right-to-life advocates were in a toe-to-toe, inch-by-inch, trench-by-trench pitched battle with the right-to-abortion activists. In the present 'fog of war' it was entirely unclear which side would win, but all the while the toll of victims increased daily, the abortion rate being up to 60,000 per year.

It made for a deep uneasiness among the politicians. Pierre Trudeau had resigned in June of that year; Prime Minister John Turner was the Liberal contender in the upcoming September federal election. His opponents, Progressive Conservative leader Brian Mulroney and NDP chief Ed Broadbent, all were, despite their distaste in so doing, compelled to face the abortion issue. It simply would not go away.

Notes
Chapter 24
Filthy lucre, lucky lawyers

[1] "Joe Borowski 'supremely confident' of court victory," Tom Blackwell, *Regina Leader-Post*, December 16, 1985.

[2] Interview with Paul Formby, September 2002.

[3] Author Anne Collins tells the tale with great detail in her 1985 book, *The Big Evasion, the Issue that Won't Go Away* (Toronto: Lester and Orpen Dennys Limited, 1985), p. 50.

[4] "Hold donations, anti-abortionist tells supporters," Pat McNenly, *Toronto Star*, May 14, 1983, p. A4.

[5] Op. Cit., Anne Collins, p. 50.

[6] Op. Cit., Anne Collins, p. 52.

[7] "I set before you life and death: Abortion—Borowski and the Constitution" Morris Shumiatcher, *University of Western Ontario Law Review*, 24 (1987) p 22.

[8] "Borowski set to appeal his case," Stan Koma, *Catholic Register*, October 29, 1983.

[9] "Abortion law is valid, court rules," *The Ottawa Citizen*, October 14, 1983, p. 1.

[10] "Canada abortion law valid—a fetus is not a person, court rules" *Toronto Star*, October 14, 1983, p. 1.

[11] Op. Cit., "Borowski set to appeal his case."

[12] Janet Somerville, ed. *Catholic New Times*, May 8, 1983.

[13] Ibid.

[14] "Premature verdict," *Globe and Mail*, October 21, 1983.

[15] "Morgentaler and his staff 'probably guilty,' judge says," *Toronto Star*, October 20, 1983.

[16] Morgentaler was granted leave to challenge the abortion law; Manitoba Court of Queen's Bench Justice Ben Hewak, at the November 7 arraignment, allotted a week in mid-January for arguments on the constitutionality of the law. ("Morgentaler granted legal challenge to abortion law," *Ottawa Citizen*, November. 8, 1983, p. 5.)

[17] Op. Cit., Dunphy, p. 235.

[18] "Morris Manning's courtroom triumphs," Elaine Carey, *Toronto Star*, December 2, 1984.

[19] "Did a strapping save Morgentaler," Jack Cahill, *Toronto Star*, February 21, 1988.

[20] Ibid.

[21] "Morgentaler lawyer bids to quash charges," *Ottawa Citizen*, November. 22, 1983, p. 2.

[22] These included American Dr. Phillip Stubblefield, a board member of Planned Parenthood of America, Christopher Tietze, board member of the National Abortion Federation, and Dr. Henry David, a psychologist and member of the Trans-National Family Institute, which promotes worldwide abortion and is funded by the pro-abortion John D. Rockefeller Foundation. Canadian witnesses included Carolyn Egan, active member of the Ontario Coalition for Abortion

Clinics, Dr. Wendell Watters, McMaster psychiatrist, board member of CARAL and DRAL (Doctors to Repeal the Abortion Law), and Dr. Augustin Roy, president of the Quebec Association of Physicians and Surgeons, who when he served as a defence witness in Morgentaler's Montreal trials in 1973, also had his name on the letterhead of the Morgentaler Defence Committee at that time, and "who fought tenaciously in 1975 to prevent the disciplinary committee of that College from reviewing Morgentaler's practise of medicine," a review which did take place and which resulted in the suspension of Morgentaler's licence. (*The Interim*, December 1983 p. 2.)

[23] "Development of fetus is termed irrelevant in abortion law motion," Kirk Makin, *Globe and Mail,* December 15, 1983, p. 4.

[24] "Fetal development questions raised in Morgentaler trial," *Ottawa Citizen,* November 29, 1983, p. 5.

[25] "Morgentaler challenge called irrelevant," *Globe and Mail*, December 17, 1983, p. 5.

[26] "Did a strapping save Morgentaler," Jack Cahill, *Toronto Star*, February 21, 1984.

[27] "Thinking on his feet for 18 long days," June Callwood, *Globe and Mail*, March 1, 1984.

[28] "Recognize the rights of fetus, court asked in abortion trial," Kirk Makin, *Globe and Mail*, March 21, 1984, p. 5.

[29] "'Unacceptable' to leave decision on abortions to women, court told," Bill Walker, *Toronto Star*, March 21, 1984, p. 2.

[30] Op. Cit., "Recognize the rights of fetus," Makin.

[31] Op. Cit., "'Unacceptable' to leave decision on abortions," Walker.

[32] "Abortion rights not guaranteed, court told," Bill Walker, *Toronto Star*, March 22, p. A23.

[33] "Morgentaler fights abortion charge of Laskin loophole," *Ottawa Citizen*, March 29, 1984 p. 3.

[34] Op. Cit., Morton, p. 182.

Chapter 25

The years when
we knew misfortune

Comforter, where, where is your comforting?
Gerard Manley Hopkins
No worst, there is none

JOE AND HIS WIFE RETURNED FROM THE SUN-DRENCHED SHORES OF Australia in time to do a bit of politicking of their own before the nation cast its ballots that fall. In this effort, Joe and his Alliance Against Abortion worked in conjunction with Jim Hughes' national lobby group to identify pro-life candidates.

Joe paid for 20,000 copies of *The Interim* to be distributed, and continued to support the national pro-life paper for many years. Much later it was discovered that the so-called distributor had unceremoniously dumped the tidy bundles of *The Interim* into a ravine, Jim Hughes related. But Joe, being the Christian gentleman he was, did not take the man to court once this treachery had been discovered. Instead, "I think Joe accepted the man's apology, " said Hughes.[1] Nevertheless, it was undeniable that "without Joe's money in the early years, *The Interim* newspaper would not have been able to get off the ground."

Brian Mulroney emerged victorious in September 1984, but public attention was soon diverted from the smooth-talking Prime

Minister when the trial for Henry Morgentaler and his cohorts began, scarcely a fortnight later, in Toronto.

It had all the makings of a sensational case, involving a notorious newsmaker, a volatile issue, and an ambitious and articulate defence lawyer. Yet, according to one reporter, "the atmosphere was curiously flat" that first day, the courtroom scarcely full, and public interest fixed instead on a drug trial taking place across the hall. Moreover, "proceedings were sluggish" as judge and lawyers became immediately preoccupied with ground rules for jury selection.[2]

While Manning had come with a list of 25 questions to pose to potential jurors, Judge Parker quickly nixed that idea.[3] It was finally agreed that three questions would be asked to sift through the pool of 132 jury candidates:

- Do you have beliefs on abortion that might cause you to convict or acquit regardless of the evidence?
- Have you formed opinions as to the guilt or innocence of the accused?
- Would you be able to set aside beliefs to reach a verdict based on the evidence and the law?

It took four days to select the jury. Manning was permitted to reject up to 36 candidates, while Crown lawyer Alan Cooper could reject four. Cooper could also request—up to 48 times if need be—that a potential juror "stand aside." Jury selection was made more unwieldy by the use of "triers"—initially, two potential jurors drawn randomly from the pool, who questioned their peers and had a say in their ultimate acceptance or rejection. The triers changed constantly, however; each new juror selected became a trier while his or her predecessor moved to the jury box.[4]

After five jurors were selected, the triers proved to be particularly fastidious and rejected candidate after candidate, much to the bemusement of Judge Parker. "Excellent" jurors were being turned away, he protested, "for some reason we don't know about."

"It's their gut reaction, My Lord," responded Manning.[5]

The lawyers could reject or approve the triers' decision, but Manning took an extra step: he conferred with two mysterious women sitting at his bench. Reporters' curiosity was piqued, but unsatisfied when Manning, and the women themselves, refused to divulge their identity. One said only that she was "working for Mr. Manning."[6]

It was *Toronto Star* reporter Bill Walker who soon revealed that the two ladies were American professional jury consultants Marjorie Fargo and Catherine Marks, the former of whom had helped select a "sympathetic jury" for the California cocaine conspiracy trial of John De Lorean. "It is believed," wrote Walker, "to be the first Canadian case in which U.S. consultants have been enlisted to help the defence screen citizens called for jury duty."[7]

Manning drifted into the habit of asking more questions than the agreed upon three; despite Cooper's objections, the judge permitted this practise to continue. The lawyer asked candidates if they were married and had children, what jobs they held, what they knew of the court case or if they had discussed it. Nothing escaped the defence lawyer's sharp and sweeping gaze. A tiny rose lapel pin prompted Manning to enquire as to its significance: "It's for right-to-life," the man replied. Needless to say, he was ousted summarily.

Cooper brought a laugh from spectators when he approached the next candidate, pointed his finger and demanded: "What's that brooch you have on?"

Yet a man ultimately accepted for the jury was identified on the registry as "coin collector." When asked to explain, he said he collected quarters from payphones: "I figured it would fool a few people."[8]

Finally, the roster was filled. The jury, described as "split perfectly," consisted of six men and six women. Six were married and had children (but none had more than two); six were single and childless.[9] Seven looked to be less than thirty years old.[10] The selection process had been "a high stakes poker game," agreed Crown attorney Alan Cooper: "I think it is the most important thing we will do here."[11]

After a trial that lasted nearly three weeks, Morgentaler, Scott and Smoling were acquitted by jury verdict, on November 9, 1984.

Public reaction exploded. Particularly controversial was the issue of such calculated jury selection. Marjorie Fargo, one of the jury consultants, admitted in an article published the day of the acquittal that their dream jury would have included "several work-ing women in their thirties who didn't attend church regularly."

The consultants didn't want regular church-goers, because they, most likely, would be "anti-abortion." They also figured that housewives, young people and older professionals would be unsympathetic to the abortionists. Because Manning was limited to three questions, the consultants were hampered in their efforts, Fargo claimed. They had to rely heavily on body language and other clues, rejecting potential jurors who stared intently at Manning or Morgentaler, who made aggressive gestures or who answered questions flippantly or indifferently.[12]

These admissions incensed the right-to-life lobby, including Joe Borowski, who reacted to the acquittal with "shock, horror and anger. The whole thing was an expensive sham—a platform for Morgentaler and his bunch to promote their anti-life view," he growled.[13]

Jim Hughes denounced the verdict as well. "It was a joke," said the president of Campaign Life, "People who have a number of children or who go to church—Canada's mainstream—couldn't get on the jury."[14] Mary Clarke, speaking on behalf of the Council for the Protection of Human Life, decried the "susceptibility of the jury to the histrionics of Mr. Manning. Morgentaler clearly broke the law. The jury based its decision on the abortion issue and not on Morgentaler's actions."[15]

It was true that Manning's dramatic address to the jury, during which he bellowed and thumped the lectern, focused on the puta-tive travail of women. "Think about it!" he roared. "If you haven't got reproductive freedom to decide whether to have a child or not, what have you got?" He also played to the vanity of the hand-ful of ordinary citizens who sat, riveted, before him. "You have become, for Canadian women, the 12 most important people in the country," wheedled the plump advocate. "You have become the key to a locked door, a door that is locked for many women. Just one woman who cannot get a swift abortion is one woman too many.

"Send a message to Mr. McMurtry saying 'stop prosecuting doc-tors for trying to help people.' You are the only independent body that can do this. Politicians can't. They are dependent on votes. You can say we can't stand for this any more. That we won't stand for this any more.

"You are this country. An independent country. A country which is not tied to any political party bosses. You can bring freedom, as the jury is the lamp by which freedom is lit."[16]

For his part, Crown attorney Alan Cooper warned that anarchy would prevail if the three abortionists, so obviously guilty, were acquitted. "Breaking the law in an attempt to change a law one doesn't like is like plunging a knife into the very heart of democracy. I say the ends do not justify the means."

It was small wonder that the Morgentaler proceedings received sober scrutiny from the legal community—although when Manning turned up at the lawyers' dining hall at Osgoode Hall on the day of the acquittal, the oak-paneled walls of that venerable room reverberated with spontaneous applause from about 300 of his colleagues.[17]

Right-to-abort activists and their supporters wildly praised Manning's accomplishment. The *Globe* called for Parliament to change the law, so that the decision to abort rested with the "prospective parents and their doctors, not with a committee acting on vague and varying guidelines. ... If there is no joy in seeing Dr. Morgentaler willfully defy the laws of Canada, there is less joy in seeing Parliament stubbornly hold on to those laws while juries, province by province, stand in rebellion."[18]

Journalist Anne Collins, whose book *The Big Evasion* was scheduled for publication the following year, typed a quietly exuberant essay, "The meaning of Morgentaler" for the November 19 issue of *Maclean's*, in which she, too, claimed that the jury had told the country the abortion law was unenforceable. The 12 people "chosen out of a random lot of 132 citizens of the city of Toronto" also revealed that Canadian conservatism had rejected "American add-ons...a right-wing image of God and family which relegates women to the kingdom of the home."

Such "esoteric heights of hysteria" drew a response from the frequently acerbic but unfailingly lucid publisher of the weekly newsmagazine, *Alberta Report*, who penned his own 'meaning of Morgentaler' under the headline: "The appalling implications of Morgentaler's unjust acquittal." The opinions of juries selected from the citizenry of Toronto and Montreal are not representative of all Canadians, many of whom reside in neither city; indeed, in no city at all, wryly observed Ted Byfield.

The 12 jurors were in no sense randomly selected, and given

that "any suspicion of religious 'taint' or of respect for authority, or of adherence to a strong moral code instantly disqualified any prospective juror," it thus should come as no surprise that one juror appeared at a "pro-choice rally" the day after the trial ended. "The perversion of justice implied by such a spectacle becomes therefore evident." The remedy for such a miscarriage of justice was left to Ontario's attorney-general, Roy McMurtry, who had a "clear and inescapable duty" to appeal the verdict.[19]

Byfield accurately captured the prevailing sentiment among pro-life folk, from whom a steady and persistent refrain had been heard since that chilly November afternoon. They were calling on Roy McMurtry, a call that took on the insistence of a steadily beating drum: Appeal. Appeal. Appeal.

McMurtry, who was contending for the leadership of the provincial Conservative party at the time, rose to his feet on December 4 in the Legislature, after nearly a month of dodging the issue. With Morgentaler himself peering down from the visitors' gallery, the attorney-general announced his decision. He would appeal.

Grounds for this action were the alleged errors in law committed by Judge Parker: he permitted the defence of necessity despite the lack of constituent legal elements required for such a defence; he did not instruct the jury properly regarding the defence of necessity; and he permitted defence counsel to address the jury in a manner that "was inflammatory and calculated to cause the jury to disregard their oath in rendering their verdict", and that urged jurors "to render a verdict based on their assessment of whether the law was a 'good' law or a 'bad' law."[20]

Morton meticulously recounted Judge Parker's travail. After his initial four-hour summation of evidence and instruction to the jury on the defence of necessity and how it did not apply, he was berated by Manning as soon as the jury had been sequestered. The judge then sent word that the jury cease deliberation while he studied the legal issues further. He re-charged the jury the following Monday, but even that address was criticized by Manning.[21]

Pro-life activists were surprised that the issue of jury selection was not one of the grounds for appeal, but such selection tactics were not illegal. The right-to-life groups went so far as to apply for intervener status at the appeal to raise this issue themselves, but were denied.[22]

They hailed McMurtry's decision to appeal, but were stingingly critical of his non-interventionist approach in the interim. He would not seek an injunction to prevent Morgentaler and his cronies from re-opening the Harbord Street clinic, as pro-life groups had been asking him to do, nor would he lay new charges should the abortionists begin again to ply their grisly trade. "To proceed with another prosecution without the law being clarified would clearly not be in the public interest," he intoned.[23]

Solicitor-General George Taylor, however, publicly contradicted his colleague and said that the police would probably raid the clinic if it re-opened.

The clinic re-opened on December 10, 1984. A state of *de facto* anarchy ensued, as pro-lifers picketed the abortuary and, in the face of inaction by the government and police, at one point sat on the steps and refused to budge.[24] This spontaneous act of non-violent civil disobedience occurred when Metro police cancelled a raid on the clinic they had planned for that day, due to a purported "political squabble" between their top brass and McMurtry's office. Instead, officers ended up hauling away seven pro-life activists and charging them with trespassing, while the illegal clinic activities carried on uninterrupted.[25]

The confusion stemmed in part from McMurtry's statements in the Legislature two days earlier. He stood to plead with Morgentaler to voluntarily close his establishment pending the appeal, "as an act of profound social responsibility." Such "restraint" would be a "demonstration of restraint for the rule of law."[26]

Nothing doing, came the answer, not from Morgentaler himself (who was on vacation) but from Judy Rebick, of the Ontario Coalition for Abortion Clinics. The clinic "had a right to stay open," she declared; she further accused McMurtry of "veiled threats."[27]

Finally, on the evening of December 20, police arrested Robert Scott. They issued a warrant for the arrest of Morgentaler, who turned himself in that evening, only to be charged and released on his own recognizance. The jury, so to speak, on Henry Morgentaler and his abortion business, was still out.

The "clear loser" in this anarchic turbulence was Roy McMurtry, in the words of author Morton. He fell from being a favorite in the Tory leadership race to lose to Frank Miller, who in turn lost in the provincial election to David Peterson and his Liberals, thus "bringing to an end forty-two years of Tory rule in Ontario and putting the once invincible 'Big Blue Machine' on the road to political oblivion."[28]

Joe, observing these events from Manitoba, was as aggrieved as his fellow pro-lifers. As a former Cabinet Minister, he had more insight than most into the quandary of Roy McMurtry, and exhorted right-to-life advocates to give credit where it was due. The attorney-general had made "a wise decision and a courageous decision" to appeal. "I hope the people will appreciate that when the decision to pick the next premier of Ontario. There was a lot of pressure, I know, from the pro-abortion side not to interfere with the jury's decision."[29]

The events in Ontario had ramifications across the country, and particularly in Manitoba, where McMurtry's counterpart, Roland Penner, announced that he would not take action on the outstanding charges against Morgentaler, Scott and the abortion clinic staff until the appeal in the east was heard.

Joe Borowski then became embroiled in a bizarre episode. He claimed he had received an anonymous call at his health food store, during which the caller offered $20,000 to anyone to do away with Henry Morgentaler. Joe "didn't want to scare the guy off" and thought that there was merit in meeting with him to ascertain if he was "a nut case," he later explained to a reporter.[30]

A meeting did not occur, but such a delicate matter lent itself to easy sensationalism by the media. A *Globe* article accused Joe of attempting to be a go-between for a would-be assassin and the man with the money—a complete misrepresentation of his remarks, Joe angrily pointed out.[31]

Moreover, a truncated version of a private letter he wrote—enough to leave a sinister impression—was revealed by CBC TV in Winnipeg in early December. The newscast reported that Joe had suggested in the letter that someone would harm Morgentaler if he returned to the city to perform abortions.[32] Joe reacted bitterly. "It was a private letter and it should have stayed that way." He had written it in response to someone who wrote him asking about Morgentaler, and had thrown the original missive away. In retrospect, Joe said, it looked as though the initial communication had been a set-up, a trap to further darken his reputation.

Joe was already in hot water for remarks he made right after the Ontario acquittal. "I would give you odds that if Dr. Morgentaler comes back to Winnipeg, something terrible will happen. It's better to say it now than be faced with the actual fact later on."[33]

Roland Penner warned Joe once, then twice, that criminal charges could be laid against him if, indeed, Morgentaler came to grief in that province. The attorney-general was "shocked that someone of his position seemed to be advising illegal measures." But Joe brushed off Penner's words with some disdain, saying his sense of justice was "upside down. Here's a guy who kills babies illegally, and when I make a statement, [Penner] takes offence. Isn't that something?"

Joe's confidence in the face of a bristling press and the taint of allegations of violence was based on his ironclad convictions, and his undeniably clean record. He "categorically repudiates violence as a way of solving the problem."[34]

What Joe did do, however, was to pray for Morgentaler, and he urged others to do likewise. "I believe he will be converted before he hangs up his spurs. Prayer will convert Henry Morgentaler. I don't know how it will happen—God works in mysterious ways."

Other pro-life leaders observed the imbroglio with growing disquiet. Mary Lamont, then president of League for Life, complained about Joe's conduct in the press. "If I had one wish," she told the *Winnipeg Sun*, "it would be, please, let Joe Borowski not say another word for at least three years. Yet, you've got to admire his spirit."[35]

Morgentaler, meanwhile, was heading straight for Manitoba. He arrived in Winnipeg that January on a whirlwind fundraising tour. It had been announced by his spokesperson, Suzanne Newman, that the Corydon Avenue abortuary would reopen in mid-March. Joe repeated his dire predictions: "If he does open it, then he's risking his own life." He and other pro-life groups chose to stay away when Morgentaler came to town. "The situation is so volatile I felt that if we went out there," Joe explained, "there would be a confrontation and there could be violence."[36]

Joe viewed illegal abortion clinics as a grave threat, for a number of reasons. It could take two or more years before the Supreme Court ruled on his lawsuit, but the decision would be meaningless if by then there were "a string of abortuaries operating across the country," he admitted. The politicians would simply not have the courage to shut them down.[37]

The Winnipeg abortuary opened on March 23, but was raided by police five-and-a-half hours later; Morgentaler was arrested, and subsequently released. That evening, angry pro-abortion demonstrators besieged the home of Roland Penner, shouting down the beleaguered former Communist while he strove to defend his actions. The police have a duty to uphold the law, a duty "they cannot avoid," he cried.[38]

And they did their duty. Twice more the police raided 883 Corydon Avenue, and seized a total of $9,000 in equipment. Still Morgentaler was determined to keep his clinic open.[39]

Joe Borowski, in the meantime, launched his own campaign. He had, according to one scribe, "moved a bit back in the phalanx of Manitoba anti-abortionists" battling Morgentaler.[40] Conspicuously absent from mass demonstrations and political pressure tactics of his peers, such as the Jury for Life postcard campaign organized by Manitoba's League for Life, Joe had come to consider picketing, petitions and letter-writing as demonstrably ineffective, and had told his pro-life colleagues so. "I keep reminding them that they've been doing it for 15 years and that is not enough. We can walk in front of the clinic until we freeze to death, but it won't do any good."[41]

Joe's strategy, revealed in a letter to Premier Howard Pawley in late March, was to engage in acts of civil disobedience and to encourage all other pro-life activists to do the same, to the point where they would be jailed. "I think this is a sensible, measured response to a very serious problem. It seems to me that non-violent civil disobedience is the only moral option open to me and others[42] ...I think I'd be guilty of gross betrayal if I didn't do anything."[43]

However, unlike pro-life activists in Toronto (or "rescuers" in the United States)[44] Joe planned to break laws that had nothing to do with abortion. He would not wear a seat belt, would not collect the 6 per cent provincial sales tax, and would sell raw milk. He also urged civil servants to conduct a one-hour work stoppage on Fridays, similar to actions taken by Solidarity in Poland. He exhorted prisoners to carry out peaceful demonstrations against the government. "I deliberately chose laws that would not hurt people. I want [supporters] to disobey laws that are not going to endanger anyone's health or life," Joe elaborated at a press conference.

His plan was ridiculed by the *Winnipeg Sun*, which ran an article headlined "Joe's planning a life of crime" followed by an editorial which likened the whole affair to a "three-ring circus" and a "simple one-upmanship that is singularly stupid." The *Sun* also berated right-to-abortion agitators, and Morgentaler in particular, for "legal theatrics."[45]

Stung, Joe sent a letter in reply, in which he pointed out that Gandhi, in his fight for his country's independence "defied colonials by picking up a pinch of British salt from India's shores." The circus, if there was one, was being orchestrated by Morgentaler and those in authority who, by refusing to stop him, were "guilty of aiding the commission of a crime spree."

Joe pithily denounced the Montreal abortion doctor: "He is spreading a deadly plague throughout this beautiful and peaceful land of ours by not only promoting and practising private capital punishment for the child in the womb but in brazenly breaking the law and hiring staff to break the law with him. He is guilty of the worst form of child abuse in existence—murder. He is a relentless slanderer and hate-peddler of anti-Catholicism—indeed, the Zundel of the left."[46]

But Joe's campaign of civil disobedience proved unnecessary, as "the Zundel of the left" was finally compelled to obey the law. In early April, after League for Life had tried and failed to get an injunction to prevent Morgentaler from opening, assistance came from an unexpected quarter.[47] The College of Physicians and Surgeons of Manitoba stopped Henry Morgentaler.

It had suspended the abortionist's medical privileges on March 30 for seven days because of "apparent willful and deliberate" use of a non-hospital facility for "surgical procedures." Morgentaler ignored the suspension.[48]

Faced with such defiance, the College went to court on April 5 and obtained an interim restraining order. This time, Brodsky said, his client would abide by the order of Court of Queen's Bench Justice Archibald Dewar. "The injunction," admitted Morgentaler, "is quite strict and the penalty severe."[49]

The battle then shifted to yet another courtroom, when Henry Morgentaler was summoned to the Ontario Court of Appeal—his case expedited, it would appear, for political reasons. On April 29, 1985, what was billed "the broadest and most controversial challenge...under the Charter of Rights and Freedoms" to ever face the court began with a flourish of publicity.[50]

As for Joe's appeal, it had lain fallow in Saskatchewan for over a year-and-a-half. In March a restive Joe complained about the delay, and was told that federal Justice Department lawyer Ed Sojonky had not yet fully prepared his arguments. In June, Joe received word his case would be heard on December 16, 1985.

Notes
Chapter 25
The years when we knew misfortune

[1] Interview with Jim Hughes, April 2002.

[2] "Morgentaler jury faces selection with morals quiz," Kirk Makin, *Globe and Mail*, October 16, 1984.

[3] Op. Cit., Morton, pp. 183-184.

[4] Ibid. p. 184.

[5] "First five jurors selected in Morgentaler trial," Kirk Makin, *Globe and Mail*, October 17, 1984, p. M3.

[6] Ibid.

[7] "Selection of jury slowed down again at Morgentaler trial," Bill Walker, *Toronto Star*, October 17, 1984, p. A3.

[8] "Six men, six women form Morgentaler jury," Kirk Makin, *Globe and Mail*, October 19, 1984.

[9] "6 men, 6 women in jury for trial of Morgentaler," Bill Walker, *Toronto Star*, October 19, 1984.

[10] Op. Cit., "Six men, six women form Morgentaler Jury," Makin.

[11] Op. Cit., "6 men, 6 women in jury for trial," Bill Walker.

[12] "Religion called key in selecting jurors," Peter Goodspeed, *Toronto Star*, November 9, 1984.

[13] *Toronto Sun*, November 9, 1984.

[14] "Anti-abortion groups call for immediate appeal," Dana Flavelle, *Toronto Star*, November 9, 1984.

[15] *Toronto Sun*, November 9, 1984.

[16] "Anarchy foreseen if Morgentaler freed," Kirk Makin, *Globe and Mail*, November 3, 1984, p. 13.

[17] "Victory in abortion case sends defence lawyer into legal stratosphere," William Bragg, *Toronto Star*, November 9, 1984.

[18] "Abortion acquittal", editorial, *Globe and Mail*, November 9, 1984.

[19] "A letter from the publisher," *Alberta Report*, November 1984.

[20] "McMurtry's reason for appeal," *Toronto Star*, December 1984, p. A23.

[21] Op. Cit., Morton, pp. 191-192.

[22] Op. Cit., Morton, pp. 206-207.

[23] *Ottawa Citizen*, December 6, 1984, p. A8.

[24] "Seven demonstrators arrested outside Morgentaler," William Clark and Bill Walker, *Toronto Star*, December 13, 1984, p. A1.

[25] Ibid. "Abortion clinic raid today halted by 'political squabbles,'" *Toronto Star*, morning edition, December 13, 1984, p. A1.

[26] "McMurtry asks Morgentaler to close clinic," Nick Martin, *London Free Press*, December 12, 1984, p. A5.

[27] "Abortion clinic will stay open defiant backers tell McMurtry," Susan Pigg and Bill Walker, *Toronto Star*, December 12, 84, p. A2.

[28] Ibid.

[29] "Manitoba puts abortion case on hold," *Ottawa Citizen*, December 5, 1984.

[30] "Borowski prays for 'conversion' of Morgentaler," Michael Tenszen, *Globe and Mail*, April. 6, 1985.

[31] "Pro-life leaders deplore threats of violence," Cathy McLaughlin, *Western Catholic Reporter*, January 28, 1985, p. 7.

[32] "Borowski letter prompts warning," Brian Cole, *Winnipeg Free Press*, December 7, 1984.

[33] "Borowski sees danger in Morgentaler return," Brian Gory, *Globe and Mail*, November 17, 1984.

[34] "Op. Cit., "Pro-life leaders deplore threats of violence," McLaughlin.

[35] "Abortion foe under fire," Shirley Muir, *Winnipeg Sun*, January 11, 1985, p. 3.

[36] "Morgentaler visit to city draws few protesters," Bob Cox and Beth Marlin, *Winnipeg Free Press*, January 19, 1985 pp. 1 and 5.

[37] Borowski sees illegal clinics as grave foe," Peter Fleck, *Alberta Sunshine News*, February 5, 1984.

[38] "Morgentaler arrested, freed," Beth Marlin and Tom Goldstein, *Free Press*,

[39] "Judge refuses to grant injunction against Winnipeg abortion clinic," Brian Gory, *Globe and Mail*, April 2, 1985.

[40] "Borowski prays for 'conversion' of Morgentaler," Michael Tenszen, *Globe and Mail*, April 6, 1985.

[41] "Abortion foe under fire," Shirley Muir, *Winnipeg Sun*, January 11, 1985, p 3.

[42] Borowski urges law breaking as 'sensible' abortion protest," Bob Cox, *Free Press*, March 22, 1985, p. 3.

[43] "I'll go to jail to stop Morgentaler, crusader says," *Montreal Gazette*, March 22, 1985, B1.

[44] See Chapter 28, note 37.

[45] "Clinic circus is sickening," *Winnipeg Sun*, March 24, 1985, p. 20.

[46] Unpublished letter to the *Sun* dated March 24, 1985.

[47] "Judge refuses to grant injunction against Winnipeg abortion clinic," Brian Gory, *Globe and Mail*, April 2, 1985.

[48] "Morgentaler to defy lifting of MD licence," Michael Tenszen, *Globe and Mail*, March 30, 1985.

[49] "Injunction stops Morgentaler from practising in Manitoba," Brian Gory, *Globe and Mail*, April 5, 1985.

[50] The five judges who heard the appeal were: Chief Justice William Howland, Associate Chief Justice B. J. MacKinnon, Charles Dubin, G. Arthur Martin and John Brooke. ("Morgentaler appeal opens biggest Charter case so far," Kirk Makin, *Globe and Mail*, April 30, 1985, p. M6.)

Chapter 26

Appeal, appeal, appeal

Though parched and exhausted with waiting
I have not forgotten your commands.
How long must your servent suffer?
Psalm 119:81

WHILE THE STREET SCENE WAS COMPARATIVELY QUIET IN WINNIPEG, such was not the case in Toronto. The Ontario Tories had been defeated in the June 1985 election and Liberal Premier David Peterson had appointed as his attorney-general Ian Scott, a man who sympathized with the right-to-abortion crowd.

According to Campaign Life, Scott played on the public's anxiety over violence—an anxiety whetted by media sensationalism—to divide the pro-life movement, and divert attention from the fact that the Morgentaler abortion clinic operated outside the law. Pro-life supporters were determined to keep this last fact squarely before the public. All through the summer and fall of 1985, Campaign Life, along with Baptist Minister Ken Campbell's Choose Life Canada, engaged in sit-ins, attempted citizen's arrests and started to sidewalk counsel distressed women going into the clinic for abortions.[1] Often, 50 to 100 pro-life picketers would be down on Harbord Street during the clinic's operating hours. Metro police were routinely dispatched to guard the establishment.[2]

Ian Scott appealed to both Norma Scarborough, head of CARAL, and to Emmett Cardinal Carter, to encourage a limit on the picketers. The Cardinal had strongly condemned abortion in a pastoral letter released while Roy McMurtry was agonizing over whether or not to appeal the Morgentaler acquittal. Morgentaler had then proposed to meet with the prelate, but as trenchant *Toronto Sun* columnist Claire Hoy observed, the latter, "no mean political force himself, was not about to be used as a pawn by a man whose main claim to fame is his skill in killing unborn babies quickly for a fee."[3] The infamous abortionist was rebuffed by the famous churchman, who, through his spokesman, declared that he had no patience for publicity stunts. (It was a pity, Hoy commented, that "Carter didn't adopt the same tough position three years ago when he met privately with Pierre Trudeau on the then-proposed and now-imposed Charter of Rights. Had Carter hung tough then, rather than compromising, and insisted on inserting protection for the unborn in that document, it might be easier to congratulate his current activities on behalf of the unborn.")

But now Cardinal Carter dismayed, and arguably, failed the pro-life movement when he agreed with Ian Scott that pickets at the Morgentaler clinic should be limited to five. No doubt he was convinced that the possibility of violence was real, yet from his correspondence with the attorney-general, it appeared that he accepted at face value a skewed portrayal of the events on Harbord Street.

"I am informed," he wrote to Scott, "that the authorities of the police department are highly concerned about the tendencies to violence, even through the use of weapons, which tend to manifest themselves."[4]

Was the Cardinal referring to the July 29 incident? But then, it was a trio of pro-life picketers, including a Jesuit priest and an 11-year-old child, who were terrorized when a woman pointed a shotgun at them and threatened, "I'll blow your heads off."[5]

What aggrieved Campaign Life, then coordinating the picketing and sidewalk counseling outside the Harbord Street abortuary, was that the Cardinal had not consulted them before agreeing to a reduction of pro-life picketers. It was yet another brick in the wall of miscommunication and misunderstanding being constructed between the Catholic prelate and the grassroots pro-life activists in Toronto.

Campaign Life, along with Toronto Right to Life and Choose Life Canada, refused to accept Carter's suggestion. The highly publicized disagreement, however, was quickly overshadowed by the announcement that the Ontario Court of Appeal would soon be releasing its much-anticipated decision on Morgentaler, Scott and Smoling's November 1984 acquittal.

On October 1, 1985, the Court released its ruling. Morgentaler and his co-accused lost.

The Court overturned the acquittal. The "errors at trial were so fundamental," the judges unanimously decided, "that there has been no trial according to law." A new trial was directed. The Court also found that the abortion provisions of the Criminal Code were "not in violation of Section 7 of the Charter." The judges severely reprimanded Morris Manning as well. His contention that the jury was a proper tribunal to change the legislation was "a serious misstatement of the law" and his argumentation in this regard constituted "a direct attack on the role and authority of the trial judge and a serious misstatement to the jury as to its duty and right in carrying out its oath."[6]

Despite this ruling, Attorney-General Ian Scott refused to close down the Harbord Street abortion clinic, and he instructed Metro Toronto Police Chief Jack Marks not to lay any new charges. The police chief told a press conference that he could not very well disregard the attorney-general's advice, but his force was then powerless to do more than monitor the situation and collect evidence for possible future use. The controversy at the clinic was "without a doubt, one of the most difficult problems that this police force, or I as chief, has ever faced," said Marks.[7]

Scott also dismissed a proposal to lay new charges and, as a condition of bail, require that the clinic remain closed pending trial. "I, frankly, as a Crown officer, do not regard the purpose of the laying of charges to be to get a bail application," he elaborated.

Morgentaler and his co-accused appealed to the Supreme Court.

The '80s were in full swing. Pop groups like Duran Duran topped the charts, music videos were all the rage and fashionable young men wore their sunglasses at night and, like Don Johnson of *Miami Vice*, neglected to shave daily. Not so Joe Borowski, who, four days after his 53rd birthday, was clad in his usual suit and tie, as he slid into one of the oak benches at the Victoria Avenue courthouse in Regina. He was confident that the Saskatchewan Court of Appeal would rule in his favour "because I happen to believe there is a God somewhere."[8]

He was fresh from a late-November arrest in Toronto, in solidarity with his beleaguered comrades there. On Harbord Street, Joe knocked on the abortuary's rear door, climbed an outside staircase, knocked on another door, and was accosted by a police officer and security guard. He refused to leave and was taken into custody. It took a little over a half-hour from his initial exertions to his escort into a police car. Five other protesters followed his example and were arrested for refusing to move from the steps and, together with Joe, were charged with trespassing.

"As an experienced prisoner," Joe told his Toronto counterparts, "I can tell you that people in jail are treated better than many living in slum housing.[9]...There is no line to be drawn and no price that can't be paid. I would gladly give my life to stop this thing. The very least I should be prepared to do is go to prison, whether it is for a month, a year or life."[10]

On this day and in this court, however, Joe did not face the threat of jail. He was there to observe as Morris Shumiatcher laid out again, like a well-used garment newly pressed, his arguments. Reporters wearily scribbled that these remained essentially unchanged from his summations in 1983. The three judges of the Court of Appeal, two men and one woman, listened intently as Shumiatcher eloquently reconstructed his client's case. "Some people may have thought that capital punishment was abolished in Canada," the advocate declared but, "the unborn child is systematically put to death... We've moved the gallows. ...It's in hospitals now."[11]

The canny lawyer was also aware that the Supreme Court was scheduled to release a landmark Charter ruling, one which he was certain would have bearing, for good or ill, on the very issues of law he had been arguing for two days in the Regina courtroom. He had arranged for a courier to bring the decision hither "with all dispatch" and it arrived at 10:30 on the morning of the last day of the appeal. Shumiatcher asked for a recess so he could assess the relevance of the decision.

It did not disappoint.

The decision, the *B.C. Motor Vehicle Reference* case, was, as Charter analyst F. L. Morton explained, "relatively unimportant with respect to the policy issue at stake" but went on to become "one of the most important and most cited Charter precedents."[12] The reason was that the ruling, written by Justice Antonio Lamer, "officially sanctioned" the view that the present and future interpreters of the Charter need not seek to discover nor strictly adhere to what the original architects of the document intended. Rather, similar to the "living tree" argument put forward by Lord Sankey in the *Persons* case, the judgment, in Morton's words, released "constitutional law (i.e. judges) from constitutional text (the meaning intended by the framers)." The consequences were breathtaking in their magnitude. The "Court had granted itself and all other Canadian judges wide discretion to read new meaning into the Charter."[13]

For Shumiatcher on that chilly December morning, the freshly minted Supreme Court decision was a bonanza. It permitted him to rebut the three key arguments put forward by Edward Sojonky.

The Crown lawyer had urged the Court to rely on Parliamentary debates that revealed the architects of the Charter did not intend the "everyone" of Section 7 to include the unborn child. But the Supreme Court decision referred to so enthusiastically by Shumiatcher, ruled "that debates in parliament are irrelevant and ought not to be considered by the Court."[14]

Sojonky had further requested the appellate judges to apply decisions made under the Canadian Bill of Rights. But the Supreme Court "held that interpretations under the Bill of Rights have no application to the Charter."[15]

Thirdly, Sojonky submitted that the phrase "fundamental justice" in Section 7 referred to procedural justice, not to the substance of law. But the Supreme Court held that the term was "not to be confined merely to procedural matters." The fundamental justice with which Section 7 was concerned could also be "of a substantive quality to be applied in testing the fairness and fundamental justness of an issue."[16]

Shumiatcher was delighted with this turn of events, and Joe Borowski was beaming. The judges, Tom Wakeling, S. J. Cameron and Marjorie Gerwing reserved their decision. Little did Joe realize at the time, but the justices would ruminate on the matter for a year and five months before delivering their verdict.

Anyone driving north on Winnipeg's St. Anne's Road has an unimpeded view of the wall of the Borowski Health Food Store. The ever-enterprising Joe did not let this natural billboard space go to waste, but used it in his continuing educational efforts—although not without the occasional controversy. In the summer of 1985, Joe had a 9 by 14 foot mural painted on that broad expanse which depicted a cemetery. "N.D.P. Morgentaler has a place for unwanted babies—but they can't live there," read the message: "No babies, no future."

In June, the sign was splattered with black and red paint. Joe offered a $1,000 reward to anyone who had information that would lead to the arrest and conviction of the vandal or vandals, who were presumably pro-abortion. "It's the colour of their trade," Joe said in disgust. "They talk about freedom of speech, but when it comes to us, they're denying freedom of speech."[17] But NDP supporters were calling him to complain, and soon, officialdom became involved.[18]

After ignoring an order to remove the mural, Joe was convicted in municipal court of maintaining an illegal advertising sign, and given 30 days to remove it. No fine was levied.[19] The charge, Joe protested, was "politically inspired. I would even suggest that it borders on harassment."[20]

Meanwhile, yet another educational attempt by Joe and the Alliance Against Abortion was marred by a strange incident. They had purchased VHS and Beta videotapes of Bernard Nathanson's dreadful film *The Silent Scream*—an ultrasound depiction of an actual abortion—through a Toronto distributor. The videos had already been sent to hospitals, the three Catholic archbishops of Winnipeg, Premier Howard Pawley and others, when it was discovered that the Beta format tapes contained six minutes of X-rated sex scenes about 10 minutes into the film. The tapes were hastily recalled, and the police vice squad undertook to discover who had tampered with them, but to no avail.[21]

As he awaited the Court's decision, Joe kept up his speaking, fund-raising and educational efforts. He altered his controversial wall mural to read: "Pro-choicers have a place for unwanted babies," rather than "N.D.P. Morgentaler." (He was ultimately vindicated in the struggle to keep his sign by claiming Charter rights to freedom of speech. The Crown, after looking into these arguments, decided to drop the charges.[22])

Meanwhile, Henry Morgentaler—with whose fate in the justice system Joe's was now, unbeknownst to either man, inextricably and inexorably linked—was battling with the College of Physicians and Surgeons of Manitoba, while he kept up elsewhere his aggressive assault on any legal or procedural constraint on his abortion business. The College held firm, even though that put it at odds with Court of Queen's Bench Justice Peter Morse, who in February 1986, quashed its original decision not to approve the Morgentaler clinic for therapeutic abortions, for the reason that the abortionist had not been given a chance to argue his case.[23]

College registrar Dr. James Morison retorted that the decision had "mind-boggling ramifications" if it meant the College was expected to notify every doctor before granting accreditation.[24] Nevertheless, as directed by the Court, the College reconsidered Morgentaler's application to perform abortions at his clinic on Corydon Avenue. On May 14, 1986, it turned him down. Morgentaler's clinic, it argued, was not an accredited hospital nor private facility approved by the provincial health department.[25][26]

Morgentaler, piqued, found a doctor who was willing to act as medical director of his Winnipeg clinic, in his stead, in order that business at the Corydon Avenue establishment could carry on.[27]

Meanwhile, far to the east, Robert Scott, long a practitioner of abortion in Morgentaler's clinics, struck out on his own. In late May 1986, Scott opened an illegal abortion clinic on Toronto's Gerrard Street.

Intrepid Ontario pro-life activists kept up the pressure despite the intractability of Attorney-General Ian Scott and his boss, Premier David Peterson. The latter was dogged by pro-life picketers every time he made a public appearance. Even when he hosted a public relations skate-fest on Ottawa's Rideau Canal, nimble protesters whizzed by, bearing signs reminding him of his duty to uphold the law, until the energetic premier left them in the icy dust.

Life was also made slightly uncomfortable for Ian Scott. An Ontario Provincial Police officer began shadowing the lanky politician in June of 1986; the government had taken seriously a persistent rumour that right-to-life activists were planning to place Scott under citizen's arrest. (Ken Campbell, head of Choose Life Canada, had shortly before asked a justice of the peace to charge Scott for refusing to close the Morgentaler clinic.) "It was not my idea, and frankly, I find it kind of boring," complained the attorney-general.[28] Scott's ennui deserted him when Morgentaler, Robert Scott, and Nikki Colodny, an abortion doctor affiliated with the Morgentaler clinic since 1985, were arrested on September 24, 1986, on the authority of Metro Police Chief Jack Marks.

The police boss and the politician denied any clash between their respective departments, but Marks insisted his force had "said all along that we'd lay charges if there was an increase in activity." When Robert Scott opened the second abortion clinic in violation of the law, the police launched a three-and-a-half month investigation—at the behest of the attorney-general, who foresaw that new charges might well result. The police, reasoned Marks, had "an obligation" to present their painstakingly accumulated evidence before the court.

The politician, strangely, did not concur. "Visibly miffed" at his press conference, Ian Scott moved quickly to secure a stay of proceedings for the malfeasant trio. It was not the charges that galled him, but the timing of the arrests. In two short weeks, Henry Morgentaler's appeal would be heard by the Supreme Court. "It is clear," barked the attorney-general, "that whatever charges are laid today and any other day, there can be no trial of those charges until the Supreme Court of Canada makes its decision." Thus, the three abortionists were released scant hours after their arrests and returned to work the same afternoon.[29]

Pro-lifers were disgusted by this decision, but the *Globe* approved. "To proceed with one case in a lower court while its substance was being considered by the highest court would amount to badgering of the accused, not justice," it pontificated.[30]

Such was the course of events when the glare of the spotlight once again fell on Morris Manning and his notorious client as they climbed the stairs to the Supreme Court on October 7, 1986. They had secured a hearing before the highest court in the land while Joe Borowski's lawsuit on behalf of the unborn languished still before the Saskatchewan Court of Appeal.

The Supreme Court had been deliberating for eight months on the Morgentaler matter when the Saskatchewan Appeal Court released its ruling on Joe Borowski's claim on April 30, 1987. He lost.

In a 44-page ruling, the three justices ruled that granting the unborn child legal status as a person "would be a major departure from tradition." They concurred with Justice Matheson that the "everyone" of Section 7 did not include the child in the womb. "The Charter is neutral in relation to abortion," wrote Madame Justice Marjorie Gerwing, who penned the unanimous ruling: "It remains for Parliament, reflecting the will of the Canadian people, to determine without reference to the Charter in what circumstances the termination of a pregnancy will be lawful or unlawful."[31]

According to the decision, a scrutiny of the history of the rights and protections accorded to unborn children in Britain, Canada and other countries revealed that while "respect for life and its fundamental sanctity have been part of the common law tradition for centuries...within this tradition for long periods of time, destruction of the fetus has been permitted...despite full knowledge of the scientific principles of fetal capacity for life urged upon us by [Mr. Borowski]. Such treatment of the fetus would not have been consistent with full status as a person."[32]

"I'd just expected the Court would have more courage and spine than the courts have had up to this point," an angry Joe told reporters.[33] It took him three weeks to "sufficiently recover" before he could sit down and write calmly to his supporters. "I have never been so disappointed and frustrated in my entire life!" he admitted in a newsletter. Now came the time for a momentous decision: proceed to the Supreme Court, or abandon the lawsuit completely.

"Cost of the two appeals will be approximately $125,000 plus ongoing day-to-day expenses," wrote Joe. "For the first time in nine years, since we launched the court action, I am going to leave the decision solely up to you, my friends and supporters. Your letters and donations will be a vote to go ahead with the case to the Supreme Court. If you do not respond, your vote will mean drop it, and I will understand and respect your decision."

It's hard to believe that Joe Borowski would have actually dropped the case and walked away—although the provocation or temptation to do so was undeniably great. However, press reports following the Appeal Court decision have Joe claiming he would sell his health food store so that he could devote himself full time to the pro-life cause. While he did not do that, he did ultimately decide to continue his legal journey.

The appeal motion to the Supreme Court was filed in 1987 on June 22—the day Catholics honour the memory of St. Thomas More, the holy lawyer. At one time, Thomas More was close advisor and confidant to his choleric monarch, Henry VIII, and, as Lord Chancellor of England, one of the most powerful and influential men in the kingdom. But in the end, he was beheaded for refusing to acknowledge either Henry's divorce from Catherine of Aragon, or Henry's claim to be head of the Church in England. As St. Thomas knelt to receive the blow of the axe, he remarked: "I die the King's good servant, but God's first"—words that could well be applied to our man Joe.

Notes
Chapter 26
Appeal, appeal, appeal

1. Campaign Life newsletter, September 1985.
2. This set the scene that led David Packer, a father of five children and 10-year veteran of the Toronto police force, to decide that he could not guard an abortion clinic. The story of Packer's refusal, in 1987, to "do his duty," the reprisals he suffered at the hands of the police force and his subsequent difficulties, is told in the book *A Matter of Conscience*, written by his wife, Anne. (Anne Packer, *A Matter of Conscience* (Toronto, Interim Publishing, 1988)
3. "Roy must do his duty," Clair Hoy, *Toronto Sun*, December 2, 1984.
4. Letter from Cardinal Carter to Ian Scott dated August 22, 1985.
5. "Shotgun pointed at anti-abortionist," Sean Fine, *Globe and Mail*, July 30, 1985.
6. Op. Cit., Morton, p. 213; October 1 press release from Campaign Life.
7. "Police to monitor but not shut Morgentaler clinic, chief says," Bill Schiller, *Toronto Star*, October 4, 1985; "Metro Police plan no more charges over abortion clinic," Mary Gooderham, Globe and Mail, October 4, 1985.
8. "Joe Borowski 'supremely confident' of court victory." Tom Blackwell, *Regina Leader-Post*, December 16, 1985.
9. "Manitoba anti-abortion crusader achieves speedy arrest in Toronto," Don Downey, *Globe and Mail*, November 26, 1985, p. A18.
10. Op. Cit., "Joe Borowski 'supremely confident'," Blackwell.
11. "Unborn face capital punishment appeal hearing on abortion told," *Toronto Star*, December 18, 1985.
12. Op. Cit., Morton, pp. 214-216.
13. Ibid. p. 214.
14. Op. Cit. "I set before you life and death," Shumiatcher, p. 23
15. Ibid. p. 24.
16. Ibid.
17. "Anti-abortion sign defaced," *Ottawa Citizen*, May 10, 1985.
18. "Pro-life poster vandalized," *The Interim*, June 1985.
19. "Borowski ordered to remove mural," *Winnipeg Free Press*, September 24, 1985.
20. "Borowski on charge," Stan Koma, *Catholic Register*, July 13, 1985.
21. "Anti-abortionists find sex scenes in their own film," *Globe and Mail*, May 29, 1985, p 3.
22. "Charges dropped against Borowski," news briefs, *Globe and Mail*, February 4, 1987.
23. "Henry wins one," Winnipeg Sun, February 18, 1986.
24. "Morgentaler hails ruling on clinic bid," Brian Gory, *Globe and Mail*, February 19, 1986.
25. "College nixes abortion bid," Bruce Owen, *Winnipeg Sun*, May 16, 1986.
26. The College was itself wracked with disagreement over how to handle Henry Morgentaler. The president, Pat Doyle, had resigned in protest in March 1985

when the College granted the abortionist a medical licence. But registrar Morison claimed the College "acted according to our regulations" in issuing Morgentaler a licence to practise medicine in Manitoba, required by all out-of-province physicians. "It's not a licence to practise abortion."
("Abortion controversy," Radha Krishnan Thampi, *Winnipeg Sun*, March 12, 1985, p 3.)

[27] "New abortion doc," Bruce Owen, *Winnipeg Sun*, May 14, 1986.

[28] "Bodyguard provided for Attorney-General,"*Globe and Mail*, June 3, 1986.

[29] "Miffed at timing of abortion charges, Scott blocks trials until top court rules," Susan Delacourt and Robert MacLeod, *Globe and Mail*, September 25, 1986.

[30] "Staying the charges" editorial, *Globe and Mail*, September 26, 1986.

[31] "No rights for a fetus," Tom Philip and Richard Cairney, *Western Report*, May 18, 1987, p. 48.

[32] Ibid. p. 49.

[33] "Borowski loses abortion appeal," *Free Press*, May 2, 1987, p. 9.

Chapter 27

That little marble building down the street

God did not make death,
nor does He rejoice in the destruction of the living.
For He fashioned all things that they might have being;
And the creatures of the world are wholesome.
Wisdom 1:13

GWEN LANDOLT WAS ON THE PHONE. THE LATE AFTERNOON SUNLIGHT tumbled through her comfortable north Toronto home, gilding in the light of a fading day the crimson-leafed trees outside her window. But Landolt's gaze was fixed, instead, on a looming crisis. Henry Morgentaler's constitutional challenge to the abortion law would soon be heard by the Supreme Court.

Landolt was convinced that pro-life groups had to be there to speak for the unborn child. "I pleaded, I pulled my hair, I yelled, I screamed, I did everything to try to convince pro-life people to intervene in the [Morgentaler] case."

That particular day, she was trying to persuade Anna Desilets, executive director of Alliance for Life.[1] Desilets was adamant that "all the money, all of the time has gone into the Borowski case," and that the pro-life movement simply could not afford to "shift over and get involved in the Morgentaler case", recalled Landolt.

"And I remember putting down the phone...I said, 'Well, that's it.'I knew the game plan." The Supreme Court justices would "shoot down" the abortion law and Joe Borowski's case would be "after the fact. I mean, they wouldn't put Borowski first and have to deal with the abortion law—heaven forbid," elaborated Landolt. "These guys are politicians, really, politicians in lawyer's gowns."

A plea to Joe himself was to no avail. His case was before the Saskatchewan Court of Appeal, and Joe was convinced he would win. Moreover, he concurred with Desilets, who argued that the pro-lifers had, in Landolt's felicitous phrase, "put all their eggs in the Borowski basket." It seemed unnecessary to intervene at the Morgentaler hearing.

Well does Landolt recall, after the Morgentaler verdict was delivered, making "that ghastly trip to Ottawa." It was in February, "a terrible, cold, miserable, freezing day as only Ottawa can have." Resolutely, the blunt-spoken lawyer set herself to the task of going through the dockets of the Morgentaler case. Page after page of the thousands she scanned: "Every one was pro-abortion, pro-abortion—not one single pro-life reference, not one counter-manding word to back it."

"It was the loneliest, saddest day of my life."

It was at that point she vowed that "never again will I ever allow a case to go to the Supreme Court without having balance." Her reasons were twofold: "I always knew that history has to show that pro-life was there"—that the voice of the unborn child would be, at the very least, part of the record of the court.

The second reason—and this intuition was vindicated in the years following the *Morgentaler* decision—was that "I didn't want the Court to be able to exonerate itself or excuse itself, and say, 'What could we do, nobody argued any differently?' And that's exactly what the Chief Justice [Antonio] Lamer said one time in a subsequent abortion case: 'Well, what could we do in the Morgentaler case? Nobody else argued any differently, there was no pro-life or anti-abortion content,' and [he] used that."[2] There was a pause as Landolt reflected, and although there was no trace of bitterness in her voice, her next words conveyed a sense of bleak resignation. "I knew he would."

In October 1986, Antonio Lamer was one of seven Supreme Court justices who assembled to hear the Morgentaler case. Joining him on the bench for the historic hearing were Chief Justice Brian Dickson, Willard (Bud) Estey, Jean Beetz, Bertha Wilson, William McIntyre and Gerard La Forest. While the full court consisted of nine justices, Justice Julien Chouinard was ill, and, to avoid the possibility of an evenly split judgment, Gerald Le Dain was dropped from the roster.

It was not clear if the latter justice was asked to stand down, or volunteered. But the absence of these two justices augured well for Manning and Morgentaler, as pointed out by F. L. Morton in his analysis. Both Chouinard (who later died of cancer) and Le Dain were part of the "judicial restraint" component of the court.[3]

The questions in the Morgentaler appeal were complex and varied: there was the constitutional challenge to the abortion law, as well legal issues stemming from the 1984 jury acquittal, such as the use of the defence of necessity, and what latitude juries should have in interpreting the law.

The debate on this last matter provided the only high-voltage exchange in a hearing remarkable principally for its dullness. For the most part, the justices listened passively while Manning plodded methodically through his Factum; no pointed questioning on his constitutional arguments occurred. This contrasted sharply with the American Supreme Court hearings, where lawyers have only 30 minutes to present their oral arguments, forcing the judges to question them on the salient points of law.[4]

However, when the arguments turned to the question of the jury's duty and discretion, five of the seven justices became "visibly perturbed."[5] Manning was "battered" by the justices regarding his invitation to the jurors to ignore the law. After almost a half-hour of "rapid-fire exchange," he conceded that no Canadian, British or Commonwealth judgment supported him.[6] "The jury has a right to be perverse," he protested nevertheless, "That's one of the benefits of trial by jury."

In the final analysis, however, the Charter challenge to the abortion law would trump any legal questions regarding the propriety of the trial. In finding abortion law invalid, the Supreme Court could conceivably sidestep the tricky legal questions.[7]

Arguing the constitutional case for the Ontario government was Bonnie Wein, who at 35 had capped an already brilliant legal career when appointed senior counsel in the attorney-general's constitutional branch, just a week before the Morgentaler hearing.[8] Representing the federal attorney-general—the only intervener in the case—was none other than Edward Sojonky, who argued, along with Wein, that Section 251 struck a reasonable balance between the rights of the woman and the rights of the child *in utero*.

But none of the legal briefs, neither Morgentaler's nor the two Crown submissions, contained "arguments about the rights of the unborn," noted Peter Calamai, who, as Supreme Court reporter for Southam newspapers, routinely filed dispatches laced with analyses and behind-the-scenes revelations. The Ontario Crown's Factum brushed aside such concerns: "Whether or not life begins at the time of conception, or birth, or some stage in between, need not be determined in a judicial sense in the context of the issue raised by the appellant."

Writing that the "other half" of the abortion issue—Joe Borowski's challenge on behalf of the child in the womb—remained "mired in Saskatchewan's highest court," Calamai echoed Gwen Landolt's concern. "So the Supreme Court faces the prospect of deciding whether legalized abortion violates the constitutionally guaranteed right to life, liberty and security of the person (Section 7 of the Charter) based solely on the submissions about the danger to women."[9]

It was precisely to avoid situations such as this, that Chief Justice Brian Dickson had repeatedly pleaded with lawyers to include in their submissions on Charter cases "all the relevant material and not just legal precedents," the Southam scribe pointed out.[10]

Morris Manning did that and more. Relying "as heavily upon facts about the effects of Canada's abortion law as upon purely legal arguments" he exhorted the justices, in front of a courtroom crammed with spectators and media, to "look at exactly what the Canadian people are doing."[11] The burly barrister derided the "balancing concept" put forward by the Crown. "The Court is in a position of comparing a person with constitutional right to a fetus, or a potential life or an entity or whatever, which hasn't yet been given constitutional rights."[12] Moreover, the government spoke out of both sides of its mouth, he accused. While federal representative Sojonky argued here that the legislation was concerned with protecting fetal life, in the Borowski litigation, he had argued that the child in the womb had no constitutional rights at all.[13]

Nestled among Manning's constitutional arguments was an appeal to Section 15, dubbed the "equality rights provisions," which came into effect three years after the Charter was proclaimed. Crown prosecutor Wein asserted that while Manning's argument that the law violated a woman's right to equality had some initial attraction, it could not stand up under scrutiny.[14] But Justices Lamer, Estey and Wilson were a little testy regarding Wein's claim that the abortion law treated women equally. It would take "legislative blindness" to disregard the fact that many hospitals choose not to perform abortions, Justice Estey stated.[15] Still, Crown lawyers insisted that Section 251 was fair in its treatment of both mother and baby. Manning's claim that Parliament did not consider the life of the fetus when it crafted the legislation was "nothing short of astounding," Wein asserted.[16]

A former articling student of Morris Manning, Wein shone when she tackled head-on "the question of judicial activism that lurks over this entire appeal," as described by Calamai. In "an argument remarkable for its understatement," she used the judges' own "pronouncements against becoming a shadow Parliament" to make her case. "The constitutional interpretation of rights, such as liberty, should not compel the court to make decisions that are essentially legislative in nature," she told the Court (quoting American Supreme Court Justice Sandra Day O'Connor).[17]

Sojonky, for his part, urged the Court not to style itself after the American Supreme Court, which, in its far-reaching 1973 *Roe v. Wade* abortion ruling, discovered a constitutional "right to privacy" that included unimpeded access to abortion. He called on the judges to repudiate "the historical, legal and constitutional analysis which appears to have rendered a disservice to the political and judicial machinery of that country."[18]

Outside the sober venue of the high court and clear of the somnolent effect of the dry constitutional disputations, Manning and Morgentaler mounted a public relations "assault," reported Calamai. Mid-way through the hearing, the abortion doctor hosted a reception attended not only by his supporters, but also by a majority of the journalists covering the hearing. This deliberate courting of the media by the appellants was a marked contrast to the attitude of Crown counsel; Bonnie Wein "recoils as from a leper when a journalist tries to clarify a purely legal question."[19]

After four days, the case adjourned. "Obviously," said a weary Chief Justice Dickson, "this Court reserves judgment."[20]

The history of the right-to-life struggle in Canada is replete with "days of infamy." It seemed that scarcely had one judicial decision or development that further entrenched the "culture of death" occurred than another, even more devastating, followed on its heels.

But within the "days of infamy" that pro-life Canadians remember, January 28, 1988, deservedly stands out. On that frosty morning, deep in the heart of the Canadian winter, the abortion law came crashing down.

The Supreme Court ruled, in a 5 to 2 decision, that the law violated the "security of the person" right guaranteed in Section 7 of the Charter, because the provisions determining when abortion was permissible were, in practise, "unfair and arbitrary." It also found that the law failed the means test of Section 1 of the Charter—the legislative safeguards erected for the unborn child were judged to be neither reasonable nor demonstrably justified in a free and democratic society.

The much-anticipated decision brought elation to the right-to-abort faction, while the reaction from pro-life advocates was one of weary disbelief. They had no love for the old law—although it purported to protect the child in the womb, Section 251 virtually permitted abortion-on-demand. The government's insistence that the law was a reasonable balance between the rights of the mother and the unborn child struck pro-lifers as the essence of hypocrisy: putative state interest in protecting the child *in utero* could not hold up under the weight of evidence that therapeutic abortion committees functioned as rubber-stamps, that abortions routinely were permitted for socio-economic reasons.

What dismayed pro-life people on January 28, 1988, was the very real spectacle of the Supreme Court, using the leverage of the Charter, engaging in judicial activism and usurping so brazenly the role of Parliament. This was precisely the turn of events predicted six years earlier by Gwen Landolt and other opponents of the Charter, when they fought vigorously against its entrenchment.

Pro-life lawyers were unhappy but unsurprised. "This decision goes a long way to prove what Sterling Lyon said about the Charter of Rights," sighed Winnipegger Ernie Wehrle, a supporter of Joe Borowski: "That it would create a situation where the courts are the supreme authority in the country. It removes control from elected representatives of the people, the power to make decisions, even on contentious issues like this."[21]

Media response was laudatory. "Women released from bad law," the headline of the *Vancouver Sun* editorial (Jan. 29, 1988) pithily summed up the tenor of comment immediately following the decision. But as pundits were quick to point out, a distinct legislative void now existed.

The Supreme Court ruled explicitly that Parliament had a legitimate interest in protecting the unborn child. It was back to the politicians, some of whom fumed at this turn of events, laying the blame squarely at the feet of a certain former Liberal Prime Minister. "The politicians made the laws but Trudeau gave the final word to that little marble building down the street," raged London Tory MP Jim Jepson. "The law is made by Parliament, is disobeyed by individuals and is remade by the courts," shrugged Reg Stackhouse, (PC for Scarborough West). "We now have government by judges and they are not accountable to the people."

"It makes it clear now that the Charter is predominant and that judges are going to make laws," pointed out Alex Kindy, Calgary Tory. He added bitterly: "It's Pierre Elliott Trudeau's last legacy."[22]

As for the justices themselves, Chief Justice Brian Dickson had once told the press that the burdensome task of interpreting the Charter had not been sought by the Court but had been thrust upon it. The judiciary, he said, would not shirk its responsibility.[23]

The 1988 *Morgentaler* decision was a murky affair.

The five justices who formed the Supreme Court majority followed different paths to reach the same destination, and to the layman's eyes, they gave every appearance of making up the rules as they went along. Three separate reasons for judgment were released between them. Chief Justice Brian Dickson wrote one, with the concurrence of Justice Lamer; Justice Beetz penned his reasons with which Justice Estey concurred, and the lone woman on the bench, Bertha Wilson, came up with yet another piece of work.[24]

This last opinion was by far the most radical. Unsupported by her fellow members of the bench, Wilson discovered a constitutional right to abortion, but conceded that the state had—perhaps, she opined, "somewhere in the second trimester of pregnancy"[25]—an interest in protecting fetal life. Relying on American abortion decisions, particularly *Roe v. Wade*, Wilson concluded that the right to liberty of Section 7 of the Canadian Charter of Rights "guarantees to every individual a degree of personal autonomy over important decisions intimately affecting their private lives." The decision of a woman to "terminate her pregnancy falls within this class of protected decisions."[26]

She also found that the decision to abort fell within the rights of freedom of religion and conscience as protected in Section 2(a) of the Charter. The decision is "essentially a moral decision, a matter of conscience." To the question she posed, "Is the conscience of the woman to be paramount or the conscience of the state?" Wilson could not but believe that "in a free and democratic society it must be the conscience of the individual" that was paramount.[27] Madame Justice went on to pen some remarkable observations regarding the plight of the expectant mother, comments which more closely resembled an impromptu hectoring at a feminist rally than a learned and impartial contribution to Canadian jurisprudence:

> It is probably impossible for a man to respond, even imaginatively, to such a dilemma not just because it is outside the realm of his personal experience (although this is, of course, the case) but because he can relate to it only by objectifying it, thereby eliminating the subjective elements of the female psyche which are at the heart of the dilemma. The right to reproduce or not to reproduce, which is in issue in this case, is one such right and is properly perceived as an integral part of modern women's struggle to assert her dignity and worth as a human being.[28]

Wilson's four male colleagues on the majority confined their reasons for judgment to measuring the procedural standards of Section 251 against Charter guarantees, but they came up with different reasons for their final conclusions.

Justices Beetz and Estey found that the right to "security of the person" guaranteed in Section 7 of the Charter "must include a right of access to medical treatment for a condition representing a danger to life or health without fear of criminal sanction." The procedural requirements of the Criminal Code which permit abortion under certain circumstances were "manifestly unfair" because, opined Justice Beetz, these "significantly delay pregnant women's access" to abortion and accordingly "result in additional risks to the health of the pregnant women."[29]

It was the unnecessary delays created by the "administrative structure" that violated the principles of fundamental justice.[30] "This does not preclude, in my view," wrote Justice Beetz, "Parliament from adopting another system, free of the failings of Section 251(4), in order to ascertain that the life and health of the pregnant woman is in danger, by way of a reliable, independent and medically sound opinion." Parliament is justified in so doing "in order to protect the state interest in the fetus."[31]

Justices Dickson and Lamer went a good deal further.

"Section 251 clearly interferes with a woman's physical and bodily integrity," wrote Chief Justice Dickson. "Forcing a woman, by threat of criminal sanction, to carry a fetus to term unless she meets certain criteria unrelated to her own priorities and aspirations, is a profound interference with a woman's body and thus an infringement of security of the person." Moreover, the means chosen by Parliament to balance the "competing interests" [between the abortion-seeking mother and the child within her womb] were "not reasonable or demonstrably justified in a free and democratic society," and therefore could not be saved under Section 1 of the Charter.[32]

Having said that, Dickson insisted that the Court's scrutiny at this time was limited to procedural requirements, not to the substance of the impugned legislation. "I wish to reiterate that finding a violation of security of the person does not end the Section 7 inquiry," he wrote. "Parliament could choose to infringe security of the person if it did so in a manner consistent with the principles of fundamental justice."[33]

The dissenting opinion was written by Justice McIntyre, with La Forest concurring. The former pointed out the inherent contradictions of his colleague Brian Dickson's reasoning. While the chief justice did not specifically say the pregnant woman has a right to an abortion, "his whole position depends for its validity upon that proposition," and his statement that "a law which forces a woman to carry a fetus to term unless she meets certain criteria unrelated to her own priorities and aspirations interferes with security of her person" would make sense only in that context.

"If compelling a woman to complete her pregnancy interferes with security of her person, it can only be because the concept of security of her person includes a right not to be compelled to carry the child to completion of her pregnancy. This, then, is simply to say that she has a right to have an abortion."

However, all laws "have the potential for interference with individual priorities and aspirations. In fact, the very purpose of most legislation is to cause such interference," McIntyre wrote. Obedience to the Income Tax Act no doubt interfered with an individual's priorities and aspirations, but that did not make the Act unconstitutional—"the ordinary taxpayer enjoys no right to be tax free." It was only when legislation "goes beyond interfering with priorities and aspirations, and abridges rights, that courts may intervene."[34]

The crucial question then, was could it be shown that a right to abortion exists in the Charter? Justice McIntyre concluded not. The Charter was silent on abortion, and the framers of the document were explicit in their intent to preclude the Court from using the Charter to override Parliament's authority to legislate on abortion.[35]

Yet here was the Supreme Court poised to do exactly that, and Justice McIntyre was absolutely opposed. The Courts, he wrote, should interpret the Charter according "to the purposes given expression in the Charter"; that is, to the intent of the legislators who drafted it. "This approach prevents the Court from abandoning its traditional adjudicatory function in order to formulate its own conclusions on questions of public policy, a step which this Court has said on numerous occasions it must not take." The Court could not second-guess Parliament by defining or protecting a right in a way that was unrelated to what the politicians meant to do.[36]

The view of Parliament that abortion "is, in its nature, 'socially undesirable conduct' is not new," he wrote. Section 251 of the Criminal Code did not confer "any general right to have or to procure an abortion. On the contrary, the provision is aimed at protecting the interests of the unborn child and only lifts the criminal sanction where an abortion is necessary to protect the life or health of the mother."[37]

The dissenting justices also discounted Chief Justice Dickson's finding that the defence provided in Section 251(4) was "illusory" because, according to the evidence of the appellants, the defence itself made abortion unavailable to many women in Canada. Justice McIntyre was left to wonder about this "evidence." He made the point early in his judgment that the charge was conspiracy to breach the disputed section of the Criminal Code: "There is no female person involved in the case who has been denied a therapeutic abortion, and, as a result, the whole argument on the right to security of the person, under Section 7 of the Charter, has been on a hypothetical basis."[38]

He returned later to this question with more vigorous criticism. "Precise evidence on the question raised is, of course, difficult to obtain and subject to subjective interpretation depending upon the views of those adducing it," he wrote. What was presented at the trial was "based largely on Ontario experience." As for the published material, reports and studies introduced at trial, "from which the Court was invited to conclude that access to abortion was not evenly provided across the country and this could be a source of much dissatisfaction," Justice McIntyre was dismissive. "I would prefer to place principal reliance upon evidence given under oath in court in my consideration of the factual matters." As far as that went, "no woman testified that she personally had applied for an abortion anywhere in Canada and had been refused, and no physician testified to his participation in such an application."[39]

Therefore it could not be held that Section 251 offered a defence from criminal sanction that was "illusory." Moreover, the aim of Section 251 (4) was "to restrict abortion to cases where the continuation of the pregnancy would, or would likely, be injurious to the life or health of the woman concerned, not to provide unrestricted access to abortion."

The problem was not the law, but the fact that there "has been a flood of demands for abortions" far beyond the scope of that contemplated by Parliament. (Significantly, many of the appellants' clients, McIntyre noted, "did not meet the standard set or did not seek to invoke it and that is why their clinic took them in.") Even though the external circumstances indicate a general demand for abortion "irrespective of the provisions of Section 251," concluded McIntyre, "It is not open to a court, in my view, to strike down a statutory provision on this basis."[40]

Gwen Landolt was on the phone. A light snow fell outside as she conferred with her steadfast ally and friend, the redoubtable Laura McArthur. Landolt was deep in tactical discussions—she had just received a copy of the Morgentaler decision, and the pungent odour of judicial impropriety came wafting through the 196 pages.

"When I read the judgment I nearly jumped off my chair," she recalled. The cause of her agitation was that "the majority of the Court" made use, in its ruling, of the *Powell Report*.[41]

It was not only the fact that Marion Powell, the director of the Bay Centre for Birth Control in Toronto, was "an old-pro-abortionist from years back," that scandalized Landolt. It was that the report, commissioned by the Ontario government under Liberal Premier David Peterson, had been released in January of 1987— and the Supreme Court had heard the Morgentaler appeal three months *before*, in October of 1986.

The justices, so it seemed, had relied heavily on a document that had not even been formally accepted by the Court. But Landolt was willing to give them the benefit of due process: she combed through the dockets of the case, searching for a notice of motion that would state the *Powell Report* had been adduced as evidence, but in vain. The findings of Marion Powell were used "to knock out the abortion law" yet no one else was privy to its assertions; the Crown was given no opportunity to read or refute it.

Powell's effort was, in Landolt's blunt phrase, "totally one-sided crap" that relied upon, among others, Henry Morgentaler as an authority. Pro-lifers denounced the report's proposal to create legal abortion centers across the province, just as they had vigorously denounced the initial appointment of Powell as a one-woman committee—the purpose of which was to make recommendations to the government on improving access to abortions.

It had been a purely political move on the part of Premier Peterson, pointed out Jim Hughes of Campaign Life. The premier appointed Powell because he was in favour of abortion clinics.

(Robin Badgley, who produced the 1977 *Badgley Report*, echoed this view. He told a friend, in a private conversation, that Premier Peterson knew what the result would be if he appointed Marion Powell.) "It's disheartening when elected officials attempt to deceive the public by trying to pass this off as a legitimate study," Hughes observed in disgust. "What else would she come back with except what the premier wanted in the first place?"[42]

It was especially galling to see so noxious a source quoted so liberally in a judicial decision of such magnitude, but Landolt and McArthur had no recourse to redress this injustice. They finally decided to lay a complaint with the National Judicial Council, although they knew that that body did not deal with questions of evidence. (The Council investigated complaints of bias or judicial misconduct.) Moreover, they were well aware that the president of the Council was none other that Supreme Court Chief Justice Brian Dickson. The reply of the Council to McArthur's letter stated that her complaint "raises no issue of judicial misconduct for investigation by the Council pursuant to its mandate under the Judges Act."[43]

Landolt hadn't expected much from the National Judicial Council, but she wanted to leave a "paper trail"—to record for posterity that the Supreme Court justices had used a biased document that was not validly introduced to support its decision to strike down the abortion law. It was, in her words, a "scurrilous" act.

And she lived to witness a breathtaking admission. Lamer publicly confessed, 10 years after the *Morgentaler* decision, the real reason he ruled as he did in that case. There was no legal basis for his siding with the majority. He relied on what he thought was public opinion, Lamer told a University of Toronto law conference in early 1998. "My reasoning is that unless you have a vast majority of people to think something is criminal, you should not make it a crime. That is why I gave my concurrence." Parliament, no doubt, was grateful for his help.[44]

In the fallout from the *Morgentaler* decision, right-to-life advocates had no way of knowing how the government would deal with the lawlessness surrounding abortion. Joe Borowski surveyed the present situation with a battle-weary fatalism. "I'd like to put the Supreme Court on trial....If they can find a master murderer like Morgentaler innocent, then what's the point of going before a corrupt judiciary? I'm just devastated. Maybe by the end of the day I'll have to think of a new word for disgust."[45] He again considered non-violent civil disobedience. "That's what Morgentaler did for years, and today the Supreme Court said that's okay. If he can get away with it, so can we. Henry proved it's okay to say to hell with you and your laws."[46]

While Morgentaler readied his Winnipeg abortion, Joe was again tempted to abandon his Supreme Court appeal. "We've spent nine-and-a-half years and over $600,000 proving medically and scientifically that abortion is murder. Maybe it's because I've been too close to the issue for so long, but I'm very close to the end now."[47] But he was persuaded to continue when the directors of his group, Alliance Against Abortion, voted unanimously not to give up the fight. Morris Shumiatcher released a statement on his client's behalf, asserting that the Court had not decided the key issue in the Borowski case: do Charter rights encompass the child conceived but not yet born? "We shall press on, and I am confident that the Court will recognize that an unborn child is not a mere tumour to be excised at will," the lawyer promised.

Joe, himself, was at this point of a different mind: "It's an exercise in futility. We're going to lose. I'm sure we cannot win. But we've come this far already. At least we'll put the judges on the spot."[48]

Notes
Chapter 27
That little marble building down the street

[1] President of the national education group was Heather Stillwell, of Vancouver.

[2] Landolt said that Lamer made this off-the-cuff remark during the Supreme Court hearing of the *Nova Scotia v. Morgentaler* case in 1992. True to her vow, Landolt, was there on behalf of REAL Women, the group she founded in 1983, to argue the pro-life side.

[3] Op. Cit., Morton p. 223.

[4] Ibid, p. 243. Indeed, as F.L. Morton wrote: "What should have been one of the most exciting and engaging legal debates of the decade turned out to be one of the greatest bores."

[5] "Abortion gets its day in (high) court," William Walker, *Toronto Star*, October 11, 1986, p. B4.

[6] "Morgentaler lawyer battered by judges," *Vancouver Sun*, October 9, 1986, p. A10.

[7] Op. Cit., "Abortion gets its day in (high) court," William Walker.

[8] Her co-counsel, Jim Blackstock, handled the criminal law issues, including the controversial jury address and the use of the necessity of defense. ("Abortion: putting ball in the Supreme Court," William Walker, *Toronto Star*, October 4, 1986.)

[9] "Abortion law on trial," Peter Calamai, *Hamilton Spectator*, October 6, 1986.

[10] Ibid.

[11] "Court asked to end abortion laws," Peter Calamai, *Ottawa Citizen*, October 8, 1986. (It must not escape notice that these 'facts' were drawn from the testimony of committed defenders of abortion.)

[12] "Charter denies rights to fetus, court told in Morgentaler case," William Walker, *Toronto Star*, October 11, 1986, p. A9.

[13] Ibid.

[14] "Little legal backup for jury's 'right' to ignore abortion law, court warns," Kirk Makin, *Globe and Mail*, October 9, 1986.

[15] Op. Cit.,"Abortion gets its day," Walker.

[16] Op. Cit., "Little legal backup," Makin.

[17] "Luck of the draw may decide abortion issue," Peter Calamai, *Hamilton Spectator*, October 11, 1986.

[18] "Abortion law on trial," Peter Calamai, *Hamilton Spectator*, October 6, 1986.

[19] "Luck of the draw may decide abortion issue," Peter Calamai, *Hamilton Spectator*, October 11, 1986.

[20] "Charter denies rights to fetus, court told in Morgentaler case," William Walker, *Toronto Star*, October 11, 1986, p. A9.

[21] "Lawyers praise, criticize ruling as harbinger of court's new role," *Free Press*, January 29, 1988.

[22] "Tory MPs fault Trudeau and Charter for decision," Heather Bird and David Vienneau, *Toronto Star*, January 29, 1988.

[23] Ibid. This was reiterated by Antonio Lamer in an address to the Empire Club in

Toronto on April 13, 1995, "that the members of the judiciary did not seek these enormous powers under the Charter, but rather, had them thrust upon them." According to a brief by Real Women on the Charter, August, 1995, "This is a disingenuous argument. Although, it is true that the judiciary did not seek these new powers, it is a fact that once their powers were conferred, judges cast aside all restraints."

[24] George Grant, Canadian cultural critic and Order of Canada recipient, wrote of the Supreme Court's decision that "the judges used the language of North American liberalism to say 'yes' to the very core of fascist thought." He warned that the modern strain of fascism—a "growing possibility in advanced industrial countries"—enshrines the concept of "the triumph of the will." No longer "the appropriate choosing by rational souls" as understood in Christianity, the will is, in this ideology, "the resolute mastery of ourselves and the world." (This concept of the will fuelled the Nazi ideology and found its purest expression in the writings of German philosopher Friedrich Nietzsche.) Feminists who clamour for abortion on demand have absorbed this idea of will, although this does not necessarily imply "that such advocates are in any sense a core for fascist politics," observed Grant. "They simply give us a taste now of what politics will be like when influential groups in society think meaning is found in getting what they want most deeply at all costs. They illustrate what pressure this puts upon a legal system rooted in liberalism, whose leaders have not been educated in what that rootedness comprises." Grant, emeritus professor of political science at Dalhousie University in Halifax, N.S., pointed out that "even in its highest ranks the legal system in its unthinking liberalism simply flounders in the face of those who find meaning in the triumph of the will…When society puts power into the hands of the courts, they had better be educated." (From an esay entitled, "The Triumph of The Will" published in *The Issue is Life*, Burlington, Ontario: Welch Publishing Company Inc., 1988), pp. 156-166.

[25] *Morgentaler v. The Queen*, 1988 *Supreme Court Reports* (SCR) Vol. 1, p. 183.

[26] Ibid. p. 171.

[27] Ibid. pp. 176-177.

[28] Ibid. pp. 171-172.

[29] Ibid. pp. 81-82.

[30] Ibid. p. 119.

[31] Ibid. p. 110.

[32] Ibid. p. 32-34.

[33] Ibid. p. 56.

[34] Ibid. p. 142.

[35] Ibid. p. 143. McIntyre quoted from the Minutes of the special Joint Committee of the Senate and House of Commons on the Constitution of Canada, the words of Justice Minister Jean Chrétien, who in the debate over the phrase "due process" was asked by David Crombie: "What effect will the inclusion of the due process clause have on the question of marriage, procreation or parental care of children?" Jean Chrétien: "The point, Mr. Crombie, that it is important to understand the difference is that we pass legislation here on abortion, Criminal Code, and we pass legislation on capital punishment; Parliament has the authority to do that, and the court at this moment, because we do not have the due process of law written there, cannot go and see whether we made

the right decision or the wrong decision in Parliament. If you write down the words, 'due process of law' here, the advice I am receiving is the court could go behind our decision and say that their decision on abortion was not the right one, their decision on capital punishment was not the right one, and it is a danger, according to legal advice I am receiving, that it will very much limit the scope of the power of legislation by the Parliament and we do not want that; and it is why we do not want the words 'due process of law'. These are the two main examples that we should keep in mind. You can keep speculating on all the things that have never been touched, but these are two very sensitive areas that we have to cope with as legislators and my view is that Parliament has decided a certain law on abortion and a certain law on capital punishment, and it should prevail and we do not want the courts to say that the judgment of Parliament was wrong in using the constitution." (For more details on the "due process" debate, please refer to Chapter 12, p. 158.)

[36] Ibid, pp. 138 and 140.

[37] Ibid. pp. 134 and 136.

[38] Ibid. p. 133.

[39] Ibid. p. 150.

[40] Ibid. p. 155.

[41] Chief Justice Brian Dickson made note of it six times, while Justice Beetz relied on it nine times. (Morton, p. 247.)

[42] "Pro-life group calls report 'unbelievable,'" *Toronto Star*, January 29, 1987.

[43] The Council also noted that it was not atypical for the Supreme Court "to cite articles, books or other publications which might not have been referred to by the parties to the litigation." (Morton, 248.) F. L. Morton regarded the Court's use of the *Powell Report* as "more a questionable procedural decision than misconduct." The Council's response, however, in treating the matter as an example of "judicial notice," was also questionable. This practise permitted judges to include in their decision social information that was relevant to the issue at hand, but had not been not introduced as evidence. But such social facts had to be "widely recognized and uncontroversial"—which the *Powell Report* most definitely was not. (Morton, p. 249.)

[44] "Retiring justice did not deserve adulation," Rory Leishman, *London Free Press*, August 1, 1999.

[45] "Borowski decries 'rot' in Supreme Court," *Winnipeg Sun*, January 29, 1988.

[46] Ibid.

[47] Ibid.

[48] "Winnipeg clinic may be open by April," Geoffrey York, *Globe and Mail*, January 30, 1988.

Chapter 28

Dies Irae

Why do sinners' ways prosper? and why must
Disappointment all I endeavour end?
Wert thou my enemy, O thou my friend,
How wouldst thou worse, I wonder, than thou dost
Defeat, thwart me?

Gerard Manley Hopkins
Thou Art Indeed Just, Lord

WHILE JOE LOOKED FOR THE CHANCE TO PUT THE JUDGES ON THE spot, it was the politicians who occupied that uncomfortable zone in the aftermath of January 28, 1988.

Prime Minister Brian Mulroney hesitated. "It is the most complex issue to have confronted the Parliament of Canada in probably 25 years," he elaborated after a marathon meeting of Conservative MPs and senators. Despite eight hours of discussions, the gathering broke up with nothing substantial decided—although the idea of a free vote on the issue had been floated.[1] While Mulroney begged for time "to get my own thoughts in order", pro-life groups insisted on immediate action. In this they were strongly supported by Cardinal Emmett Carter of Toronto, who in late February sent an unambiguous letter to the parliamentarians, exhorting them to craft quickly a permanent law that would protect the unborn child, and provide an interim measure to reverse the current anarchy. "We are in a state of lawlessness," wrote the prelate, "Seldom have the people of Canada who are dedicated to the concept of the sanctity of and value of human life been so concerned, disturbed and outraged."

No half-measures would be acceptable: "We will not be satisfied with anything less than legislation which respects human life at all stages…Nor will we accept a compromise based on any length or stage of pregnancy. A human fetus in the womb three weeks old or one week old is as much an individual and as valuable to society in the sight of God and in our sight, as a child of 24 weeks." Although "it is not within the purview of the Church to instruct our people how to vote" Catholics "must ask politicians of all parties where they stand on the protection of human life at all stages."[2]

The letter had "tremendous impact" on politicians, said Jim Hughes. The president of Campaign Life Coalition, who endorsed the Cardinal's communiqué along with a host of other pro-life and Christian groups, had been engaged in his own quiet discussions.[3] "The pro-life politicians I've spoken to indicate that the caucus is worried about the Cardinal's statement and it will give them all cause to stop and ponder about the abortion legislation that will be put before them." The letter will prove "a rallying point" for pro-life advocates of all faiths, he predicted.[4]

This moment of accord between the pro-life political lobbying group and a member of the Catholic hierarchy was more the exception than the rule in a relationship that already bore the scars of past wrangling over tactics. Three months later, the Catholic bishops would be embroiled in a dispute with the Campaign Life Coalition—only this time, alleged the latter, the rift was not just about tactics, but substance.

The Conservatives had already faltered on their first attempt to grapple with the abortion issue. They wanted to test the waters, so proposed a motion with three options, which would be non-binding and subject to a free vote. The opposition balked and accused the Mulroney government of evading its responsibility to propose specific legislation. The three-pronged proposal was an attempt to appease dissent within the Tory caucus, they charged. Nevertheless, deputy government House Leader Doug Lewis, who was himself in favour of abortion-on-demand, announced shortly afterwards that the Conservatives would use their majority to press on with the resolution. On May 24, 1988, the government tabled its motion with three options, of which the first was reputedly "pro-life."

It wasn't. Option A was, in fact, more liberal than the 1969 law, Campaign Life Coalition pointed out. The group urged its supporters to lobby politicians to reject all three options, and to demand truly pro-life legislation.[5]

That's why a letter to the MPs and senators by Archbishop Hayes that June stunned the pro-life lobbyists. President of the Canadian Conference of Catholic Bishops, Hayes wrote that the government's three options were "all objectionable from the standpoint of Catholic teachings. Amendment A, however, is the least objectionable."

"In forming their consciences," Hayes continued, "legislators should take serious account of the concern expressed by many pro-life Members of Parliament that abstention from voting, because the perfect law has not been presented, may indirectly contribute to the passage of the government's main motion which allows for the totally unacceptable gestational approach."

Jim Hughes was compelled to denounce the CCCB's contribution. "We deny that any person or group of persons may exonerate the conscience of legislators in voting for the legalization of abortion on the grounds that a 'perfect' law is not likely to be passed in the immediate future," he said. "Such an exoneration is nothing less than a betrayal of both nation and church."[6]

All through that long, hot, humid summer, parliamentarians debated over not only the abortion issue but also the niceties of the constitutional Meech Lake Accord, as well as free trade in North America. The fractiousness of both the Tory caucus and the opposition over the "three-headed monster" (so dubbed by NDP leader Ed Broadbent) that was their abortion resolution, forced Mulroney, Justice Minister Ray Hnatyshyn and beleaguered quarterback Doug Lewis to pull it off the order paper.

After a brief huddle, they called the next play. Hoping still to get a sense of the mind of the House before drafting a law, they put forward a "one-headed monster"—another non-binding resolution to be subject to a free vote by MPs. This motion, which satisfied neither pro-lifers nor pro-abortionists, differed from its predecessor in one important respect: amendments were allowed.[7]

In the dying days of July—a month renowned for spawning rev-
olutions—the politicians sweated it out on the abortion debate for
two days and two nights. Ninety of the 281 MPs rose to speak during the 25-hour-long marathon. Twenty-one amendments were
proposed; all but five rejected by Speaker John Fraser. When the
voting began, Brian Mulroney and Liberal leader John Turner
were conspicuously absent: the Prime Minister had earlier stated
he would vote—when there was proposed legislation.

On July 28, 1988, all amendments were defeated, the government motion repudiated. It was left to Mulroney to try again.

Remarkably, a pro-life amendment put forward by Conservative
MP Gus Mitges (Grey-Simcoe) nearly passed. That amendment,
which would have banned abortion except where the life of the
mother was threatened, was defeated 118 to 105.[8]

Joe Borowski stood under the merciless glare of the midday
summer sun, and surveyed the south wall of his health food store
with grim satisfaction. It was adorned with a new mural, a gaudy
and controversial caricature.

"The great betrayal" trumpeted the caption, while the illustration beneath depicted a prostrate figure, labeled the CCCB
(Canadian Conference of Catholic Bishops), kissing the feet of
another figure, identified as "P. M. Mulroney" who was in turn
prostrate and kissing the feet of a large besandled female—the
personification of the "pro-choice feminist."

It was the pictorial encapsulation of a bitterness to which Joe
gave full vent in a full page ad he placed in the August 22 edition
of the *Western Report*. His bishops had let him down.

"If there was a major disappointment for Joe Borowski, it was
the failure of the Catholic Church in Canada to take a major role
in the fight against abortion. He saw the Pope out there doing his
thing, he saw Mother Teresa doing hers, he saw individual bishops
and individual priests doing their job, but by and large he thought
there was a huge vacuum at the top and he was quite upset about
it," was the way Jim Hughes remembers it all. "If anything—he was
angry at Trudeau, he was angry at the federal Liberals, he was
angry at the NDP, he was angry at the Conservatives as well—but I
think he was just really shocked by the failure of the Catholic

Church in this country to provide a leadership role in the battle and I think that hurt him more than anything."

In the summer of '88, Joe's disappointment found its voice. "I was born and raised a Catholic but I never dreamed that the Catholic bishops or clergy would ever sell out on any issue of principles," he admitted in his advertisement. His critique was touched off by Archbishop Hayes' June letter to the MPs and senators. The missive "gravely undermines 20 years of hard work by pro-lifers from every walk of life and from every religious belief." Not since the English bishops—save for St. John Fisher—capitulated to the demands of Henry VIII in his defiance to Rome had there been such a sell-out, charged Joe. At least those "gutless traitors" of yore faced death if they refused to swear allegiance to Henry as head of the Church.

But the Canadian bishops had no such excuse. "I along with many pro-lifers am writing to the Holy Father about this mass betrayal and disobedience to the teachings of the Church. It is up to the Pope, not us, to deal with rebels." What was up to them was to "disobey the bishops on the specific issue of abortion" as they had been "disobedient to Rome."

There dwelt, in Winnipeg at that time, three archbishops: Latin-rite Adam Exner, Ukrainian-rite Maxim Hermaniuk and Archbishop Antoine Hacault of the French diocese of St. Boniface.

Archbishop Exner had always been vocal in defence of life, and, together with his brother bishops, had provided particularly strong leadership in the spring of 1985 when the three prelates led a march of 3,000 to protest the government inaction against Henry Morgentaler. Specifically, they demanded that Manitoba Attorney-General Roland Penner seek an injunction to stop the abortionist from operating his illegal clinic. The archbishops had also declared a day of prayer and fasting. "The lives of many unborn babies are at stake. They look to us for help," wrote Archbishop Exner in a letter to his flock. "We must not fail them. We must act and now."[9]

"I think the right to life is one of the most basic human rights there is; there is not another more basic," Exner told reporters at that time. "I feel I cannot remain silent. I cannot sleep unless I speak out." Moreover, he acknowledged, it was necessary to confront society: "I think I have to be heard by the public, not only the people in the pews. Talking to the people in the pews is talking to the converted."[10]

For this reason alone it could be assumed that Archbishop Exner was stung by Joe's assault. It wasn't long before Joe received a letter from his shepherd. It was "the toughest letter I've ever received," the ex-miner, ex-politician conceded. Joe refused to release the missive to the press without the archbishop's permission. But he did reveal that the latter had rebuked him for "misguided zeal." Joe's public manifestations of discontent were "unjust and harmful."[11]

Exner admitted that "the letter of the CCCB president to the MPs and senators is not beyond reproach" and was based on an erroneous assumption that "the only option open to the MPs was to vote on one of the three options placed before the House of Commons."

"On the strength of this incorrect assumption, the letter suggested to MPs that they choose the lesser evil." The CCCB acted on the "legal and political information and advice available" to it at the time. "In this regard," wrote Archbishop Exner, "the president and his council can be blamed for not availing themselves of the expertise of pro-life leaders through consultation and dialogue."

That did not excuse Joe. "To say 'you haven't done a good job' is one thing," the archbishop pointed out. "To say 'you have abandoned the cause, you have betrayed it en masse deliberately and therefore you are disobedient to the teachings of the Church' is quite another matter and calls for redress."[12]

Joe gave redress, promptly and generously. He had the sign taken down from his wall that very day. He took out a second ad in the *Western Report* and clarified matters. The CCCB letter suggested that "politicians could opt for the lesser of three bad pro-abortion options. In checking with higher authorities, I was informed that settling for a lesser evil is not permitted where human life is at stake. I believe the bishops of Canada, through the CCCB, were wrong in writing that letter. They were wrong in not consulting us in the pro-life movement before issuing their letter," ran Joe's ad. "I also believe that in spite of their letter every bishop is pro-life. But, I think that I went too far and was too harsh in my condemnation of the CCCB and the Canadian bishops. So to set matters right, I want to publicly apologize to the bishops of Canada, and to reaffirm my loyalty to the Church, and my obedience to the bishops of our country."[13]

Lost in this public drama was the pertinent fact that Archbishop Hayes had sent a further letter, dated July 25, to the MPs and senators, in which he explicitly condemned the government's new motion and left it at that; he did not endorse any amendments. The government's resolution "proposes the totally unacceptable gestational approach for a new Canadian abortion law," Hayes wrote. "The gestational approach is scientifically and ethically indefensible because it draws an arbitrary dividing line between life which is worthy of protection and life which is not." The position of the Catholic Church "is that human life begins at conception and must be valued, respected and safeguarded from the beginning."

Lost, too, in the dazzle of publicity given to the original CCCB letter was a July 25 communiqué by Cardinal Carter, which denounced the government motion. "You are being asked to begin debate on a motion which is not worthy of you as elected representatives nor is it worthy of the people of Canada whom you represent," the Cardinal wrote. "As the Catholic Archbishop of Toronto I hereby solemnly and explicitly state that in my judgment no Catholic legislator can vote for the proposal on abortion as now presented, with an easy conscience....It is against humanity itself to take innocent life and no appeal to freedom of choice can justify it. There is no choice here. No choice for the mother; no choice for the sworn medical practitioner, guardian of life; no choice for the legislator, also the protector of life."[14]

This episode appeared, in retrospect, to be a practise run for that turbulent period that began in November of 1989, when the Mulroney government introduced Bill C-43, which, after finally being passed by the House of Commons on third reading on May 29, 1990, was defeated by a historic tie vote of 43 in the Senate on January 31, 1991.

Once again, as this bill progressed torturously through debate and committee, Campaign Life Coalition found itself at loggerheads with the CCCB when it denounced Bill C-43 as irremediably pro-abortion. The bishops cautiously advised that a Catholic politician could vote for the bill as a containment of abortion. The political lobbyists were of the mind that the legislation would result in *de facto* abortion on demand, and they were further dismayed that once again, the CCCB did not avail itself of their expertise and insight, experience which, it could be noted, had been heartbreakingly and painfully gained through the decades-long battle over permissive abortion.[15]

It was a long, hot summer for other reasons. The Tories, mired in their abortion resolution debacle and facing a fall election, tried to persuade the Supreme Court to postpone Joe Borowski's appeal indefinitely—or until they brought in a new abortion law.

Ed Sojonky appeared on July 19 to argue the government's case at the behest of Justice Minister Ray Hnatyshyn. Before a packed courtroom, Sojonky admitted to Chief Justice Brian Dickson that no legal precedent existed for his request.[16] Nevertheless, now that the old law had been struck down, the Borowski case was concerned only with "naked, abstract questions" about the meaning of certain sections of the Charter, Sojonky argued. "They do not ask about the validity of any statute…They do not raise questions that are precise enough to be answered."

Morris Shumiatcher, in turn, accused the government of acting improperly in asking the Court to change its agenda "simply to suit the political aspirations of a government." Such a request "is really an abuse of the position of that high office."[17]

The Chief Justice ruled in Joe's favour: "I am in no way persuaded this is a case which should be postponed."[18]

Joe was delighted at the victory. "I think you can say justice is alive and well and not an endangered species," he exulted. Shumiatcher, too, was pleased. The chief justice made "a splendid judgment." The reaction of Justice Minister Ray Hnatyshyn was philosophical: "We thought it would be appropriate to have the Borowski matter heard in a legislative context. But that's the way it goes."

It did not, however, augur well that the other side was also pleased with the decision. In fact, according to author F.L. Morton, they had actually influenced the outcome. Morton gives the behind-the-scenes account of this last episode, detailing how LEAF (Legal and Educational Action Fund) was becoming increasingly alarmed at the government's handling of the Borowski case. LEAF lawyer Mary Eberts tipped off *Toronto Star* reporter David Vienneau that the government was intending to ask for an indefinite postponement of the Borowski case, until it came up with a

law. Vienneau wrote three articles that stirred up immediate opposition to the Hnatyshyn motion, which the Justice Minister intimated was motivated out of fairness to Borowski. "Rather than be
negative, I have taken an action which is supportive of having the
Borowski case heard at an important time in the future when
Parliament has spoken on this very sensitive issue," Hnatyshyn
told Vienneau. The motion, which was originally to be heard in
chambers, was moved to open court at the Vienneau's request.[19]

When Joe arrived back in Winnipeg after his jaunt to Ottawa, his
exuberance at the victory quickly evaporated. He was hit with bills
from Shumiatcher totalling $79,000 for that latest court caper, and
forced to pull $35,000 out of his health food business while trying
to drum up cash through advertisements and press releases.
"We've never had money problems before. Now we do and it's
embarrassing," he confessed.[20] The latest bills were purportedly
for research, preparation and presentation costs, but Joe was
flummoxed. There had been no case law to support the latest government's motion. What research was needed? What preparation?

Joe's skepticism was echoed by the pro-life newspaper, *The
Interim*. In an article signed only by "*Interim* Staff" it was pointed
out that when Joe first met Shumiatcher in 1978, they agreed to a
cost of $100,000, for the trial. Then came the demand of a
$350,000 guarantee even before the case began in 1983.[21]

"After the trial was over and the bills paid, little did [Joe] think
it would cost him another half million to see the paperwork pass
from one court to another, " read the critique. (That estimate was
a bit high—including the latest bills, Joe had paid out $760,000 in
total.) "Where do these massive legal bills come from?" questioned
The Interim. "Simply because this law firm, like others, charges for
everything under the sun, from opening a file folder, answering a
telephone call, going for lunch, to appearing in court." Concluded
the article somberly: "Some people feel that Joe Borowski is being
milked dry."

Jean Borowski remembered her husband arguing with his
lawyer over items on the statement. "Joe said, 'Hey, wait a minute,
you're going too far, what was that guy doing—or two lawyers
other than you—doing in Toronto for a week? Why were you staying at this expensive hotel and charging me? There's something
wrong now, Morris, come on.' And he'd always say, 'Well...I need
this and I need that.'" Finally, Jean said, her husband put his foot

down. "Joe says, 'No, that's it, you're not getting any more, do what you will, that's it. You went over the perceived budget.'"

Joe, being the man he was, would carry no underlying resentment toward his lawyer when they returned to the Supreme Court for the final battle on October 3, 1988. He had spoken his piece and dealt with it. He was an inside-out man: himself through and through. But the heart of Morris Shumiatcher was more difficult to penetrate, not being, as was Joe Borowski's, of the translucent variety. A case could be built to argue that, when he arrived at the Supreme Court, Shumiatcher's heart was not in it.

Even before the sun rose on that October day, a crowd had gathered outside the Supreme Court building to witness Joe Borowski's last stand. His appeal on behalf of the unborn child had reached its final destination.

The atmosphere in the courtroom was thick with anticipation and anxiety as the seven justices spent the better part of the first day deciding whether they could even rule on the appeal in the absence of a law. Hearing the Borowski appeal were Chief Justice Brian Dickson, Antonio Lamer, William McIntyre, Bertha Wilson, Gerard La Forest, Claire l'Heureux-Dubé, John Sopinka.

Justice Antonio Lamer was particularly flustered. On what basis could he find that the unborn child was protected under the Charter: "Where do I find my jurisdiction? I can't relate it to a law. I can't strike it down, I can't uphold it. I can only express an opinion on what the law should be... I don't minimize the seriousness of the issue. I'm concerned that if the Court can make such a pronouncement, then it is an acknowledgment by this Court that it has the power to tell Parliament that it should enact a law and that if it doesn't, Parliament is in violation of the Charter. ..That might be so. But it is a very serious step for a court to take in our system of government. If we take it, we are saying it is within our reach to scrutinize a lack of legislation."

Shumiatcher argued that his client's appeal found its legal justification in the Charter. "If the Court doesn't tackle the issue, what will the public perception be? It will be that there is no need for a law. Failure to make a decision is to make a decision."

Justice Lamer also voiced displeasure at the Crown's handling of the case. It was not clear from Edward Sojonky's written argument what the Crown was asking from the Court, other than advising that the appeal not be heard until an abortion law was in place. "I realize you follow instructions." Lamer told Sojonky, "We can allow, dismiss or quash. You would like us to quash, but you just don't want to ask for it."[22]

Finally, the Court reserved judgment on the "mootness" issue, and agreed to hear arguments. Morris Shumiatcher proceeded to attempt to convince the Court to extend constitutional protection to the child in the womb.

His job was not made any easier when the next day, Joe Borowski showed up in the lobby of the Supreme Court building with the bodies of two unborn babies, preserved in formaldehyde in glass jars, which he showed to one television reporter before his lawyer discovered what he was doing.

Joe hoped that the judges would be able to pass around the jars, one of which contained a 10-week-old human embryo, and another which contained the body of a child of seven months gestation. But a clearly annoyed Shumiatcher nixed this plan, and told Joe not to show the bodies to any other reporters, who questioned Joe about his actions. He became defensive.

"It's not a question of indignity," he protested. "We didn't dig up the grave. These are fetuses brought in from Europe and I thought it would be appropriate to show the court." The older fetus was the result of a miscarriage.[23] The judges "would see very clearly that that's a perfect baby. It's got the fingers, the eyes, the nose, it's got all the features of a miniature baby."

When one reporter labeled the action "a grotesque form of grandstanding," Joe angrily responded: "I think it is no less grotesque that the people who are killing babies."[24] The surreal episode took a cloak-and-dagger turn in the account of one reporter, who claimed that pro-life supporters denied Joe even had the tiny corpses—"but a nun was seen carrying the airline travel bag that contained the vials."[25]

Also present at the Supreme Court hearing was Gwen Landolt. True to her vow, the lawyer was intervening at the Borowski case on behalf of REAL Women the lobby group she founded in 1983 (the acronym stands for Real, Equal, Active, for Life). It was her contention that Joe received "inadequate representation at the Supreme Court level." Perhaps it was just a matter of one lawyer critiquing another, but Landolt thought Shumiatcher's Factum needed a little dusting off: his legal argument was replete with references to the now defunct Section 251 of the Criminal Code.

She stood at the bottom of the stairs with fellow lawyer Angela Costigan after the hearing was completed, and watched as the right-to-abort contingent, headed by LEAF lawyer Mary Eberts, chatted with reporters, seemingly confident of victory.[26] Then they caught sight of Dr. Shumiatcher "walking down the stairs all by himself."

It did not bode well.

On March 9, 1989, Joe Borowski's health food store was a scene of tense confusion. Radio reporters and pressmen mingled as TV crews fumbled at outlets, set up lights, checked angles. All of Joe's family were there, including Karen's three sons, who scampered amid the cables. Debbie had come straight from working the night shift at the youth center.

"We were waiting for the phone call, the news crew was already waiting there," she recalled. "They had the camera in his face when he got the phone call—you know, the reaction thing—and they followed him next door where he had kind of set up."

They have a photograph of the day, Sandy broke in. "Dad looked sick, he looked green around the gills...."

"We all looked sick," said Debbie. She remembered her dad "being so angry and saying—trying to choose his words—he says, 'If the Supreme Court justices were here, I'd, I'm not a violent man but I would punch them'—he was so mad...He couldn't believe that they put him through that—"

"And all those delays," interjected her sister.

"And all that money, dragged it on, really, I guess we all realized it ... they were dragging it on until the law was changed so they could say, 'Well, you're challenging a law that's no longer—'"

"You know," Sandra interrupted again, "to me, that's when the life went out of Dad in a lot of ways—it was like, there's nothing to fight for..."

At the time, however, as she watched her father struggle through that terrible press conference, Sandra badly wanted to speak out, to penetrate the professional indifference of the media.

Because she was, herself, eight months pregnant. "I wanted to say, 'You know what, this affects me, I am a pregnant single mother'. ...I wanted to point to here. 'There is a child in here and that's what he's been fighting for, it's so that people like you, who just think that it's nothing, there is something here to be protected,' and I was just—and I didn't know if—I thought, no, this is not the time, it was one of those—" And her voice trailed off.

In the end, she chose not to speak because it was her dad's moment, and because, although Joe Borowski doted on his granddaughter, born the next month, there was also at that time an underlying realization that no one could gainsay that, as Sandy herself shyly put it, "He felt funny about the whole thing."

She trusted the small intuition that said, no, wait—that voice in her heart that saw her father at his worst moment, saw him, accepted him, loved him, and because of that, suffered silently for him.

"The judges are gutless," Joe Borowski was at that moment expounding.

So sure had he been of victory that he had a bottle of champagne on hand to celebrate. "I'll dump the champagne in the toilet or send it to the judges after I spike it."[27]

The Supreme Court, in a unanimous decision, declined to rule on the constitutional protection of the unborn child because it lacked the authority to do so in the absence of a law. Not only was Joe's plea "moot," ruled the justices, but he had lost his standing when the section of the Criminal Code he was challenging was struck down in January.

"They are responsible for that situation," fumed Joe. "For them to use that as an excuse is the ultimate cop-out and is political sleaze of the worst kind. I can only conclude they were dead drunk or bought off by someone to make such a stupid and idiotic decision."[28]

His lawyer was more circumspect. Reached in Regina, Morris Shumiatcher observed that the justices had drawn "very fine-line distinctions," in their ruling. "When you come down to it, it's entirely a matter of discretion. They had the discretion to hear it and they should have, I think."

He had attempted to get the Borowski appeal heard before the Supreme Court made its ruling on Morgentaler, but had been stymied by the federal government, Shumiatcher said. (The Morgentaler constitutional challenge to the abortion law was heard by the top court in October 1986, the ruling released on January 28, 1988. The Court had announced in the summer of 1987 that it would hear the Borowski appeal. Conceivably, it could have heard and ruled on Borowski challenge before rendering its verdict on Morgentaler.) "Then Morgentaler comes out and they say—ha, ha, ha—well, your legs are chopped off because all you've got is a theoretical issue now."[29]

The Borowski decision was widely publicized. The abortion issue crackled with heat and the ruling by the Supreme Court threw the question back to Parliament. Brian Mulroney had publicly declared in November 1988, after the Tories won an election campaigning on free trade, that his government would deal with abortion after the Borowski case had been decided. Now the media reminded him of his statement. It was not, however, until November of 1989 that the Conservatives put forward the ill-fated Bill C-43.

As for the Borowski ruling itself, it was written by newly appointed John Sopinka who noted that when the abortion law disappeared, so did the "substratum of Mr. Borowski's appeal." Lacking a "live controversy...which affects the rights of the parties," the suit was moot.[30] Not only was the question moot because there was no law, but Joe had lost his legal standing.

Moreover, any "abstract pronouncement on fetal rights in this case" might well be challenged in a future litigation, as it was likely any future abortion law would be scrutinized by the Court. "In a legislative context any rights of the fetus could be considered or at least balanced against the rights of women guaranteed by Section 7. A pronouncement in favour of the appellant's position that a fetus is protected by Section 7 from the date of conception would decide the issue out of its proper context."[31]

To illustrate this point, he related a portion of the intervention by REAL Women, whose counsel was asked, in the event that the Court granted constitutional protection to the unborn child, what would a hospital do if a pregnant woman required an abortion to save her life. "The answer was that doctors and legislators would have to stay up at night to decide how to deal with the situation.

The state of uncertainty would clearly not be in the public interest. Instead of rendering the law certain, a decision favourable to the appellant would have the opposite effect."

Finally, "what the appellant seeks is to turn this appeal into a private reference," the justice wrote. "He now wishes to ask a question that relates to the Canadian Charter of Rights and Freedoms alone. This is not a request to decide a moot question but to decide a different, abstract question. To accede to this request would intrude on the right of the executive to order a reference and pre-empt a possible decision of Parliament by dictating the form of legislation it should enact. To do so would be a marked departure from the traditional role of the court."[32]

The Court also mildly rebuked the government for moving to adjourn the appeal rather than asking that it be quashed. The Tories' refusal to request the latter, either initially or after their motion for adjournment was denied, has "resulted in needless expense of preparing and arguing the appeal before this Court."[33] It therefore took the unusual step of awarding court costs to Joe Borowski.

He, however, was not impressed: costs would cover court-time his lawyers logged in and nothing more, and would not even begin to offset the $850,000 he estimated the litigation had cost him. "We will get the princely sum of $1,000."[34][35]

So there it was. Joe Borowski had lost, and along with him, thousands of Canadian pro-life advocates and thousands upon thousands of mothers and unborn children. "The nice guy time is over," he asserted. "The gloves are off. The question is, how far do we go?"[36]

Some people had, as Joe had himself over his lifetime, gone as far as jail.

Operation Rescue—non-violent intervention where pro-lifers block the entrances of abortion clinics with their bodies to save the lives of unborn children and protect their mothers—had begun in earnest in Canada that year.[37]

In January, 140 people, followed in February by 102 people—including Catholic priest Vincent Hawkswell—had been arrested and charged with criminal contempt for blocking the Everywoman's abortion clinic in Vancouver (it took 13 policemen 35 hours to clear the rescuers away from the door in the latter event).[38] Two days before the Supreme Court ruling, three of these—Karen and James Hanlon and David Forsyth—were sent to jail for three months. They had been jailed already for breaking the injunction at the clinic, and returned to the abortuary a day after being released.[39]

Three days after the Supreme Court ruling on Borowski, a rescue took place in Toronto. In January, 160 pro-life activists had been arrested; 109 followed suit on March 13.[40]

Joe heartily endorsed these efforts. Doing time was not a big deal: "Ninety days out of someone's life is a small price to pay for saving the life of the unborn."[41] But he also urged another tactic: demonstrations, even sit-ins, within the hallowed halls of justice. Because "they've chosen to act like politicians" judges were no longer exempt from the citizen's manifest discontent, Joe charged. "The veneer of infallibility and untouchability will be stripped away from the courts because of this court case, and they can expect to be targets in their courts throughout the land."

He himself would be taking part in non-violent civil disobedience in the future. "I expect to be in jail very soon. I've always believed the generals should lead the way, and not just send the troops into battle. The war goes on. There is no end to this fight, and certainly no compromise. They are the enemy. It's a war.

"Our side has one advantage. We pray. They don't."[42]

Notes
Chapter 28
Dies Irae

[1] "PM weighing free vote in Commons on abortion," David Vienneau, *Toronto Star*, March 7, 1988. [2] "Catholic leaders step up push to ban abortion," Ann Rauhala, *Globe and Mail*, March 1, 1988 p. A1.

[3] "Cardinal's abortion letter seen affecting Parliament," Bonnie Byrne, *Catholic Register*, March 19, 1988, p. 1.

[4] Ibid.

[5] In a pamphlet "Baby Talk" five flaws of Option A were listed: it resembled but was more liberal than the 1969 legislation; it allowed abortion when either the life or health of the mother is threatened; only two doctors (rather than three) need approve an abortion; abortions would be done outside hospitals; abortions would be done for vague reasons such as depression or suicidal tendency. For a pro-life law, the pamphlet referred to Senator Haidasz's Bill 16.

[6] "Bishops' stance on abortion bid 'a betrayal' group charges," Michael McAteer, *Toronto Star*, June 29, 1988. [7] "Both sides furious at abortion motion," *Toronto Star*, July 23, 1988, A1.

[8] "MPs veto abortion options," David Vienneau, *Toronto Star*, July 28, 1988, A1.

[9] "Winnipeg Catholic leaders call for abortion protest at legislature," David O'Brien, *Free Press*, March 4, 1985.

[10] Matt Maychak, *Toronto Star*, March 8, 1985.

[11] "Borowski scolded for 'misguided' zeal," David Roberts, *Winnipeg Free Press*, September 13, 1988.

[12] "Bishops betrayed church teachings: Borowski," Judy Wager, *Prairie Messenger*, October 17, 1988.

[13] *Western Report*, October 1988. ed.

[14] In preparing this letter, Cardinal Carter did consult with Campaign Life Coalition.

[15] Campaign Life Coalition's main objection to the bill was that it sanctioned abortion if medical practitioner—not even necessarily a medical doctor—concluded that the continuation of the pregnancy would endanger the mother's health or life. However, it would be disingenuous to suggest that a rift did not occur within pro-life ranks over the bill. A number of pro-life advocates, many of whom were lawyers concurred with the view of the CCCB that Bill C-43 was better than no law, and could be supported by pro-life politicians as a containment of abortion. (Campaign Life Coalition noted that Kim Campbell, then Conservative Justice Minister, publicly assured doctors that not one of them would be prosecuted under this law; pro-life advocates of Bill C-43 dismissed Campbell's statements with skepticism, stating that she could not foresee that this would indeed be the result of the legislation.) Right-to-life Catholics who supported the bill claimed vindication in retrospect when Pope John Paul II issued his encyclical *Evangelium vitae* in 1995. In Section 73 the pope carefully discussed the moral issues surrounding "the passage of a more restrictive law, aimed at limiting the number of authorized abortions, in place of a more permissive law already

passed or ready to be voted on... When it is not possible to overturn or completely abrogate a pro-abortion law, an elected official, whose absolute personal opposition to procured abortion was well known, could licitly support proposals aimed at limiting the harm done by such a law and at lessening its negative consequences at the level of general opinion and public morality. This does not in fact represent an illicit cooperation with an unjust law, but rather a legitimate and proper attempt to limit its evil aspects." CLC argued that the moral precepts articulated in section 73 simply did not apply in the case of Bill C-43, which was a bill that would allow virtually unlimited access to abortion, and which recognized the licitness of abortion. The legislation fell unambiguously into the category of intrinsically unjust laws, the lobby group believed, and as *Evangelium vitae* reiterated, traditional Catholic moral teaching asserts that "in the case of an intrinsically unjust law, such as a law permitting abortion or euthanasia, it is therefore never licit to obey it, or to take part in a propaganda campaign in favour of such a law, or vote for it." The dispute, which obviously involved the deepest questions of law and morality, was literally a life and death matter for thousands of unborn children, not to mention the reality of the incalculable harm done to their mothers. It is a small wonder that the controversy left palpable bitterness in its wake, and has made it extraordinarily difficult for those holding opposing views to work together harmoniously.

[16] "Supreme Court rejects bid to delay abortion hearing," David Vienneau, *Toronto Star*, July 20, 1988.

[17] "Top court refuses to delay hearing on rights of fetus," Graham Fraser, *Globe and Mail*, July 20, 1988.

[18] Ibid., *Toronto Star*, July 20, 1988.

[19] Op. Cit. Morton, p.258.

[20] "Borowski's crusade in financial distress," Heidi Graham, *Free Press*, August 24, 1988.

[21] "Borowski's legal costs skyrocket," *Interim* Staff, November 1988, p. 8.

[22] "Court might not rule on abortion appeal," David Vienneau, *Toronto Star*, October 4, 1988; "Supreme Court confused by lack of abortion law," Ken MacQueen, *Montreal Gazette*, October 4, 1988.

[23] "Pro-life activist brings remains of two fetuses to Supreme Court," David Vienneau, *Toronto Star*, October 5, 1988.

[24] "Anti-abortionist brings fetuses to court," Ken MacQueen, *Montreal Gazette*, October 5, 1988.

[25] Ibid., "Pro-life activist brings remains," Vienneau, October 5, 1988.

[26] This outward jauntiness belied the very real misgivings LEAF had over the Court's handling of the Borowski case, as Morton relates in detail in his 1992 book. When the Supreme Court did not move to declare the Borowski case moot in the aftermath of the *Morgentaler* ruling, LEAF became worried that the Court perhaps retained some sympathy for the right-to-life position. This anxiety manifested itself in a move by LEAF to block REAL Women from intervening in the Borowski appeal when the case was finally heard by the Supreme Court. LEAF was represented in this attempt by John Laskin, nephew of the late Chief Justice Bora Laskin and later, an Ontario Appeals Court Justice. The move backfired. Justice Antonio Lamer was enraged that LEAF would try to bar REAL Women from intervening, even though the latter group had missed the filing

deadline by six months. Lamer, who, according to Morton, literally shook with anger, regarded the pro-abortion group's motion as unwarranted interference in the Court's business. Morton speculates that the Court was perhaps conscious of the appearance of partiality in its use of the *Powell Report* for its reasoning in the *Morgentaler* decision, and this motivated it to extend wide latitude to REAL Women. (Morton, pp. 252-256 and 249.)

[27] "Opponents climb back to the political ramparts," *Montreal Times-Transcript*, March 10, 1989.

[28] "Borowski vows judicial 'war' in abortion row," Derek Ferguson, *Toronto Star,* March 10, 1989.

[29] "Fetal rights ruling reaffirms Parliament's role in national debate," Gerald McNeil, *Montreal Gazette*, March 10, 1989.

[30] "Why the court didn't rule on fetal rights," *Toronto Star*, March 10, 1989, p. A20.

[31] Ibid.

[32] Ibid.

[33] Ibid.

[34] "Supreme Court refuses to rule on fetal rights," Kirk Makin, *Globe and Mail*, March 10, 1989.

[35] The right-to-abortion side was pleased with the result, although the stalwartly pro-abortion *Globe* thought things could have gone a little better. Under a headline "One decision the Court can't put off indefinitely," a legal expert accused the Court of expediency because it refused to slam the door shut on the unborn child. "The recognition of fetal rights by the courts remains a very real possibility," warned Osgoode Hall law professor Allan Hutchinson. The Supreme Court seemed not to have considered the possibility that Parliament might not act, but "a decision not to do anything is as much government action as a decision to legislate. The Court's persistent failure to recognize this invalidates much of its jurisprudence to date." Hutchinson concluded that, as Ottawa "is actively involved in providing abortion services by its financing of such operations and regulation of hospital faculties" it was "patently false" to declare, as had Judge Sopinka that, "in the absence of legislation, there is no government action to bring the Charter into play." The "only one sensible and just course" the Court could pursue was to "plainly declare that the fetus does not qualify for constitutional protection in the Charter's guarantees of personal liberty." (*Globe and Mail*, March 16, 1989.)

[36] "Borowski: 'the nice guy time is over,'" *Montreal Times-Transcript*, March 10, 1998, p. 9.

[37] Rescue began in the United States as early as 1975 when groups such as the Pro-Life Non-Violent Action Project discovered that this non-violent intervention saved lives, by physically preventing the mother from entering the abortion clinic —and by influencing the hearts and minds of those who did not believe that the unborn child deserved protection. While regarded by some as an inherently political action, "rescue" (the name is derived from Proverb 24:10-12: "Rescue those unjustly led to slaughter") is, at its heart, an act of radical solidarity with the child in the womb.

[38] "Protesters off to jail," Suzanne Fournier, *Vancouver Sun*, February 10, 1989.

[39] "Three anti-abortionists sent to jail," *London Free Press*, March 8, 1989.

[40] "Anti-abortionists claim victory despite arrest of 109 protesters," Caroline Bourque, *Globe and Mail*, March 13, A12.

[41] "Abortion foes told to fill jails," *The Province*, Friday, March 10, 1989.

[42] "Borowski vows judicial 'war' in abortion row," Derek Ferguson, *Toronto Star*, March 19, 1989.

Chapter 29

Voca me cum benedictis[1]

Yet I was always in Your presence,
You were holding me by my right hand.
You will guide me by Your counsel,
and so will lead me to glory.

To be near God is my happiness,
I have made the Lord God my refuge.
I will tell of all Your works
at the gate of the City of Zion.
Psalm 73

FAR BELOW THE BUSY CORRIDORS OF ST. BONIFACE HOSPITAL, WHERE the trolleys rattled and nurses bustled on their rounds, the noonday traffic roared and rumbled. But in a quiet room removed from the pitch and pull of every day life, a recumbent figure lay and scarcely stirred, save for the immense effort it took to breathe in, breathe out.

Joe Borowski was leaving.

In the province of his boyhood, under the arc of the calm blue sky, golden waves of wheat trembled then fell rippling in the wake of the combine's sharp blade. It was harvest time.

Almost a year before, Joe had received the prognosis that his cancer was too advanced, too aggressive, too lethal to be stopped. He had tried unorthodox methods to thwart and defeat, or at least, contain the malignant tissue gnashing away at his body. But that had proved disastrous.

The consequence of his 28-day treatment at the so-called cancer clinic of Dr. R. Devgon in Newmarket, Ontario, in the fall of 1995, was severe urine bleeding, and accelerated growth in a tumour that was once the size of a golf ball. In a couple of months, it compared with a tennis ball.[2]

Not only that, but the "doctor" charged Joe $10,000 for his treatments, which Joe concluded were illegal. He lodged a complaint with the College of Physicians and Surgeons, and told his old friend, Jim Hughes, what had befallen him. "So I said, 'Well, we'll picket the guy.' So I got a picket together, went out and picketed the guy's office for several days." The doctor finally reimbursed Joe's money. "I think Joe sent us a couple of hundred dollars to thank us," chuckled Hughes. "'Take the group out to lunch or something,' he said."

Joe got his money back, but the cancer got him. His condition was, by then, such that "my own doctor has stated that I only have a short time to live, even though I underwent major surgery on my bladder and prostate."

It was at this time that Sr. Rose Bouchard, the tiny nun with the warm brown eyes, again crossed paths with the Borowski family. "I met Joe as a patient at St. Boniface at the time that he was diagnosed with cancer, and he had only one year to live. I remember him pacing in his room over that, his family was called in and I was there when they discussed it," she recalled. "Jean, she said, 'Well, if things get out of hand over the year, the coming year…maybe he could go to palliative.' I was working there.

"So he agreed to that, if things got out of hand."

After the Supreme Court judgment on his case, Joe never really got back his stride, despite his initial reaction. "Joe told everybody, 'I guess it's time to go play golf, we've lost.' And before that, he had been making comments like, 'God won't let me, won't allow me to lose,' and I tried to talk to him, I said, 'Joe, this is the wrong thing to say, how do you know what God's mind is, what, what God has in store for us all?'" recounted Jim Hughes.

"He did change after the court case. He wasn't the same guy. He put everything he had into the effort. I think he was a much more mellow guy afterward, much more philosophical," asserted Hughes. "It was very difficult after that to deal with him—he was still a great friend and I still talked to him from time to time, but it took an awful lot of cajoling to get him to come round. In the end he had come around, thank God but…he was very, very despondent."

It broke his heart, conceded his wife. "He had a lot of surprises. He'd say, 'I can't believe it, I thought he or she was a strong pro-lifer, a strong Catholic,' and they'd say, 'Well, don't you think you should just drop it, don't you think it's enough of that? People are getting tired of hearing abortion and abortion, it was there, it always will be—just give it up.' Joe says, 'No,' he says, 'I'm going to do it for all it's worth, and once and for all we'll know where we stand.'

"But he was just devastated" by the Supreme Court decision, Jean continued. "It was, like Joe says, 'I wouldn't in a million years have expected it, never in a million years. That's it.' And you know, there really wasn't a big follow-up or anything. Okay, the big Supreme Court says, so that is the end. God has spoken sort of thing."

It was not as if Joe disappeared entirely. He was just flying low.

He promoted a Referendum for Life in 1992, following the December 1991 Saskatchewan referendum on abortion and medicare. The province voted that abortion should not be paid for by public funds.[3] Similar measures should be taken in all provinces, Joe suggested, and he began gathering funds for just such a purpose. Those who donated over $1,000 were promised a piece of the real "Berlin Wall" mounted on a plaque of the province of Manitoba.

True to his promise, he began paying his taxes after his lawsuit concluded.[4]

He and Jean often vacationed in Arizona, where Joe could get in a few rounds of his beloved golf. He was in that desert when Bill C-43 was defeated in the Senate in January 1991, and had not heard the news when a curious reporter called him up some days later. The event, apparently, did not make the Arizona papers.[5]

On January 9, 1996, Joe received one of the highest honours the Vatican can bestow on a layman, the *Pro Ecclesia Et Pontifice*

(For Church and Pontiff) medal. "When I first found out about it, I joked that it seems to me they only give this award to people who are very old or who are about to die," Joe told reporters. "I'm neither, so yes, it did come as a surprise. In fact, I feel greatly honoured. Let me tell you, it's not because I'm Mr. Nice Guy. If they only gave it out because of that, I'd never get it."[6]

Gruff, kindly Fr. Patrick Morand, who recommended Joe for the award, had been spiritual overseer to the Borowski family for years. When his daughters talked about dream analysis, or started subtly doing healing therapy along with dispensing herbal remedies and vitamins, Joe would refer them to the priest for adjudication on these unorthodox matters.

While circumspect about his famous penitent, Fr. Morand admitted that Joe "was kinda down a bit" after his court case ended so disastrously. "I can remember once it seems to me, talking to Jim Hughes about that, and where he had figured well, that's it, ball game over. I think it hit him pretty hard there. But, he wouldn't stay down though, and I was impressed with his religious fervour."

It was this last that defined Joe Borowski in the end.

After the Supreme Court ruling came down, Joe told the press, "I'm going to sit down and write the Lord a letter." What went on between the two must remain between them. Did Joe argue with God, as did Job? Like the afflicted Old Testament innocent man, Joe's faith did not falter. Ultimately, he embraced the cross, from which "the source of life, the 'people of life' is born and increases."[7] In the economy of God, death leads to the fullness of life, and worldly failure can hide that which is pleasing in His eyes—a gloriously humble heart that has spent itself in the service of love.

Sister Rose recognized this in Joe. He "drew his strength from his life of prayer. The family recognized his need to attend at Mass every day, and when he came back, they were saying, as long as he's got his Mass, he'll be all right with the day—because his health food store is his toy," she laughed.

Things had gotten out of hand. A year to the month that he was diagnosed Joe Borowski entered St. Boniface Hospital palliative care unit "a very sick man."

"He came in oh, very weak, barely talking, misery in itself," related Sr. Rose. He was there about a week, and while for the first two days he had strength to get up, after that, he did not leave his bed. The cancer had invaded his bones. "He had asked me to come in and pray with him every moment I had, and there was never enough. So, of course, his friends came in and his sister from Regina."

Jean was by her husband's side almost constantly. "Sometimes she would tell me, 'We're all going now,' as if I can go in to be with Joe and talk to him," Sr. Rose recounted. "I said, 'Well, Joe, you geared up for many challenges and now, God is challenging you to give, surrender your life.' But he had already done that. Over the year, or before that. It's as if he had let go of everything and he knew that he was going to meet his Creator. So all he wanted was prayers.

"And he would always carry a little booklet in his pocket, a booklet of prayers. I saw him sometimes at Mass here and there, and if Mass didn't start right away he would take out a little prayer book from his pocket and he would read, he would pray that, so he had that same book with him.

"And he said, 'Okay, this prayer is on page'—he knew where the pages were—so I said, 'Fine.' I would pray that with him. Finally, he couldn't even talk so I chose, I named the prayer, and he would approve." And if he wanted her to pray a different prayer, Sister Rose remembered, Joe would move his finger slightly and she would page through the book until he signaled.

"But he went in peace, very much a peaceful man, having let go of all what is important to him, and just focusing on his journey ahead with his prayers that we, or at moments of silence, that people had around in the bed or a chat with his friends when he could, at the beginning. Some came, and he could chat a little bit, but, similar to the other patients, he didn't want long discussions, couldn't hold that, and they don't want that.

"They want a presence with them so that …they're not alone…and Joe wanted more and more prayer… I think it's normal that people are afraid of the unknown, of dying, so with a presence there, they are kind of soothed, that they…receive comfort and I think Joe, Joe received that from his family, from the prayers we gave him. And from his friends that came in at his last."

Joe Borowski died in the forenoon on September 23, 1996.

For months after his death, his wife Jean found his rosaries, hanging on trees, on fence posts, scattered over the property at La Salle. Joe always wanted to have a rosary handy with which to pray as he walked in the cool of the evening—Jean gathered up hundreds and passed many of them on to fellow pro-lifers.

In his encyclical *Evangelium vitae (The Gospel of Life)*, released on the feast of the Annunciation, March 25, 1995, Pope John Paul II wrote words that could easily describe his countryman, Joe Borowski. "There is certainly an enormous disparity between the powerful resources available to the forces promoting the 'culture of death' and the means at the disposal of those working for a 'culture of life and love'. But we know that we can rely on the help of God, for whom nothing is impossible.

"Filled with this certainty, and moved by profound concern for the destiny of every man and woman, I repeat what I said to those families who carry out their challenging mission amid so many difficulties: a great prayer for life is urgently needed, a prayer that will rise up throughout the world...Jesus himself has shown us by his own example that prayer and fasting are the first and most effective weapons against the forces of evil (cf Mt 4:1-11). As he taught his disciples, some demons cannot be driven out except in this way (cf Mk 9:29).

"Let us therefore discover anew the humility and the courage to pray and fast so that power from on high will break down the walls of lies and deceit: the walls which conceal from the sight of so many of our brothers and sisters the evil of practises and laws which are hostile to life. May this same power turn their hearts to resolutions and goals inspired by the civilization of life and love."[8]

Or, as Joe Borowski would have said: "Pray to God and row for shore."

Notes
Chapter 29
Voca me cum benedictis

[1] Call me among your blessed.

[2] Letter to College of Physicians and Surgeons from Joe Borowski, December 28, 1995.

[3] The referendum was non-binding; its author, Premier Grant Devine, had been defeated during the course of its administration.

[4] "Borowski calm about abortion," Neil Scott, *Regina Leader Post*, February 11, 1991.

[5] Ibid.

[6] "Pope honors anti-abortion crusader," Bruce Owen, *Winnipeg Free Press*, January 7, 1996.

[7] John-Paul II, *Evangelium vitae*, no.50.

[8] Ibid. no. 100

Life of Joe Borowski
and other significant events along the way

1932
Dec. 12: Born in Wishart, Saskatchewan, Canada

1952
Aug. 20: Marries Jean Zelinski in Wynyard, Saskatchewan

1965
April 1-7: Camps out on the steps of the Manitoba Legislature to protest lack of self-government for the town of Thompson, Manitoba

1966
Sept. 20 - Nov. 21: Camps out, lives in a trailer and pickets on the steps of the Manitoba Legislature to protest Tory government's cabinet members' salary increase, and to effect an increase of Manitoba's minimum wage

1968
Jan., Feb., and June: Convicted of refusing to collect provincial sales tax on items sold at his souvenir store in Thompson; served 7 days, 21 days, and a month in jail respectively

1969
Feb. 20: Elected as NDP opposition Member of the Legislative Assembly (MLA) for what was then the Churchill constituency, in a by-election
June 25: Elected as an MLA in Ed Schreyer NDP government, for the constituency of Thompson. Appointed Minister of highways; later given the portfolio of public works as well

1971
April 28: Convicted of contempt of court for threatening to have a magistrate "defrocked and debarred" during the many events comprising the curious saga of the Dauphin, Manitoba "highways scandal"
Sept. 8: Resigns as Minister of highways and public works because of government funding of abortion

1972
July: Resigns from NDP caucus in protest

over government policy on abortion and film censorship

1973
Feb.: Leaves the NDP, sits as an Independent for the remainder of his term. Founds the Alliance Against Abortion
June 25: Defeated in provincial election in the Winnipeg riding of Point Douglas by NDP candidate

1975
March 26: Supreme Court of Canada rules against Henry Morgentaler, who had appealed the Quebec Court of Appeal decision of April 1974. (The Court had overturned a jury acquittal of the Montreal abortionist on charges of procuring illegal abortions, and had substituted the verdict of guilty.)
May 12: Joe is convicted of failure to file income tax return for 1973, choses five days in jail rather than pay fine
Oct. 21: Joe convicted of failure to file 1974 income tax return. Choses 20 days in jail rather than pay fine

1976
Jan.: Quebec Court of Appeal upholds jury acquittal of Henry Morgentaler on further charges of procuring illegal abortions brought by the Bourassa government. The Supreme Court refuses to hear the Crown appeal. Federal Liberal Justice Minister Ron Basford overturns previous conviction and orders retrial of Morgentaler
Sept.: Henry Morgentaler is acquitted in Quebec after retrial
Nov.: Parti Quebecois comes to power in Quebec; all charges against Henry Morgentaler are dropped

1977
May 2: Joe and Jean open the Borowski Health Food store on St. Anne's Road in Winnipeg

1978
Aug.: Lien on Borowski property in La Salle by Revenue Canada

Sept. 5: Morris Shumiatcher files Joe Borowski lawsuit on behalf of the unborn child at the Court of Queen's Bench in Regina, Saskatchewan

Nov. 16: Revenue Canada agents seize Joe's new car, and attend at his store to obtain information; he escorts them off the premises

Nov. 17: Revenue Canada agent lays charge of common assault against Joe Borowski

Nov. 27: Revenue Canada seizes $37,000 from Alliance Against Abortion bank account

Dec. 5: Revenue Canada returns funds to Alliance Against Abortion bank account

1979

April: Joe convicted of common assault, sentenced to 50 hours community service, and a year's probation

June 14: Found guilty of contempt of court for refusing to comply with a court order to disclose information on his assets to Revenue Canada, sentenced to 14 days in jail and $800 and 90 days if fine not paid. Further trouble with Revenue Canada is forestalled by the formation of "Friends of Joe", who negotiate a settlement with the government on Joe's behalf

1980

April 1: Saskatchewan Court of Queen's Bench rules it has jurisdiction to hear the Borowski lawsuit. The Crown appeals

Nov.: Saskatchewan Court of Appeal rules that the Saskatchewan Court of Queen's Bench has jurisdiction to hear Borowski lawsuit

1981

Jan. 8: Campaign Life delegation appears before the Joint Committee of the House of Commons and the Senate on the Constitution to oppose the proposed entrenched Charter of Rights and Freedoms

April 3: Cardinal Emmett Carter of Toronto publicly removes his opposition to the proposed Charter when Trudeau guarantees that it will not affect abortion legislation

May 1: Joe begins his fast to protest the lack of protection for the unborn child in the proposed Charter

May 27: Morris Shumiatcher argues the case for Joe's legal standing, and the jurisdictional question, that the case can be heard in the Saskatchewan Court of Queen's Bench, before the Supreme Court of Canada.

May 27: Joe Borowski ejected from a Supreme Court of Canada hearing (the first, and perhaps the only, person to have been so)

July 19: Joe ends his "Fast for Life"—80 days later, more than 50 pounds lighter

Sept. 28:The Supreme Court rules on the Liberal government plan to unilaterally amend the Constitution, declares the plan is legal but violates unwritten constitutional convention

Nov. 4-5:The Trudeau federal Liberals reach an accord on the Constitution with a majority of the provinces, Quebec being an exception

Dec. 1: The Supreme Court rules that Joe Borowski has standing to pursue his lawsuit on behalf of the unborn child. Jurisdictional questions are deferred to ruling on similar cases and are ultimately decided in Joe's favour: the case can be heard in the Saskatchewan court

Dec. 2: House of Commons passes the Constitutional package, including an entrenched Charter of Rights and Freedoms

1982

April 17: The new Constitution of Canada is proclaimed and patriated

1983

Feb.: Joe informed by his lawyer Shumiatcher that a guarantee of $350,000 is needed before Shumiatcher will proceed to court. Larry Henderson, editor of the Toronto archdiocese weekly, The *Catholic Register*, writes of Joe's dilemma; thousands of donations pour in

May 5: Henry Morgentaler opens an illegal abortion clinic in Winnipeg.

May 9: "Trial for Life"—Joe Borowski's civil suit on behalf of the unborn child—begins in Regina

May 13: Joe tells pro-life supporters to stop sending donations to fund the court case, as the required sum has been reached and surpassed

June 3: Police raid Morgentaler clinic in Winnipeg

June 15: Henry Morgentaler opens illegal abortion clinic in Toronto

July: Toronto police raid Morgentaler clinic on Harbord Street

Oct. 6: In Winnipeg, Justice Stevanson concludes there is enough evidence against Henry Morgentaler and his co-accused to proceed to trial on conspiracy to commit abortions

Oct. 13: Joe's challenge to the abortion provision of the Criminal Code fails. Justice Matheson of the Saskatchewan Court of Queen's Bench rules that the unborn child is not a person under the law. Joe appeals the decision

Nov. 21: Morgentaler's Toronto lawyer, Morris Manning, challenges the constitutionality of the abortion law. (Henry Morgentaler, Robert Scott and Leslie Smoling have been charged with conspiracy to commit abortions)

Dec. 8: In Manitoba, NDP Attorney-General Roland Penner drops conspiracy charges against Morgentaler et al and substitutes the charge of performing illegal abortions

1984

July 20: Morgentaler's challenge to the abortion law fails. Justice William Parker of the Ontario Supreme Court rules that Section 251 of the Criminal Code is valid. Morgentaler, Scott and Smoling to be tried as charged.

Sept.: Brian Mulroney is elected as prime Minister of Canada

Oct. 15: Jury trial of Morgentaler, Scott and Smoling in Toronto. Morris Manning uses "jury consultants"

Nov. 9: Morgentaler et al acquitted by jury. A month later, Conservative Ontario Attorney-General Roy McMurtry announces his government will appeal the verdict

Dec.: Joe Borowski warned by Manitoba A-G Penner to refrain from intemperate remarks regarding the safety of Henry Morgentaler while he is in Manitoba

1985

March: Morgentaler's Winnipeg abortion clinic is raided by police. Joe Borowski announces his plan of "civil disobedience"

Oct. 1: Ontario Court of Appeal overturns the November 1984 jury acquittal of Henry Morgentaler et al. Manning appeals the decision on behalf of his clients

Dec. 16: Joe Borowski's appeal of Justice Matheson's decision is heard by the Saskatchewan Court of Appeal

1986

Sept..: Morgentaler, Scott and Nikki Colodny are arrested in Toronto. Ontario Liberal Attorney-General Ian Scott stays charges, pending Henry Morgentaler's appeal at the Supreme Court

Oct. 7: The Supreme Court hears Henry Morgentaler's appeal, including a constitutional challenge to the abortion law

1987

April 30: The Saskatchewan Court of Appeal upholds Justice Matheson's decision and rules against Joe Borowski. Morris Shumiatcher appeals to the Supreme Court

1988

Jan. 28: The Supreme Court rules, in the Morgentaler decision, that Section 251 of the Criminal Code violates the Charter of Rights and cannot stand

July 19: The federal government's request to the Supreme Court that it postpone hearing Joe Borowski's appeal until an abortion law is in place is denied by the Court

July 28: The federal Mulroney government attempt to achieve consensus on tentative abortion legislation comes to naught; all amendments to a government resolution are defeated; the resolution falls

Aug.: Joe is reprimanded by Winnipeg's Archbishop Adam Exner for accusations Joe makes against the Canadian bishops. Joe apologizes

Oct. 3: The Supreme Court of Canada hears Joe Borowski's appeal

1989

Mar. 9: The Supreme Court rules that, as a result of the 1988 Morgentaler decision, Joe's case is moot and that he has lost his standing

1990

May 29: Bill C-43, the Mulroney government's legislation to govern abortion, is passed in the House of Commons

1991

Jan. 31: Bill C-43 is defeated by a tie vote of 43 in the Senate

1995

Oct.: Joe goes for unorthodox treatment for his cancer to a clinic outside Toronto, Ontario; his condition worsens

1996

Jan. 9: Joe is awarded one of the highest honours that the Catholic Church bestows on laymen, the *Pro Ecclesia et Pontifice* (for Church and Pontiff) medal, having been recommended for this award by his good friend and confessor, Fr. Pat Morand of Winnipeg
Sept. 23: Joe Borowski dies of cancer at St. Boniface Hospital, Winnipeg

Index

About the author

Lianne Laurence was born in Alberta, one of 11 children, and obtained her Bachelor of Arts in Journalism and Communications from the University of Regina. She worked as a reporter/photographer for the Edmonton Catholic weekly, the *Western Catholic Reporter,* and was active in the pro-life movement in Alberta in the late 80s and early 90s. She relocated to Toronto in 1994 to work at the *Catholic Insight* Magazine, first as assistant to the publisher and later, as managing editor. In January 2002, she undertook the writing of the Joe Borowski biography. A contributor to *Catholic Insight*, Lianne presently lives in Alberta, where also reside her parents, most of her siblings, and numerous nieces and nephews.